JUSTICE AND POWER IN SOCIOLEGAL STUDIES

FUNDAMENTAL ISSUES IN LAW AND SOCIETY RESEARCH

BRYANT G. GARTH AND AUSTIN SARAT, EDITORS

JUSTICE
AND
POWER
IN
SOCIOLEGAL
STUDIES

Edited by

BRYANT G. GARTH

AUSTIN SARAT

NORTHWESTERN UNIVERSITY PRESS

THE AMERICAN BAR FOUNDATION

Northwestern University Press
Evanston, Illinois 60208-4210

Printed in the United States of America

ISBN 0-8101-1432-1 (cloth)
ISBN 0-8101-1433-X (paper)

Library of Congress Cataloging-in-Publication Data

Justice and power in sociolegal studies / edited by Bryant G. Garth,
    Austin Sarat.
        p.   cm.—(Fundamental issues in law and society research ;
    v. 1)
    Includes bibliographical references.
    ISBN 0-8101-1432-1 (cloth : alk. paper).—ISBN 0-8101-1433-X
(pbk. : alk. paper)
    1. Justice.   2. Power (Social sciences)   3. Sociological
jurisprudence—Research.   I. Garth, Bryant G.   II. Sarat, Austin.
III. Series.
K240.J88   1997
340'.115—dc21   97-45537
                                                            CIP

This material is based on work supported by the National Science Foundation under Grant No. SBR-9410902. Any opinions, findings, conclusions, or recommendations expressed in this material are those of the authors and do not necessarily reflect those of the National Science Foundation.

CONTENTS

ACKNOWLEDGMENTS

This volume is the first in a series based on a succession of summer institutes organized under the auspices of the Law and Society Association. These institutes brought together junior scholars and leading established scholars around a theme thought to be central to the field. Each volume in the series will examine one of these central themes. Each volume will look at one central aspect of the field of law and society by bringing together scholars from a variety of perspectives and disciplines. We wish to thank all those who have made this series possible. It is never easy to coordinate the timing for the publication of collections of essays, and we are therefore very grateful to all the people who have persevered on behalf of this series. We are also grateful to the participants at the institutes for their enthusiastic interest and sharp insights.

Within the Law and Society Association, we thank especially Ron Pipkin and Lissa Ganter, both of whom devoted considerable energy into the organization of the institutes. At the American Bar Foundation, special thanks go to Brenda Smith, who has patiently worked with these manuscripts as an add-on to an already overloaded schedule; and to Carole Silver, who provided useful editorial services and in general helped bring the project to fruition. We are also grateful to the organizations that have supported these institutes and publications, including the National Science Foundation, which has made three grants to support these summer institutes: SES 9211969, SBR 9422669, and SBR 9410902. We also are grateful for the commitment of resources by the Law and Society Association—and for the smaller commitments by our own home institutions.

Finally, we would like to thank Felice Levine, now the executive director of the American Sociological Association, who served with us on the commitee that began these summer institutes. Her vision of "law and society" as a field of scholarship with its own distinctive questions, approaches, and literature, which she developed first at the ABF and then in her work for the National Science Foundation, has been a key inspiration for these volumes and the scholarly identity of the Law and Society Association.

JUSTICE AND POWER IN LAW AND SOCIETY RESEARCH: ON THE CONTESTED CAREERS OF CORE CONCEPTS

❖

BRYANT G. GARTH

AUSTIN SARAT

I. INTRODUCTION

To speak about law is always and necessarily to be engaged in a discourse about both justice and power. Law's relationship to justice is everywhere contingent and uncertain, yet law completely divorced from power is unthinkable. And, while law need not be virtuous to be law, if it had no effect in the world it could hardly be said to merit the name law. Recognizing these facts, law and society scholarship has tried to connect an understanding of culture's normative ideals with examination of the complex ways that law works in the world (see Silbey 1996). It is the distinctive contribution of that scholarship to insist that justice is inseparable from social practices (see Sarat and Kearns 1996) and to analyze law as one form of power, one way of constituting, controlling, and changing those practices (Silbey 1985).

The concepts of justice and power, we argue in this essay, have had distinctive "careers" in law and society scholarship. Moreover, we suggest that the development of the field can be described in terms of those careers and the contests that have marked them. Roughly speaking, early commitments to substantive justice have become less dominant in the face of an emerging interest in procedural justice. Explicit concerns for substantive justice tend therefore to live on as critical perspectives on both law and law and society scholarship (see Trubek 1984). Paralleling this trajectory, law and society research that began with a largely instrumentalist conception of power has witnessed the emergence of a constitutive view. As new approaches to justice and power have emerged, fierce but productive debates have erupted about both the instrumental and constitutive power of law (see Sarat and Kearns 1993), and about the place of justice in the social study of law (Sarat and Kearns 1996). Such debates about core concepts both enliven the law and society community and help to build law and society scholarship as a coherent field of inquiry (Levine 1990; Levine and Pipkin 1988).

Beginning with the idea of justice, it is clear that this idea can sponsor a variety of different approaches. Philosophers from Plato to Derrida (1990) have written extensively on the connections between law and justice and the forms that justice might take. Most legal scholars develop their legal analyses in relation to what they believe to be accepted or acceptable understandings of justice. They argue, for example, in favor of particular outcomes of jurisprudential debates, or particular interpretations of statutes or lines of cases; but in either event they situate their arguments, implicitly if not explicitly, within what is taken to be the range of acceptable possibilities made available by contemporary understandings of justice. Other legal scholars more explicitly employ ideals of justice as critical perspectives on accepted understandings of law (Balkin 1994). They see justice as an unrealized, perhaps unrealizable, yet always present aspiration for a better future (Young and Sarat 1994).

Within law and society, there are parallel developments and approaches. Empirical research, for example, may show that the "law in action" is a far cry from the "justice" that the law was supposed to promote. Empirical research might also be used to make the case for remedy of a particular "injustice." Again, justice may be employed as a standard of acceptability, or it may serve as a basis to argue for deeper legal and social change. One self-conscious strand of law and society research from the early days of the Law and Society Association, therefore, has questioned whether empirical research contributes to some form of actual social improvement—that is, social justice (e.g., Abel 1980; Friedman 1986; Trubek 1984; Trubek and Esser 1989; Harrington and Yngvesson 1990; Sarat 1990). That does not mean, however, that most researchers have chosen directly to address concerns about justice in their research. Quite the contrary, as Marianne Constable points out in this volume. Yet this silence cannot hide the role tacit understandings about justice play in structuring research.

While avoiding discussions that directly address justice, most law and society researchers have no such qualms about the concept of power. One reason is an assumed academic division of labor. The study of power is relatively easy to frame as legitimate social science, while the study of justice seems normative or political—assigned mainly to philosophers and philosophically oriented law professors. Social scientists typically claim their expertise in domains other than in the production of theories or analyses of the requirements of justice. In contrast, interest in the power of law and law as power has been one of the mainstays of work in the field of law and society (see Hunt 1992; Silbey 1992). That interest emerges not only in the mapping of "law in action," but also in inquiries about what difference law makes and in explorations of where, when, and how law makes a difference.

In asking what difference law makes, for example, one of the most common types of law and society research treats the power of law in terms of the impact of particular legal decisions (see Blumberg 1967).[1] Law and legal rules are portrayed, in this kind of scholarship, as "tools" whose power consists in their ability to realize certain goals and advance the interests of particular people or groups (Silbey and Bitner 1982). As presented, rules and legal processes are used or avoided in the everyday world to facilitate the accomplishment of various ends, goals, or purposes whose origins tend to be treated as substantially independent of law itself. In this sense, law becomes, in White's (1985: 686) words, "reducible to two features: policy choices and techniques of their implementation. Our questions are 'What do we want?' and 'How do we get it?' In this way the conception of law as a set of rules merges with the conception of law as a set of institutions and processes. The overriding metaphor is that of a machine."

Recently, legal scholars have begun to examine the operation of law, and of various legal institutions and actors, in the generation and reproduction of structures of meaning or what Geertz calls "webs of signification" (1983; see also Harrington and Yngvesson 1990; Trubek 1984). For these scholars, law is "part of a distinctive manner of imagining the real" (Geertz 1983: 184); it is "a mode of giving particular sense to particular things in particular places (things that happen, that fail to, things that might)" (Geertz 1983: 232; see also Trubek and Esser 1989). So conceived, law is inseparable from the interests, goals, and understandings that shape or comprise social life. Law is part of the everyday world, contributing powerfully to the apparently stable, taken-for-granted quality of that world and to the generally shared sense that as things *are*, so *must* they be. To acknowledge that law has power is to acknowledge that social practices are not logically separable from the laws that shape them and that those practices are unintelligible apart from legal norms that give rise to them. In this view, law permeates social life, and its influence is not adequately grasped by treating law as a type of external, normative influence on independent, ongoing activities.

Examination of debates about power and justice shows that, despite substantial differences in theory and in approach, law and society scholars share a vocabulary and a set of common concepts which make it possible to speak to each other across relatively distinct areas of specialization. This book looks at the field through the lens of that vocabulary and those concepts.[2] Justice and power, as we have suggested, not only provide key organizing concepts for law and society scholarship. They also reveal challenges to the field and clues to how it is transforming.[3]

The remainder of this essay is divided into five parts, reflecting different approaches to power and justice and different stages in their contested careers

in law and society. Part 2 examines "gaps and social justice," drawing particularly on the field's formative period. Part 3 focuses on challenges to the gap
perspective. Part 4 then turns to the constitutive power of law. Part 5 examines
the explicit engagement with justice found in research on procedural justice
and asks what that research tells us about the power of law to legitimate itself
and the social relations in which it is embedded. The conclusion suggests
that, by attending to the contested careers of justice and power in the law
and society tradition, we can begin to understand the way legal policy takes
shape and the way law operates in and through social relations.

2. GAPS AND SOCIAL JUSTICE

In the generation of law and society research which emerged with the formation of the Law and Society Association, scholars found themselves in an
implicit political alliance with the state and the legal order. To simplify, we
can say that the state was considered a positive force, law a tool that could
be used effectively to solve social problems, and legal justice equated with
social justice (Sarat 1985). Lawyers at that time were feeling optimistic about
the prospects for using law to "do good" (Auerbach 1976), and that feeling
brought individuals into law practice as well as into the social study of law.
Social justice, in turn, was seen primarily in distributive terms. Commitment
to substantive equality through legal means was in the background, if not the
foreground, of such pioneering law and society studies as Carlin, Howard,
and Messinger's *Civil Justice and the Poor* (1967), Caplovitz's *The Poor Pay
More* (1967), Galanter's "Why the 'Haves' Come Out Ahead" (1974), and
Handler's *Social Movements and the Legal System* (1978). It can also be seen in
Nonet and Selznick's depiction of a "responsive law [that] brings institutional
competencies to the quest for justice" (1978: 116).

   At this stage in the development of law and society research, there was
a taken-for-granted understanding of the nature of justice and an unembar-
rassed commitment to the project of using social research to promote justice
through law. If law could be used as a resource in the creation of a more
just society, then understanding what made law powerful was one way of
contributing to the achievement of justice. Researchers thought of the power
of law largely in instrumental terms as they allied themselves with the effort
to promote a more efficacious legality. What stood in the way were a variety
of administrative and implementation problems that prevented "law on the
books" from being translated into practice. Thus law and society scholars
took up the "gap" problem; closing the gap meant insuring that the full force
of a justice promoting legality could be realized in social relations (see the
discussion in Trubek 1990).

   Studies of criminal justice and regulation, for example, identified the exercise of discretion among regulators and the police as one barrier to closing
the gap. Discretion, discovered in the American Bar Foundation Survey of

Criminal Justice in the 1950s and 1960s, prevented the criminal justice system from operating consistently with the emerging progressive goals and values of the Warren Court. The task of criminal justice research was "to begin to identify gaps in the procedures of review [of discretion]" and to move toward "full enforcement" (Goldstein 1993: 17). Similarly, one of the key features underlying studies of regulation has been the idea that "reasonable regulation" (Bardach and Kagan 1982) should be enforced. The focus then becomes on explaining gaps or failures in the regulatory ideal, whether through industry "capture" or a host of other theoretical explanations. Implicit in most of this research was the assumption that the state regulatory policies, like the goals of the criminal justice system, represented an appropriate starting point for a researcher strongly committed to social justice. Among researchers there was genuine anger and frustration with the inability of the federal government to deliver legality in the form of civil, criminal, and regulatory justice, all terms that seemed to have had an agreed upon meaning not very long ago.

While studies of the legal profession long have been a mainstay of law and society, the link to gap studies is not quite so obvious. However, one of the key concerns of this literature was the autonomy of lawyers with respect to their clients. Preoccupation with this question in the early years of the law and society movement arose as researchers tried to determine whether lawyers could resist pressures from powerful clients who wished to circumvent the progressive intent of laws and regulations (see Heinz and Laumann 1982; Nelson 1988). An independent lawyer, according to the implicit assumption, would serve as one of the engineers of compliance with the benign, justice-oriented regulatory goals of the state (cf. Gordon and Simon 1992). Here we can see how discoveries that lawyers were not as independent as we had hoped were linked to a commitment to the attainment of social justice through law (Kagan and Rosen 1985).

Today gap studies remain mainstays of research in the law and society community. Because of what they can reveal about the efficacy of policy initiatives or particular institutional practices, they have the advantage of a ready-made market of consumers, namely policymakers and the legal profession. Among questions addressed in this genre of work are: Can juries be trusted to do what juries are supposed to do? Does alternative dispute resolution meet its goals? And even though the long social scientific engagement with the death penalty did not do away with the death penalty, defenders of capital punishment found themselves confronted with powerful scientific studies documenting the ways the death penalty fails to meet the standard of equal justice under law.

As theoretical constructs, both power and justice were central in gap research. Justice was taken for the most part as a given, though, as we have argued, the particular understanding of justice was most often linked to a concern for redressing the most egregious injuries of the system of social stratification. Power was treated as instrumental; it was defined in terms of the law's capacity to intervene (mainly positively) in social life. Given the political inclinations of the Supreme Court and the regulatory state during the 1960s and 1970s, failures of law's power were taken to be failures to achieve justice.

3. OUT OF THE GAPS: LAW AGAINST JUSTICE

Critics of gap studies soon raised questions about the ability of the liberal state, even in the best of times and with the best intentions, to realize social justice (Abel 1980; Sarat 1985). They claim that the liberal state is incapable, or unwilling, to undertake the substantial social changes necessary to promote real substantive justice. For them law inhibits or distorts socially progressive action. While these critics share with those committed to gap research an explicit interest in the connection between law and justice, they worry about the alliance between law and society research and state policy which, in their view, does not go far enough in addressing issues of inequality and injustice (Sarat and Silbey 1988). Where they differ most substantially from the earlier work is in the conception of power that they bring to the analysis of law. As against an instrumentalist account, critics of gap research suggest that law's power is more pervasive and less benign (Sarat 1985).

In the face of such criticism, in area after area, the early view that by studying the power of law one would also be making a contribution to the realization of social justice quickly faded. Thus, for example, many researchers on regulation came to the view that the entire regulatory effort is some kind of hoax, unlikely ever to contribute to the progressive goals implicit in early enthusiasm for regulation (see Reichman, this volume). Scholars also now express skepticism about the power of litigation to promote social change (Rosenberg 1991; Galanter 1974), about claims of right generally (Scheingold 1974), about the helpfulness of due process hearings for welfare recipients (Handler 1978), the usefulness of consumer rights (Macaulay 1979), the proliferation of alternative dispute resolution mechanisms (Abel 1981), and the autonomy of the legal profession (Heinz and Laumann 1982; Nelson 1988).

Some of this research questions the power, if not the motivation, of legal officials and the efficacy of legal reform. It suggests that the way to social justice is only through "politics," not the revelation of gaps between legal ideals and practices. This perspective grants little efficacy to law in bringing us closer to substantive justice and perhaps even little importance to law and society research. The focus on politics, however, also presents problems in an era when a changed political climate offers limited prospects for egalitarian reform.

Loss of confidence in research-inspired progressive legal reform led law and society scholars to turn away from the strategy of "delivering legality" as a way of delivering justice (Galanter 1976).[4] Some began to study lawyers in politics (Heinz et al. 1993). Others focused on "private ordering" (e.g., Galanter 1981; Macaulay 1986), or refocused on foreign domains, like India (Galanter 1989), where they had initially developed their interests in law and society. Others committed themselves to the more critical and overtly political posture of critical legal studies, which came along late in the 1970s (Trubek 1984). Still others turned to research on legal pluralism (see Merry 1988) as a way of responding to the failure of law and society's early justice-oriented, progressive agenda.

That research responds to the failures of official law by making explicit other, competing forms of legality and regulation. The emphasis here is less on law as a force for change than on understanding how law helps reproduce social relations and maintain social order. Yet critics of legal pluralism (Robert Kidder, this volume) understandably focus on the conceptual confusion that arises in research that holds onto state law and its norms of "universalism" while celebrating "nonstate law" as equally important. Carol Greenhouse's criticisms (this volume) of efforts to use "community" to find a better law with a more progressive understanding of justice underline difficulties in the legal pluralist project. Yet the appeal of a research program that attempted to locate a progressive "law" and "justice"—"contrasting forms of law and politics" (Kidder, p. 202)—outside of the state also must be recognized. It was almost as if the discovery of the right "law" could be used to advance goals of social justice. Research on legal pluralism is, no doubt, open to the identification of other forms of justice, but the search, as Kidder shows, was for a more equal justice akin to that sought from the state in the earlier days of law and society.

We can see a similar dynamic in the "dispute processing" literature. This literature suggested that the legal process, or the translation of a dispute into the language and institutions of law, typically narrowed disputes and distorted them. This finding was in line with the growing pessimism that we have already discussed. But, like the legal pluralism literature, this new approach held out some hope for what authors saw as the original law and society project. The approach suggested that it was possible for disputes to be expanded, which, in turn, could lead to justice-promoting change (e.g., Felstiner, Abel, and Sarat 1980–81; Mather and Yngvesson 1980–81). For those interested in justice, the purpose of research then becomes to understand the conditions that lead to such expansion of disputes. Again, while there was little explicit discussion of justice in the dispute transformation literature, it is fair to say that it remained linked to a vision of substantive justice that, we are arguing, was especially evident in an earlier generation of law and society research. An interest in power also was explicitly present in these approaches to research. Indeed many disputing studies considered the conditions under which law could be empowering for disadvantaged groups.

4. POWER EVERYWHERE

In the next turn in the contested career of the concept of power, it began to be defined in constitutive rather than instrumental terms. Attention was now focused on the question of how law and legal ideology help keep people in place rather than promote egalitarian reform (Gordon 1984; Sarat and Kearns 1993). This new concern was not only with whether and when law could serve progressive goals, but also with how law worked more generally in shaping social relations. The study of ideology and legal consciousness, in particular, became part of the quest for an understanding of this side of law's power (see Hunt 1985). From this perspective, as Susan Silbey observes (this volume), "The law is a principal agent in the construction of the world because—in its concrete legal norms, in its general principles and values, and in its form and processes—it is a means of apprehending the world" (p. 291).

With the recognition of the constitutive dimension of law, the study of power in law and society scholarship today is thriving. Some of the essays in this collection exemplify the move in recent years, inspired largely by neo-Marxists and by Foucault (whose work is used in at least five of the essays), to see law as "constitutive" of social relations, not merely as a tool that may or may not be manipulated instrumentally for social change (see also Munger 1993). More and more, law is portrayed as an organizer of our thoughts, our approaches, and our sense of possibilities: "Law constrains not by force but by creating the very categories of action that define social life" (Reichman, this volume, p. 250). In terms of power and justice, most of the emphasis on the constitutive power of law is on law as social control, or even law as a stage in the evolution of social control (Ewick, this volume). Law contributes to social control by, for example, eliding persistent class, racial, and gender differences in the organization of social life. Yet criticisms of law based on these differences, as Kidder observes in his discussion of legal pluralism, tend to be built on the bedrock of universalism that reinforces the power of law (p. 198).

Studying the power of law as social control has led scholars to consider the mechanisms through which liberal legality works to limit our conceptions of justice as well as our efforts to promote social change. Those who focus on law's constitutive power see law as implicated in the maintenance of inequality rather than its amelioration. The commitment to substantive justice and the tradition in law and society of searching for a way of empowering the disadvantaged, perhaps through law, perhaps through resistance to law, continues even as the conception of law's power broadens.

In much of the research that examines law's constitutive power there is an implicit hope that law and society scholarship will identify, and therefore bolster, movements that might engage in what is now termed "transformative" behavior (cf. Hunt 1993: 248). In this sense there is a strong justice claim in this literature (Silbey, p. 275). This claim may involve a refusal to be a prisoner of hegemonic categories, or it may be seen in an effort by researchers to identify counterhegemonic strategies (see Handler 1992; Ewick 1992; McCann 1992). The justice claim, however, enters only implicitly in research that concentrates on law's power. As Nancy Reichman notes about studies of regulation, "While the notion of contest, if not explicitly power, has been a recurring current in sociolegal scholarship, discussions related to justice have been remarkably few," and, when they do emerge, they "are related to questions of bias in enforcement or implementation," which draw on traditional legal values (p. 256).

Several of the essays in this volume present case studies of the constitutive power of law. Thus Carol Greenhouse describes the way the concept of community—and law in community—was used to understand urban "riots" and the claims for equality associated with them. Both the civil rights texts and the social control discussions that were prominent in the aftermath of the Rodney King riots in Los Angeles focus on the problem of transforming "diversity into civility." What the civil rights texts and the newspaper accounts of the riots share, in Greenhouse's terms, is "their construction of the public space as a site of engagement among 'groups,' and the law as having a central role in mediating those engagements." The state offers "protection from the consequences of difference through law (civil rights) or through law enforcement (policing)" (p. 122). In terms of the constitutive power of law, we see how law actively takes control of social phenomena and turns them into "timeless," "universal," diversity-obliterating categories.

The Hartog essay (this volume) carefully—indeed, almost tantalizingly—refuses to generalize from a fascinating account of power and justice in the struggles around "John Barry's rights." Consistent with a focus on the constitutive power of law, we cannot say if the use of law by John Barry or Eliza Barry was "empowering" or "enfeebling," or, if one or the other, why. We can only see a process by which a highly ambiguous case made out of intense personal and ideological conflict became part of an arsenal of legal "arguments." These arguments could be employed by different sides in different ways over time as the legal management of their conflict changed. However, it is relatively easy to see the constitutive role of the law in the details of the story.

In contrast to Hartog's approach, Joel Handler (this volume; also Martha Fineman) directly engages with the literature on the constitutive power of law. Drawing on case studies of the welfare poor, he tries to identify a path through which welfare recipients could gain some power in relation to the legalized system of charity that we call the social welfare system. The skill of Handler's analysis, however, only underscores the difficulty of the task (Ewick 1992; McCann 1992). Embracing Foucault as a theoretical point of departure while, at the same time, remaining committed to instrumental social reform movements is surely a considerable task. This is because research on law's constitutive power generally shows how law disciplines potential challengers to the social order rather than serving to promote change and reform. In this literature, the separation of law and justice is almost complete. Justice becomes at best an external, political critique—and otherwise an inevitable disciplinary ally of law's hegemony.

5. JUSTICE REGAINED

Recognition of law's hegemony and its constitutive power undermined the optimism of the vision of "social justice through law" that animated so much early scholarship. For those committed to distributive justice, it is clearly no longer sufficient simply to take the side of the state and identify the conditions of a more powerful (efficacious) legality. Even in contemporary gap studies, scholars are less eager to promote the "givens" of the legal profession or legal policymakers as the standards by which legal institutions are to be measured. In part, this is because those "givens" have changed and are now less attractive to much of the law and society community. The effort to keep an unspoken but accepted vision of justice alive through new scholarly approaches has also been difficult. That is why so many scholars would say that they now study power, not justice.

Further, law and society's growth and institutionalization as a social scientific field means that a justice-oriented, "legal-political" scholarship seems increasingly out of place. But, paradoxically in the career of the idea of justice, it is from one of the most scientist sectors of the law and society community that an explicit engagement with that idea has reemerged. In this line of research, a concern for distributive justice and with the contributions of law to the redress of social inequality is displaced by an interest in the contribution of procedural justice to the legitimacy of law itself (e.g., Lind and Tyler 1988; Tyler and Mitchell 1994; Tyler, this volume). Here the internal needs of law for legitimacy take precedence over the impact of law on society (see Sarat 1993).

In the literature on procedural justice, justice is "operationalized" as a subjective perception against which no normative standard is juxtaposed. Procedural justice research treats justice solely as an empirical concept and, in so doing, offers little support for a general "social justice" agenda (Sarat 1993). Individuals, indeed, are shown by procedural justice research not to care very much whether they win or lose, or whether they are disadvantaged by legal decisions, as long as they are able to present their story and are treated with dignity and neutrality by relevant legal officials.

In this collection, Tom Tyler's explanation and defense of "procedural justice" suggests the importance of the question of legitimacy, or of "how . . . the legal system [is] maintained" (p. 336), to this body of scholarship. He also argues that the study of procedural justice represents "a reenactment among scholars of the dynamic found among respondents" (p. 338). Procedural justice research, in other words, finds that individuals care more about the procedures of dispute processing, including the opportunity to tell a story to a neutral third party, than the nature of the outcomes. Similarly, since scholars cannot agree on such normative issues as how much equality there ought to be in a given society, they focus on the "justice" of procedure, a justice that allegedly can be studied from a "neutral" position. Thus concern for justice—though justice understood very differently—is no longer left implicit.

The power of procedural justice concerns as a research and analytical tool is evident also in the essay by William Felstiner (this volume) on power and justice in lawyer-client relations. Felstiner notes that "if this [procedural justice] theory of status definition is correct, then we can see that a lot of ordinary behavior in the lawyer-client context is charged with much greater significance than lawyers either realize or intend." In particular, lawyer inattention to clients, he says, "may inflict serious psychological trauma" (p. 65). Accordingly, Felstiner advocates research into how lawyers treat their clients and how that treatment relates to the procedural justice literature.

Interestingly, the focus of procedural justice on legitimacy parallels the concerns of other law and society scholars with legitimation (Sarat 1993). Law's constitutive power, so these scholars contend, depends on its ability to legitimate its power, and law's social utility depends on its ability to legitimate existing social relations (Hay 1975). As emphasized here in Patricia Ewick's essay, "Punishment, Power, and Justice," "within the official discourse, justice demarcates the limits of penal power by announcing standards against which power can be held accountable" (p. 36). The ability to hold power accountable, or to be seen to do so, is crucial to legitimation. Moreover, both Kidder (pp. 202–5) and Silbey (pp. 275, 291) insist in their essays that scholars sometimes unwittingly participate in this aspect of legitimation by treating the universalizing categories of law as just (see also Constable, p. 22).

The justice that is described in research on procedural justice is fully compatible with, and may be an essential part of, the processes through which law legitimates itself and *unjust* social arrangements. Thus, in the contested careers of power and justice, studies of procedural justice may tell us less about justice as an ideal and more about the power of law to get its way. As Ewick emphasizes, "Justice is a necessary and integral part of power" (p. 42). Furthermore, what is represented as justice cannot be examined ahistorically, for it changes in relation to changes in power. Justice cannot be defined "in terms of a single, unchanging, and peculiarly modern, value," whether procedural or substantive (p. 41).

6. CONCLUSION: CONTESTING JUSTICE AND EXERTING POWER

The focus on procedural justice and its relationship to the legitimacy and legitimation of law reminds us that different ideas of justice frequently provide a site for contests over the meaning and content of law itself. This is made especially evident in the Ewick essay, which allows us to see changes in technologies of social control in relation to contested conceptions of justice. This understanding of the way different conceptions of justice underlie debates about legal policy is also the basis for Reichman's assertions about the need to imagine alternative justices, in particular those based on feminist principles, and for Greenhouse's statement about the need to find a better way to understand law's relationship to diversity.

The essays by Martha Fineman and Lewis Kornhauser (as well as the Handler essay discussed earlier) describe and in some sense actively participate in contests about the meanings of justice—and their significance in shaping policy—in the particular domains of the family and private justice. Fineman's essay notes a close relationship between power and justice, observing that "justice is the societal conclusion legitimating and condoning what might otherwise be viewed as inappropriate coercive maintenance of certain traditional family forms and expressions of individual power within families" (p. 81). Her essay therefore describes factors that have shaped the meaning of legal justice in the family. Fineman suggests that while challenges to the "traditional family" seemed to develop a model of the "egalitarian family" (p. 92), the conservative idea of the "private-natural family" (p. 98) remained central in law and is, in part, implicated in the conception of justice in the family that elevates formal equality over the needs of mothers and their children. Fineman thus suggests that "the concept of justice must be reformulated so that punitive and mean-spirited laws designed to discipline women and children into patriarchy are not seen as appropriate. Transforming justice requires an attack on the underlying ideology that valorizes the nuclear family" (p. 102).

Lewis Kornhauser's essay on "interest, commitment, and obligation" is concerned mainly with developing a systematic method for understanding and evaluating how individuals act in relation to law. There is a sense, however, in which the essay is also about different and competing approaches to justice—justice as a condition in which individuals treat norms as matters of preference vs. treating norms as matters of obligation. As Kornhauser notes, the model of norms as preferences is especially well-developed in the economic literature, and we could say that the idea of norms as obligations is a traditional view found in legal scholarship. Kornhauser's argument shows how contested meanings of justice inform debates about the limits of law. Indeed, this essay helps to show how attitudes toward law in the academy have changed in the past twenty years toward a justice that is grounded more on economic models of behavior (and legitimacy) than on the traditional model of strict allegiance to positive law.

The essays by Fineman and Kornhauser, each produced by a law professor who is also active in the domain of law and society, suggest that contests about the meaning of justice, whether about the requirements of procedural justice or the claims of substantive justice, are themselves part of the process of legal change and the legitimation of law. As scholars of procedural justice have shown, the question of how law is legitimated—as compared, for example, to authority grounded on family, the bureaucracy, the party, or economic growth—ought to be a central concern of law and society research. Contests about the meaning of justice in established domains, or the requirements of justice in new social domains or geographic areas, help to extend or maintain the position of the law as a central regulatory authority and, in so doing, to explain its power.

Law and society scholars must take seriously and even participate in contests about the meaning and requirements of justice, especially since the field of law and society is inevitably implicated in those debates whether we admit it or not. In our view, concepts of justice and power furnish building blocks for a field in which both political commitment and scientific standards have their place. By being open about our engagements with ideas of power and justice, and aware of how contests about those concepts relate to the construction of law's legitimacy, we may push the boundaries of the law and society field and, at the same time, make possible strategic alliances with scholars beyond those boundaries.

The development of law and society as a field during the past thirty years is marked by particular interventions in contests about justice and particular ways of talking about the power of law. While there has been a discernible shift in emphasis from distributive justice to procedural justice and from an instrumental to a more constitutive conception of power, these have been neither linear nor consistent trends. Neither the concern for distributive justice nor an instrumental conception of power have been dislodged or displaced. Quite to the contrary, distributive justice remains a strong background concern in much scholarship, and an instrumentalist conception of power remains quite prevalent in our community. These layered and interlocking ideas, and the contested careers of which they are a part, not only frame debates within the field but also provide a shared vocabulary and knit us together as a research community and as an evolving field of interdisciplinary inquiry.

As we look to the future careers of justice and power, we must find ways to understand the social construction of justice and how it relates to the legitimacy and power of law. The processes of social construction can be represented as primarily an internal story of change within a field, part of which has been presented in this essay,[5] but the internal story can also be related to what can be seen as an external story of economic and social change. Justice disciplines power, but it also legitimates power; and law serves its role partly by adjusting to political and social changes that can be seen as occurring outside of the legal domain (even if still, to some extent, framed in legal terms) (Dezalay and Garth 1996). We have seen, in the period of the life of the Law and Society Association, major changes in the economy and society of the United States (and many other countries). The social activism of the state, for example, has given way to a neoliberal, more "economized" model. Transformations in the field of law and society—and visions of justice and power—relate to those complex changes.[6] That does not mean that the internal story is dictated by outside developments, especially since some of the external developments are framed and interpreted according to the language of the law. But we must recognize that positions taken and ideas developed within the field have an important, and so far unexplored, relationship to what happens in the larger social and economic context. Attending to that relationship will, in the future, help us understand the power of our academic labors and the justice to which those labors ultimately do, or do not, contribute.

NOTES

1. This discussion of different conceptions of power in law and society research is taken from Sarat and Felstiner 1995: chap. 1.

2. The effort, therefore, is different from the reviews that have focused on particular subfields of law and society (e.g., Lipson and Wheeler 1986). Our ambition is to explore the ways in which subfields could speak to each other. The contributions contained in this volume developed initially out of plans for a summer institute designed to attract scholars at early stages of their careers into the activities of the Law and Society Association. The selections were designed therefore both to represent a range of work by scholars in the association and a theme—power and justice—which unites that group around core issues. Toward that end, we divided law and society scholarship along three dimensions. We start with basic subjects of law and society research, the institutional locations of legal work: civil justice and dispute processing; criminal justice; the legal profession; and regulation. The second dimension involves four recognizable social settings in which law is generated or received: community, family, class (with a special emphasis on the welfare poor), and "private justice" regimes. Finally, we selected four topical approaches in law and society research and asked how ideas of power and justice emerge in each approach: legal pluralism, language, ideology, and legal history. We sought with these selections to highlight some traditional research approaches as well as some that are relatively new to the field.

   While this volume articulates a distinctive vision of law and society, it also brings together individuals with different academic training and research approaches, including anthropology, economics, history, law, psychology, and sociology. Each of the essays makes its own contribution, both generally and to the subfield that it examines through the lens of power and justice. We will not attempt to review each in detail in this introduction. Rather, we will draw freely on the insights of these essays to reexamine the state of law and society research and to ask how the field engages with, and is constituted by, ideas of justice and power.

3. Instead of focusing on law and society as a field, we could instead present the body of scholarship about law and society as an aggregation of distinct disciplinary perspectives aimed at understanding an area of social life—namely law. We do not believe it is necessary to choose between the two opposing perspectives, and indeed a creative tension between the two can help to advance scholarship in traditional disciplines and in law and society. For the present volume, however, our concern is with the particular dimension of the law and society story that focuses on its development as a distinctive field of inquiry.

4. At the same time, the growth of the field of law and society also brought a greater attention to questions of method and the requirements of rigorous social science. Part of the tension in law and society marked the difficulty of reconciling the commitment to rigorous social science with the ideal that research should make a difference in the struggle for a more just society.

5. A key focus of any sociological story of the transformation of meanings of justice would have to be law schools and law professors—who are at the center of debate and production of justice theories and conceptions. Apart from a few historical studies, law and society scholars have not taken up this challenge (Brandwein 1996; Kalman 1996; Schlegel 1995; Shamir 1995).

6. At the very least, such a study would require empirical work on the rise of law and economics, the transformation of legal scholarship, and the position of academic knowledge in the world of economic power. We are not in a position here to develop the connections between the internal story of law and society and the larger picture—to explore, in other words, the social legitimacy of the law and the connection between academic and scholarly production in the law schools as well as in other kinds of law and society research.

BIBLIOGRAPHY

Abel, Richard. 1980. Redirecting Social Studies of Law. 14 *Law and Society Rev.*, 805.

———. 1981. The Contradictions of Informal Justice. In *The Politics of Informal Justice*, ed. R. Abel. New York: Academic Press.

Auerbach, Jerold. 1976. *Unequal Justice: Lawyers and Social Change in Modern America*. New York: Oxford Univ. Press.

Balkin, Jack. 1994. Being Just with Deconstruction. 3 *Social and Legal Studies: An International Journal*, 393.

Bardach, Eugene, and Robert Kagan. 1982. *Going by the Book: The Problem of Regulatory Unreasonableness*. Philadelphia: Temple Univ. Press.

Blumberg, Abraham. 1967. The Practice of Law as a Confidence Game. 1 *Law and Society Rev.*, 15.

Brandwein, Pamela. 1996. Dueling Histories: Charles Fairman and William Crosskey Reconstruct "Original Understanding." 30 *Law and Society Rev.*, 289.

Caplovitz, David. 1967. *The Poor Pay More: Consumer Practices of Low-Income Families*. New York: Free Press.

Carlin, Jerome, Jan Howard, and Sheldon Messinger. 1967. *Civil Justice and the Poor: Issues for Sociological Research*. New York: Russell Sage.

Derrida, Jacques. 1990. Force of Law: "The Mystical Foundation of Authority." 11 *Cardozzo Law Rev.*, 919.

Dezalay, Yves, and Bryant Garth. 1996. *Dealing in Virtue: International Commercial Arbitration and the Construction of a Transnational Legal Order*. Chicago: Univ. of Chicago Press.

Douzinas, Costas, and Ronnie Warrington. 1994. The Face of Justice: A Jurisprudence of Alterity. 3 *Social and Legal Studies: An International Journal*, 405.

Eisner, Marc. 1991. *Antitrust and the Triumph of Economics*. Chapel Hill: Univ. of North Carolina Press.

Ewick, Patricia. 1992. Postmodern Melancholia. 26 *Law and Society Rev.*, 755.

Felstiner, William, Richard Abel, and Austin Sarat. 1980–81. The Emergence and Transformation of Disputes: Naming, Blaming, Claiming. 15 *Law and Society Rev.*, 631.

Foucault, Michel. 1979. *Discipline and Punish: The Birth of the Prison*. New York: Vintage.

Friedman, Lawrence. 1986. The Law and Society Movement. 38 *Stanford Law Rev.*, 763.

Galanter, Marc. 1974. Why the 'Haves' Come Out Ahead: Speculations on the Limits of Legal Change. 9 *Law and Society Rev.*, 95.

———. 1976. Delivering Legality: Some Proposals for the Directions of Research. 11 *Law and Society Rev.*, 225.

———. 1981. Justice in Many Rooms. 19 *Journal of Legal Pluralism*, 1.

———. 1989. *Law and Society in Modern India*. Delhi: Oxford Univ. Press.

Geertz, Clifford. 1983. *Local Knowledge: Further Essays in Interpretive Anthropology*. New York: Basic Books.

Goldstein, Joseph. 1993. "Criminal Justice Administration." In *Commemorating Forty Years of Research*. Chicago: American Bar Foundation.

Gordon, Robert. 1984. Critical Legal Histories. 36 *Stanford Law Rev.*, 57.

Gordon, Robert, and William Simon. 1992. The Redemption of Professionalism. In *Lawyers' Ideals/Lawyers' Practices: Transformations in the American Legal Profession*, ed. R. Nelson, R. Solomon, and D. Trubek. Ithaca, NY: Cornell Univ. Press.

Handler, Joel. 1978. *Social Movements and the Legal System*. New York: Academic Press.

———. 1992. Postmodernism, Protest, and the New Social Movements. 26 *Law and Society Rev.*, 697.

Harrington, Christine, and Barbara Yngvesson. 1990. Interpretive Sociolegal Research. 15 *Law and Social Inquiry*, 141.

Hay, Douglas, et al., eds. 1975. *Albion's Fatal Tree: Crime and Society in Eighteenth-Century England*. New York: Pantheon.

Heinz, John, and Edward Laumann. 1982. *Chicago Lawyers: The Social Structure of the Bar*. New York: Russell Sage.

Heinz, John, Edward Laumann, Robert Nelson, and Robert Salisbury. 1993. *The Hollow Core: Private Interests in National Policy Making*. Cambridge, MA: Harvard Univ. Press.

Hunt, Alan. 1985. The Ideology of Law: Advances and Problems in Recent Applications of the Concept of Ideology to the Analysis of Law. 19 *Law and Society Rev.*, 39.

———. 1992. Foucault's Expulsion of Law: Toward a Retrieval. 17 *Law and Social Inquiry*, 1.

———. 1993. *Explorations in Law and Society: Towards a Constitutive Theory of Law*. London: Routledge.

Kagan, Robert, and Robert Rosen. 1985. On the Social Significance of Large Firm Law Practice. 37 *Stanford Law Rev.*, 399.

Kalman, Laura. 1996. *The Strange Career of Legal Liberalism*. New Haven, CT: Yale Univ. Press.

Knight, Frank. 1963. On the Meaning of Justice. In *Justice*, ed. Carl Friedrich and John Chapman. New York: Prentice-Hall.

Levine, Felice. 1990. Goose Bumps and "The Search for Signs of Intelligent Life" in Sociolegal Studies: After Twenty-Five Years. 24 *Law and Society Rev.*, 7.

Levine, Felice, and Ronald Pipkin. 1988. Graduate Programs in Sociolegal Studies: A Requisite for the Future." 4 *Focus on Law Studies*, 1:4.

Lind, Allan, and Tom Tyler. 1988. *The Social Psychology of Procedural Justice*. New York: Plenum.

Lipson, Leon, and Stanton Wheeler, eds. 1986. *Law and the Social Sciences*. New York: Russell Sage.

Macaulay, Stewart. 1979. Lawyers and Consumer Protection Laws. 14 *Law and Society Rev.*, 115.

———. 1986. Private Government. In *Law and the Social Sciences*, ed. L. Lipson and S. Wheeler, 445–518. New York: Russell Sage.

Mather, Lynn, and Barbara Yngvesson. 1980–81. Language, Audience, and the Transformation of Disputes. 15 *Law and Society Rev.*, 775.

McCann, Michael. 1992. Resistance, Reconstruction, and Romance in Legal Scholarship. 26 *Law and Society Rev.*, 733.

Merry, Sally. 1988. Legal Pluralism. 22 *Law and Society Rev.*, 868.

Morris, Clarence. 1963. Law, Justice, and the Public's Aspirations. In *Justice*, ed. Carl Friedrich and John Chapman. New York: Prentice-Hall.

Munger, Frank. 1993. Sociology of Law for a Postliberal Society. 27 *Loyola Law Rev.*, 89.

Nelson, Robert. 1988. *Partners with Power: Bureaucracy, Professionalism, and Social Change in the Large Law Firm*. Berkeley: Univ. of California Press.

Nonet, Phillippe, and Philip Selznick. 1978. *Law and Society in Transition: Toward Responsive Law*. New York: Harper and Row.

Plato. 1992. *The Republic*. Trans. G. M. A. Grube. Indianapolis: Hackett.

Rosenberg, Gerald. 1991. *The Hollow Hope: Can Courts Bring about Social Change?* Chicago: Univ. of Chicago Press.

Sarat, Austin. 1985. Legal Effectiveness and Social Studies of Law: On the Unfortunate Persistence of a Research Tradition. 9 *Legal Studies Forum*, 23.

———. 1990. Off to Meet the Wizard: Beyond Validity and Reliability in the Search for a Post-Empiricist Sociology of Law. 15 *Law and Social Inquiry*, 155.

———. 1993. Authority, Anxiety, and Procedural Justice: Moving from Scientific Detachment to Critical Engagement. 27 *Law and Society Rev.*, 647.

Sarat, Austin, and William Felstiner. 1995. *Divorce Lawyers and Their Clients: Power and Meaning in the Legal Process*. New York: Oxford Univ. Press.

Sarat, Austin, and Thomas Kearns. 1993. Beyond the Great Divide: Forms of Legal Scholarship and Everyday Life. In *Law in Everyday Life*, ed. A. Sarat and T. Kearns. Ann Arbor: Univ. of Michigan Press.

———. 1996. Legal Justice and Injustice: Toward a Situated Perspective. In *Justice and Injustice in Law and Legal Theory*, ed. Austin Sarat and Thomas Kearns. Ann Arbor: Univ. of Michigan Press.

Sarat, Austin, and Susan Silbey. 1988. The Pull of the Policy Audience. 10 *Law and Policy*, 97.

Scheingold, Stuart. 1974. *The Politics of Rights: Lawyers, Public Policy, and Political Change*. New Haven, CT: Yale Univ. Press.

Schlegel, John Henry. 1995. *American Legal Realism and Empirical Social Science*. Chapel Hill, NC: Univ. of North Carolina Press.

Shamir, Ronen. 1995. *Managing Legal Certainty*. Durham, NC: Duke Univ. Press.

Silbey, Susan. 1985. Ideals and Practices in the Study of Law. 9 *Legal Studies Forum*, 7.

———. 1992. Making a Place for Cultural Analysis of Law. 17 *Law and Social Inquiry*, 39.

———. 1996. Globalization and the Possibilities of Justice. Presidential Address to the 1996 Annual Meeting of the Law and Society Association.

Silbey, Susan, and Egon Bitner. 1982. The Availability of Law. 4 *Law and Policy Quarterly*, 399.

Silbey, Susan, and Austin Sarat. 1987. Critical Traditions in Law and Society Research. 21 *Law and Society Rev.*, 165.

Trubek, David. 1984. Where the Action Is: Critical Legal Studies and Empiricism. 36 *Stanford Law Rev.*, 575.

———. 1990. Back to the Future: The Short, Happy Life of the Law and Society Movement. 18 *Florida State Univ. Law Review*, 1.

Trubek, David, and John Esser. 1989. Critical Empiricism in American Legal Studies: Paradox, Program, or Pandora's Box. 14 *Law and Social Inquiry*, 3.

Tyler, Tom, and Gregory Mitchell. 1994. Legitimacy and the Empowerment of Discretionary Legal Authority: The United States Supreme Court and Abortion Rights. 43 *Duke Law Journal*, 705.

White, James Boyd. 1985. Law as Rhetoric, Rhetoric as Law: The Arts of Cultural and Communal Life. 52 *University of Chicago Law Rev.*, 684.

Young, Alison, and Austin Sarat. 1994. Introduction to "Beyond Criticism: Law, Power and Ethics." 3 *Social and Legal Studies: An International Journal*, 324.

REFLECTIONS ON LAW
AS A PROFESSION
OF WORDS

MARIANNE CONSTABLE

Law is a profession of words.
— *David Mellinkoff (1963)*

I. INTRODUCTION: THE NAMING OF CATS

The Naming of Cats is a difficult matter,
  It isn't just one of your holiday games;
You may think at first I'm as mad as a hatter
When I tell you, a cat must have THREE DIFFERENT NAMES.
— *T. S. Eliot (1940)*

During the past two decades, sociolegal scholars, like scholars in other fields, have turned their attention increasingly to discourse. Sociolegal studies of discourse point, almost unanimously, to the *power* of language. Such power, to be sure, is neither uniform nor conceptually consistent across studies, but the articulation of its presence is explicit. The studies' concern for the power of language—and of law—thus contrasts noticeably with the studies' pronouncements, or rather lack of pronouncements, about *justice*, whether that of language or of law. The ostensible inattention to justice in sociolegal studies of language and discourse seems to underscore an unbridgeable distance between law, of which the studies do speak and whose words and power they analyze, and justice, for which and of which no word appears.

Law, by contrast to whatever unspoken concern for justice may lie in these studies, then, is a matter of words. And words, or more precisely, the deployments of language explored in these studies, whatever their differences, are matters of social power. For some, power lies in a speaker-actor's manipulation of the more or less powerful tool of language. For others, power lies in aspects of language itself or in (those who control) the social context that shapes linguistic possibilities. For yet others, a dynamic between the social formation of language and the linguistic construction of social reality suggests the potential of language for both oppression and resistance.

The appearance in recent years of bibliographies and review essays on sociolegal studies of language and discourse make it unnecessary to devote much space to the background and classification of studies and approaches here (Danet 1980; Goodrich 1984; Levi 1982, 1994; see also Brenneis 1988; O'Barr and Conley 1985: 61–91). Elizabeth Mertz's (1992) "Language, Law, and Social Meanings: Linguistic/Anthropological Contributions to the Study of Law," in particular, provides an up-to-date overview of anthropological and linguistic approaches to language in general and reviews work on legal language that focuses on its contextual or social character. Rather than duplicating Mertz's efforts, section 2 illustrates approaches to language and power through passages drawn from particular sociolegal studies of discourse. Section 3 then shows how thinking about law as a profession of words captures much that is of interest in studies of law more broadly construed. Section 4 then suggests that the silence about justice in sociolegal studies of discourse reveals aspects of law that remain inaccessible to strictly sociolegal study. The essay concludes by gesturing toward possibly nonsociolegal reflections on law, justice, speech, and silence.

2. EVERYDAY NAMES: LANGUAGE AND POWER

> First of all, there's the name that the family use daily,
> . . . all of them sensible everyday names.
> — *T. S. Eliot (1940)*

Sociolegal studies of language often appeal explicitly to "power" for understanding legal discourse. As noted above, some studies view language as a tool or instrument by which an independently ascertainable world or reality is affected (if not effected) through the "power" of a speaker. Susan Berk-Seligson, for instance, shows how the bilingual courtroom interpreter "plays a far more active verbal role than the [American legal] system could ever imagine, [which role] is very much tied to the linguistic control of 'legitimate' [non-interpreter] participants in judicial proceedings, a degree of control that often is tantamount to linguistic coercion" (Berk-Seligson 1990a: 156; see also Berk-Seligson 1990b).

In many studies, power or control belongs less to a speaker such as an interpreter than to some aspect of language—narrative, story, or style, for instance—which may or may not be in the control of a determinate agent. Like Berk-Seligson's study, these studies often focus on language use in legal institutions, looking at rules and practices in legal or judicial proceedings to analyze language as a matter of control. The control in these studies belongs to the studies' subject-matter: the object of study seems to serve as the subject or agent with power, as its status as grammatical subject indicates: "narrative forms," for Douglas W. Maynard (1990: 89, citing Schudson 1982: 98), for instance, "shape and narrow the range of what kinds of truths can be told." He concludes that

> [c]ase characteristics and legal matters . . . are not irrelevant, but neither are they self-invoking or self-evident features of the negotiational process. . . . [T]hey are "talked into being" by way of narrative and narrative structure. As an aspect of the interaction order, this structure shapes the content of the case and clearly *effects* the course of negotiations. The exact ways in which it also *affects* outcomes cannot be ascertained until more is known. (Maynard 1990: 92, citing Heritage 1984)

Bennett and Feldman's investigation into "some underlying judgment scheme" that makes it possible "for different people with different relationships to the law to communicate meaningfully about the issues in legal cases" (1981: 11) leads them to the view that "stories *produce* a clear definition of an action and the conditions surrounding it" (1981: 10, emphasis added). The seminal work of O'Barr and his colleagues on speech styles in the courtroom focuses on the effects of the particular dimension of style considered "powerful" and "powerless" on the perceptions of legal actors (Erickson, Lind, Johnson, and O'Barr 1978; O'Barr 1982). Recent experimental and ethnographic research on the effects of style or what some call "the power of language" extends such work beyond its original courtroom context to, for instance, adjudication and mediation (Morrill and Facciola 1992).

These socio- and psycholinguistic studies of institutional legal discourse often affirm a speaker-agent's control at the same time as they treat the speaker-agent as him/herself determinable: Berk-Seligson accords to the court interpreter both the status of "actor" and of "variable" or "intrusive element" (1990a: 198). Maynard suggests that "narratives and their components may be devices for 'doing' the identities by which principal actors in the discourse are known" (1990: 87). Bennett and Feldman's "ordinary people in criminal trials" transform evidence into stories that themselves establish the contexts for "social action" or frameworks for judgment (1981: 3, 7).

Sociolegal studies of discourse also move beyond formal legal processes. Some continue to focus on the power of legal and other professionals, even as they can only speculate as to motives or intentions. Edelman, Abraham, and Erlanger, for instance, argue that in conveying ideas about (wrongful discharge) law, legal and personnel professionals and their journals help shape employment law and construct a particular legal environment (1992).

Yet other law and society scholars treat legal language as an even less singularly determinate—less agent- or subject-centered—social force. These studies often concern themselves with the authority and legitimation of law. They turn to the interstitial space in which "law" interacts with "society" to explore, for instance, everyday language for societal conceptions of law and justice or the conversations between those belonging to the legal profession and those ostensibly outside of it. At issue in these works are the linkages that lie in what earlier law and society scholars took to be the "gap" between law in action and law on the books. Now the gap between the everyday and official law is filled with legitimating discourse, made manifest to the observant sociolegal scholar who renders such discourses coherent and can thereby investigate their effectiveness in producing meaning. Yngvesson thus attributes power to "exchanges" and "interaction." She shows how

> exchanges between [the court] clerk and citizens produce legal and moral frameworks that justify a decision to handle a case in a particular way. The clerk plays a dominant role by controlling the language in which the issues are framed. . . . But the definition of events during a hearing is also shaped by these working, middle, and lower class people. (1988: 410)

Sarat and Felstiner show how divorce lawyers' explanations justify their authority and invite client dependence as well as dissatisfaction (1988); they go on to view the interactions of lawyers and clients as a site for the generation and conveyance of "meaning," where "power" is present: "Power is seen in the effort to negotiate shared understandings, and in the evasions, resistances, and inventions that inevitably accompany such negotiations." The "meaning-making power" of law is not unidirectional, however; it is "interactive, dynamic, and strategic" and invites "adaptation and change in the practices of judges, lawyers and other officials." (1995: 13, citations omitted).

Such scholarship, with its focus on the shaping of law through linguistic interactions that are themselves to some degree shaped by law, merges into scholarship adopting even more reflexive interpretivist approaches. Acknowledging and self-consciously reflecting on their own language and complicity in worlds of particular sorts of language, these scholars dwell on the constitutive aspect of legal discourse and its capacity or potential to both oppress and resist. Taking to heart that one cannot get outside either language or society, their exploration of the interaction between discourse and social world leads these scholars to consider explicitly their own positions as actors and speakers (Harrington and Yngvesson 1990; White 1991).

Such reflexivity seems most prominent in the work of law professors at the moment. Some critical race theorists, for instance, whose stated aim is admittedly less the analysis of discourse than the pursuit of "racial justice," have adopted a self-consciously "subjective" stance. Critical race theory draws on "personal histories," as well as "parables, chronicles, dreams, stories, poetry, fiction, and revisionist histories" (Matsuda et al. 1993: 5) to reveal the "dominant narratives" and "liberal premises" that shape the problem of race (Delgado 1995: xiii, citation omitted). In their criticisms of "assaultive speech" as well as in their turn to "the words of law and politics to fight the words that wound and exclude," critical race theory clearly makes language an issue of power (Matsuda et al. 1993: 15). As law professor Mary Joe Frug puts it in another context,

Identifying the gendered character of the discourses [of law] can . . . be a feminist strategy for challenging the extensive and complicated network of social and
cultural practices which legitimate the subordination of women. The assumption
underlying this strategy is that language is a mechanism of power, that there is
always more at stake in the relationship of gender and language than "just"
a question of literary style—indeed that style itself can constitute a powerful
socializing apparatus. (1992: 112)

All of the studies mentioned so far conceive of language and power together, as somehow social, even when they do not go so far as to construct
what, for instance, Patricia Ewick and Susan S. Silbey call a "sociology of
narrative." Ewick and Silbey's sociology "recognizes that narratives are social
acts performed within specific contexts that organize their meanings and
consequences" (1995: 205). Their work fits with what Mertz calls "an integrative approach" to language and social context. Using Sally Engle Merry's
*Getting Justice and Getting Even: Legal Consciousness among Working Class
Americans* (1990) and John M. Conley and Willam M. O'Barr's *Rules versus
Relationships: The Ethnography of Legal Discourse* (1990) as examples, Mertz
describes a recent move to view language as neither simply "reflectionist"
(language mirrors society) nor "instrumentalist" (language as the transparent
instrument of a social actor) (1992: 418, 417). This ostensibly new approach acknowledges what Mertz calls "a moment of linguistic creativity."
The "resistance or unpredictability" Mertz identifies in these studies still
belongs to a language which is primarily *social,* however: language in these
studies, Mertz writes, is both a "process whereby cultural understandings are
enacted, created, and transformed in interaction with social structure" and
itself "structured in crucial ways by its social context," such that "social power
is implicated at every level of contextual influence on language" (1992: 423).
Or, as Mertz puts it in her own work:

The approach taken here views language as a key mediator in human interaction,
and as socially-grounded. In both respects, language is ideological. As work
by linguists and semioticians has demonstrated, language filters and channels
the stories speakers tell. Language is also the medium through which much
of our social interaction is accomplished. Thus language is socially grounded,
structuring and being structured by social context. (1988: 662, citation omitted)

At stake in understanding language and law as essentially social is a particular worldview. This worldview insists on the primacy of a social framework
from which there is no escape or outside. Social processes, such as language or
law, function simultaneously as subjects modeled on traditional conceptions
of human agency and control and as the objects and tools of human mastery.
While this view may be correct as far as it goes, it only goes so far—as the
studies' ostensible neglect of "justice" suggests. Only by transforming justice
into power—and into human or social power at that (in the same way as
sociology of religion transforms faith into social power)—does scholarship

informed by such a worldview deal with justice (Constable 1994a; de Certeau 1988). Hence Levi, for instance, makes the justice of jury instructions a question of (social) "desire": "One question in this context is just what a 'desirable' level of comprehensibility would be in the setting of a jury trial—and how such a level might be decided." As a social matter, judgment as to justice is deferred and becomes a matter of social policy: "This question is patently not one for psycholinguists alone but rather is an issue of public policy that must be addressed by the legal profession *in the light* of relevant empirical research" (Levi 1990: 22).

Many sociolegal studies of discourse thus seem to defer issues of justice or to simply lack explicit reference to it. Some studies of discourse do suggest that an absence of words—the absence of stories and voice, the absence of history as articulation of a past, the absence of a tradition that knows itself—constitutes silence in the face of powerful official institutions and texts or silence in the face of a powerful and discursive law. They implicitly or explicitly identify law with authoritative declarations and characterize silence as an absence of power to which they give various names—hegemony and hierarchy (Messick 1988), repression and domination (Kessler 1993), subordination (White 1991; Frug 1992), oppression (Mertz 1988: 684)—that give rise to calls for "further action" (White 1991: 58), "resistance" (Engel 1993), and "empowerment" (see Merry 1991, 1995). Meanwhile "justice" remains unspoken.

When scholars do use cognates of the term "justice," such usage usually points to some aspect of social power. Mertz, for instance, refers to South Africa's homeland apartheid policy as "this unjust system" (1988: 661). Injustice in this context indicates a lack of power and voice: "The power behind the imposition of law was evident in its summary treatment of indigenous people's history and rights—indeed in its exclusion of their voices and stories," writes Mertz (1988: 668).

Studies that focus on others' usage of the term "justice" also point to connections between law and power. Sally Falk Moore, in her careful analysis of a British colonial directive to officers in charge of African local courts in Tanganyika, considers among other issues the particularity of the British conception of "justice" in what the document states "is the main function of a court—to dispense justice" (1992: 18, citing document). Moore's essay suggests in part the extent to which British commitment to "the rule of law" is grounded in an "ideal of rule standardization" that she associates with H. L. A. Hart's positivist model of a legal system (1992: 22). For Moore, the simultaneous British "commitment to discovering and respecting the authentic African legal 'tradition' " that was not simply a set of rules *and* "to writing it down in the form of rules" indicates an ambivalent tension in a colonial administration (Moore 1992: 24) whose "aims of empowerment" and "aims of control" were "bound to face in opposite directions" (1992: 40).

Moore's analysis could equally well be taken to point to tension in Hart's own concept of law, a sociological and legal positivist account of the modern "municipal legal system" that implicitly underlies much sociolegal scholarship (Hart 1961: v, 17; Constable 1994b). Recall that, for Hart, the existence of a legal system requires two kinds of rules: first, the rules recognized as valid by the system's ultimate criteria of validity and generally obeyed by citizens, from whatever motive; and, second, the rules specifying such criteria and accepted by officials (1961: 113). The "unification" of rules that Hart associates with the emergence of a modern legal system thus combines the propositionally articulated customs of a people with the similarly propositional secondary rules of the officials. This unification involves "as a matter of history," for Hart, the "mere reduction to writing of hitherto unwritten rules," although "what is crucial is the acknowledgement of reference to the writing or inscription as *authoritative*, i.e. as the *proper* way of disposing of doubts as to the existence of the rule" (1961: 92). Moore's analysis points to the instability of this crucial second step, the acknowledgement of a mark of authority, in Tanganyika. Can one ascertain a time about which it can be said that the Africans in question acknowledged the authority of the British or of their rules to determine the validity of articulations of local custom? Moore implies that the answer is never a full-hearted yes: "not only has much of the British-designed structure of the courts been inherited, but so have many of the resistances to it and circumventions of it" (1992: 21). She thereby suggests that, at least in Tanganyika, the emergence of the Hartian positivist legal system of the British directive is—perhaps perpetually—incomplete.

Such incompleteness indeed seems to be an attribute of the positivist legal system that Hart and Moore's British officials describe. Although those officials take the English common law as their model of an existent legal system, the "crucial step" for its emergence as a legal system also remains indeterminate as a matter of history. While the existence of Hart's positivist legal system requires the past occurrence of an acknowledgement of authority, historians of the common law locate such acknowledgement in a perpetually receding moment of origin (see Constable 1994b: 67–95; see also Fitzpatrick 1992). The inaccessibility of this moment for both Tanganyika and the English common law suggests an eternal deferral of the coming-into-existence of any actual positivist legal system.

That system nevertheless maintains its hold on the sociolegal imagination that views law as a socially powerful system of discourse or as the official declarations and statements of rules that most people obey most of the time. A study of legal discourse of sorts, Tom R. Tyler's *Why People Obey the Law* is a case in point. Tyler's analysis of interviewees' responses to telephone questionnaires in effect explores the first condition of Hart's legal system by investigating the influence on compliance "of what people regard as just and moral as opposed to their self-interest" (1990: 3). Hart had argued that

> the first condition [that rules of behavior which are valid according to the system's ultimate criteria of validity must be generally obeyed] is the only one

which private citizens *need* satisfy: they may obey each "for his part only" and from any motive whatever; though in a healthy society they will in fact often accept these rules as common standards of behavior and acknowledge an obligation to obey them, or even trace this obligation to a more general obligation to respect the constitution. (1961: 113)

Tyler is concerned to show that attitudes toward law fit what he calls a normative model rather than a model that focuses on outcomes or instrumental ends. "Normative commitment through personal morality means obeying a law because one feels the law is just; normative commitment through legitimacy means obeying a law because one feels that the authority enforcing the law has the right to dictate behavior," he writes (1990: 4). He concludes that people generally obey law because of its legitimacy and their perceptions of the procedural justice or fairness of the system.

In so doing, Tyler seems to affirm the "crucial step" in Hart's description of the emergence of a modern legal system—acknowledgement of the authoritativeness of law. It is telling however that for Tyler, the "experiences, attitudes, and behavior" that contribute to such affirmation on the part of his respondents are still grounded in "the process of socialization" (168) "through which a society or organization communicates values within a group concerning the meaning of 'fair' procedures and 'fair' outcomes" (1990: 176). Turning to the communication of values through socialization to ground an acknowledgement of authoritativeness of law, as Tyler does, reintroduces social power or what Hart had called "social pressure" (1961: 84) as determinative of the existence of a legal system or, in other words, as crucial to the emergence of a legal system. Moore's British administrators, whatever the difficulties in their knowledge of and attitudes toward Africans and African law, named their own conformity to British rules and the rule of law "justice." Tyler, Hart, and most sociolegal scholars of discourse, on the other hand, consider acknowledgement of authority to be the effects of socialization or of the social production of meaning and take conformity to statements of rules to be indicative of such power.

In his classic articulation of a positivist conception of law, Hart argues that, unless one considers "control by rules" to amount to a "necessary connection between law and morality," the rules of a positivist legal system are not necessarily moral or just (1961: 202). Sociolegal studies of discourse go further. In turning "justice" into purely sociological terms, in deferring issues of justice, or in simply failing to mention "justice" at all, these studies imply that the justice of the law they study is nothing more than social power, that they have nothing to say on the matter, or that it is nonexistent. They may in fact be correct on all counts. Yet insofar as one is concerned with justice as something more or other than a social construct, one must reach beyond these studies' assertions. For while sociolegal studies of discourse successfully draw attention to law as a profession of words, they dwell on the social power of law and language and remain silent as to justice.

3. DIFFERENT NAMES: PROFESSIONS OF WORDS

> But I tell you a cat needs a name that's particular,
> A name that's peculiar and more dignified,
> Else how can he keep up his tail perpendicular,
> Or spread out his whiskers, or cherish his pride?
> — *T. S. Eliot (1940)*

The sociolegal scholarship cited in section 2 construes the power of legal language in a variety of ways—as instrumentality, structure, force, potential, as shaping or being shaped in a world of which it is not part or as shaping its own world. Despite this range of construals of the power of legal language, such scholarship takes the character of both law and language to be essentially social and continually defers, if it does not simply neglect, justice. In dealing with law as a profession of words, such scholarship nevertheless draws our attention to a relatedness of language and law that characterizes, even when it is not the ostensible focal point of, many other studies of law. Almost all studies of law engage, one way or another, with law as a profession of words, even when they do not adopt a strictly power-oriented or legal positivist and "social" conception of law.

"Profession" here has three relevant meanings: an open declaration or public avowal; an avowal in appearance only or a pretense; and an occupation, vocation, calling, or business in which proficiency or expertise is claimed. While studies of the legal profession, a significant subfield in law and society studies, draw the third definition into play most clearly, other studies engage— contest and affirm—other senses of the phrase. That phrase, "profession of words," is complicated not only because of the multiple senses of "profession" but also because "of" has two grammatical senses. "Knowledge of God," for instance, may mean (roughly) either "knowledge belonging to God [that God possesses]" or "knowledge [one possesses that is] about God." "Profession of words" thus has six—or more, depending on the constancy of "words"— different senses. Most studies of law engage continually with one or more of these aspects of the profession of words that is law. In doing so, they do not simply accept a particular meaning of the phrase as definitive of law; instead they explore relations between law and language that they may express in terms of power but that also have implications—which may or may not be verbalized as such—for justice. (The appearance of a theme such as that of this collection of essays from various sociolegal fields attests to the possibility that justice, as well as power, may be at stake. The question for scholars of law and language then becomes whether the essays manage to avoid turning "justice" into a subcategory of power relations.)

Law in the first sense of a profession of words, as an open declaration or public avowal of words, may be taken to affirm words, principles, rules as proper ways of dealing with disputes and controversies. Although one usually thinks of a declaration or avowal as taking place through words, it need not.

Public declarations of law may occur through statements and enactments, but they may also occur through the actions of legal actors or institutions who display rather than verbally articulate a commitment to speech. Hence historical studies, pursuing this first sense of law as a profession of words, may consider the extent to which public declarations of law—statements or actions—affirm the value of speech, or of particular rules of law, or of a rule of law. Innumerable studies of the U.S. Constitution's First Amendment— including those which would critique or qualify the jurisprudence that has developed around it—attest to the significance granted to declarations about speech in the United States. Impact studies or policy analyses evaluate the past or future effects of particular rules and standards in almost all areas of contemporary law by in effect analyzing the type and extent of legal institutions' and practices' commitments to what has been or is about to be said. And, finally, analyses and critiques of the rule of law explore public commitment to and legal avowal of government by rules.

In the second sense of law as a profession of words, the avowal made by law occurs through words or consists of words. In constitutional theory as well as in anthropology of law, scholars turn to particular language as evidence of what is called law (even when such language paradoxically serves to recall the listener to a silent or exemplary rather than propositional law). Social psychologists and other researchers use judges' instructions as standards by which to measure jury performance and accept such statements as law. Some scholars point explicitly to the use of claims and counterclaims to express legal differences (Perelman and Tyteca 1969); many others take for granted that argument and interpretation characterize law, filling law journals with the fruit of their participation in such activity. The stature of written vs. spoken texts, the authoritativeness of the U.S. Constitution as a founding document, controversies over so-called activist judges' deviations from established legal doctrine, and discussions of judicial decision-making all concern the words through which law makes public declarations.

While some theorists, such as Ronald Dworkin and Jürgen Habermas, seek the conditions of law as conditions under which a sincere exchange of words may occur, other scholars suggest that viewing law as an exchange of words (as in the second sense of a profession of words) or as a commitment to speech (as in the first) is naive, disingenuous, or worse. Invoking a third and a fourth sense of law as a profession of words, such scholars see law as a pretense of words—as involving a falseness that belongs either to words themselves or to law insofar as it claims to be about words rather than something else. Claims as to the obfuscation produced by legal language or of the inability of language of any sort to map reality involve this third sense; claims as to the falseness of legal assertions of neutrality or law's commitment to speech over violence involve the fourth sense of a profession of words, in which law's avowal of words is contrasted to its less neutral, or even violently oppressive or irrational, conduct.

In a fifth sense, law as a profession of words is the subject matter of studies of the legal profession which draw attention to how the occupation, vocation, calling, or business of law claims proficiency or expertise about words. Even studies that do not focus on legal training acknowledge that learning law is like learning a language (or unlearning one) and that practicing law involves communication, if not traditional skills of oratory and argument (Plato; White 1985, 1990; Wydick 1994).

Finally, if the fifth sense of law as a profession of words refers to a vocation or calling that specializes in or is about words, a sixth sense takes the "profession of words" to refer to a calling belonging to words. That is, while the expertise of the legal profession is linguistic, the occupation or business of words concerns law; their vocation or calling lies in or consists of law. But while the first five senses of law as a profession of words may or may not involve justice, this sixth sense is different. For the concern of speech with law, its calling to law, is a call for justice, never a call for mere power.

4. ONE NAME LEFT OVER: THE SILENCE OF JUSTICE

> But above and beyond there's still one name left over,
>   And that is the name that you never will guess;
> The name that no human research can discover—
>   But THE CAT HIMSELF KNOWS, and will never confess.
> — *T. S. Eliot (1940)*

Sociolegal studies of discourse, as section 2 showed, consider law and language to be powerful. In these studies, words call to law as power. In the absence of words, sociolegal scholars—and others—suppose an absence of power whose rectification lies in empowerment. This call for empowerment and voice is a call for justice of sorts, although it often occurs without the word "justice" and calls for what lies beyond existing law. The sixth sense of law as a profession of words in section 3 suggests by contrast a call for justice that lies precisely in language and in law. Reflecting on the latter calling of words, one is led to wonder at the absence of "justice" in sociolegal study and its law. Law as the calling of words, that is, leads us to ponder sociolegal studies' simultaneous garrulousness about power and silence about "justice." It leads us to wonder at the silence of justice.

Indeed, even more broadly than in sociolegal studies of discourse, "voice" today lends itself to a variety of causes, most of which seem to presume that an absence of voice means an absence of power and an absence of justice while, conversely, voice means empowerment and justice. While it is commonsense at some level to claim that speech may fail to correspond to power and that silence—as in the right to remain silent—may point to possibilities of justice, at another level such claims challenge the equation of voice with power and justice that characterizes the way many at least talk about politics and write about law. A critique of the voice = power = justice equation highlights the particular configuration of legal positivism, liberalism, and social science that holds sway in modern American law and politics and which will only be sketched briefly below.

The discussion in section 2 supports a suggestion made elsewhere that the conventional natural law/positive law distinction is less important for understanding contemporary law than what may be called the "sociologiza-tion" of law (Constable 1994a, 1994c). Sociologization involves, first, the uniform insistence by modern legal thinkers in a variety of fields that law is a social, and hence sociologically knowable, phenomenon; and, second, the pervasive privileging in the liberal society of the United States and its legal institutions of the kind of truth-claims or propositional knowledge that constitutes the social sciences, such that even law comes to be thought of as propositional statements of rules. Sociolegal studies of discourse that take both law and language as social power in part testify to the sociologization of law. Acknowledging the complexity of a language and voice that may be neither powerful nor just leads to alternative—nonsociological—conceptions of law whose justice may lie, at least in part, in silence.

Modern Western law, jurisprudence, and sociolegal study posit a relation between sovereign and subject in which speech—or command—is the right or privilege of power. By contrast, Pierre Clastres's *Society against the State* describes a people for whom speech is the *duty,* rather than just the privilege, of the chief (1987: 41). Inverting the Austinian relation in which the speech of master or state dominates subjects "bound to the silence of respect, reverence, or terror" (1987: 151), Clastres describes Indian societies in which "the tribe demands to hear" the chief (1987: 153). And yet "there is so little necessity for the chief's discourse to be listened to that the Indians often pay no attention to it" (1987: 46), "or rather, they feign a lack of attention" (1987: 153). For "the word of the chief is not spoken in order to be listened to" (1987: 153). It is an "empty speech" (1987: 154) in that

> the chief, for all his prolixity, literally says nothing. His discourse basically consists of a celebration, repeated many times, of the norms of traditional life: "Our ancestors got on well living as they lived. Let us follow their example and in this way we will lead a peaceful existence together." That is just about what the discourse of a chief boils down to. One understands why those for whom it is intended are not overly disturbed by it. (1987: 153–54)

In its diversion from the "function of communication" immanent in modern propositional language (1987: 46), the word of the leader is not a discourse of power. In primitive societies, in societies without a State, power is not found on the side of the chief: it follows that his word cannot be the word of power, authority, or command. An order? Now there is something the chief would be unable to give: that is the kind of fullness his speech is denied. A chief forgetful of his duty who attempted such a thing as an order would be met by a sure refusal of obedience, and a denial of recognition would not be far behind. (1987: 154)

Whatever one makes of Clastres's ethnography or political anthropology, his account alerts us to the significance of speech in both modern law and liberal politics. Clastres's societies of "nonseparate" law refuse the "separate power" of a society divided into sovereigns who command silent subjects (Austin) or officials who declare rules that citizens obey (Hart). Although this "primitive society is the place where . . . society itself . . . is the real locus of power" (1987: 154), such society also rejects the modern liberal democratic politics of power that valorizes the voice or speech of the citizenry. Contemporary liberal accounts of politics, Clastres helps one to see, view citizens as minisovereigns who are not only the free and equal individuals capable of owning things and bearing rights about which one hears so much but are also speaking subjects. According to liberalism, legitimate government, or government whose authority society acknowledges, requires speech—or, more precisely, requires general public participation and individual opportunity to participate. Liberal theorists invent speech forums; they project speech onto silence and name it "consent." Liberal politicians take mixed messages, the results of surveys of what pollsters warn are transitory public opinions, as clear mandates. Liberal scholars strive to find consistency over incoherence to such a degree that almost any public expression is read as acquiescence or resistance.

The refusal of Clastres's "primitive societies" to equate language and law with communicative and political power hints at a blind spot in current political debates over liberalism. Critiques of liberalism generally rely on appeals to the reality of social power. Despite the importance of speech to liberalism, its critics tend to dwell on liberal construction of autonomous rights-bearing subjects, rather than on liberalism's construction of speaking subjects. Standard critiques of liberalism claim either that liberalism disregards the social embeddedness of persons (e.g., communitarians such as Sandel [1982] on Rawls, liberal feminism) and/or that liberalism disregards the way that as a theory it is itself implicated in existing structures of power (e.g., Marx, critical legal studies; [Unger 1983; Fitzpatrick and Hunt 1987], critical race theory, feminists such as MacKinnon [1989]). Both these critiques challenge the neutrality of the liberal rights-bearing subject by grounding themselves, like the sociolegal studies of discourse mentioned in section 2, in a reality that privileges social power: sociologically determinable characteristics and/or social structure constitute the frame from which both sorts of critiques of liberalism are launched.

In contrast to the sociological approach of critics of liberalism, reflection on law as a profession of words leads one—to some extent like liberalism and sociolegal study of discourse—to attend to the language and texts of and about the positive law of a liberal state. In contrast to the focus on the power of speech of both liberalism and sociolegal studies of discourse, however, such reflection attends, like Clastres, to the limits of speech and to places where the texts of liberalism, positive law, and sociolegal study fall silent. In these places, one encounters the limits of liberalism, legal positivism, and sociolegal study: the justice of which they do not speak. One encounters in reflection on modern texts the inextricability of law with a justice that remains unsaid, if not unsayable.

Students of law and language do well to recall the limitations and limits of a discourse—that of sociolegal studies of discourse—which ostensibly neglects justice in favor of power and construes empowerment as justice. These limits beckon: they mark the place where a silent justice encounters the powerful articulated and propositional declarations of the law of sociolegal study and legal positivism. This encounter with justice—*contra* the theoretical claims of legal positivism—is necessary to law and for law. Yet if this essay is to retain its focus on the sociolegal studies of discourse that grasp law exclusively as powerful social discourse, it can pursue the matter of this limit and encounter no further. It can only gesture toward a nonsocial law and language—that of Pierre Clastres (1987), Drucilla Cornell (1992), Peter Fitzpatrick (1992), Peter Goodrich (1990, 1995), Martin Heidegger (1971a, 1971b), and Philippe Nonet (1995), perhaps—that calls our attention back to the mutually sustaining speech and silences of (in and about) modern law and justice.

> When you notice a cat in profound meditation,
> The reason, I tell you, is always the same:
> His mind is engaged in a rapt contemplation
> Of the thought, of the thought, of the thought of his name:
> His ineffable effable
> Effanineffable
> Deep and inscrutable singular Name.
> — *T. S. Eliot (1940)*

NOTES

The author thanks Bryant Garth and Austin Sarat for their patience and support, and for the challenge presented by the original (summer 1992) terms of the assignment: a "playful" piece about "conceptions of justice and power in law and society studies of language and discourse," which is "not a review of the literature" but will provide "a sense of the topic" that will educate readers and develop the field while suggesting a "potential research approach." The author thanks Jennifer Culbert for research assistance.

BIBLIOGRAPHY

Bennett, W. Lance, and Martha Feldman. 1981. *Reconstructing Reality in the Courtroom.* New Brunswick, NJ: Rutgers Univ. Press.

Berk-Seligson, Susan. 1990a. Bilingual Court Proceedings: The Role of the Court Interpreter. In *Language and the Legal Process,* ed. J. Levi and A. Walker, 155–201. New York: Plenum Press.

———. 1990b. *The Bilingual Courtroom: Court Interpreters in the Judicial Process.* Chicago: Univ. of Chicago Press.

Brenneis, Donald. 1988. Language and Disputing. 17 *Ann. Rev. Anthropology,* 221.

Clastres, Pierre. 1987. *Society against the State.* New York: Zone Books.

Conley, John M., and Willam M. O'Barr. 1990. *Rules versus Relationships: The Ethnography of Legal Discourse.* Chicago: Univ. of Chicago Press.

Constable, Marianne. 1994a. Genealogy and Jurisprudence: Nietzsche, Nihilism and the Social Scientification of Law. 19 *Law and Social Inquiry,* 551.

———. 1994b. *The Law of the Other.* Chicago: Univ. of Chicago Press.

———. 1994c. Thinking Nonsociologically about Sociological Law. 19 *Law and Social Inquiry,* 625.

Cornell, Drucilla. 1992. *The Philosophy of the Limit: Justice and Legal Interpretation.* New York: Routledge.

Danet, Brenda. 1980. Language in the Legal Process. 14 *Law and Society Rev.,* 445.

de Certeau, Michel. 1988. *The Writing of History.* Trans. Tom Conley. New York: Columbia Univ. Press.

Delgado, Richard, ed. 1995. *Critical Race Theory: The Cutting Edge.* Philadelphia: Temple Univ. Press.

Edelman, Lauren B., Steven E. Abraham, and Howard Erlanger. 1992. Professional Construction of Law: The Inflated Threat of Wrongful Discharge. 26 *Law and Society Rev.,* 47.

Eliot, T. S. 1940. The Naming of Cats. In *Old Possum's Book of Practical Cats.* London: Faber and Faber.

Engel, David. 1993. Origin Myths: Narratives of Authority, Resistance, Disability and Law. 27 *Law and Society Rev.,* 785.

Erickson, B. E., E. A. Lind, B. C. Johnson, and W. M. O'Barr. 1978. Speech Style and Impression Formation in a Court Setting: The Effects of "Powerful" and "Powerless" Speech. 14 *Journal of Experimental and Social Psychology,* 226.

Ewick, Patricia, and Susan Silbey. 1995. Subversive Stories and Hegemonic Tales: Toward a Sociology of Narrative. 29 *Law and Society Rev.,* 197.

Fitzpatrick, Peter. 1992. *The Mythology of Modern Law.* London and New York: Routledge.

Fitzpatrick, Peter, and Alan Hunt, eds. 1987. *Critical Legal Studies.* Oxford and New York: Basil Blackwell.

Frug, Mary Joe. 1992. *Postmodern Legal Feminism.* New York: Routledge.

Goodrich, Peter. 1984. "Law and Language: An Historical and Critical Introduction," 11 *Journal of Law and Society,* 173.

———. 1990. *Languages of Law: From Logics of Memory to Nomadic Masks.* Littleton, CO: Rothman.

———. 1995. *Oedipus Lex: Psychoanalysis, History, Law.* Berkeley: Univ. of California Press.

Harrington, Christine B., and Barbara Yngvesson. 1990. Interpretive Sociolegal Research. 15 *Law and Social Inquiry,* 135.

Hart, H. L. A. 1961. *The Concept of Law.* Oxford: Clarendon Press.

Heidegger, Martin. 1971a. *On the Way to Language.* Trans. by Peter D. Hertz. New York: Harper and Row.

———. 1971b. *Poetry, Language, Thought.* Trans. by Albert Hofstadter. New York: Harper and Row.

Heritage, J. 1984. *Garfinkel and Ethnomethodology.* Cambridge: Polity Press.

Kessler, Mark. 1993. Legal Discourse and Political Intolerance: The Ideology of Clear and Present Danger. 27 *Law and Society Rev.,* 559.

Levi, Judith N. 1982. *Linguistics, Language and the Law: A Topical Bibliography.* Bloomington: Indiana Univ. Linguistics Club.

———. 1990. The Study of Language in the Judicial Process. In *Language in the Judicial Process,* ed. J. Levi and A. Walker, 3–35. New York: Plenum Press.

———. 1994. *Language and Law: A Bibliographic Guide to Social Science Research in U.S.A.* Chicago: American Bar Association Commission on College and University Legal Studies, Teaching resource bulletin, no. 4.

Levi, Judith N., and Anne Graffam Walker, eds. 1990. *Language in the Judicial Process.* New York: Plenum Press.

MacKinnon, Catherine A. 1989. *Toward a Feminist Theory of the State.* Cambridge, MA: Harvard Univ. Press.

Matsuda, Mari J., Charles R. Lawrence III, Richard Delgado, and Kimberle Williams Crenshaw. 1993. *Words That Wound: Critical Race Theory, Assaultive Speech and the First Amendment.* Boulder: Westview.

Maynard, Douglas W. 1990. Narratives and Narrative Structure in Plea Bargaining. In *Language in the Judicial Process,* ed. J. Levi and A. Walker, 65–95. New York: Plenum Press.

Mellinkoff, David. 1963. *The Language of the Law.* Boston: Little, Brown.

Merry, Sally Engle. 1990. *Getting Justice and Getting Even: Legal Consciousness among Working Class Americans.* Chicago: Univ. of Chicago Press.

———. 1991. Law and Colonialism, Review Essay. 25 *Law and Society Rev.,* 889.

———. 1995. Wife Battering and the Ambiguities of Rights. In *Identities, Politics, and Rights,* ed. A. Sarat and T. Kearns, 271–306. Ann Arbor: Univ. of Michigan Press.

Mertz, Elizabeth. 1988. The Uses of History: Language, Ideology, and Law in the United States and South Africa. 22 *Law and Society Rev.,* 661.

———. 1992. Language, Law and Social Meanings: Linguistic/Anthropological Contributions to the Study of Law. 26 *Law and Society Rev.,* 413.

Messick, Brinkley. 1988. Kissing Hands and Knees: Hegemony and Hierarchy in Shari'a Discourse. 22 *Law and Society Rev.,* 637.

Moore, Sally Falk. 1992. Treating Law as Knowledge: Telling Colonial Officers What to Say to Africans about Running "Their Own" Native Courts. 26 *Law and Society Rev.*, 11.

Morrill, Calvin, and Peter C. Facciola. 1992. The Power of Language in Adjudication and Mediation: Institutional Contexts as Predictors of Social Evaluation. 17 *Law and Social Inquiry*, 191.

Nonet, Philippe. 1995. Judgment. 48 *Vanderbilt Law Rev.*, 987.

O'Barr, William. 1982. *Linguistic Evidence: Language, Power and Strategy in the Courtroom.* New York: Academic Press.

O'Barr, William, and Conley, John. 1985. Litigant Satisfaction versus Legal Adequacy in Small Claims Court Narratives. 19 *Law and Society Rev.*, 661.

Perelman, Chaim, and Obrechts Tyteca. 1969. *The New Rhetoric: A Treatise on Argumentation.* Notre Dame, IN: Notre Dame Univ. Press.

Plato, *Gorgias.*

Sandel, Michael. 1982. *Liberalism and the Limits of Justice.* Cambridge: Cambridge Univ. Press.

Sarat, Austin, and William L. F. Felstiner. 1988. Law and Social Relations: Vocabularies of Motive in Lawyer/Client Interaction. 22 *Law and Society Rev.*, 738.

———. 1995. *Divorce Lawyers and Their Clients.* New York: Oxford Univ. Press.

Schudson, M. 1982. The Politics of Narrative Form. 111 *Daedalus*, 97.

Tyler, Tom R. 1990. *Why People Obey the Law.* New Haven, CT: Yale Univ. Press.

Unger, Roberto. 1983. *The Critical Legal Studies Movement.* Cambridge, MA: Harvard Univ. Press.

White, James B. 1985. *Heracles' Bow: Essays on the Rhetoric and Poetics of Law.* Madison: Univ. of Wisconsin Press.

———. 1990. *Justice as Translation: An Essay in Cultural and Legal Criticism.* Chicago: Univ. of Chicago Press.

White, Lucie E. 1991. Subordination, Rhetorical Survival Skills, and Sunday Shoes: Notes on the Hearing of Mrs. G. In *At the Boundaries of Law*, ed. Martha Albertson Fineman and Nancy Sweet Thomadsen. New York: Routledge (reprinted from [1990] *Buffalo Law Review* 1).

Wydick, Richard. 1994. *Plain English for Lawyers.* 3d ed. Berkeley: Univ. of California Press.

Yngvesson, Barbara. 1988. Making Law at the Doorway: The Clerk, The Court, and the Construction of Community in a New England Town. 22 *Law and Society Rev.*, 409.

PUNISHMENT, POWER, AND JUSTICE

PATRICIA EWICK

I. INTRODUCTION

The connections between punishment, power, and justice are abundant, obvious, and complex. Whereas in many social institutions, such as schools, families, or hospitals, power lurks, submerged within dominant and often competing discourses of enlightenment, love, or benefaction, within penal institutions the operation of power is rarely disguised or denied by those who deploy it. Despite historical variations in the form, purposes, or rationalities of penal power, it is always conspicuously, publicly, and deliberately exercised. In the acts of surveillance, confiscation, detention, incarceration, reformation, and execution that constitute penality, the state claims for itself the right and obligation to commit acts of violence and transgression that are otherwise forbidden. Whether for expressive (retribution) or instrumental (deterrence or reformation) reasons, in the very act of punishing, penal power announces itself.

In announcing itself, penal power does not, however, present itself as limitless. Systems of penality also define themselves in term of justice. One need only consider the locution "criminal justice system" as an example of such self-definition. Within the official discourse, justice demarcates the limits of penal power by announcing standards against which power can be held accountable. A commitment to distributive justice, for instance, demands that the pain and deprivation that constitute penality be evenly and fairly exacted: like cases will be treated alike. Similarly, standards of justness require that punishments must be reasonable, not cruel, unusual, or excessive. To the extent that it contains and regulates the state's power to punish and afflict pain, justice legitimates that power. By holding itself accountable to standards of justice, the power to punish is made palatable. Wherever penal power is invoked, it is accompanied by some understanding of justice.

The capacity of justice to impart legitimacy to penal power depends, at least in part, on these ideals being construed as stable and transcendent, or "beyond culture and outside of history; a kind of absolute which is unaffected by change or by convention" (Garland 1990: 205). Justice may be breached, violated, or miscarried in specific situations, but these are to be understood as distortions of what are essentially the unchanging ideals of justice. The variations and transformations in penal practice that can be observed historically are understood to be accounted for by changes in power—who has it, how it is exercised, against whom, and for what purpose. These changes merely represent better or worse approximations of those transcendent values of justice.

Despite the transcendent quality that is claimed for justice, Garland (1990) has also observed,

> Even if past generations believed that their invocation of justice was an appeal to an absolute value, it is clear that the conceptions of what this value demanded, and of what justice implied, have changed over time in important ways. Precisely because justice was understood as unchanging, any changes in the conventions whereby justice was enacted have tended to be gradual and unannounced. Nevertheless, historians of criminal justice have begun to uncover important changes in the mentalities through which justice was conceived and enacted at different times, and these changing conceptions have been an important determinant of penal practice and its evolution. (1990: 205)

Garland's insight is important insofar as it suggests a different relationship between power and justice than that which is commonly recognized. The historically variable character of justice implies that it does more than simply harness, delimit, or discipline power by specifying a point beyond which power cannot go. Characterizing conceptions of justice as "important deter-minant[s] of penal practice" is to attribute to them the capacity to catalyze, not simply contain, power. Justice calls forth power; it demands action as much as it limits it. Moreover, to the extent that conceptions of justice are historical constructions themselves, whose articulation and acceptance needs to be explained, power is implicated in the construction of justice. In other words, just as the exercise and character of penal power is determined by conceptions of justice, notions of justice are likewise defined by the power against which they are poised. Justice, like mercy, is "given meaning by its contingency. It is the obverse of coercion, terror's conspiracy of silence" (Hay

1975: 62). The history of penal practices can be read, then, as the dialectic between power and justice.

2. PENALITY AND POWER

Despite the historically variable meaning of justice and its role in shaping penality, most recent histories of penal practice have focused almost exclusively on power. Power has been accorded a central and determinative role in constituting not only penality but criminality as well. Beginning in the 1960s, theories of social control and crime claimed that social control responses to criminal and deviant behaviors have the perverse effect of exacerbating or even constructing that which they would cure or condemn. Despite a century and a half of penal reform, criminological research, and sociological critique, the project to contain, curb, or cure criminality had, by all accounts, failed. More significantly, the failure seemed unavoidable, leading many social theorists to reevaluate the ostensible goals of the social control project and to conclude that its real objective has never been to eradicate crime or criminals, but rather to construct categories of crime and to produce criminals (Cohen 1985; Foucault 1979; Garland 1985, 1990). According to the various theoretical perspectives subscribing to this view, the delinquent is a result of either the psychological effects of labeling (Lemert 1951; Scheff 1984), the biophysical effects of disciplinary power (Foucault 1979), or the needs of a capitalist economy (Chambliss 1964; Rusche and Kirchheimer 1939). Power, as Foucault would have it, is not deployed negatively to eradicate or suppress criminality but positively to create the delinquent.

The inversion of the relationship between control and deviance has had a number of theoretical and conceptual consequences. First, it shifted the analytic and theoretical focus of criminologists and sociologists away from the criminal actor and systems of criminal behavior and directed it toward the systems and agents of control that have been devised to produce such actors and behaviors. The shift in focus entailed an abandonment of questions regarding etiology and individual depravity, poverty, or powerlessness. In fact, according to Cohen (1989),

> the tendency [within these perspectives] is to see the object of social control (whom or what is being controlled) as a *tabula rasa*, a blank space which is given identity and form only through the operation of social control. Deviance is an artifact of social control, virtually a reflection of this active and autonomous force which has a life of its own. (1989: 349)

Following from this view, the central questions that have concerned criminologists and sociologists of deviance in the past few decades have been about power and social control with a primary, although not exclusive, focus on the organized power of the state as it has been deployed against crime. The questions that have preoccupied these sociologists concern the different forms and technologies of power that have been used to produce delinquency; the ideological bases of the power to punish or cure; and the ways in which these forms of power and the ideologies that they have produced have been transformed historically.

In addition to making questions of power and its deployment central in the study of penality, the inversion of the relationship between crime and control also led to a radical reconceptualization of power. Once it was noted that the real objective of punishment was not to eradicate crime, a narrative history of penal failure was transformed into a unmitigated success story. Whatever was being done within the courts, prisons, probation offices, and community-based control centers was, appearances notwithstanding, precisely what was *supposed* to be happening. Obviously, this rendition of penal history required a radical reconceptualization of power (in this case the power to control or punish). No longer is power defined as a resource deployed by discrete persons or organizations, operating within particular relationships, animated by identifiable but specific capacities, interests, or motives, the realization of which is historically contingent or problematic (i.e., power might fail, be ineffective, or successfully resisted). Power is instead recast as an ineluctable force that follows a rationale, logic, or a master plan that belies its apparent failures and ineffectiveness and which, in some self-fulfilling process, cannot help but realize its objectives (Cohen 1989; O'Malley 1993). This conceptualization of power has been most clearly and self-consciously articulated by Foucault. However, weaker versions of it predate Foucault: vestiges of it can be found in Durkheim's functional analysis of social control, and a similar, albeit theoretically less elaborated, understanding of power underwrites some of the earliest versions of labeling theory.

So central and exclusive a position has power been accorded in histories of penality that transformations in its form have provided the principal basis for historical periodization. In other words, it has been transformations in the forms and technologies of power that have been used to mark discontinuities in penal epochs. According to Foucault, for instance, disciplinary forms of control succeeded the ancien regime's control over the body, because of its greater efficiency in producing docility among larger populations with a minimum of resources. The critical break or discontinuity that occurred in the eighteenth century marked a radical transformation in technologies of power.

Other scholars have extended Foucault's genealogy of power, noting a third and in some cases a fourth period, each representing a new form or technology of (more efficient, more effective) power. It has been proposed, for example, that modern disciplinary regimes have been supplemented by processes of normalization and the operation of actuarial forms of control (Reichman 1986; Simon 1988). Others have written of commodity culture and market control as the newest form of control in a "postdisciplinary" society (Ewick 1993; O'Malley 1993). In each of these accounts, justice, if it is mentioned at all, plays a subordinate role to power. Conceptualizing power as a technology that can be assessed in terms of such technical criteria as effectiveness and efficiency has rendered justice marginal or epiphenomenal in the history of penal change. Justice is either depicted as an ahistorical, transcendent set of values against which new technologies of power can be assessed, or, where changes in cultural understandings of justice are acknowledged, they are attributed to changes in the operation of power. In short, cast as the ideological handmaiden of power, conceptions of justice are thought to simply follow from transformations in power.

Without rewriting the by now familiar history of penal power that has been offered by Foucault and elaborated by many others over the past few decades, I would like to retell it from a slightly different perspective, recasting justice in a more central and pivotal role in the constitution of penal practice.

3. ANALYZING JUSTICE

Social scientists are somewhat ambivalent about justice, and this ambivalence manifests itself, in part, in the conceptual confusion and vagueness that surrounds the term. Unlike power, which can be observed in its behavioral or material form, justice requires a subjective assessment of the meaning of some behavior or decision: was it just, fair, appropriate? To engage in that assessment is to leave the value-free realm of positivist social science. To avoid such epistemological exile, the concept of justice is often deployed as I have used it thus far in this essay: as a vague but often unspecified marker for some set of equally unspecified value commitments having something to do with the distribution of costs and benefits.

Despite the general reluctance of empirical social scientists to analyze justice, there is general agreement, often implicit, that there are different sorts of justice. Consequently, the term is often preceded by an adjective connoting the various distinctions that have been drawn: procedural, substantive, or distributive, for instance. Unfortunately, there is less agreement regarding the precise practices or values to which these dimensions refer or regarding what relationships might exist among these various dimensions of justice.

For instance, in their study of why people obey the law, Lind and Tyler (1988) identify two types of justice considerations that shape people's attitudes and assessment of the law: procedural and distributive. For Lind and Tyler, procedural justice refers to the process of legal decision-making, more specifically whether the decision-making processes are "fair." Distributive justice refers to the fairness of distributions (i.e., the costs and benefits that derive from legal decisions). Their conceptual dyad suggests that there are two aspects of legal practice (decision-making and decisions) each of which might be assessed in terms of a single justice value: fairness.

In contrast to the particular justice dyad Lind and Tyler propose, Reiss (1974) suggests that,

Two related but different ideas inhere in traditional definitions of justice. The first idea grapples with the accuracy, fairness, reasonableness, or "justness" of the application of particular sanctions to particular conduct (or in a particular instance). At issue is the appropriateness of the rewards and costs as standards for and when applied to particular conduct. For example, is capital punishment for an offense just? The second idea refers to the distributive property of justice. Are equals treated equally regardless of the reward or the cost? (1974: 693)

Whereas Lind and Tyler mark differences in types of legal practice (decision-making versus the substantive outcomes that follow these decisions) and assess them in relation to a single value (fairness), Reiss's distinction relies on the identification of different values (justness versus fairness) without specifying the particular legal practice to which these criteria might be applied. Both of these definitions of justice illustrate similar conceptual deficiencies. Insofar as each of these typologies obscures a different dimension of justice, they are, I would suggest, singularly underspecified. Additionally, these definitions of justice are ahistorical. In identifying the distributive aspect of justice, Reiss, like Lind and Tyler, defines it in terms of equity (like treatment accorded like cases), without acknowledging or allowing for the possibility of historically variable definitions of "just" rules of distributions. In both cases, distributive justice is simply equated with equitable distributions, an equation that reflects the ahistoricism referred to previously by Garland insofar as it defines justice in terms of a single, unchanging, and peculiarly modern, value. A consequence of this definitional specificity has been to impede precisely the sort of historical analysis proposed here in that it defines justice "outside of history and culture."

In place of these dyadic conceptions of justice, I would like to propose that an adequate typology of justice would need to recognize at least four different dimensions of justice. For instance, the *procedural* dimension of justice refers to an epistemology of legal decision-making in that it defines the assumptions, rules, and conventions used in determining, producing, or uncovering the truth (e.g., of guilt, fault, responsibility). The *substantive* dimension of justice refers to some quality or qualities of the outcome of those decisions. These two different sorts of legal acts can, in turn, each be evaluated in terms of their justness or reasonableness and in terms of some distributive aspect. Thus, legal procedures, as well as legal outcomes, may each be assessed in terms of how reasonable or appropriate they are *and* in regard to the terms of their distribution. For example, relying on the contemporary American definition of distributive justice, a particular procedure for ascertaining the truth (torture, for instance) might be found inappropriate (and, thus, deemed unjust) even were it to be used consistently on all like cases. The same determination might be made for substantive outcomes. Capital punishment might be rejected as unjust even if it could be shown (which it cannot) that it is applied fairly and evenly across all like cases. Conversely, a particular procedure or outcome could be deemed reasonable or appropriate but still defined as unjust because it is not evenly or "fairly" applied to all like cases. As the following diagram suggests, both legal procedures and substantive outcomes can each be assessed in terms of their distributive aspects, as well as their justness, that is, their appropriateness or reasonableness.

Procedural
(decision-making)

Justness criteria   Distributive criteria

Substantive
(outcomes)

Relying on this elaborated typology of justice, it is possible to map historical transformations in penality and power according to changes in the definition and operation of these various dimensions of justice.

4. THE JUSTICE OF TYRANTS: PENALITY AND THE ANCIEN REGIME

The canonical history of penal practice typically begins by describing the period immediately predating the modern period, a period that has been variously labeled the ancien regime or the "classical" period. As a result of Foucault's arresting image, premodern penality is emblemized by the scaffold, a symbol that evokes the public, excessive, corporeal, and ritualistic quality of penal power during this time. Power was directed toward the body of the condemned. It was exacted within the community before an assembled audience. It was excessive and spectacular. And, in proclaiming and avenging the power of the sovereign, it had a face and a name.

But what about justice during this period? By contemporary definitions, justice was conspicuously absent from premodern or classical penality. The secret nature of legal proceedings, the absence of almost all guarantees of due process, the reliance on torture to extract confessions or determine guilt, and the use of hideous forms of execution to punish those convicted of serious offenses all conjure up the image of a system of penality without any operable concept of justice.

Yet, just as we recognize premodern forms of power, we should be prepared to recognize premodern forms of justice. As suggested earlier, justice is not an optional component of penality or power. Justice is a necessary and integral part of power. Given the public, excessive, brutal, and capricious nature of premodern power, demonstrations of justice were as, if not more, important than they would become in subsequent epochs. Because punishment during this period was theatrical, performed before the community to dramatize the power of the sovereign, penality required the belief, support, and legitimacy of the audience assembled to view it. It required, in short, strong and persuasive demonstrations of justice. According to Douglas Hay (1975), the eighteenth-century English gentry "were acutely aware that their security depended on *belief*—belief in the justice of their rule, and in its adamantine strength. Hence punishment at times had to be waived or mitigated to meet popular ideas of justice, and to prevent popular outrage from going too far and thereby realizing its own strength" (1975: 51).

Acknowledging the necessity and centrality of some form of justice in premodern penal systems is not to suggest that the meaning of justice during this period conformed in any recognizable way to modern notions of justice. For one thing, the distinction that has been so meticulously drawn between procedural and substantive justice was blurred or nonexistent in premodern systems. Second, although contemporary definitions of justice accept punishment and the infliction of some measure of pain as a reasonable and just outcome in cases where there has been a finding of guilt, they do not allow that procedures of investigation and adjudication should produce or inflict pain or deprivation. So committed are we to the value of nonpunitive procedures that social scientists have successfully condemned the legal system with the charge that the "process is the punishment," a phrase intended to evoke a portrait of a system of justice where something has gone terribly wrong. Yet the phrase would stand as nothing more than a bland description, rather than critique, of premodern penal practice.

In the premodern penal system "investigation and punishment had become mixed" (Foucault 1977: 41). During this period, the accused would be routinely subjected to torture during interrogation as a way of extracting a confession. "The body interrogated in torture constituted the point of application of the punishment and the locus of extortion of the truth. And just as presumption was inseparably an element in investigation and a fragment of guilt, the regulated pain involved in judicial torture was a means of *both punishment and investigation*" (1977: 42).

In practice, the distinction between legal procedural and substantive outcomes, and thus the distinction between procedural and substantive *justice*, was erased. This blurring of the boundaries between the processes of interrogation and punishment should be seen and understood as a reflection of a premodern, prepositivist epistemology that conceived of truth and methods of its discovery in radically different ways than they are currently understood. Knowledge did not conform to a dualistic system, in which facts or circumstances could be determined to be true or false or defendants to be guilty or not guilty (Foucault 1977). According to this premodern epistemology, there were degrees of truth and gradients of guilt. At each moment in the process of criminal adjudication the evidence revealed more or less guilt, thus warranting more or less punishment. To the degree that the process revealed guilt, it was *supposed* to be punitive. This premodern epistemology also underwrote the importance placed on confession and legitimated the use of torture in interrogation. Unlike their positivist counterparts in the modern period, investigators placed considerably less reliance on or faith in the physical or material world to reveal guilt or innocence through forensic evidence. The testimony of persons, typically in the form of the confession, reflected a commitment to religious practices of receiving truth through revelation and reflection rather than as something gained through scientific methods of observation and deduction. The ideological capacity of confession to legitimate and affirm the power of the sovereign rests in these popular understandings of truth and the means of its discovery.

Modern understandings of the *justness,* or appropriateness, of substantive outcomes are almost invariably based on the calculation of proportion. The belief that the punishment should "fit" the crime, or that the convicted should receive their "just deserts," are typically interpreted in some quantitative way: lesser crimes, or lesser guilt, should receive lesser punishments. In the classical period of penality, however, there was no expectation that there would be a quantitative equivalency between crime and punishment. In fact, the objective of punishment was to produce an excess of pain and suffering on the part of the convicted: not simply to execute but to torture. As Foucault has argued, the principle objective of the scaffold was to demonstrate to the audience assembled the awesome, unrestrained power of the sovereign rather than match the severity of punishment with the seriousness of crime. "The punishment is carried out in such a way as to give a spectacle not of measure, but of imbalance and excess" (Foucault 1977: 49). Rather than a failure of justice, the intended goal of punishment was to achieve a deliberate *dissymmetry* between the crime and its punishment.

The distributive aspects of premodern penality are as alien to the modern consciousness of justice as are the justness aspects. The modern idea of like cases being treated alike begs the question of what constitutes a like case. As an operating principle of legal practice, it assumes a schema of circumstances, persons, and crimes within which specific cases can be fit, compared, and evaluated. Thus, modern notions of *distributive justice* as being synonymous with *equitable outcomes* rest on a type of order that categorizes and classifies that which comes to constitute "like" cases. Yet, as Hay (1975) has noted, most eighteenth-century Englishmen "tended to think of justice in personal terms, and were more struck by understanding of individual cases than by the delights of abstract schemes" (1975: 39). Distributions of punishment in the eighteenth century were based on idiosyncratic, personal relations. Modern constructions of distributive justice require systematic, rational, and bureaucratic administration of penalties. In contrast, eighteenth-century justice was characterized by the apparently capricious system of excessive capital sentences relieved by royal pardons. As Hay points out, the system of pardons, doled out to gentlemen on the basis of class favoritism and to the lower classes on the basis of paternalistic ties to gentlemen, was an integral and sustaining feature of penal power at this time. Particularism and biography, rather than membership in an abstract cultural category, were considered legitimate bases for determining the application of a sanction or the rewarding of a pardon. Just as power, in the person of the monarch, had a face and a name, the objects of penal power were also known in the particularities of their character and relationships.

Excessive, capricious, bloody, and implacable, premodern penality appears to be characterized by power unfettered by the restraints of justice. This appearance of unrestrained power, however, is dependent on justice being defined in terms of measure, proportion, and equity, on a type of justice cast in peculiarly modern terms. Alternatively, where justice is defined as that which renders power intelligible as a set of legal operations—as that which does not so much limit power as gives it content—we can observe the operation of justice in the very excesses it "fails" to contain.

While premodern penality was clearly not characterized by the same criteria that appear in contemporary understandings of justice, there were, nonetheless, other criteria of justice to which power was held accountable. For instance, although there was no attempt to achieve a proportionality between the crime and the punishment, some meaningful correspondence between the two was enforced. More specifically, the relationship that was sought between the sanction and crime was mimetic rather than proportional. Punishment was a production designed to be the theatrical realization of the crime, rather than simply a matching of it in terms of intensity or severity. Executions would occur at the location where the crime was said to have taken place, the specific forms of torture would represent the type of crime (the tongues of blasphemers would be pierced, the hands of murderers cut off), or the condemned would be made to carry the weapon with which he committed the crime. In these ways, the punishment would broadcast its own justification to the audience.

Within the practices of premodern penality the appropriateness, or justness, of sanctions was determined not just in relation to the crime but also in relation to the legal procedures that preceded the sanction. The gallows speech, the *amende honorable,* and the death song, as integral parts of the execution, served as proof of the crime as well as of the legitimacy of the procedures. "They pursued that mechanism by which the public execution transferred the secret, written truth of the procedure to the body, gesture and speech of the criminal. *Justice required these apocrypha in order to be grounded in truth*" (Foucault 1979: 66, emphasis mine).

The mimetic quality of justice in this period reflected the premodern episteme: a theory of knowledge based on resemblance rather than comparison, on similitude rather than difference. The modern passion for classification and taxonomy rests on the recognition of abstraction, difference, and complexity that was absent in this period (Foucault 1973). This absence marked virtually all aspects of classical or premodern justice. The proportionality that would come to define "just" sanctions, the commitment to "equitable" distributions, even the distinction drawn between procedures and substantive outcomes, all derive from distinctly modern epistemologies and ontologies. Most important, these aspects of justice emerge out of the social construction of the individual subject who can be abstracted from the particularities of biography and social relationships and who, thus, can be "known" in a way that was historically unprecedented. The knowledge of such individuals and the calculations and procedures that such knowledge enables was to come to underwrite a new form of penal power in the nineteenth century, a form of power that operated with respect to entirely different purposes, objects, technologies, and, notably, incorporated a radically different sense of justice.

5. MODERN PENALITY: THE JUSTICE OF INSTITUTIONS

Modern penality, a period that is traced to the early nineteenth century, is distinguished by its relative lack of cruelty, excess, and passion. Penal power appears at this time to be fettered by what are, today, familiar constraints of justice. We see, for instance, the abandonment of torture and other cruel and expressive forms of punishment for measured, rationally administered penalties. We see in place of an inquisitorial model that blurred interrogation and punishment the development of guarantees of due process. And we see the emergence of a new sense of distributive equity that invalidates the particularism, and with it the capriciousness, of the classical period.

At one level these changes can and have been understood as the result of the civilizing process. As human societies mature and evolve, the story goes, they adopt more humane (i.e., less primitive or barbaric) forms of penality. We can read in this narrative a teleological, and thus transcendent, view of justice. Systems of penality are seen as maturing as power defers to the values of justice. Rather than a cluster of historically contingent value commitments that collaborates with power to constitute penality, justice is seen in these accounts as that which counters and civilizes raw judicial power.

An alternative reading of this history views changes in the meaning of justice as being of a piece with transformations in penal power, both a result of political and cultural developments that extended beyond the realm of penality.

First, what were understood to be "just" legal procedures reflected an epistemological transformation that redefined the nature of truth and invalidated the earlier ways of discovering and establishing it. Modern definitions of procedural justice are founded on the positivist notion of the truth as an objective fact that must be demonstrated through empirical evidence. The necessity of that demonstration underpins the central commitment of modern procedural justice: the presumed innocence of the defendant until such "proof" is forthcoming. According to Langbein (1976), the abolition of judicial torture, then, was a result of changes in the law of proof in which the judicial evaluation of evidence came to replace the old Roman canon law of statutory proofs.

In fact, most of the specific guarantees and protections that constitute procedural justness work to preserve the objectivity of the methods through which data is obtained and interpretations are made. Recall that the epistemological assumptions that underwrote the use of torture and the extraction of confessions included the belief that "semi-proofs produce semi-truths and semi-guilty persons" (Foucault 1977: 97). Truth, conceived in this way, blurred the line between process and outcome, adjudication and punishment. However, once truth was conceived as existing in the nature of things, that is, apart from its apprehension or the method of its discovery, a separate sphere of legal procedures emerged and with it a radically new understanding of what constituted procedural justice. The truth of guilt or innocence was no longer understood to be a construction or consequence of the judicial process. In the new episteme, the fact of guilt or innocence was recognized to exist prior to and, thus, independently of that process, whose function is now simply to reveal that truth through investigation, observation, and logic. Accessing the truth of the matter, that is, establishing guilt or innocence, necessitated adopting the same standards of objectivity, validity, and logic that defined empirical scientific research.

"With the multiplicity of scientific discourses, a difficult, infinite relation was then forged that penal justice is still unable to control. The master of justice is no longer the master of its truth" (Foucault 1977: 98). The procedural guarantees that characterize modern penality reflected a modern ontology as well as epistemology. As Foucault has argued, beginning in the nineteenth century the object of punishment shifted away from the body of the condemned to the soul of the prisoner, where the soul represented the knowable, and thus calculable, individual. Perhaps the most salient change in penality in the nineteenth century, the invention of the prison, reflected this shift (Foucault 1977; Rothman 1971). The penitentiary replaced the scaffold as the principal venue and instrument for the operation of penal power. Within the walls of the prison, those subject to penal power were observed, knowledge regarding them was collected, and here they were exposed to the normalizing effects of disciplinary power. Most significantly, however, the modern individual was not merely subjected to this penal discipline, he or she was produced by the operation of these regimes of power. Out of the meticulous and minute regulation of gestures, the spatial deployment of bodies, and the temporal structuring of days emerged the individual with a soul, that is, a portable, knowable self that was recognized as having an existence outside of the web of hierarchical social relationships. This modern individual could, thus, be invested with capacities and fundamental human rights that transcended the exigencies of time, place, or association. Disciplinary power, in constructing such a subject, also redefined the meaning of justice and, thus, the limits of its own legitimate exercise. Against the barbarity of the scaffold and the inhumanity of judicial torture was pitted the humanity of this new being. It was "a 'man-measure'; not of things but of power" (Foucault 1979: 74). Accordingly, what was deemed reasonable, and thus just, punishment was defined at its boundary by this "man-measure."

Humans were not only redefined in terms of their universal humanity, they also came to be understood in their variety, in terms of the diversity of human types. Classical penality, in claiming that crime was a result of the exercise of free will, attributed a criminal potential to all humans (Pasquino 1991). By contrast, in modern penality, the *type abstrait* so beloved of classical jurisprudence has been radically undermined, along with the strict uniformity of treatment which its notion of justice entailed. From the point of view of this new system, there no longer exists a universe of free and equal subjects which coincides with the sane adult population. Now there are categories which pose exceptions to the rule (Garland 1985: 25).

These newly wrought individuals could be assessed, classified, and thus acted upon, according to their various mental, physical, social attributes and capacities. Thus, recognition of both the universal and the variable among humans came to define modern penal justice. That dimension of justice that we have labeled procedural justness, that is, the reasonableness of processes of investigation and adjudication, reflects a recognition of the autonomous juridical subject to whom certain unalienable and universal rights could be attached. Similarly, that dimension of justice that we have called substantive justness, the appropriateness or reasonableness of sanctions or outcomes, is now measured in terms of proportionality, a correspondence between the seriousness of the crime, the responsibility of the criminal, and the severity of the penality. Finally, modern notions of distributive justice as it would apply to either process or outcome relies on the construction of difference and likeness upon which calculations of equity are based.

All of these changes were predicated on the construction of the modern individual. The object of intense supervision, observation, classification, and regulation, individuals subjected to penal power became visible and known. Meanwhile, penal power itself receded and disappeared from direct view. Whereas, in the premodern period, power, in the shape of the sovereign, had a name and a face, in the modern period, penal power exists but as a disembodied and faceless force. In the modern period, power assumes the form of the impregnable prison walls, the imposing courthouse, the rational schedule of penalties, and the professional expertise of legal functionaries. In short, the social organization of modern punishment takes the form of a highly articulated bureaucratic structure: the specification and differentiation of roles, the interdependence that comes from a division of labor, a centralized hierarchy of authority, and a reliance on rules and regulation. Rationalized and dispassionate, the power to punish seems to work without human agency or human sentiment. This structure, as is true of all social structures, allows legal actors to operate by proxy, that is, to produce results that they could not, or perhaps would not, achieve on their own (Connell 1987). For instance, the bureaucratic structure of modern penality is the context that links the judge's "word" with the violent acts of the jailer or the executioner.

The context of a judicial utterance is institutional behavior in which others, occupying preexisting roles, can be expected to act, to implement, or otherwise to respond in a specified way to the judge's interpretation. Thus, the institutional context ties the language act of practical understanding to the physical acts of others in a predictable, though not logically necessary, way (Cover 1986: 1611). Even while it divides labor and diffuses responsibility, the bureaucratic organization of punishment enables action. These structural properties of modern penality are similarly recognized as critical components of modern justice. For, as part of the same historical process of rationalization, justice, like power, has been redefined as the passionless, objective, and measured infliction of just the right amount of pain and suffering.

In sum, knowable, calculable individuals, and the categories they would come to constitute, called forth an economy of power that would match taxonomies of crimes and criminals against gradients of punishments, maximizing their effectiveness while minimizing their cost. The result was not simply the abolition of public executions or judicial torture—a civilizing change at the so-called frontiers of punishment—but the creation of an entire schedule of complex and differentiated penalties and professionals designed to deter without excess and punish without anger or enthusiasm (*sine ira ac studio*) (Weber 1958: 214). Justice, lodged in the dehumanized interstices of bureaucratic institutions, appears as power without passion.

6. POSTMODERN PENALITY: THE ECLIPSE OF POWER AND JUSTICE

While the transition from classical penality to modern penality appears as a clean break, the third moment in this history of penal power and justice lacks such distinctiveness. In the spirit of all that is postmodern, it exists as an amalgam of that which went before: elements of ancien regime penality are juxtaposed with modern techniques and both are overlaid with forms of control that are historically unprecedented. The most distinctive feature of postmodern penality lies, then, in the simultaneous operation of parallel control systems, each system defined, in part, by who and what it excludes.

Modernist disciplinary institutions, such as the prison, survive and expand. Despite the movement toward decarceration and deinstitutionalization, rates of imprisonment have continued to increase in the past few decades, dispelling any notion that discipline as a form of penal control is moribund (Cohen 1985). At the same time, alternative, postdisciplinary forms of social control have also emerged and expanded (O'Malley 1993; Simon 1993). These technologies of control are unusual insofar as they appear as totally nonpunitive. In general, the ensemble of postdisciplinary techniques avoid being punitive by managing *opportunities* for behaviors, as opposed to manipulating behaviors themselves.[1]

Postdiscipline control is largely accomplished through the regulation of space, including how it is designed, distributed, and inhabited. Space is made "defensible," for instance, by closing off escape routes or opening up vantage for surveillance (Newman 1972, cited in Simon 1993). Similarly, contemporary office buildings and amusement parks are located and designed to discourage certain types of behaviors or visitors (Shearing and Stenning 1984; Shields 1992). Indeed, if the scaffold is the emblem of power under the ancien regime and the prison of modern penality, the shopping mall has come to symbolize postmodern control.

Of course, the regulation of space has always been an integral component of modern disciplinary (as opposed to postdisciplinary) control. According to Dreyfus and Rabinow (1983),

> Discipline proceeds by the organization of individuals in space, and it therefore requires a specific enclosure of space. In the hospital, the school, or the military field, we find a reliance on an orderly grid. Once established, this grid permits the sure distribution of individuals to be disciplined and supervised; this procedure facilitates the reduction of dangerous multitudes or wandering vagabonds to fixed and docile individuals. (1983: 54–155)

What makes postdisciplinary control distinctive, then, is not the regulation of space per se but the use of particular spatial practices. As the quote from Dreyfus and Rabinow suggests, discipline proceeds through the "enclosure of space" and, once that is achieved, through the containment of individuals within these enclaves. Individuals are located within prisons, schools, or factories, and, once inside, subjected to discipline and surveillance. By contrast, postdisciplinary use of space operates less through containment than through selection and exclusion. The location and architectural design of the modern mall, for example, does not so much contain potentially disruptive populations as it discourages their entry, reserving occupancy for already docile individuals. Along these lines, Jonathan Simon (1993) has observed that postmodern control relies on "channeling" out "those segments of the population that are more likely to pose risks than benefits to the space being controlled" (1993: 7).[2]

Shields, writing of the West Edmonton Mall (the third largest tourist attraction in North America after Disneyland and Disney World), describes the contradictions of such a highly regulated semiprivate space:

> Although the promoted image is one of freedom, unfettered impulse buying, and liminality, the reality is one of control. . . . In Canada, this contradiction has already engendered a series of constitutional challenges to mall-owners' right to bar people selectively, in one case a 60-year old cripple, from malls on the grounds of loitering. (1989: 160)

Invoking the shopping mall as the emblem of postmodern control is even more appropriate if we consider a second distinctive feature of this type of control, its use of market-based technologies to shape and control identity and behavior (Ewick 1993; O'Malley 1993; Rose 1990). The subjects who are channeled into the regulated spaces—whether a mall, a private residential treatment facility, or a high-rise condominium, are constructed as consumers. O'Malley (1993) has written that in such a commodified sphere, "the exercise of power is thus decoupled, for now the autonomous citizens regulate themselves through organizing their lives around the market. Management of commodity circulation implies that government of things replaces, or acts as a relay for, the government of persons" (1993: 172–73).

Postmodern control is promotive rather than reactive, voluntary rather than coercive, and is based more on choice than on constraint. Within such a market, power seems to have no place. Whereas power in a rationalized bureaucratic context appears passionless, here, eclipsed by the image of individual choice, it seems to disappear altogether. Yet, the orderliness of persons and behaviors within these spaces belies the image of unconstrained individual freedom. Describing the youth culture within the Edmonton Mall, Shields writes,

> To congregate in such spaces as the West Edmonton Mall requires that one observe bourgeois norms of social docility and conservatism both in dress and action. The displays of "peacock clothing" or "punk spectacle" . . . are relegated to just outside the doors of this Mall. Instead, the clothing adopted is a fashion industry edition of punk or gothic style. [T]he credo is: One must always look as if one has bought something or is about to buy. Hence their uniform, classless appearance. Also, there are thus no hangouts. The greatest rebellion is the act of sitting down on the floor, ignoring benches, defying the planned environment in a gesture which questions the conventional discourse of space at the Mall. Movement after a few minutes is often essential to avoid the security guards patrolling for loiterers. (1989: 160)

As many have noted, even outside of confines of such spatialized markets, the "invisible hand" regulates individuals. In particular, through the production of need and the ordering of choice, the market, advertising, and a "culture of consumption" operate to regulate not only the behavior but the imagination and identities of citizens (Ewen and Ewen 1982; Ewick 1993; Spitzer 1983; Shearing and Stenning 1985). As Rose has written, "the same forces that de-legitimate 'public' interference in 'private life' [and] open the details of wishes, desires, and pleasures to a plethora of new regulatory forms, [are] no less powerful for being decoupled from the authoritative prescriptions of the public powers" (1990: 255).

While it is no doubt true, then, that power of some sort is operating within these semiprivate spaces and public markets, it is certainly not a form of penal power. In fact, it is the near total absence of penal power within the regulated hyperspaces that makes its operation elsewhere—in the abandoned spaces of the city: the projects, the dangerous neighborhoods—all the more significant. Only those who can qualify as consumers, those who are on "the inside of freedom" to use Simon's evocative phrase, are eligible for this type of postmodern control. All others, the chronically unemployed, the insane, the socially marginal, are excluded and subjected to the traditional disciplines as practiced by the police and other public officials.

7. CONCLUSION

I began with the thesis that power and justice mutually define one another within systems of penality. Power is thus made intelligible through justice, just as justice is given meaning through the exercise of power. Relying on a rather conventional history of penal practices, I have attempted to read beyond the typical focus on power to excavate a parallel history of justice. This history indicates that as penal power deploys different technologies of control it activates different conceptions of justice, that is, varying understandings of what are reasonable, appropriate, or fair procedures and distributions. Embedded within these conceptions, moreover, are varying ontological and epistemological commitments. As cultural understandings of knowledge and the possibilities of its apprehension are redefined, power itself is transformed. As the subjects of penal power are differentially constructed, the power that is brought to bear on them is shaped and reshaped.

It follows from this thesis that the bifurcation and stratification of power that has occurred in the postmodern period and, in particular, its submergence within a discourse of choice and freedom, has predictable consequences for the definition of justice. Specifically, as power is effaced within the sanitized, selective spaces of a consumption society, so too is justice. Considerations of just distributions or reasonable and appropriate procedures and interventions become irrelevant once "public" powers to adjudicate and punish disappear or defer to individual choice and "private" regulation. Indeed the ontology that previously underwrote modern definitions of justice, the autonomous individual invested with fundamental unalienable rights, is replaced within a postmodern regime by a new ontology of the individual: that of the consumer.

"Merely to be in attendance at the 'court of commodities' (Benjamin 1973) is to claim one's status as a consumer which under a capitalism which reduces people to their function in an economist equation, is to assert one's *existence* and to be recognized as a person. Being a consumer, with the right to attend these rituals seems to have almost overtaken the importance of being a citizen" (Shields 1989: 159). Given this, it is perhaps not coincidental that, within the United States, both rates of imprisonment and frequency of executions have increased in the past few decades, a time when the postindustrial decay of our inner cities produced an increasing disparity between those who could be regulated via the relays of the market and those who are likely to be perpetually outside of the reach of the "invisible hand." In short, for those denied access to the "court of commodities," the penal power of the state continues to operate, but now with a diminished sense of citizenship and with it a stunted definition of justice.

NOTES

1. Recently, for instance, Nynex converted 250 of its public telephones in New York City from pushbutton to rotary dials in an effort to thwart drug dealers from paging customers.

This was the latest in an arsenal of tactics used by the company against drug dealing. Previously the company had disabled approximately 8,400 of its public telephones from receiving incoming calls in addition to moving phones away from problem areas and improving lighting (*New York Times,* January 10, 1993, p. 1).

2. In 1993 homicides, while declining, were increasingly concentrated in specific areas of New York City. "Safe" neighborhoods became safer, at the same time other neighborhoods witnessed a rise in the rate of homicide (*New York Times,* January 10, 1993, p. 23).

BIBLIOGRAPHY

Chambliss, William. 1964. A Sociological Analysis of the Law of Vagrancy. 12 *Social Problems,* 67–77.

Cohen, Stanley. 1985. *Visions of Social Control.* New York: Oxford Univ. Press.

———. 1989. The Critical Discourse on "Social Control": Notes on the Concept as a Hammer. 17 *International Journal of the Sociology of Law,* 347.

Connell, R. W. 1987. *Gender and Power.* Stanford, CA: Stanford Univ. Press.

Cover, Robert. 1986. Violence and the Word. 95 *Yale Law Journal,* 1601.

Dreyfus, Hubert, and Paul Rabinow. 1983. *Michel Foucault: Beyond Structuralism and Hermeneutics.* Chicago: Univ. of Chicago Press.

Ewen, Stewart, and Elizabeth Ewen. 1982. *Channels of Desire: Mass Images and the Shaping of American Consciousness.* New York: McGraw-Hill.

Ewick, Patricia. 1993. Corporate Cures: The Commodification of Social Control. 13 *Research in Law, Politics and Society,* 137.

Foucault, Michel. 1973. *The Order of Things: An Archaeology of the Human Sciences.* New York: Vintage.

———. 1977. *Discipline and Punish: The Birth of the Prison.* New York: Vintage.

Garland, David. 1985. *Punishment and Welfare.* Brookfield, VT: Gower.

———. 1990. *Punishment and Modern Society.* Chicago: Univ. of Chicago Press.

Hay, Douglas. 1975. Property, Authority and the Criminal Law. In *Albion's Fatal Tree: Crime and Society in Eighteenth-Century England,* ed. Douglas Hay, Peter Linebaugh, John G. Rule, E. P. Thompson, and Cal Winslow, 17–63. New York: Pantheon.

Langbein, John. 1976. *Torture and the Law of Proof.* Chicago: Univ. of Chicago Press.

Lemert, Edwin. 1951. *Social Pathology: A Systematic Approach to the Theory of Sociopathic Behavior.* New York: McGraw-Hill.

Lind, E. Allan, and Tom R. Tyler. 1988. *The Social Psychology of Procedural Justice.* New York: Plenum Press.

O'Malley, Pat. 1993. Containing Our Excitement: Commodity Culture and the Crisis of Discipline. 13 *Research in Law, Politics and Society,* 159.

Pasquino, Pasquale. 1991. Criminology: The Birth of a Special Knowledge. In *The Foucault Effect: Studies in Governmentality,* ed. Graham Burchell, Colin Gordon, and Peter Miller. Chicago: Univ. of Chicago Press.

Reichman, Nancy. 1986. Managing Crime Risks: Toward an Insurance Based Model of Social Control. 8 *Research in Law and Social Control,* 151.

Reiss, Albert J., Jr. 1974. Discretionary Justice. In *Handbook of Criminology*, ed. Daniel Glaser. Chicago: Rand-McNally.

Rose, Nikolas. 1990. *Governing the Soul: The Shaping of the Private Self*. New York: Routledge.

Rothman, David J. 1971. *The Discovery of the Asylum*. Toronto: Little, Brown.

Rusche, G., and O. Kirchheimer. 1939. *Punishment and Social Structure*. New York: Columbia Univ. Press.

Scheff, Thomas J. 1984. *Being Mentally Ill*. New York: Aldine.

Shearing, Clifford D., and Philip C. Stenning. 1984. From the Panopticon to Disney World: The Development of Discipline. In *Perspectives in Criminal Law*, ed. Anthony N. Doob and Edward L. Greenspan, Q.C. Aurora, Ontario: Canada Law Books, Inc.

Shields, Rob. 1989. Social Spatialization and the Built Environment: The West Edmonton Mall. 7 *Society and Space*, 147–64.

———. 1992. *Places on the Margin: Alternative Geographies of Modernity*. New York: Routledge.

Simon, Jonathan. 1988. The Ideological Effects of Actuarial Practices. 22 *Law and Society Review*, 771.

———. 1993. From Confinement to Waste Management: The Postmodernization of Social Control. 8 *Focus on Law Studies*, 4.

Spitzer, Steven. 1983. The Rationalization of Crime Control in Capitalist Society. In *Social Control and the State*, ed. Stanley Cohen and Andrew Scull. New York: St. Martin's Press.

Weber, Max. 1958. Bureaucracy. In *From Max Weber: Essays in Sociology*, ed. H. H. Gerth and C. Wright Mills. New York: Oxford Univ. Press.

JUSTICE, POWER,
AND LAWYERS

WILLIAM L. F. FELSTINER

We can think of justice in lawyer-client relations in both substantive and procedural terms. Substantively, the traditional position is that lawyers produce justice by counseling clients to do the right thing. They are counsel for the situation, they transform their clients' objectives into socially acceptable goals, they are statespersons as well as advocates, they mediate between their clients' illegitimate objectives and the social interest, they refuse to do the clients' most destructive and antisocial bidding, even if it is technically legal. Of course it is not easy for a commentator to define "the right thing" nor, on many occasions, for a lawyer to identify it. But, for the moment, let us assume that some counsel tends more toward socially acceptable ends than others, and that such advice is intended to turn clients away from the most aggressive behavior and selfish objectives. Procedurally, justice in these relationships would mean that lawyers treat clients well—that lawyers are accessible, responsive, empathetic, communicate effectively, pay prompt attention to their clients' affairs, and are motivated by professional values rather than financial returns. In sum, the procedurally just lawyer treats her clients with respect.

In this chapter, I will briefly elaborate on the notion of constructive counseling and then present the conventional case that American lawyers have generally abandoned that role. I will then analyze the theory of power in the lawyer-client relationship that is embedded in the abandonment thesis. That theory of the power balance between lawyers and clients will be contrasted with the quite different perspective that is reflected in Austin Sarat's and my work on divorce lawyers and with the available data about how lawyers in fact tend to treat their clients. I will conclude by summarizing the factors that seem to account for the transformation in the roles of American lawyers, if there has indeed been one, and by considering how all this has happened in the face of the idealism with which recent college graduates enter law schools.

I. LAWYERS AND JUSTICE: SOCIALLY CONSTRUCTIVE COUNSELING

Where does the idea that, when there are choices, lawyers ought to counsel their clients along socially constructive paths come from in the first place? It is not a notion that is self-evident. If the lawyer is thought to be an agent for her client, to do that which the client would do for herself had she the requisite technical skills, then the lawyer's conception of goodness, morality, social acceptability, constructive means, or the spirit of the law would be irrelevant. But the lawyer has long been normatively considered more than an agent. Inherent in the idea of a profession, incorporated in repeated codes of ethics, enshrined in countless speeches by legal officials and pronouncements by official bodies is the idea that lawyers are accountable to court and public, have responsibilities to society that have priority over their own interests, and, although particular instances are hotly contested and even litigated, over the interests of their clients.

Empirically, the case that law is a public calling and that lawyers have assumed—have ever assumed—a special responsibility to advance the public good (see Kronman 1995: 4) is not that obvious. The major works that are concerned with the social role of lawyers provide only a shallow picture of the profession in action. For example, take Gordon's "Independence of Lawyers" (1988), Kagan and Rosen's "On the Social Significance of Large Law Firm Practice" (1985), Nelson's *Partners with Power* (1988), Simon's "Ideology of Advocacy" (1978), Kronman's *Lost Lawyer* (1993), and Shamir's *Managing Legal Uncertainty* (1995). Simon's paper, a monster even by law review standards, provides elaborate arguments about the failure of philosophical and practical underpinnings for the conventional rationalizations of law practice, but it almost never provides empirical support for the scores of positions and insights that it presents, subtle as they may be. Moreover, though Simon endorses the ideal of lawyer and client jointly formulating client goals—an instance of the important exhortatory literature that reaches its apex in Binder, Bergman, and Price's (1991) client-centered approach to counseling—he believes that the lawyer's counseling role, that is the efforts that she is supposed to make "to discourage the client's short-sighted pursuit of his interests" (1978: 78), may be psychologically doomed.

Kronman's book is elitist in conception. He talks about lawyers and the legal profession in general, but when it gets down to the details he is concerned only with the posture of large firm lawyers as they face a transformation in institutional structures armed only with the (flawed) preparation provided by top-tier law schools. The only references in almost four hundred pages of text to empirical work on lawyers are to the triumvirate of major works on the large firm (Smigel 1964; Nelson 1988; and Galanter and Palay 1991; plus a couple of citations to *The American Lawyer* and *The National Law Journal*), and even these references are limited to changes respecting branch offices, specialization, house counsel, firm hierarchies, and marketing practices (1993: 273–83), all tangential to the ultimate question of whether law is a public calling. Kagan and Rosen, on the other hand, focus directly on that issue: they consider whether large firm lawyers are doing more or less work of social significance as in the past and how much that more or less is. It is less and the less is not much (1985: 430–34), but the caveat is that their conclusion, interesting as it is in the details, is based on only fourteen responses to twenty-five questionnaires (1985: 431).

Of these major commentators, only Nelson and Shamir have conducted extensive empirical work. Nelson's findings (1988: 335) contradict Smigel's notion that lawyers mediate between their clients' unreasonable demands and the social interest. Nelson's lawyers do not struggle with clients over basic questions of social morality, for the most part because their views on such issues are rarely out of step with those of their clients (1988: 256, 258). Shamir's study of elite New Deal lawyers reaches the same conclusion. But his extremely sophisticated analysis suggests that these lawyers not only took public positions aligned with their clients' interests, but at the same time promoted their own interests in protecting the legal turf from New Deal innovations that would displace the involvement of lawyers (1995: 171). In fact, when these two objectives came into conflict, as in the struggle over the National Industrial Recovery Act, the lawyers provided only qualified support for the legislation although it was favored by many of their most important clients (1995: 21, 24).

Gordon makes several distinctions that are important in analyzing lawyer responsibilities and behavior. The first is just that, the difference between how we would like lawyers to behave and how we believe they do in fact behave (1988: 13). The second is between the lawyer fulfilling public responsibilities through action that is, in one way or another, a matter of law reform, or through action that is in the service of particular clients on particular matters (1988: 33–34). If we are to conclude that law is a public calling, then we must focus on one side only of these distinctions. It is obvious that our interest must be in what lawyers do rather than what we want them to do or what they say they do. I believe that it is equally important to focus on what they do for clients. A definition of a public calling that is primarily grounded in law reform takes the incidental and sporadic and places it at stage center, enabling the everyday behavior of everyday lawyers to glide smoothly away from the arena of responsibility.

Gordon's argument is subtle. He acknowledges that his case about lawyers in public service in the past is limited to a few accounts of the lives of leaders of the metropolitan bar, but says that is the only information that is available (1988: 31). He acknowledges that the case is primarily based on what he calls "outside representation" rather than "in the course of representation" because the guts of the lawyer-client relationship are virtually impenetrable (1988: 49; but see Sarat and Felstiner 1995). He nevertheless can assert that this vision of lawyering has real historical and current content because the conditions for its exercise, which he elaborates with great ingenuity, were and are present and because he can conjure up business-related legal decisions in which coming to grips with social as well as technical difficulties appear unavoidable. He provides a powerful critique, but empirically it is without reference to the way that ordinary lawyers treat most clients: it has next to nothing to say about how lawyers actually confront personal injury, workers' compensation, consumer, divorce, bankruptcy, and estate cases, while it exempts criminal defense work from the general problem.

When we turn to evidence of the actual behavior of lawyers, we see that the notion that lawyers are motivated more by financial returns than professional values has wide currency in the sociolegal world. This is, of course, the familiar litany that law practice has been transformed from a profession into a business. This refrain has been heard for many decades (Solomon 1992: 145, 173; Nelson and Trubek 1992a: 12), but self-flagellation by the profession seems to have gained force and credibility in the last ten years (see Galanter 1994: fn. 154 [collecting references]; Commission on Professionalism 1986; Scottsdale II 1978: 3). An extreme example of such behavior, quoted in Flood's (1994: 400) recent review of two books about large law firms, is Steven Kumble of Finley, Kumble etc., instructing junior lawyers that they should "praise the adversary. He is the catalyst by which you bill your client. Damn the client. He is your true enemy." Sarat and Felstiner (1995), in a study of lawyer-client interactions, encountered several divorce lawyers who refused to take further steps in cases until their retainers had been replenished even if their clients were put at a disadvantage by this inaction. Blumberg's (1967) famous Mr. Green, the fictional witness who was a signal to judges that defense counsel had not been paid, reappears in Phillips's (1978) autobiographical account of a famous murder trial in the South Bronx. That the sociolegal community believes that tort lawyers routinely subordinate their clients' financial interests to their own is reflected in the voluminous literature on conflicts of interest in contingency fees (see Johnson 1981: 569; Kritzer et al. 1985: 252–53; on lawyers' conflicts of interest generally, see Shapiro 1995). Finally, the conventional understanding of the "courtroom workgroup" is that criminal defense lawyers are more interested in their relationships with other court regulars than they are in serving their clients (Eisenstein and Jacob 1977: 50).

Interestingly, where empirical support for socially responsive lawyering can be identified at all, it is in the area of divorce. For instance, both O'Gorman (1963) and Kressel, Hochberg, and Meth (1983) found that many divorce lawyers describe their roles in terms that would fit well with Brandeis's notion of counselor for the situation. Hotel and Brockman (1996) found that 50 percent of the divorce lawyers to whom they put a series of hypothetical questions recognized the moral costs of their positions and alleged that personal morality would play an active role in the way that they behaved professionally. The reason for such postures is obvious. In divorce practice lawyers constantly are aware of the consequences of their action for the children of the marriage who are both vulnerable and unrepresented. However, there is even some doubt that divorce lawyers actually behave as they say they do in these accounts to researchers (Sarat and Felstiner 1995: 148); Cavanagh and Rhode (1976: 148) report that divorce lawyers often believe that they risk malpractice unless they inform divorce clients about the outer boundaries of the clients' rights and the tactics that are available to achieve them.

The thin trickle of empirical evidence supporting the socially constructive role of lawyers is overwhelmed by a tide of studies that depict lawyers in the opposite posture, sacrificing their clients' interests in favor of their own (Carlin 1962, 1966), paying more attention to the courtroom workgroups in which they practice than to their clients' interests (Sudnow 1965; Eisenstein and Jacob 1977), putting their clients' cases into cold storage to suit their own capacity for work (Hensler et al. 1985), permitting fee arrangements to dictate strategy (Johnson 1981), describing the legal system in exaggeratedly negative terms to distance themselves from poor case results (Sarat and Felstiner 1995), subordinating clients' positions to the bureaucratic exigencies of their offices (Hosticka 1979), not pushing their clients' cases fully for fear of annoying other lawyers or jeopardizing future business (Macaulay 1979), doing more work than is necessary in order to pad fees (O'Gorman 1963: 146; Bartlett 1982), and engaging in group settlement practices that enhance fees at the expense of individual clients (Hensler et al. 1985).

Whatever the reality and extent of lawyers counseling their clients toward socially responsible behavior in the past, the conventional wisdom is that most lawyers have now abandoned that role. The difference is most patent in the case of the large corporate law firm (see Galanter and Palay 1991: 68–69; Gordon 1988: 60), probably because that is the most salient practice site where such behavior was debated by scholars in the first instance. That the large firm and the corporate client attracted such attention may well reflect a commonsense drive to use professional counseling to restrain the behavior of powerful corporations, especially in periods of low regulation. But whatever the site, the lawyer-client relationship now seems dominated by the bottom lines of both clients and lawyers. Clients are assumed, probably correctly in the case of business firms (see Reich 1996), to give priority to economic returns when faced with competing social responsibilities. Because lawyers are intensely focused on their own economic returns (Commission on Women in the Profession 1988: 16), they are desperate to secure and retain clients. They therefore adopt what they take to be clients' views of their objectives, a profit-margin oriented view that in lawyers' hands is incompatible with a socially sensitive counseling function. In short, clients are assumed to want aggressive lawyers who will deliver economic returns (but see Gordon and Simon 1992: 245), and lawyers who value their own returns over *their* social effect will do whatever the clients want, counseling be damned, as long as they do not run a real risk of being indicted for something.

2. LAWYERS AND POWER: CONTROL OVER CLIENTS

This abandonment thesis incorporates a view of power as well as justice in the lawyer-client relationship. It sees power in the hands of clients and lawyers as agents that are willing simply to do their bidding. On the other hand, the line of research that focuses on power rather than justice suggests a much more complicated relationship. The predominant, but not exclusive, image of the lawyer-client relationship is one of professional dominance and lay passivity (see Heinz 1983: 892; Becker 1970: 96–97; Johnson 1972: 53; Bankowski and Mungham 1976; Cunningham 1989; Alfieri 1991). The lawyer governs the relationship, defines the terms of the interaction, and is responsible for the service provided. This image is bolstered by studies of a wide range of legal situations and types of legal practices. Thus, Hunting and Neuwirth (1962), writing more than thirty years ago, found that the majority of litigants in automobile accident claims in New York City had no idea what their lawyers were doing in their cases and had no say in when to settle or how much to accept. Legal services lawyers of the kind studied by Hosticka (1979: 604) rarely even ask their clients what they want them to do. Such lawyers habitually engage in maneuvers that "exploit and reinforce client dependency on the lawyer's specialized knowledge and technical skill" (Alfieri 1991: 2132). Kritzer's review of a national survey of lawyers and clients in litigated cases finds low client involvement in case development and strategy (1990: 66). Both Blumberg (1967) and Macaulay (1979), writing about entirely different fields of practice, describe the ability of lawyers to control case development and strategy as unidirectional. Lawyers exercise power by manipulating their clients' definitions of the situation and of their role. The actions and reactions of clients, and the consequence of their presence, are barely visible. This unequal relationship is accentuated in franchise law firms that today serve tens of thousands of low-income clients (Van Hoy 1995: 705). From these studies one might think that contemporary lawyers fulfill Bakunin's nineteenth-century prediction about scientific intelligence, namely, that it would produce an aristocratic, despotic, arrogant, and elitist regime (Derber, Schwartz, and Magrass 1990).

Indeed, even when individual clients are involved in the management of their own cases, that involvement often is limited. Thus Rosenthal's (1974) notion of a high level of client participation in personal injury litigation is confined in its interactive dimensions to expressing special concerns and making follow-up demands for attention. The few clients who take an active role in their cases are considered hostile and problematic rather than helpful and persistent (Hosticka 1979: 607). In the conventional wisdom, people have "problems" and experts have "solutions" (Illich et al. 1978). This superordinate position of lawyers is alleged to prevail even with progressive lawyers dedicated to producing social change (Lopez 1992).

Other research emphasizes the context of legal practice as crucial in shaping lawyer-client interaction. Spangler (1986: 166–67, 170), for example, reports that private practitioners and corporate counsel are less likely to dictate action for their clients than are legal services lawyers. Heinz and Laumann recognize that there is considerable variation by area of law in the practice characteristic they term "freedom of action," a notion reflecting the lawyer's power to decide on strategy and to operate free of close supervision (1982: 108–9, 104).

While these scholars see variation in the locus of power by area of practice, others see variation on a case by case basis. Cain (1979) notes that the array of power between lawyer and client varies from client to client: the solicitors she observed adopted their clients' goals as the given agenda unless they had a conflict of interest or the clients exhibited unreal expectations. In the same vein, Bottoms and McClean (1976) find that the extent of participation of criminal defendants in their cases varies by culture, personality, and ideology. Still other researchers find power to be differentially distributed between lawyer and client by task. Reminiscent of Johnson's (1972: 46–47) distinction between defining needs and the manner of fulfilling them, Nelson's (1988: 264, 267) and Spangler's (1986: 60–61, 64) work on large law firms indicates that even though corporations set goals and policy independent of lawyer influence, lawyers have a major say in tactical matters.

Finally, other analysts suggest that power in the professional relationship directly reflects control over resources. Thus Flood (1987: 386–90), having observed the life history of two lawsuits as part of his ethnographic study of a large Chicago law firm, suggests that allocation of power between lawyer and client depends on whether or not the clients are likely to produce repeat business or have the ability to pay fees that command attention. Abel is, perhaps, the strongest proponent of this view. He argues that corporate clients are typically the "dominant" actors in the relationship with their lawyers while solo and small-firm practitioners "dominate" their clients (1989: 204).

In this standard analysis of the professions, lawyers are presented either as agents moving tactically toward their clients' clearly expressed goals (Kagan and Rosen 1985), as principals paternalistically operating in accordance with their sense of the clients' best interests (White 1990; Alfieri 1991), or as opportunists using the client's case to work out their own agenda (see Blumberg 1967; Casper 1972: 194; Derber, Schwartz, and Magrass 1990: 140). Given these very different images of lawyers, it is natural to pose Rosenthal's (1974) well-known question, "Who's in charge?" However, asking "Who's in charge?" implies that a single stable answer can be provided and that the possessor of power can be clearly identified.

Sarat and Felstiner (1995) present a different perspective. They found that while professionals and their clients in divorce typically occupy different and unequal positions and bring different and unequal resources to bear in their relationship, power in the lawyer-client interactions they observed was part of what Engel (1993: 126) describes as the "dynamic processes [that] characterize the interaction of law with the culture of common sense and the fluidity, negotiability and ever changing qualities of both law and everyday life." As a result of this fluidity, both lawyers and clients were sometimes frustrated by feelings of powerlessness in dealing with the other (White 1990). Often no one may be in charge: interactions between lawyers and clients involve as much drift and uncertainty as direction and clarity of purpose. Sarat and Felstiner found it difficult, at any one moment, to determine who, if anyone, was defining objectives, determining strategy, or devising tactics.

Sarat and Felstiner observed divorce lawyers only. Yet they argue (1995: 151–52) that the struggles over meaning and power between lawyers and their clients occur as well in other areas of practice. They extend their findings to law practice generally because they believe that negotiations between lawyers and clients are required across the board on issues such as client expectations and goals, the production of a consistent version of events, the timing of actions, and the division of labor between them. Law practice, they allege, rarely involves the straightforward delivery of a technical service to complacent clients: more often the interaction between lawyer and client resembles a complex, shifting, conflicted set of negotiations. To the extent that Sarat and Felstiner are on the right track, the dichotomies between social justice and client selfishness and between lawyers' interests and client interests may be drawn too sharply. If, in the legal world, client relationships are highly contextual and strongly negotiated, it is not at all unlikely that many lawyers may be at one and the same time trying to do their clients' bidding and seeking the socially responsible end (see Gordon and Simon 1992: 248–57) or trying to do well by their client as they try to secure a good return for their effort.

3. LAWYERS AND POWER: RESPECT FOR CLIENTS

Not only does the literature on lawyer-client relations suggest that clients other than large businesses or other powerful entities are often in no position to dictate goals and means to their lawyers, but a separate body of work focusing on the interpersonal dimensions of the lawyer-client relationship indicates that lawyers frequently do in fact neglect and show little respect for their clients. Clients frequently experience lawyers as condescending (see Abel 1989: 247). Legal-aid clients are particularly prone to being treated as embodiments of legal problems rather than full-fledged persons (Hosticka 1979; Cunningham 1992). Clients become exasperated when lawyers try to overwhelm them with jargon (Levine 1992: 60). Even an American Bar Association commission chaired by Hillary Rodham Clinton describes lawyers as becoming dehumanized, unable to relate to clients with compassion (Commission on Women in the Profession 1988: 16). The literature is full of assertions that lawyers are arrogant (Hengstler 1993: 62; see Menkel-Meadow 1994: 595 [criticizing the MacCrate Report for not paying enough attention to the human aspects of lawyering]) and paternalistic (see Gutman 1993: 1769; Wasserstrom 1975: 1). Public defenders instruct rather than consult with their clients while some private defense counsel are alleged by their clients to be brash, cold, inattentive, and poor communicators (Casper 1972: 109, 116–17).

Clients complain that lawyers are uncooperative, uncommunicative (Curran 1977: 230; Harris et al. 1984: 68; Abel 1985: 584), lack empathy (Hengstler 1993: 62; compare Seron 1994: 8, 273–74, 278, 300), are rude, unresponsive, evasive (Rosenthal 1974: 52), and are tardy in providing services (Levine 1992: 62). Studies of lawyer-client relations often report client files that were forgotten or lost (see Rosenthal 1974: 48; Felstiner and Sarat 1992: 1475–76). The most common client complaint about lawyers is that they do not respond to phone calls and letters (Seron 1994: 6–216; Stevens 1994; Sussman 1993; see Samborn 1993; Scottsdale II 1978: 13; Abel 1985: 585), even though communications specialists allege "nothing says as much to people that I don't care about you as unanswered phone calls" (CLE videotape "One Client at a Time"). In criminal defense work, both assigned counsel and public defenders have been found to ration severely the time they spend with clients (see Casper 1972: 102, 106, 108; Mather 1979: 24). Two of the most common types of lawyer malpractice, "blowing" the statute of limitations and suffering default judgments for failure to appear, can be considered as "inattention" in the extreme.

Problems in communications with clients exist despite the high importance training in such skills is accorded by both law students and their prospective employers (see Garth and Martin 1993). Lawyers fail both to listen (Seron 1994: 8–270) and to explain legal matters adequately in lay terms (Vogel 1989: 23): both are matters of capacity (Jaquish and Ware 1993) and of disposition (Gutman 1993: 1759). Rosenthal (1974: 19) quotes advice given to lawyers by the Wisconsin Bar Association: "Get at the client's problem immediately and stick to it. Don't bother to explain the reasoning process by which you arrived at your advice. . . . This not only prolongs the interview, but generally confuses the client."

In addition, lawyers are frequently indifferent to clients' feelings and to the pace of their affairs. The irrelevance, if not contaminating effect, of client feelings is axiomatic in traditional definitions of the lawyer's role (Binder et al. 1991). Sarat and Felstiner (1995: 128–33) provide extensive accounts of lawyers both refusing to engage with their clients' emotions and schooling clients about the need to separate their emotions from their objectives (see also Cunningham 1992: 1300–1 on literature in poverty and civil rights practice to the effect that lawyers routinely silence their clients even while "purporting to tell their stories"). A refusal to engage with clients' feelings has an effect on the quality of service provided: clients whose feelings are ignored or discounted have difficulty in responding to the legal counsel that the lawyer provides as well as to the lawyer herself (see Sarat and Felstiner 1986: 123–24). A common complaint of clients is that no action is taken in their cases over long periods of time (see Sarat and Felstiner 1995: 59–62; Mansnerus 1995: 8). Lawyers may or may not have good reason to delay attending to their clients' affairs, but in either case the clients' frustration is exacerbated by the lawyers' frequent failure to explain the sources of delay.

It is not at all clear what proportion of clients are merely annoyed by the bad manners and consultative postures of lawyers and how often these behaviors inflict serious social or psychological traumas. Procedural justice theorists have found in a wide range of contexts that people are remarkably sensitive to the process that they experience in encounters with authority figures like lawyers. This sensitivity to process has been found to outweigh outcome concerns in politics and in organizations as well as in a wide variety of legal settings including those of misdemeanor and felony defendants and citizens in their encounters with the police and when involved with divorce, mediation, and small claims courts.

Before procedural justice researchers turned their attention to tort litigation (see Lind et al. 1990), litigant satisfaction was assumed to reflect only considerations of outcome, cost, and delay. Economic analyses of procedures, and the proposals for reform that they lead to, assume that litigants are primarily concerned with recoveries and payouts and with how much it costs and how long it takes to bring a case to closure. Lind and his colleagues (Lind 1994; Tyler and Lind 1992; Lind et al. 1990), on the other hand, have found that what they call "dignitary process" issues are even more important than objective outcomes because respectful and dignified treatment implies that the recipient is a full-fledged, valued member of society, a belief that goes to the core of the way that we define our self-identity.

When applied to the question of the level of attention that lawyers give to clients, the procedural justice argument goes like this. People learn about how they stand in the world, they search out and learn about their status, from the quality of their treatment by people in positions of authority, by people who have power over them (see Freeman and Weihope 1972: 30). These encounters provide people an opportunity to learn where they stand in society; they provide an opportunity to test their social identity. When a client, for instance, is treated politely and with dignity and when respect is shown for and attention is paid to her needs and opinions, her feelings of positive social status are enhanced. On the other hand, when a lawyer treats a client disrespectfully or impolitely, when he ignores her needs or her existence, the client's self-definition is affected and her self-respect is threatened.

If this theory of status definition is correct, then we can see that a lot of ordinary behavior in the lawyer-client context is charged with much greater significance than lawyers either realize or intend. Not answering a phone call or, worse, ignoring a string of phone calls, not answering the mail, not sharing plans and developments with clients, not pushing a client's affairs on to closure, are no longer just bad manners or the inescapable social abrasions inflicted by busy people on those who have hired and depend on them. Instead, suggests the theory, such behavior may inflict serious psychological trauma. Thus, lack of respect for clients reflects not only the power of lawyers to behave without considering the effect of that behavior on their clients, but it may involve the power to cause serious injury to those on whose behalf one is supposedly acting.

4. THE CONDITIONS OF PRACTICE

There are hundreds of thousands of American lawyers, and collectively they have millions of clients. Any generalizations about the reality of power and justice in their relationships will no doubt have thousands of exceptions. The documented changes seem to involve the relationship of the large law firm to its corporate clients, and even there the documentation is currently sporadic and unsystematic. The origins of the changes in behavior of large firm lawyers, whether they represent central or marginal adjustments, are generally alleged to lie in the changes in the nature of client relationships, the structure of firms, the level of competition, the struggle to control costs and increase output, the amount of information about firms that is publicly available, the spectacular growth of corporate litigation, the costs of maintaining firm infrastructures (Galanter and Palay 1991: c. 4; Gordon 1985: 273; see Committee on the Profession and the Courts 1995: 1–2, 18), and particularly in the business environment in which law firm clients operate which forces managers to focus on earnings without regard to the effect on employees, customers, or the public (Reich 1996).

These changes in the culture and context of large firm practice do not, by and large, affect lawyers working in the personal services hemisphere of the profession. For these lawyers the intriguing question is not the substantive side of justice, for empirically hardly anyone has made the case that a socially responsible practice has at any time in the past hundred years been high on the agenda of a substantial proportion of this set of lawyers (this is not to say that it has not, but rather that we do not know, and that what we do know about law practice a generation ago points in the other direction; see Carlin 1962, 1966; Blumberg 1967; Sudnow 1964; Rosenthal 1974). Rather, the interesting question is on the procedural side—why does a significant proportion of these lawyers treat their clients so badly? There are apparently several causes including socialization into practice norms, occupational stress, substance abuse, and the image that lawyers hold about what clients want (see Lind and Felstiner 1995). But the most powerful influence may be the workload that these lawyers face.

We start with a simple proposition. Almost all lawyers want to be overcommitted, and a large proportion of them actually are (see Hensler et al. 1985: 90–91; Dingwall and Durkin 1995: 375–76; Sarat and Felstiner 1995: 61). This drive is as true of lawyers handling criminal cases on a private basis as it is of lawyers in civil matters (see Casper 1972: 102; Mather 1979: 24). The incentive structure pushes in that direction. Lawyers generally cannot assure future business by contract. Many do not have clients who know that they will require legal services of any particular volume in the future, and those that have them frequently find that those clients are unwilling to commit that future business to their current lawyers (Gordon 1988: 63; Nelson and Trubek 1992a: 14). The typical lawyer and law firm response is to take on all the work that they can get. Their only insurance for the future is the backlog of the present (see Carlin 1962: 73). No amount of history seems to cure this habit; the lawyer's drive to assure that the clients required to pay the overhead and profits in the future will be on tap seems more to reflect some deep prudential urge than it does reasonable management planning.

Government lawyers, particularly public defenders and legal aid attorneys, are naturally unconcerned with maintaining a large caseload for personal economic reasons. But the limited extent of public financing of legal services for the indigent frequently puts these lawyers in the position of facing very large, if not crushing, caseloads. Thus, we see in the literature the familiar picture of public defenders who spend very little time with individual defendants (Sudnow 1964: 265), even in felony cases (Casper 1972: 106), and legal aid attorneys who appear forced to adopt the same working practices (Abel 1985: 572). Large caseloads are imposed on government lawyers rather than created by them as is the case with private lawyers, but the effect is likely to be the same on their ability to relate to clients in a deliberate and considerate manner.

I have in another context analogized the lawyer's backlog to a form of inventory of raw materials. Before the inventory can be sold (the clients' business brought to closure), it must be processed (the lawyer must do that which is legally required, e.g., prepare cases for trial). But there is a limited amount of processing machinery (lawyers' time).

> If the supply of raw materials is large, the limits of processing machinery mean that much of the raw material will either sit on the shelf for long periods before it can enter the production line, or move through the production phase more slowly than it would if more machinery were available. It is here that the analogy between [legal business] and ordinary production breaks down. In the ordinary case, the manufacturer would not permit a large supply of raw materials to build

up: it is improvident to invest money in resources that cannot be put to ready use. [But in law practice], a large stock of raw materials is an asset to the lawyer, and an asset for which the lawyer does not initially pay much. Cases are a scarce resource, rather than one generally available, and thus represent future profits rather than current expenses. (Hensler et al. 1985: 90–91)

The same risk aversion that moves lawyers to taking on more business than they can handle often precludes them from hiring the assistance that they require to process the existing inventory. The concern, of course, is that a decrease in future business will saddle them with unnecessary overhead.

The connections between lawyer overload and their inattention to clients are obvious. Even if they follow a killing regime, lawyers can do just so much. The clients either do not understand that their affairs are, for the time at least, in cold storage or refuse to accept that posture, and so they make overtures of various kinds that would require the lawyers' attention. But matters that do not absolutely require immediate attention may receive either no, or a glancing, response. Clients who are on the receiving end of such behavior experience neglect, rejection, and disrespect. The lawyers whom Seron (1994: 8–275) studied say that they are aware that "an entrepreneurial concern to be fast and cheap must in fact be balanced by the demands to be responsive and caring," but the general report from clients indicates that the responsive and caring side of the balance is slighted. McEwen, Mather, and Maiman (1994: 157–58, 173), for instance, report that the Maine divorce lawyers that they studied had hundreds of cases, paid attention to each only when faced by some sort of deadline and at other times delayed or avoided responding to clients because they had "nothing" to report. Overloaded, harassed lawyers with their eyes directed to the returns from their efforts are all too likely to be short-tempered, impatient, highly focused on the instrumental dimensions of their work and little inclined toward caring, empathy, responsiveness, cooperation, sharing, and patience.

Overwork is not the only situational source of lawyer neglect of clients. Stress, distress, and substance abuse may as well be implicated. Benjamin et al. (1986) suggest that the sequence begins in law school and may even be a hidden agenda of legal education. They begin with the finding that while prelaw students score within the normative range on nine scales of psychological distress, the levels they report increase significantly within their first year of law school. These high levels of distress and the symptoms that accompany them such as substance abuse and excessive anger were found not to decrease within the first few years of law practice. Thus they suggest that the psychological disorders that follow students into practice seem to be in part a product of legal education.

Benjamin and his colleagues believe that the causes of this distress are the intense competition of the law school environment coupled to classroom pressure to remain unemotional and neutral in the face of issues that in other contexts would evoke feelings and partisanship. They find that the interesting question is not whether law schools cause high levels of distress in students, but why they continue to maintain those pedagogical practices that cause such distress. They suggest that legal educators may encourage students to relate to law and their roles as future professionals in a manner that results in significant levels of psychological distress because they view such distress as a beneficial and adaptive aspect of being a lawyer (see Guinier, Fine, and Balin 1994: 63). For instance, they raise the questions of whether the jobs that lawyers must perform require qualities that accompany phobic anxiety or paranoid ideation, or whether the clients for whom they will work are assumed to require qualities that are found in psychologically distressed people.

Thus the question is whether an indoctrination regime that produces people who are capable of becoming simultaneously angry and unemotional, who are hyperaggressive, highly stressed, sleep deprived, work excessively long hours, and have little social support is doing what their professional tasks require and their clients are perceived to want. To legal educators who, consciously or not, see reality in such a professional world, the psychological distress that is produced in law school may not be a cost but a responsibility, and the students themselves are not victims but rather volunteers who have assumed these burdens in order to achieve the goals of high status and liberal compensation.

When we move from law school to practice, we find many studies over the past ten years that document unusually high levels of distress and substance abuse among American lawyers (see Beck 1993; Benjamin, Sales, and Darling 1992; Kozich 1988; McPeak 1987; see also Hagan and Kay 1995: 200). As measured by reports from Washington, Wisconsin, and Florida, the incidence of depression is three to five times that of the general population (Benjamin, Sales, and Darling 1992: 114–15). Beck's (1993: 31–32) recent cross-sectional study found that over 20 percent of Arizona and Washington male lawyers at all career stages scored above the ninety-eighth percentile on standard tests for anxiety, social isolation and alienation, depression, and obsessive-compulsiveness while the scores of female lawyers were nearly as high. Both male and female lawyers scored significantly higher than the normal population mean for seven of nine items in the Brief Symptom Inventory subscales (Beck 1993: 32). Easton and his colleagues (1990: 1081–86) found that lawyers ranked fifth in major depressive disorders among the 104 occupations studied; when the rates were adjusted for sociodemographic factors, lawyers topped the list.

Another reflection of the ubiquity of distress in the legal profession is the elevated level of substance abuse among lawyers, particularly the abuse of alcohol. Benjamin et al. (1992) believe that alcohol abuse among lawyers is more than double that of Americans generally. Drogin's (1991) conservative estimate is that 15 percent of American lawyers suffer from alcoholism, a number that today would exceed 100,000 lawyers. Although Carroll's (1992) estimate of lawyers who drink "alcoholically" is a few percentage points less than Drogin's, he concludes that for every six lawyers who abuse alcohol, another one is addicted to either tranquilizers, sleeping or diet pills, heroin, cocaine, methamphetamines, or marijuana. These conditions are very much on the agenda of the organized bar, particularly since there is a high correlation between alcohol abuse and client complaints that lead to disciplinary proceedings (Benjamin et al. 1992: 118). In 1988 the American Bar Association established a Commission on Impaired Attorneys which has developed an active intervention program. State bar associations have organized lawyer assistance programs in all fifty states, double the number that existed in 1980 (Blodgett 1988: 144).

It is generally assumed that, if there is one root cause of the elevated levels of psychological distress and substance abuse among lawyers, it is the conditions under which they work. It does not seem to matter whether they are employed by large multinational firms or are in solo or small firm practice: the story all too often is one of alienated labor, overwork, anxiety over status, concern about financial returns and layoffs, intense competition, difficult relations with clients, technological changes that have transformed the pace of practice from deliberate to hectic, the strain of balancing career and family responsibilities, gender bias, moral ambiguity, truncated career ladders, and the accentuation of hierarchy (see, generally, Epstein 1994; Horne 1994; Galanter and Palay 1991; Abel 1989; Spangler 1986; Carlin 1962).

My assumption is that these conditions frequently lead to what we may think of as a kind of psychological disconnection from professional responsibility (see Drogin 1991: 158). Under such pressures the lawyer may become depressed, bored, apathetic, distracted, overwhelmed, or lose motivation and initiative. The consequence to clients may be a lawyer who is badly organized and has poor work habits; a lawyer who is unapproachable, uncommunicative, abrupt, or impolitic; a lawyer who shuns contact with the client, neglects the client's work, and treats the client as an object rather than a person.

5. LAW SCHOOL AND CLIENTS

Inroads in both the substantive and procedural side of justice in law practice are distressing from the perspective of a teacher of law-school bound undergraduates. By and large the dominance of market considerations is far from their nature or aspirations. The tale about how they are transformed as individuals into lawyers dominated by the condition of their checkbooks is familiar—the scarcity of public interest jobs, the low pay for those that do exist, high educational debt, the summer job recruitment process, and the status orientation of lawyers (see Heinz and Lauman 1982: 90–109).

But the process that leads to their neglect of their clients is more opaque, especially the role of law schools. Many law teachers believe that the capacity of law schools to affect the procedural side of justice in lawyer-client relations is extremely limited. They neither know how to integrate such considerations into their teaching efforts nor believe that whatever they do can withstand the overwhelming influence of actual law firm experience, even in the summers during law school. Other legal educators believe that law school has a potential for inculcating students with values that would lead to socially responsive counsel to clients and careful attention to the interpersonal dimensions of their practice (see Gordon 1988: 38; Kronman 1993: c. 4; Rhode 1988; Shalleck 1993; Menkel-Meadow 1988).

I will, thus, describe what I take to be problems in the way that students are typically introduced to lawyer-client relations in law school as they are exposed to the conventional perspective on the methods and content of legal education: the view that law school teaches the language of neutrality, autonomy, and distance while it systematically slights an appreciation of the relevance and humanity of the real people who are engaged in the legal process. I also note the opening for change in this powerful pedagogy that is provided by clinical courses and those on legal ethics and the legal profession.

The experience of most students in law school, particularly in the first year, is intense and distressing. Pedagogic techniques provoke anxiety. Assignments are long, difficult, confusing, and couched in an unfamiliar vocabulary. Competition in the sense of the comparative quality of fellow students is stiff. The stakes appear high: grades influence first job opportunities and first jobs have a significant effect on career possibilities. Expenses are high and usually lead to relatively high debt burdens. These unfamiliar conditions and formidable concerns make students unsure of themselves and vulnerable to the professional suggestions of the faculty, the only guides that they have over this difficult intellectual and emotional terrain. What, then, are the explicit faculty agendas and the implicit faculty messages about clients embedded in the work of the classroom?

Legal education is a professionalized experience. This means that the focus of legal education is on professional resources such as rules, their origins and interpretations, professional actors such as lawyers, judges, administrators, and legislators, and professional results such as legal regimes and their connection to social policies and consequences. Left out or trivialized in this professionalized education is concern for individual people, for the very clients whose cases are hyperanalyzed in the classroom dance around precedents, issues, consistency, efficiency, balances, and policies.

Most law professors assume that the habits of analysis, the intuitions, and the values of beginning law students require adjustment. They assume that their students are entering the boot camp of the mind with an inclination toward particularistic values that give priority to the fates of the actual people whose legal difficulties they are asked to analyze. They assume that, if undirected and uncorrected, law students will view case situations in terms of the life effects of the participants in those cases, will respond to the emotional pull that various actors in the case dramas will evoke, and will put into play their first-order inclinations toward justice and fair dealing (Granfield 1992: 74).

To counter these tendencies, these law professors try to habituate students to value the rational response over the emotional, the general effect over the particular, the efficient solution over the seemingly just result, and the unpalatable outcome in preference to the awkward exception (see Harris and Shultz 1993: 1773–76; Guinier, Fine, and Balin 1994: 54–55). As Menkel-Meadow (1992: 305) notes, students learn "to block feelings, analyze intellectually, and deal with abstractions." In the words of a Penn student quoted in Guinier (1994: 50), it is the difference between talking about "how a woman feels having to have a baby" and talking about a constitutional right to privacy. This effort to separate personal values from legal issues is part of what Nelson and Trubek (1992b: 186) call the " 'hidden' curriculum that is embodied in the way schools are organized, classes conducted and values transmitted in informal ways."

In this law school indoctrination, the actual parties to the cases get left out in two senses. They are slighted in the classroom interaction as, the students soon learn, their interests are subordinated to general categories of people, like tenants or bondholders, or abstract concepts such as efficiency or due process. Moreover, the general practice of demanding that students argue both sides of a case, or be prepared on a moment's notice to jump from one side to the other, reduces the client to a token piece representing the side the student happens to be arguing at that moment (Shalleck 1993: 173; Rowe 1992: 40). In other words, the client becomes an unimportant part of the legal process, the occasion for a legal controversy but not powerfully connected to it (Shalleck 1993: 1731). Just as students are tutored to quash their own emotional reaction to reported cases, they are rewarded in the classroom when they strip the parties of those dimensions of their humanity that are not directly connected to the resolution of "legal" issues and are punished by their instructors and classmates when they seek to include the full scope of the parties' humanity in the analysis (Granfield 1992: 75–81).

Parties in reported cases are also left out of the classroom as they are clients of lawyers (see Gutman 1993: 1759, 1770–71). That is, the classroom discussion will rarely pay any attention to them as clients, to their predicaments, limitations, reactions, and needs as lay people in the hands of powerful professionals with their own affiliations and agendas and operating on their own turf. Issues are abstracted from the problems in which they are embedded and little attention is paid to what Menkel-Meadow (1994: 620) calls "empathy training." As an example of the disjuncture between the way law is practiced and taught, Sarat and Felstiner (1995) illustrate the extent to which negotiations between lawyer and client are frequently as time consuming and consequential as those between opposing parties in litigation: yet the appellate reports, and thus the classroom discussion, are absolutely silent about this dimension of professional tension and practice.

In other words, outside the possible reach of instruction in clinical or professional responsibility classes, the lesson from most law school classrooms is that clients do not matter, that they simply provide the setting in which the people who do matter, that is judges and lawyers, are able to carry on their professional task of analysis and argument. If this is an accurate picture, then law students run the risk of leaving school and becoming lawyers imprinted with a set of priorities in which the only client concerns that are valued are those closely tied to their narrow legal posture, and everything else about the clients' lives is subordinated to the lawyers' technocratic function (Condlin 1983: 379).

Is there a contradiction between this view and the conventional wisdom that basic moral and political values are generally unaffected by the law school experience (see Granfield 1992: 229 [collecting references]). Because personal contact with faculty is rare, students are mature on arrival, the student body is diverse in gender, social origins, and experience, and the bar exam influences course selection, Abel (1989: 212–14), for example, believes that there is reason to doubt the effect of law school as a socializing agent. But none of the scholars who see law school and practice as politically and morally discontinuous have considered the connection between them with respect to lawyers' relations with clients. There law school influences are persistent first impressions, nearly univocal, and have no competitors.

In principle, there ought to be two exceptions to the pedagogical trivialization of clients—courses in professional responsibility and instruction and experience in clinical programs. Since most ethical problems concern the temptations and threats that lawyers and clients pose for each other, one would think that clients would play a major role in classes on professional responsibility. This is, however, an open question. Shalleck (1993: 1737–39) suggests that the clients that are constructed in these courses are once again stick figures in a decontextualized posture. They are, she alleges, assumed to have no goals other than wealth or freedom, their subjective interests are generally constituted prior to their interaction with a lawyer, and the process of discovering their motives is straightforward and transparent. As a result, "students have no sense of how hard it often is to identify what a client wants, nor do they develop any insight into how they themselves can participate in shaping clients' understanding of the client's goals. Students do not attend to the ways power operates within their client relationships, nor are they taught the role that it can play in the definition of client interests" (1993: 1739).

On the other hand, so-called "live-client" clinics may, for those students who engage in them, counter the conventional classroom marginalization of clients. These clinics certainly create the opportunity for students to attend to a fully contextualized version of clients' law-related problems. Depending on the objectives and skill of their supervisors, students in these relationships may learn to treat clients with respect, act with compassion, pay attention to client feelings, learn not to be arrogant or paternalistic, listen carefully, and behave responsively. The American Bar Association Task Force on Law Schools and the Profession reports on the content of courses in communication and counseling (MacCrate 1992: 256–57) in terms that could provide, but do not necessarily require, instruction in such values (see Binder, Bergman, and Price 1991: c. 2). Or clinical courses may not do the job. Shalleck (1993: 1741), for one, believes that as "lawyers in their daily practice often replicate the construction of the client within legal education," students in the clinical setting may reproduce the version of the client in which they are schooled in the rest of the curriculum. In addition, clinical courses, lower in the law school status hierarchy, irrelevant for purposes of making law review and generally graded on a pass-fail basis, may simply be less salient for law students than the regular curriculum.

Shalleck is even concerned with the actuality of the famous "client-centered" approach of Binder, Bergman, and Price (1991). Their orientation, which requires laser-like attention to client emotions and accounts and legal solutions that are cooperatively constructed, obviously puts the client at stage center. Nevertheless, Shalleck (1993: 1743–48) is concerned that Binder, Bergman, and Price provide a program that obscures differences in clients, uses a single model (chronological) for gathering information, provides a closed list of factors that are to be considered in decision making, is inattentive to the dynamics of power in the lawyer-client relationship, and, by confining clients to the nonlegal world, provides no basis on which to criticize the legal world, which is then dominated by lawyers. It is thus a matter for exploration whether clinical opportunities in law school actually train students to interact constructively with clients, can overcome the influence of the rest of the curriculum, and stick with students as they confront the realities of practice (see MacCrate 1992: 7 [employers unconcerned with whether students have undertaken clinical courses]).

6. CONCLUSION

This is a researcher's conclusion; that is, it is a call for more research. I began with the questions of whether lawyers counsel clients along socially constructive lines and whether they treat their clients with respect. If most were to do both most of the time, I believe that we ought to be quite content with the connection between lawyers and justice and lawyers and power. The truth is we do not really have a firm grip on the answers. As developed in this chapter, most of the evidence that we do have points in the other direction. Some of that tendency is probably an artifact of social research generally. It is natural to direct studies toward problematic rather than untroubled areas of inquiry; empirical researchers are more often than not cynics accustomed to revealing patterns of inequity beneath formalistic platitudes or unexamined conventional wisdom (Danet, Hoffman, and Kermish 1980: 908). This tendency is exaggerated in sociolegal studies because of the salient position for many years of studies in the "gap" between rule and behavior tradition.

Even more important, there really has not been a frontal, empirical assault on either of these questions. The evidence on the substantive side is not that, when presented with a choice, lawyers fail to take the socially responsible path with their clients, but that in the circumstances in which they have been studied they frequently put their own interests ahead of those of their clients. These are not the same thing. Even if the "circumstances in which they have been studied" had been randomized, which with the emphasis on solo practitioners and personal injury, legal aid, and criminal defense lawyers they clearly have not, we have no assurance that the advice that is given to clients is not socially responsible where the lawyers' own interests are unaffected. Moreover, I have a strong hunch that if researchers were looking at the question of socially responsible counsel rather than who is feathering whose nest, they would adopt different research strategies, ask different questions, and produce results we have no way to anticipate.

On the procedural side, the evidence that many lawyers neglect some of their clients some of the time is rather compelling. However, there has been no systematic effort to connect variation in neglect to any of the obvious contributing factors. As a result we do not know the effect of age, income, work effort, firm size, position within firm, area of law, type of practice, personal habits, lawyer psychology, educational experience, or family situation on how lawyers treat their clients. If we are concerned about the connection between lawyers and justice, now is the time to start to seek these answers.

BIBLIOGRAPHY

Abel, Richard L. 1985. Law Without Politics: Legal Aid Under Advanced Capitalism. 32 *UCLA Law Rev.*, 474.

———. 1989. *American Lawyers.* New York: Oxford Univ. Press.

Alfieri, Anthony. 1991. Reconciling Poverty Law Practice: Learning Lessons of Client Narrative. 100 *Yale Law Journal*, 2107.

Bankowski, Zenon, and Geoff Mungham. 1976. *Images of Law.* Boston: Routledge and Kegan Paul.

Bartlett, Joseph W. 1982. *The Law Business: A Tired Monopoly.* Littleton, CO: F. B. Rothman.

Beck, Connie J. 1993. A Model of Lawyer Distress. Unpublished M.A. thesis, Univ. of Arizona.

Beck, Phyllis W., and David Burns. 1979. Anxiety and Depression in Law Students: Cognitive Intervention. 30 *Journal of Legal Education*, 270.

Becker, Howard. 1970. The Nature of a Profession. In *Sociological Work*, ed. Howard Becker. Chicago: Aldine.

Benjamin, G. Andrew H., Alfred Kaszniak, Bruce Sales, and Stephen B. Shanfield. 1986. The Role of Legal Education in Producing Psychological Distress among Law Students and Lawyers. 1986 *American Bar Foundation Research Journal*, 225.

Benjamin, G. Andrew H., Bruce D. Sales, and Elaine Darling. 1992. Comprehensive Lawyer Assistance Programs: Justification and Model. 16 *Law and Psychology Review*, 113.

Binder, David, Paul Bergman, and Susan Price. 1991. *Lawyers as Counselors: A Client-Centered Approach.* St. Paul: West.

Blodgett, Nancy. 1988. "Substance Abuse: New Commission Will Aid Impaired Lawyers," 74 *ABA Journal*, 74.

Blumberg, Abraham. 1967. The Practice of Law as a Confidence Game. 1 *Law and Society Rev.*, 15.

Bottoms, A. E., and J. D. McClean. 1976. *Defendants in the Criminal Process.* Boston: Routledge and Kegan Paul.

Cain, Maureen. 1979. The General Practice Lawyer and Client. 7 *International Journal of the Sociology of Law*, 331.

Carlin, Jerome E. 1962. *Lawyers on Their Own.* New Brunswick: Rutgers Univ. Press.

———. 1966. *Lawyer's Ethics—A Survey of the New York City Bar.* New York: Russell Sage.

Carroll, John R. 1992. When Your Colleague Is Hooked. 55 *Texas Bar Journal*, 268.

Casper, Jonathan D. 1972. *American Criminal Justice: The Defendant's Perspective.* Englewood Cliffs, NJ: Prentice-Hall.

Cavanagh, Ralph C., and Deborah L. Rhode. 1976. The Unauthorized Practice of Law and Pro Se Divorce. 86 *Yale Law Journal*, 104.

Commission on Professionalism. 1986. *In the Spirit of Public Service: A Blueprint for the Rekindling of Lawyer Professionalism.* Chicago: ABA.

Commission on Women in the Profession. 1988. *Report.* Chicago: ABA.

Committee on the Profession and the Courts. 1995. *Final Report to the Chief Judge.* New York: Committee on the Profession and the Courts.

Condlin, Robert. 1983. The Moral Failure of Clinical Legal Education. In *The Good Lawyer*, ed. David Luban. Totowa, NJ: Rowman and Allenheld.

Cunningham, Clark. 1989. A Tale of Two Clients: Thinking about Law as Language. 97 *Michigan Law Rev.*, 2459.

———. 1992. The Lawyer as Translator: Towards an Ethnography of Legal Discourse. 77 *Cornell Law Rev.*, 1298.

Curran, Barbara. 1977. *The Legal Needs of the Public: The Final Report of a National Survey.* Chicago: American Bar Foundation.

Danet, Brenda, Kenneth B. Hoffman, and Nicole C. Kermish. 1980. Obstacles to the Study of Lawyer-Client Interaction: The Biography of a Failure. 14 *Law and Society Rev.*, 905.

Derber, Charles, William Schwartz, and Yale Magrass. 1990. *Power in the Highest Degree: Professionals and the Rise of a New Mandarin Order.* New York: Oxford Univ. Press.

Dingwall, Robert, and Tom Durkin. 1995. Time Management and Procedural Reform. In *Reform of Civil Procedure*, ed. A. A. S. Zuckerman and Ross Cranston. Oxford: Oxford Univ. Press.

Drogin, E. 1991. Alcoholism in the Legal Profession: Psychological and Legal Perspectives and Interventions. 15 *Law and Psychology Rev.*, 117.

Easton, William W., James C. Anthony, Wallace Mandel, and Roberta Garrison. 1990. Occupations and the Prevalence of Major Depressive Disorder. 32 *Journal of Occupational Medicine*, 1079.

Eisenstein, James S., and Herbert Jacob. 1977. *Felony Justice.* Boston: Little, Brown.

Engel, David. 1993. Law in the Domains of Everyday Life. In *Law in Everyday Life*, ed. Austin Sarat and Thomas R. Kearns. Ann Arbor: Univ. of Michigan Press.

Epstein, Cynthia F. 1994. Mixed Messages: Structured Ambiguity in the Career Lines of Wall Street Lawyers. Paper delivered at the meeting of the Law and Society Association, Phoenix, AZ, June 1994.

Felstiner, William L. F., and Austin Sarat. 1992. Enactments of Power. 77 *Cornell Law Rev.*, 1447.

Flood, John. 1987. Anatomy of Lawyering: An Ethnography of a Corporate Law Firm. Unpublished Ph.D. diss., Northwestern Univ.

———. 1994. Shark Tanks, Sweatshops, and the Lawyer as Hero? Fact as Fiction. 21 *Journal of Law and Society*, 396.

Freeman, Harrop, and Henry Weihope. 1972. *Clinical Law Training: Interviewing and Counseling*. St. Paul: West.

Galanter, Marc. 1994. Predators and Parasites: Lawyer-Bashing and Civil Justice. 28 *Georgia Law Review*, 633.

Galanter, Marc, and Thomas Palay. 1991. *Tournament of Lawyers: The Transformation of the Big Law Firm*. Chicago: Univ. of Chicago Press.

Garth, Bryant G., and Joanne Martin. 1993. Law Schools and the Construction of Competence. 43 *Journal of Legal Education*, 469.

Gordon, Robert W. 1985. Introduction to Symposium on the Corporate Law Firm. 37 *Stanford Law Rev.*, 271.

———. 1988. The Independence of Lawyers. 68 *Boston University Law Rev.*, 1.

Gordon, Robert W., and William H. Simon. 1992. The Redemption of Professionalism? In *Lawyers' Ideals/Lawyers' Practices: Transformations in the American Legal Profession*, ed. Robert L. Nelson, David M. Trubek, and Rayman L. Solomon. Ithaca, NY: Cornell Univ. Press.

Granfield, Robert. 1992. *Making Elite Lawyers*. New York: Routledge.

Guinier, Lani, Michelle Fine, and Jane Balin. 1994. Becoming Gentlemen: Women's Experience at One Ivy League Law School. 143 *Pennsylvania Law Rev.*, 1.

Gutmann, Amy. 1993. Can Virtue Be Taught to Lawyers? 45 *Stanford Law Rev.*, 1759.

Hagan, John, and Fiona Kay. 1995. *Gender in Practice: A Study of Lawyers' Lives*. New York: Oxford Univ. Press.

Harris, Angela P., and Marjorie M. Shultz. 1993. "A(nother) Critique of Pure Reason": Toward Civic Virtue in Legal Education. 45 *Stanford Law Rev.*, 1773.

Harris, Donald, Mavis Maclean, Hazel Genn, Sally Lloyd-Bostock, Paul Fenn, Peter Corfield, and Yvonne Britain. 1984. *Compensation and Support for Injury and Illness*. Oxford: Oxford Univ. Press.

Heinz, John. 1983. The Power of Lawyers. 17 *Georgia Law Rev.*, 891.

Heinz, John, and Edward Laumann. 1982. *Chicago Lawyers: The Social Structure of the Bar*. New York: Russell Sage.

Hengstler, Gary A. 1993. Vox Populi: The Public Perception of Lawyers. 79 *ABA Journal*, 60.

Hensler, Deborah R., William L. F. Felstiner, Molly Selvin, and Patricia A. Ebener. 1985. *Asbestos in the Courts: The Challenge of Mass Toxic Torts*. Santa Monica, CA: Rand Corporation.

Horne, Christine. 1994. Responses to Economic Decline: A Look at Associate Attorney Dissatisfaction. Paper delivered at the meeting of the Law and Society Association, Phoenix, AZ, June 1994.

Hosticka, Carl. 1979. We Don't Care What Happened, We Only Care What Is Going to Happen. 26 *Social Problems*, 599.

Hotel, Carla, and Joan Brockman. 1996. Legal Ethics in the Practice of Family Law: Playing Chess While Mountain Climbing. *Journal of Business Ethics* (forthcoming).

Hunting, Robert, and Gloria Neuwirth. 1962. *Who Sues in New York City: A Study of Automobile Accident Claims.* New York: Columbia Univ. Press.

Illich, Ivan, Irving Zola, John McKnight, Jonathan Caplan, and Harley Shaiken. 1978. *Disabling Professions.* London: Marion Boyars.

Jaquish, Gail A., and James Ware. 1993. Adopting an Educator Habit of Mind: Modifying What It Means to "Think Like a Lawyer." 45 *Stanford Law Rev.*, 1713.

Johnson, Earl, Jr. 1981. Lawyers' Choice: A Theoretical Appraisal of Litigation Investment Decisions. 15 *Law and Society Rev.*, 567.

Johnson, Terence. 1972. *Professions and Power.* London: Macmillan.

Kagan, Robert, and Robert Rosen. 1985. On the Social Significance of Large Law Firm Practice. 37 *Stanford Law Rev.*, 399.

Kozich, Dennis W. 1988. An Analysis of Stress Levels and Stress Management Choices of Attorneys in the State of Wisconsin. Unpublished Ph.D. diss., Univ. of Wisconsin.

Kressel, Kenneth, Allan Hochberg, and Theodore Meth. 1983. A Provisional Typology of Lawyer Attitudes towards Divorce Practice. 7 *Law and Human Behavior*, 31.

Kritzer, Herbert. 1990. *The Justice Broker: Lawyers and Ordinary Litigation.* New York: Oxford Univ. Press.

Kritzer, Herbert M., William L. F. Felstiner, Austin Sarat, and David M. Trubek. 1985. The Impact of Fee Arrangement on Lawyer Effort. 19 *Law and Society Rev.*, 251.

Kronman, Anthony T. 1993. *The Lost Lawyer.* Cambridge, MA: Harvard Univ. Press.

———. 1995. Letter to Friends and Graduates of Yale Law School, Nov. 13.

Levine, Alan P. 1992. Looking for Mr. Goodlawyer. 78 *ABA Journal*, 60.

Lind, E. Allan. 1994. Procedural Justice and Culture: Evidence for Ubiquitous Process Concerns. 15 *Zeitschift für Rechtssoziologie*, 24.

Lind, E. Allan, and William L. F. Felstiner. 1995. Professional Neglect: Origins and Consequences. Research Proposal to the American Bar Foundation, Chicago.

Lind, E. Allan, Robert J. MacCoun, Patricia A. Ebener, William L. F. Felstiner, Deborah R. Hensler, Judith Resnick, and Tom Tyler. 1990. In the Eye of the Beholder: Tort Litigants' Evaluations of Their Experiences in the Civil Justice System. 24 *Law and Society Rev.*, 953.

Lopez, Gerald P. 1992. *Rebellious Lawyering: One Chicano's Vision of Progressive Law Practice.* Boulder: Westview.

Macaulay, Stewart. 1979. Lawyers and Consumer Protection Laws. 14 *Law and Society Rev.*, 115.

MacCrate, Robert. 1992. American Bar Association Section of Legal Education and Admissions to the Bar, *Task Force on Law Schools and the Profession: Narrowing the Gap.* Chicago: ABA.

Mansnerus, Laura. 1995. Looking for an Attorney? Here's Counsel. *New York Times*, June 11, sec. 3, p. 1.

Mather, Lynn M. 1979. *Plea Bargaining or Trial?* Lexington, MA: Lexington Books.

McEwen, Craig, Lynn Mather, and Richard Maiman. 1994. Lawyers, Mediation and the Management of Divorce Practice. 28 *Law and Society Rev.*, 149.

McPeak, Allan. 1987. Lawyer Occupational Stress. Unpublished Ph.D. diss., Florida State Univ.

Menkel-Meadow, Carrie. 1988. Excluded Voices: New Voices in the Legal Profession Making New Voices in the Law. 42 *U. Miami Law Rev.*, 1297.

———. 1992. The Power of Narrative in Empathetic Learning: Post-Modernism and the Stories of Law. 2 *UCLA Women's Law Journal*, 287.

———. 1994. Narrowing the Gap by Narrowing the Field: What's Missing from the MacCrate Report—Of Skills, Legal Science and Being a Human Being. 69 *Washington Law Rev.*, 593.

Nelson, Robert. 1988. *Partners with Power: The Social Transformation of the Large Law Firm.* Berkeley: Univ. of California Press.

Nelson, Robert L., and David M. Trubek. 1992a. New Problems and New Paradigms in Studies of the Legal Profession. In *Lawyers' Ideals/Lawyers Practices: Transformations in the American Legal Profession*, ed. Robert L. Nelson, David Trubek, and Rayman L. Solomon. Ithaca, NY: Cornell Univ. Press.

Nelson, Robert L., and David M. Trubek. 1992b. Arenas of Professionalism: The Professional Ideologies of Lawyers in Context. In *Lawyers' Ideals/Lawyers Practices: Transformations in the American Legal Profession*, ed. Robert L. Nelson, David Trubek, and Rayman L. Solomon. Ithaca, NY: Cornell Univ. Press.

O'Gorman, Hubert. 1963. *Lawyers in Matrimonial Cases.* Glencoe, IL: Free Press.

Olson, Susan. 1984. *Clients and Lawyers: Securing the Rights of Disabled Persons.* Westport, CT: Greenwood Press.

Phillips, Steven. 1978. *No Heros, No Villains.* New York: Random House.

Reich, Robert S. 1996. How to Avoid These Layoffs. *New York Times*, Jan. 4, p. A13.

Rhode, Deborah. 1988. Perspectives on Professional Women. 40 *Stanford Law Rev.*, 1163.

Rosenthal, Douglas. 1974. *Lawyer and Client: Who's in Charge.* New York: Russell Sage.

Rowe, Jonathan. 1992. Loot Court: How Harvard Devours Its Young. 24 *Washington Monthly*, 39.

Samborn, Randall. 1993. Anti-Lawyer Attitude Up. 15 *National Law Journal*, 49:1.

Sarat, Austin, and William L. F. Felstiner. 1986. Law and Strategy in the Divorce Lawyer's Office? 20 *Law and Society Rev.*, 97.

———. 1995. *Divorce Lawyers and Their Clients: Power and Meaning in the Legal Process.* New York: Oxford Univ. Press.

Scottsdale II, Long Range Planning Committee, Section on Communications and Public Relations. 1978. *An Updated Communications Agenda for the Legal Profession.* Chicago: National Association of Bar Examiners.

Seron, Carroll. 1994. When Lawyers Go to Market: The Restructuring of Private Legal Practice. Unpublished manuscript.

Shalleck, Ann. 1993. Constructions of the Client within Legal Education. 45 *Stanford Law Rev.*, 1731.

Shamir, Ronen. 1995. *Managing Legal Uncertainty: Elite Lawyers in the New Deal.* Durham, NC: Duke Univ. Press.

Shanfield, Stephen B., and G. Andrew H. Benjamin. 1985. Psychiatric Distress in Law Students. 35 *Journal of Legal Education*, 65.

Shapiro, Susan. 1995. Conflicted Responsibilities: Maneuvering through the Minefield of Fiduciary Obligations. Paper presented at the meeting of the Law and Society Association, Toronto, June 1995.

Simon, William. 1978. The Ideology of Advocacy. *Wisconsin Law Rev.*, 30.

Smigel, Erwin. 1964. *The Wall Street Lawyer.* New York: Free Press.

Solomon, Rayman L. 1992. Five Crises or One: The Concept of Legal Professionalism, 1925–60. In *Lawyers' Ideals/Lawyers Practices: Transformations in the American Legal Profession*, ed. Robert L. Nelson, David Trubek, and Rayman L. Solomon. Ithaca, NY: Cornell Univ. Press.

Spangler, Eve. 1986. *Lawyers for Hire: Salaried Professionals at Work.* New Haven, CT: Yale Univ. Press.

Stevens, Amy. 1994. Lawyers' Annoying Misdeeds Targeted. *Wall Street Journal*, Sept. 1, p. B1.

Sudnow, David. 1965. Normal Crimes: Sociological Features of the Penal Code in a Public Defender Office. 12 *Social Problems*, 255–76.

Sussman, Fern S. 1993. Lawyers Have to Take the Complaints of Clients More Seriously. *New York Times*, Nov. 26, p. A18.

Tyler, Tom, and E. Allan Lind. 1992. A Relational Model of Authority in Groups. 25 *Advances in Experimental Social Psychology*, 115.

Van Hoy, Jerry. 1995. Selling and Processing Law: Legal Work at Franchise Law Firms. 29 *Law and Society Rev.*, 703.

Vogel, Howard H. 1989. *Report of ABA Task Force on Outreach to the Public.* Chicago: ABA.

Wasserstrom, Richard. 1975. Lawyers as Professionals: Some Moral Issues. 5 *Human Rights*, 1.

White, Lucie. 1990. Subordination, Rhetorical Skills and Sunday Shoes: Notes on the Hearing of Mrs. G. 38 *Buffalo Law Rev.*, 1.

JUSTICE IN LAW
AND SOCIETY

MARTHA ALBERTSON FINEMAN

I. INTRODUCTION

Whydocument hen a woman becomes a mother she performs a valuable societal function. By reproducing she benefits the state, the workforce, and the family. Historically, the significance of her task has been the justification for subjecting her as "mother" to the power of the state. She is supervised and judged according to standards that do not apply to general members of the population. Mothers owe duties of care to their children not applied to strangers. The behavior of mothers is regulated through the companion normative systems of law and family ideology. If mothers are found wanting, they may be punished. This is particularly true for poor and single mothers, but all women as mothers risk intervention and subjugation based on their status. State supervision and control of mothers, and the corresponding sacrifice of privacy, should form the basis of a claim for justice for mothers—a claim for the resources to perform the tasks society sets for them.

This will not be simple to implement. Our societal sense of what constitutes justice for families as social entities, as well as our conclusions about what is just when there are conflicts to be resolved among individuals within families, are formulated in the context of existing, historically legitimated relations of power. The model for family formation and operation was patriarchal. While pure patriarchy is no longer a dominant mode of social organization, the basic tenets remain fundamental to the ways in which we continue to define families and understand intimacy in our society. Our definition and acceptance of the family as a legal and as a social institution, and the acceptance of assigned roles to individual family members, reflect the contemporary (and temporal) resolution of struggles of power and dominance.

Conversely, our experience of "power" is filtered through our perception of "justice." Justice is the societal conclusion legitimating and condoning what might otherwise be viewed as inappropriate coercive maintenance of certain traditional family forms and expressions of individual power within families. Society's sense of justice currently allows some politicians to feel it appropriate to condemn alternatives to the preferred family arrangement as deviant and to propose subjecting those which do not conform to exercises of state power which would not typically be condoned if directed toward traditional entities. Intrusion and supervision are justified because of the deviation from state norms. At the same time, however, families that are in conformity with state standards are empowered. Our perception of justice requires that they have, by their conformity, earned a right to protection and privacy.

Justice as a normative conclusion reflects a particular ideological position. A particular ideology is tested through the interaction of power (or institutions of power, such as law) and prevalent concepts of the just. For this reason, it is artificial and inappropriate to separate the concept of justice from that of power or ideology. This notion of the inseparability of experience of power from concepts of justice is generalizable to other specific subject areas. A major premise of work in the law and society tradition is that all events, concepts, and concerns must be understood in the contexts in which they operate. Feminist scholars, in particular, have highlighted the significance of the ideological medium in which legal concepts operate (Fineman 1992a; Siegel 1992; Rhode 1991; Brophy and Smart 1985; Sanger 1989). Appreciating these grand theoretical concepts and understanding their implications in society mandates appreciating and understanding the way they effect and influence each other. In the context of the development of policy about single mothers, the law as "power" and reform rhetoric as "justice" (or justification) intersect and reinforce each other to cast nonconforming social behavior as behavior in need of punishment, supervision, regulation, containment, and control. The disciplining of women is understood as necessary and appropriate. Traditional family structures and individual roles are also perceived as necessary and, therefore, "neutral" and "just." Unequal allocations of major societal resources (both cultural and economic capital) to subsidize existing nuclear families are justified by the dominant family ideology. The subsidized nuclear family unit, mischaracterized as "self-sufficient" and "independent," is held out as the idealized norm. The subsequent successful performance of this class of families furthers the ideology of the independent family and masks or distorts the universal and extensive nature of dependency in society. Their subsidized existence solidifies the notion that successful families manage dependency without resort to the state. Challenges to the justness of formulating and implementing state family policy around a model that conforms neither to the way in which a majority of Americans live their lives, nor to the dictates of its own rhetoric, have not been successful.

The historic construct of the family in its relationship to the state also has implications for what is considered just in specific contexts. In fact, deviant intimate entities—those families that are poor (or fail to conform to the nuclear model)—are given a separate, stigmatized set of subsidies, increasingly punitive in nature and in implementation. These dependent families are vilified in public policy discourse and provided with "incentives" to replicate the ideal model. One concrete manifestation of the injustice of our policies is found in the pronounced gendered poverty gap in the United States.

American women are much more likely to be poor than are American men: a recent study indicates that American women are forty-one percent more likely to live in poverty (Casper, McLanahan, and Garfinkel 1994: 598). By contrast, poverty is more "equally" experienced in countries like the Netherlands, and marriage equalizes the ratio—poor couples share meager resources and are both poor, but one prominent factor lifting single women to the level of better off males is government benefits. In the Netherlands, for example, there is a low over-all poverty rate and an almost nonexistent gender poverty gap due to the generous welfare system. The Netherlands has a relatively high income floor beneath which no citizen is allowed to fall, independent of work history. Sweden takes a different track, encouraging women to work by providing services such as day care and paid parental leave. In Sweden, women's high employment rates substantially reduce the gender poverty gap (Casper, McLanahan, and Garfinkel 1994: 602, 600).

2. THE IDEAL

In the United States we tolerate a schizophrenic response to the disjunction between our abstract social ideals and empirical observations concerning dependency. The family as a social and political construct plays an important role in facilitating this interaction (Fineman 1995). Specifically, the continued adherence to an unrealistic and unrepresentative set of assumptions about the family affects how we perceive and attempt to solve persistent problems of poverty and social welfare. In the normative conclusions generated and reiterated in political and popular discussions about family, Americans mea-sure the justice of particular policies addressing societal problems by using contrived concepts such as the "individual" and "dependency." Unable to mask dependency by retreat within socially formed institutions like the family, single-mother caretakers in particular are stigmatized, subjected to negative epithets and scorn for embodying a dependency which we as society would rather deny.

Inconspicuously complementing the myths about individual autonomy are assumptions about the contexts in which individuals exist in our society, most relevant being the assumption that we all belong to or aspire to belong to families. The family typically imagined is a unit populated in traditional form— a husband and wife, formally married, living together with their biological children. The husband performs as the head of the household, providing economic support and discipline for the dependent wife and children who correspondingly owe him duties of obedience and respect. This assumed archetypical Family provides the normative expectations for the institution of the family.

This family is viewed as productive of individual identity and development. It is touted as the site for intimate connection, the place for individuals to retreat when seeking to satisfy human needs. We desire to be part of the Family because we experience it as a psychological conglomerate of nurture and support and/or as an emotional proving ground for individual self-development. This is reflected in the law. Long ago, the Supreme Court characterized marriage as "the most important relation in life . . . the foundation of the family and of society, without which there would be neither civilization nor progress" (*Maynard v. Hill*, 1888: 205, 211). In *Meyer v. Nebraska*, the Court recognized that the right "to marry, establish a home and bring up children" is a central part of the liberty protected by the Due Process Clause (1923: 399).

The family has also had a historic monopoly on "legitimate" reproduction. In 1949, Justice Panken of the New York Family Court stated:

> Man enters a marital relationship to perpetuate the species. The family is the result of the marital relationship. It is the institution which determines in a large measure the environmental influences, cultural backgrounds, and even economic status of its members. It is the foundation upon which society rests and is the basis for the family and all its benefits. (*Lester v. Lester*, 1949: 520)

There has been a historical "insistence on the traditional family as the sole permissible locus of childbearing" (Carbone 1994: 398). Children born outside of the traditional (marriage-based) family were labeled "illegitimate" or deemed "bastards." Use of these stigmatizing terms continues in the political debates over welfare reform (Fineman 1995: chap. 5). Other nonlegal but equally socially supported functions assigned to the family are associated with its role as an economic unit. The household is the relevant demographic measure in a variety of economic contexts. Historically the government and reformers were interested in defining or securing a "family wage," a label that assumed the role differentiation of the traditional family.[1] The family has psychological and functional dimensions, and also serves as a powerful ideological symbol with political implications. It is the intimate unit in policy and legal discussions that is given exclusive status, designated as what is normatively desirable.

The continued reliance on the traditional family as cultural icon and political anchor is puzzling, given the changes in society over the past several decades. In particular, the rejection by women of the hierarchical family, the dissolution of the conceptual lines that had been drawn at the turn of the century between the domestic or private and the market/political or public spheres, and the increased participation of women in the paid workforce (with their consequential shouldering of dual responsibilities) challenge the vitality and desirability of the traditional family (Cott 1977; Taub and Schneider 1982; Law 1984; Olsen 1983). These developments raise questions which we seem to ignore as change proceeds. As more women enter the job market, marriage rates have gone down (Carbone 1994; Siegel 1994). There has been a significant drop in the number of women who ever marry. For example, from 1975 to 1990, the number of women aged twenty to twenty-four who ever married dropped by about a third, from 63 to 38 percent; for ages twenty-five to twenty-nine, the percentage dropped from 87 to 69, and in the thirty to forty age group, from 93 to 82 percent (Norton and Miller 1992: 3).

In addition, altered expectations and aspirations about equality and economic opportunity have been the impetus for many individual women to change the ways they practice mothering. On a societal level, these changes have generated reconsideration of the meaning and implications of motherhood. This process of cultural and social rethinking presents a challenge to the dominance of the traditional family model. The rather rapid acceptance (and embrace) of the possibility of viable and desirable alternatives by certain subsets of society seems to have struck terror in the hearts of many, women and men alike. In some quarters, change is perceived as inherently destabilizing. Groups who view change as necessarily threatening often also tend to consider the family to be a foundational institution essential to civilization. Its instability is perceived, therefore, as the equivalent of a threat to society.

Policy- and lawmakers scramble to make sense of and address the implications of the changes for the family. Reflecting the deep divisions within society on these issues, some seek to impose sanctions and incentives to suppress the emerging social realities or make them conform to the old ideal. Charles Murray, Newt Gingrich, and the Republican Contract with America early on urged that if mothers cannot care for their children, primarily because they are poor, the children should be removed from them and placed in orphanages (Roddy 1995: A1). Generally, advocates for children, professional and nonprofessional, were appalled at the suggestion and "were outraged by the notion that mothers would have to give up their children simply because they were poor" (Dean 1995: 1A). In one example, The Children's Home and Boys' Town in Florida were described as places "where children end up after they have failed in foster families." What these children need, according to child welfare experts, is a "safe, stable family"; it is not good for children to lose primary caretakers, or to change homes (Dean 1995: 1A). Orphanages raise the "specter of children again being removed from their homes for no other reason than that their parents are poor" (Benson 1995: 16A). The media have followed up on this suggestion by investigating the past and current history of orphanages and children's homes in this country. In one article, the Executive Director of the New England Home for Little Wanderers, where "[t]he majority [of children] must be medicated to cope with reality," was quoted as denying the reality of the "cozy, poignant, drug-free, bruise-free, 'Boys' Town' " image of orphanages: "[i]f they do exist, I have no idea where" (Jones 1994: A10). Where they exist, they are expensive. The Good-Will Hinckly Home, which cares for approximately eighty-nine children, spends about $24,000 per year on each child and has had some success. One child, taken from the South Bronx and placed in an institution, became a high-school football star and prospective college graduate. The institution is considered a "moderately" priced one but the price tag for the success—well worth it, of course—was $200,000: five years in the institution for $173,000; then foster care at $10,945 per year. This is roughly six times the national average of $1,584 paid annually for Aid to Families with Dependent Children (AFDC) (Roddy 1995: A1).

The current incoherence between family reality and the images of family in law exposes the dominant ideology and its role in policy formation. Refusing to address and assess the continued viability of ideological assumptions, politicians and pundits resort to condemnation and repressive policy suggestions. This pattern of reaction to changing family behavior should raise questions about the responsive capabilities of our lawmaking institutions.

A. FAMILY, LAW, AND LEGITIMACY

Law performs an important societal function when it monitors or disciplines transformations and transitions in society, imposing conceptual order on the chaos generated by the perception of change. Widespread changes in behavior or rejection by significant segments of society of existing social institutions should be the impetus for a collective reconsideration of the continued viability of the old normative system. If, instead, change becomes the occasion for retrenchment and repression, inspiring the type of mean-spirited and dangerous polemics that currently pass for politics, the legitimacy of the entire legal system will eventually be undermined.

Reconsideration of basic social institutions does not take place without constraints, of course. Widely held beliefs about and insistently reinforced notions of what is natural, normal, and desirable affect how we approach change. Ideologies that reference collectively held conceptions domesticate or tame radical initiatives and impulses. In law reform, the fundamental and initial debate is always about the underlying cultural and social constructs. One indication of this is found in the *New York Times* analysis which blamed Sweden's current fiscal difficulties on its expansive welfare structure (Stevenson 1995: A1). This subtly biased article reflects how even a liberal paper may view more socialistic governments. The reported Swedish budgetary problems were cast as vindication of anti–big government attitudes and indicative of the superiority of the imperatives of capitalism and the Puritan work ethic. This article has been criticized as an unfair portrayal of the Swedish welfare system and the Swedes themselves (Rhodes 1995: A28). As components of the dominant ideological structure in which later discussions about policy will take place, these constructs direct the progression of reform. Nevertheless, when there are such fundamental shifts in family formation and functioning as we now experience, it is foolish and shortsighted merely to resort to antiquated visions and ignore the emerging social realities.

B. THE HISTORY

Historically, the American family has been our most explicitly gendered institution. The family has been justified and valorized as an institution for its perceived role in reproducing and transmitting norms of social behavior to all its members, but most particularly to the young. It continues to be gendered in its operations and expectations as well as in the values that it represents. Concurrently, the complementary legal roles of Husband-Father, Wife-Mother, and Child-Adult are formulated in the context of the relationship between the state and the legally contrived institution of the official Family. Dependency is "naturally" assigned to the family: privatized. It is not anticipated in the ideology that either the market or the state will directly contribute to or assist in the necessary caretaking—that is done in the privacy of the family. The ideology of the private family mandates that the unit both nurture and provide for the economic needs of its members. The burdens of economic support and caretaking, the costs of intrafamily dependency, must be distributed within the family, allocated to its members based on the perceived family roles they play. The state will provide assistance if the family is unable to do so, falling below the standards of self-sufficiency and independence that are part of the ideology of families in our culture. This assignment of burdens within the family operates in an inherently unequal manner—the uncompensated tasks of caretaking are placed with women while men pursue careers that provide for the family economically but also enhance their individual career or work prospects. This division of family labor has been understood as just and "natural," not as manufactured or contrived, perpetuating historic, gendered family roles.

As appealing as this traditional model may be to some, it is essential to note that even had the world once been so simple, things have changed. An examination of the current statistics on intimate associations reveals that the traditional family composes a decided minority of possible domestic arrangements. There is a change in the ratio of married couple-based families: in 1960, the census counted 53 million households; in 1990 the figure was 93 million. In 1960, married couples with children comprised 75 percent of the family households; in 1990, the figure was down to 56 percent. Conversely, the number of nonfamily households rose from 15 percent in 1960 to 29 percent in 1990 (Lugaila 1992: 15; Sorrentino 1990: 41). The Bureau of the Census estimates that one-half of all marriages entered into since 1970 could end in divorce, with the majority of the parties remarrying (Lugaila 1992: 8); married couples may be working on second, third, or later relationships. More and more individuals are living alone than in past decades. In 1989, approximately one-quarter of all households consisted of persons living alone (Report 1993). Between 1960 and 1990, the number of men living alone more than doubled to approach 10 percent; for women, the number reached almost 15 percent (Lugaila 1992: 15). Single-parent families comprised 32 percent of families with children in 1990. From 1960 to 1990, the percentage of children living with only their mother rose from 8 to 21.6 percent; children living with only their father increased in number from 1.1 to 3.1 percent. Never-married motherhood is on the rise, even among middle-class educated women. The number of white single-parent families increased from 7.1 to 19.2 percent; the number of black single-parent families increased from 21.9 to 54.8 percent. Twenty-two percent of white single-parent families have a never-married parent; for black families the number is 53 percent, and for Hispanics, 37 percent (Lugaila 1992: 36–37, 21). In addition, couples choose not to become parents in larger numbers than in prior generations. Households comprised of married couples with their biological children declined from 44.2 percent in 1960 to 26.3 percent in 1990 and other families with children increased from 4.4 to 8.3 percent. Married couples without children remained statistically the same at around thirty percent (Lugaila 1992: 15).

Furthermore, even in structurally conforming families (married with children), the traditional roles have broken down. The breadwinner/housewife model is in decline. Many women work outside of the home either in a full-time or part-time capacity, and some are as deeply committed to career and job advancement as are their husbands. In 1990, in approximately 70 percent of two-parent families with children, both parents worked. In more than a quarter of these families both parents worked full-time; in 30 percent the husband worked full-time, the wife part-time or not continuously; in 20 percent the wife worked only in the home; and in 21 percent the husband did not work full-time (Lugaila 1992: 42–43).

Looking at family reality involves more than just a reference to these empirical changes, however. The statistics have normative as well as empirical implications. The fact that America has a multiplicity of ethnic, religious, and cultural traditions supports the argument that we should develop a pluralistic social model inclusive of diverse family practices. For example, in recent years people have begun to question the received wisdom as to what should constitute the core or central family connection (Lewin 1994: A1, B7). Historically, marriage has been considered the fundamental building block of society. In the words of Chief Justice Waite over a century ago: "Marriage, while from its very nature a sacred obligation, is . . . a civil contract, and usually regulated by law. Upon [marriage] society may be said to be built, and out of its fruits spring social relations and social obligations and duties, with which government is necessarily required to deal" (*Reynolds v. United States*, 1878: 165–66). In *Loving v. Virginia*, the court reiterated that marriage was "one of the basic rights of man [*sic*], fundamental to our very existence and survival" (1967: 12). The foundational role of marriage was eulogized by

Judge Bork: "The reason for protecting the family and the institution of marriage is not merely that they are fundamental to our society but that our entire tradition is to encourage, support, and respect them" (*Franz v. United States*, 1983). More recently, Justice O'Connor, ruling that states could not prevent prison inmates from marrying while incarcerated, echoed this thought:

> [M]arriages are . . . expressions of emotional support and public commitment. These elements are an important and significant aspect of the marital relationship. In addition, many religions recognize marriage as having spiritual significance . . . the commitment of marriage may be an exercise of religious faith as well as an expression of personal dedication. . . . [M]arital status often is a precondition to the receipt of government benefits (e.g. Social Security benefits), property rights (e.g. tenancy by the entirety, inheritance rights), and other, less tangible benefits (e.g. legitimation of children born out of wedlock). (*Turner v. Safley*, 1987)

Some people continue to insist that legitimate families can only be built upon the presence of a traditional marital tie. Others refer to the significance of biological connection and minimize legalities in favor of kinship structures that form affiliations transcending current formal definitions of the family (Collins 1987; Stack 1974). For others, the preference is for an affectional family, a unit composed of those with whom we choose to connect but who may not be "related" to us either by blood or by marriage (Weston 1991; Goldscheider and Waite 1991; Swerdlow et al. 1989). Family affiliations are expressed in different kinds of affiliational acts. Some are sexually based, as with marriage. Some are forged through biological events, such as parenthood (Bartlett 1984; Treuthart 1991). Others are more relational, such as those based on nurturing and caretaking, or developed through conferral of affection and acceptance of interdependence (Anderson and Hopkins 1991: 211–13).

Each of the alternative conceptions of the central or core family connection assumes certain things about what is appropriate and desirable. Each family form carries within its confines the possibility of exclusion and stigmatization of nonconforming relationships. Each model, in defining itself, defines the parameters of what is natural or appropriate. The converse of the created ideal may become defined as deviant or pathological.

The process of articulating alternatives has attended the dominance of our official and, often, legal adherence to the unitary, heterogeneous, patriarchal family. One of the most entrenched notions about marriage is that it is an institution that can be entered into exclusively by one man and one woman. Most state statutes, explicitly or implicitly, limit marriage to "a male and a female."[2] The dominant ideological construction of the family assumes only one appropriate model of family formation—heterosexual marriage. For a short while in 1993, many gay and lesbian couples had hoped that things were changing when the Hawaii Supreme Court struck the male/female requirement as violating same-sex couples' civil right to marry (*Baehr v. Lewin,* 1993). Responding to this ruling, the Hawaii legislature quickly amended and reenacted the requirement:

> The legislature finds that Hawaii's marriage licensing laws were originally and are presently intended to apply only to male-female couples, not same-sex couples. This determination is one of policy. Any change in these laws must come from either the legislature or a constitutional convention, not the judiciary. The Hawaii supreme court's recent plurality opinion in Baehr v. Lewin . . . effaces the recognized tradition of marriage in this State and, in so doing, impermissibly negates the constitutionally mandated role of the legislature as a co-equal, coordinate branch of government. (1994 Haw. Sess. Laws, Act 217, Section 1)

The political preference for the traditional model has economic implications. The exclusivity of the heterosexual marriage model controls the political process in which the state, through its institutions and designated actors, wields the symbolic power of this normative structure in order to justify a parsimonious distribution of economic and social subsidies. Married persons receive significantly favorable treatment through estate and gift tax laws (26 USC 2056, 2523, West Supp.). Other benefits include insurance, or other health-care coverage, worker's compensation, disability, social security benefits, and in many urban areas housing benefits associated with rent control.

At the federal level, a Republican Party initiative in response to *Baehr v. Lewin* seeks to define marriage as "a legal union between one man and one woman" (Schwinn 1996: A11). The so-called "Defense of Marriage Act," now enacted into law, enables states to bypass the constitutional provision of "full faith and credit" (White 1996). Under the definition, same-sex marriages authorized by one state need not be honored elsewhere, and federal benefits are reserved for heterosexual married couples.

In the context of the current debates about the family in the United States, we focus on family form, not function. We are concerned with the number of parents and their legal status and are increasingly punitive toward those that deviate from the traditional model. A discussion of what societal role the family plays—its relationship to the obligations of the state—has not taken place. We deal in platitudes rather than assess what functions we want from the family (whatever its form) or realistic explorations of how such functions might be facilitated through public subsidy and support.

C. The Family in Politics

In spite of alternative visions and nonconforming behavior, the politically normative family remains the intact, heterosexual, formally married couple and their biological children. Intimate groups that do not conform to this model have historically been labeled "deviant"; their nonconformity has been used to justify their subjection to explicit state regulation and control.

The level of state intervention, control, and punishment is being raised, and the rhetoric directed at unmarried and/or poor women has moved rapidly from that of the disapproving patriarch to the ranting of the righteous witch-hunter. Given a patina of academic responsibility by the likes of Charles Murray, and led by the careening crusading of Newt Gingrich, the descriptive terms and accusations directed at the most defenseless people in our society stigmatize and dehumanize them. When Murray first began his crusade, many people, including feminists and politicians, dismissed him as ultraconservative, too radical even for the extreme right. Today his punitive ideas are being parroted by members of Congress and state legislators. Murray is one of the most vicious commentators on the increased rates of single motherhood, blaming them for all the ills of society: "[I]llegitimacy is the single most important social problem of our time—more important than crime, drugs, poverty, illiteracy, welfare, or homelessness, because it drives everything else" (Murray 1993: A14). We have rejected a humane social "contract"—one based on the spirit of a sense of collective responsibility and an appreciation of the generalized interdependence among all members of society—for the public, ritualistic washing of federal hands and the devolution of responsibility to states, many of which have already declared the intention to pass the problem further on down the line—eventually laying the burden on the poor themselves (Lipton 1995: D1, D4; Sawhill and Nightingale 1995: A29). We witness the creation of punitive, mean-spirited federal measures disguised as "reforms."

In the context of the welfare debates, the idealized family has become the panacea for all social ills in contemporary policy discussions. The institution of marriage is seriously offered as a uniquely appropriate form of social policy, and systems of proposed disincentives for unmarried women to reproduce are debated by a multiplicity of men in various halls of power. Women who do not conform—either by not marrying or by refusing to participate in pa-ternity proceedings—are threatened with orphanages or restrictive measures and conditions on their societal subsidies. In some states, women receiving benefits are currently required to undergo mandatory paternity proceedings as a condition of receiving their benefits. A Wisconsin enactment makes full cooperation in paternity determinations of "nonmarital" children a condition of eligibility for receiving assistance; failure to cooperate means that the custodian will be ineligible, and "protective" payments for the child will be paid to "a person other than the person charged with the care of the dependent child." Wisconsin law also requires the state attorney to file an action for paternity within six months of receiving notice that no father is named on the birth certificate of a child, if paternity has not been adjudicated, regardless of the wishes of the mother (WI. STAT. ANN. 767.45(6m)(1994)). President Clinton has sought to "lure married voters" in an election year by identifying himself with a conservative " 'values agenda' " attractive to "couples with children" (Mitchell 1996: A19). Initially, the president was quick to endorse the Wisconsin program, aligning himself with the idea of wage subsidies for "single mothers who work" (Pear 1996a: A1). On closer examination, this enthusiasm was tempered; however, in backing down, the administration focused its rhetoric on the program's harsh effects on children in poverty, and has continued to emphasize "family issues" in the context of the nuclear family paradigm (Pear 1996b: A1; Mitchell 1996: A19).

At this time, federal law provides for justified refusal to name the father for "good cause" (41 USC 602(a)(26)(B)(1988)). "Good cause" is based on the needs of the child and exists only when the child will suffer physical or emotional harm, or the mother will suffer such harm to the extent that she will be unable to care for the child adequately (43 C.F.R. 232.42 (a)(1)(i)–(iii)(1990)). In one extremely punitive application of this standard, "good cause" was denied when one woman failed to report rape to police because she feared harm to herself and her child (*Waller v. Carlton County Human Servs. Dep't.* 1989). Women who have named men later excluded by blood test or women who have said they do not know the name or location of the father have been subjected to severe scrutiny and questioning by the state agencies. In one case, after several men named by plaintiff as the possible father were excluded by blood tests or could not be found, the agency demanded a calendar on which she had supposedly written the names of sexual partners. When she refused, her benefits were cut (*Allen v. Eichler* 1990).

One of the provisions of the Personal Responsibility Act denies AFDC benefits until paternity is established, *even when the mother is fully cooperating* (emphasis supplied). If this provision had been in effect in the 1992 fiscal year, 2.8 million children would have been denied aid (News 1995: 1–4). Under the much touted Wisconsin program, women are punished by cuts in their meager public assistance awards if they have any additional children, refuse to (or cannot) name the father of their children, are unable to force their children to attend school and/or fail to get vaccinations for their children (Wɪ. Sᴛᴀᴛ. §49.50(7)(g) and (h) (1993)). The problems with these programs remain relatively unpublicized. A 1990 audit of the Wisconsin learnfare program found that 84 percent of the orders imposing sanctions were overturned by an administrative judge "because of error in record-keeping by either the schools or the welfare agency" (Taylor 1991: A3). Draconian incentive systems are proposed to tie them to the world of wage work or make work—all of this in a system that refuses to consider mothering as work. Mothering under the best conditions is work, of course. It is work that is not incorporated into the Gross National Product, however, and often overlooked for that reason by various policy makers. Poor motherhood, particularly when one is receiving AFDC, is even more work in our suspicious and demeaning system. Lines are long and forms and formalities profuse (Simon 1983).

What have these women done that make them "deserving" of harsh words and punitive measures? In large part it is the stigma of being poor. But more than poverty is at issue. The broad general target is unmarried women with children, and the attacks on these mothers is only one salvo of a reactionary plan to discipline women who do not conform to the roles they are assigned within the traditional scheme of the family. This is why all women, whether they are mothers or not, should be concerned with the nature of the debates about poverty. While the welfare debate seemingly stigmatizes only one form of mothering as pathological, the orchestration and performance of the political rhetoric reinforces, recreates, and reiterates several fundamental premises about families that will be used against all women. Paramount among these is, of course, the strong preference for formally celebrated heterosexual marriage that functions as a reproductive unit and is thus the "core" of society on which all else is founded. This preference places responsible reproduction (indeed, responsible sexuality) within the context of the traditional family, a context in which the legal consequences are clear and decisions will be considered and controlled. Motherhood outside this family will be punished and stigmatized. Nonmothers will also be disciplined—pressured and pitied as attacks on birth control and abortion extol the inevitability and naturalness of motherhood.

3. THE FAMILY IN LAW

A. THE SEXUAL ORGANIZATION OF FAMILY INTIMACY

Our conception of the family as an entity is built around a core unit— the married couple. The basic family relationship is founded on the sexual affiliation or conjugation of two heterosexual adults. This unit traditionally was considered so basic that it was referred to as the foundation of American society. This heterosexual unit continues to be considered as presumptively appropriate, and it has ongoing viability as the essential family connection. Even contemporary critics of the institution are typically revisionists, viewing marriage to be merely in need of some updating and structural reformulation. In fact, arguments that other sexual affiliations, such as nonmarital cohabitation or same sex relationships, are deserving of the same privileges afforded to marriage, far from challenging the privileged status of marriage, reinforce it by inscribing onto it the attributes of normalcy, desirability, and privilege.

B. THE EGALITARIAN ORGANIZATION OF THE FAMILY

As a result of reform movements during the 1970s and 1980s, certain aspects of the law reflect a gender neutral family ideal.[3] Our linguistic model is now one of an egalitarian family, based on the marital "partnership" of husband and wife. Gone from our formal, official discourse is the hierarchical organization of the common law marriage described so graphically by Blackstone (1862) under the doctrines of "unity" and "merger."

Female subservience is no longer assumed by the formal legal rules, nor our inherent incompetence for the business and market world seriously asserted and used as a basis for exclusion by courts and legislators. Wives and mothers are held equally responsible for the economic well-being of their families and no longer presumed by virtue of their sex to be the preferred parent in custody disputes. Many legal disabilities for nonmarital children have been removed. There is less stigma to divorce with the ascendancy of no-fault philosophy where marriages are terminated because of irreconcilable differences rather than the culpable conduct of one of the spouses.

However, rhetorical changes in law and legislation do not reflect real changes, nor can they compel them. In considering the empirical data on the operation of the family, the inescapable conclusion, rhetoric aside, is that gender divisions persist. Women continue to bear what I call the "burdens of intimacy"—the costs of inevitable dependency—in our society. Cross-cultural studies indicate that women still perform the vast majority of housework and family responsibilities, despite the existence in some countries of laws mandating shared responsibility between men and women. Mothers still perform the vast bulk of child care and housework (Labor Report 1992; Labor Conference 1993; Bane et al. 1979: 52–53; Project 1982; Fuchs 1986). Contrary to popular anecdotal information of fathers actively participating in child care, fathers today are actually participating only slightly more than they did in 1967. While there is some evidence that more fathers are becoming primary caregivers when women return to work (Report 1994: 2), a 1988 study showed that employed women still spend twice as much time with child care and housework as do their husbands (Drakich 1989: 83–87).

As a definitional note, "burden" is not the same as oppression. I use the term to signify that, clearly, there are costs associated with what women typically do in regard to caretaking in our society. These labors may provide "joy," but they are also burdensome and have material consequences to those who typically bear them but are not compensated for doing so within the private family. Not to recognize them as "burdens" is to ignore the costs and to continue to make women's labor invisible, condoning that it is also uncompensated.

A second definitional point is that, in discussing dependency, it is important to differentiate between various forms of dependency. I am interested in two specific dependencies. The first I label "inevitable dependency." It is inevitable in that it flows from the status and situation of being a child and often accompanies aging, illness, or disability. This type of dependency is biological, developmental in nature. It is universal. In this sense dependency will always be (and always has been) with us as a society and as individuals. In the current welfare debate the paradigmatic inevitable dependent is the child—also considered to be "worthy" or "deserving." There is a second, complementary form of dependency, however, that is more problematic for policy makers. Those who care for inevitable dependents are often themselves dependent—a derivative dependency, a function of their roles as caretakers and the need for resources they generate. This type of dependency is not inevitable, nor is it universal. It is socially defined and assigned, and that assignment is gendered.

To point out that the costs of caretaking associated with these dependencies continue in our society to be allocated to women should not be misunderstood to be an argument about essentialism. The allocation is accomplished and reinforced by the culture and our ideology of the family as a functioning institution. Nonetheless, to label something as a social construct does not mean it will be easy to change. In fact, change is difficult because of the tenacity of the still potent traditional ideology of the family in American culture.

We seem to be caught in an "equality trap" when discussing the family—a trap set by rhetoric generated in earlier feminist efforts to reform the family that focused on the need for a reorganization of existing gendered roles within the confines of the traditionally populated family unit. Susan Moller Okin seems to be ascribing to this view when she says:

> Only children who are equally mothered and fathered can develop fully the psychological and moral capacities that currently seem to be unevenly distributed between the sexes. Only when men participate equally in what have been principally women's realms of meeting the daily material and psychological needs of those close to them . . . will members of both sexes be able to develop a more complete human personality. (Okin 1989: 107)

Rather than challenging the basic structure, early reformers merely expected that fathers would be enlisted to share more in the domestic tasks as modern mothers spent more time and energy in market endeavors. Fulfilling egalitarian impulses, the marital partners would simply rework the parameters of their relationship into a nonhierarchical form. The marital tie, nonetheless, would continue to serve as the anchor defining and giving content to their relationship with each other as well as defining other family associations.

This approach to family reform influenced and informed the changes made in law during the past several decades: the fashioning of the "egalitarian family" from the structure of its old common law hulk. This reform vision was a particularly narrow one, considering only some family actors in its reconstituted vision. The roles of husband and wife were restructured in regard to child care and vaguely described household domestic tasks, but little thought seems to have been given to the demands on domestic time and labor represented by the less attractive specters of caring for the elderly, the ill, or the disabled. The egalitarian family was structured around sexual affiliation—the assumed inevitability of heterosexual pairing and its association with reproductive destiny were expressed in family form. No one was arguing over who got to take care of and get credit for caring for grandma in the development of the rhetoric of the "new man" in the reconstructed family story. The grand aspirations about equality are manifested in the terms we now use to discuss family relationships—"partnership" substituted for marriage; "shared parenting" substituted for mothering and fathering; "interdependency" and "contribution" substituted for need and obligatory domestic labor. Unfortunately, the equality direction had severe limitations, both practical and theoretical. In failing to recognize the gendered nature of the world in which they were demanding change, early feminists mistakenly believed that formal equality would rectify past discrimination. This was not true, and in fact could not be true. To be successful, any theory seeking to change women's lives and their relationship to mainstream culture, that is patriarchal culture, must be gendered. It must be woman centered, gendered by its very nature because it is based on women's experiences which are gendered. Women's experience is not and cannot be theorized as "neutral" (Fineman 1991a).

Reformers naively assumed that sharing could and would happen. With the egalitarian aspiration ensconced in law, women would be freed to develop their careers, men unconstrained in choosing nurturing over other endeavors. On the most basic level, such assumptions unrealistically continue the notion of husband and wife as a couple forming the basic family core in a society in which the divorce rate hovers at fifty percent and never-married motherhood is on the rise. Interestingly, it was this increase in nonmarital births among white women that seems to have been the proverbial last straw for those in power. As Charles Murray said: "the brutal truth is that American society as a whole could survive when illegitimacy became epidemic within a comparatively small ethnic minority. It cannot survive the same epidemic among whites" (Murray 1993: A14). Recent census figures show the largest percentage increase in never-married motherhood occurring among women with some college education (Bachu 1993). The Bachu report reviewed the 1990 census data for women between the ages of eighteen and forty-four who had never married and found that 24 percent of them had become mothers, as opposed to 15 percent in the 1980 census. The rate of births among unmarried women with at least one year of college increased from 5.5 percent to 11.3 percent; for women in professional or managerial positions, it rose from 7 percent to 8.3 percent.

The media gave this phenomenon a great deal of attention (Beck 1993; DeParle 1993; Whitmire 1993; Cohen 1993, Pollitt 1993; Lawson 1993; Lamott 1993). And, of course, we all recall the Quayle debacle with Murphy Brown: "Hollywood thinks it's cute to glamorize illegitimacy," Quayle told reporters; "Hollywood doesn't get it" (Yang and Devroy 1992; Whitehead 1993; Coontz 1993). Before Democrats embrace the view that marriage is the best antidote to poverty, educational failure, and psychological distress, they might consult the two-parent families devastated by layoffs in the steel, defense, timber, and auto industries, families whose children now exhibit most of the emotional and cognitive problems generally blamed on divorce.

These statistics indicate to me that it is time for us to admit that the complementarily gendered notion of the marital couple is no longer an adequate concept. We must begin to rethink the institution of the contemporary family unfettered by the limitations of the past in a way that is responsive to emerging realities. We must begin to think explicitly of family policy in terms of the functions we want the family to perform and leave behind our obsession with form. We should establish a system of sanctions and rewards that reflect as far as possible a consensus about what it is society should be protecting and encouraging through social and economic subsidies. Our meager and sporadic family policies do not facilitate or support actual families as they struggle to fulfill their own expectations and responsibilities. We do not subsidize families operating outside of the traditional context. Unlike other industrialized democracies we have no well-defined notion of collective responsibility for inevitable dependency—no basic income guarantee, no comprehensive publicly assisted day care, no universal health coverage, no societal structures and institutions to help shoulder caretaking burdens. In fact, recent welfare reforms resort to the privatized solutions of marriage and/or child support as the answer for myriad societal problems as well as child poverty.

C. THE PUBLIC ROLE OF THE PRIVATE FAMILY

In attempting to analyze the tenacity of the sexually affiliated or marriage-based notion of family in the face of forceful articulations of alternatives, we must consider the structural position of the family. In this assessment, we move away from preoccupation with the roles of individuals within the family and concentrate on the institution in relation to the state. The relevant questions are: what is the role of the family as a social institution? How does it interact with the state and how does this interaction reflect the ideological underpinnings of the structure? It is important in this regard to remember that the family is first and foremost a *social* institution. As such it is defined and given social content by significant systems of belief or knowledge with coercive potential exceeding that of law. In this regard, the family as an institution embedded in social understanding should be understood to be resistant to redefinition. Furthermore, individual understandings about family are shaped by societal forces. So, while one may "choose" to live outside of the conventional norms, one does not escape them totally and the challenge is apt to be slight. No one is exempt from the implications of the culture in which she lives—it influences our actions, our aspirations, our politics, and what we can see as possibilities.

4. THE FAMILY IN SOCIETY

Within the variety of extralegal cultural and social systems that shape our beliefs about families, there are certain core concepts or "metanarratives" that predominate and affect the law, shape and influence reform. Meta- or public narrative is essentially a modernist concept, understood to be the story or "narrative" that legitimates and controls knowledge in the Western world.

The modernist attempts to characterize the world as ultimately unrepresentable while relying on a form of narrative presentation that is familiar and recognizable and that offers the reader or listener a degree of comfort. The idea of metanarratives assumes a hierarchy of cultural representations and values. Since the Enlightenment, the central Western metanarrative has been that of progress, reason, and the individual—a narrative of Darwinian evolution and economic opportunity. Metanarratives are normative and aid in the formation of collective identities, allowing for a linear and narrow interpretation of history. For example, a single metanarrative has established public law adjudication as the paradigm for all adjudication: a system of adjudication governed by a single set of principles regardless of whether the question is one of common law, statutory construction, or constitutional interpretation (Eisenberg 1988: 8–13). In contrast, postmodern theories focus on the existence of local, interlocking language games that are asserted to replace the idea of overall, overarching structures (Wicke 1989: 562; Jameson 1991; van Reijen and Veerman 1988: 301–2). Postmodern theorists reject metanarratives and see culture and society as a complex interaction, a closely knit weave without any single exclusive or overpowering identity (Wicke 1989; Kolb 1986; Thomas 1991; Unger 1976).

There are two interrelated metanarratives about the American family that direct current social policy and limit the possibility of policy initiatives that would help to support functioning, nontraditional families. The first is that of the natural nature of the family—the belief that the family has a "natural" form. The natural family form of husband, wife, and child (the nuclear family) is built around a foundational sexual affiliation which is ultimately reinforced by reproductive biology. This natural family is postulated as predating the state, but it is also expressly viewed as a complement to the state, essential for its very existence.

The second metanarrative is that of the private family, a unit entitled to protection and assistance from the state. Freedom from state intervention has historically been conferred on the appropriately functioning family unit as a "reward" for fulfilling our societal and political expectation that the family is the natural repository for inevitable dependency. The private family is the social institution that will raise the children, care for the ill, the needy, the dependent. Ideally it performs these tasks as a self-contained and self-sufficient unit—located within the larger society, complementing the state which protects it without demanding public resources to do so. In the societal division of labor among institutions, the private family bears the burdens of dependency, not the public state. Resort to the state is failure. The idea of the private family thus is the way responsibility for inevitable dependency is directed away from the state and privatized. Responsibility for dependency is ideologically a private matter.

As with the ideals of individual autonomy and self-sufficiency, the notion of the private family has important ideological and political currency. Its existence as an ideological construct masks the universal and inevitable nature of dependency and allows our official and public rhetoric to be spun out in terms of ideals of capitalistic individualism, independence, self-sufficiency and autonomy. Significantly, the ideals of self-sufficiency and autonomy operate on two levels—they construct the ideal family as well as the ideal individual within our culture. There is as much unreality in the ideal of self-sufficiency and autonomy for the private family as there is in the same concepts applied to individuals. The many direct and indirect subsidies that such private families receive through tax, inheritance, marriage, and other laws are hidden. Employer contributions to health and life insurance policies are not counted as income (and hence, not taxed as income); transfers between spouses are not taxed as gifts; labor performed in the home is not counted as "imputed income" to the wage earner who benefits (nor is the homeworker compensated or given pension benefits for her tasks). Middle-class deductions such as mortgage interest rate or some child care expenses are considered appropriate even though they also remove income from the taxable pool. One of the rallying cries for welfare caps was that private families did not receive a raise when they had an additional child so why should welfare recipients receive extra benefits if they did. Missing from the attack was the realization that private families receive a tax deduction for each new child worth considerably more money each month than the pittance typically given to welfare mothers who have another child.

These two metanarratives—that of the natural family and that of the private family—are composed of interdependent assumptions that reinforce one another on an ideological level and perversely interact to continue gender inequality. The tasks assigned the private family mandate that the burdens or costs associated with dependency must be allocated among family members, and this allocation is gendered. In other words, our perception of the family as a social institution facilitates the continuation of gendered role divisions and frustrates the egalitarian ideal.

A. DISCIPLINING DEVIANT WOMEN

The very definition of single motherhood as an independent and significant social problem as well as the nature and direction of suggested remedies for the "crisis" show the strength of the natural and private family concepts in tandem. Under the ideal system, private families need economic resources for nurturing work. The economic portion of the equation is "naturally" supplied by the head-of-the-household, the caretaking by his wife, the adult "naturally" dependent on his economic resources for her work within the household. The reform objective for single-mother families, whether created by divorce or because the woman never married, is to reconstitute the natural family in some form—bring the male (back) in so that dependency can be properly privatized. In fact, it is striking how central the image of male as head-of-household is to all family and welfare reforms.

The very existence of these "problems" and our inability to respond to them within the confines of our family ideology are strong evidence supporting assertions about the failure of the nuclear family paradigm. They illustrate that the private-natural family is no longer viable as the sole, or even primary, institutional response to dependency. This is not the only possible response. Punitive and harsh measures designed to stigmatize those who deviate from the failed norm seem preferred by many policy makers (Fineman 1991b; 1991c).

In constructing the problems presented by, as well as the solutions for, both the never-married mother and the divorced mother, the physical absence of a male is assumed central. The male metaphysical presence in the form of economic support is induced by conferring "rights" over children. The vision is that male discipline and control will make "complete" the family in some mystical way. The economically viable male becomes social policy: "he" is the universal answer, the means offered for resolving the problems of poverty and despair. Paternity proceedings and child-support enforcement will alleviate poverty. Both divorce and welfare reforms attempt to reconfigure the natural family, to bring the father into the picture through an economic and disciplinary connection reminiscent of the traditional male role in the hierarchical private family as head of the household. Equality imagery has taken hold in this area. The argument is that fathers as equal parents are equally obligated to be with and care for children, but (the myth grows) they fail to do so because mothers have superior rights. If law gives fathers more rights over children, they will pay child support for those children. There have been some efforts to assess whether more rights actually translate into more support. The question is unresolved (Maccoby and Mnookin 1992: 251–57; Fineman 1992b). Patriarchy is thus reasserted, modified to meet new social realities.

Further consideration of the circumstances in which the social idea of the private, natural family fails will illuminate the previous abstractions. In this regard, the current economic circumstances make it unlikely that marriage is truly going to resolve the problems of most poor women and children. Unemployment, "down-sizing," and the change from manufacturing to service economy have eroded the wage scale for many men. In addition, the flight of businesses to suburbs means that many urban workers must commute, another difficulty.

Even if economic patterns do not create insurmountable obstacles to using marriage as the solution for poverty, there are significant changes in the ways in which we define family behaviors and aspirations that will have an impact. One set of difficulties is presented by the tension generated by the wide acceptance among elites of the notion of the egalitarian family. The second set of problems is found in the sense of crisis surrounding the increase in the number of women from all classes and races that are becoming single mothers as a result either of our high divorce rate or because they never married in the first place.

The egalitarian family as an articulated ideal is imposed on existing couple-based family units, and it generates tensions in so far as one of the goals to be attained by the partners is equal career or market proficiency. Equality as an ideal has developed in the context of a society that rewards and values market work, and feminist theory has reflected this. Mothering and other family work is to be "managed" so as to free women for career development. However, attempts to achieve equality in the public sphere, particularly in the market, leave the two-parent family an institution with potentially *no* available caretakers. The solution may be to hire them, but this may come with its own set of problems, as the Zoe Baird and Kimba Woods incidents indicated for professional moms.

The never-married or divorced-single-mother case presents a version of the same dilemma. Without a designated "partner," if she devotes her time to market work in order to support her child financially, no one will be available to perform her caretaker role. If she fulfills her culturally assigned obligations by sacrificing career to bear the burdens of dependency, since she is single and has no wage earner to support her, she will starve or go begging to the state. In either case her family has not dealt with its dependencies privately.

Both of these situations reveal the latent gender implications in the concept of the private family. The task assigned to the private family—its societal role as the private repository of inevitable dependency—mandates two parents and some form of role differentiation and division. The private family seems destined to be gendered and unequal. Given these demands the family will assume the traditional natural form almost inevitably.

Of course, the rhetorical resolution of the potential dilemma of no care-taker in the egalitarian coupled family has been to "share" caretaking. Rhetoric aside, empirical information indicates sharing is not what is happening. The figures are overwhelming—not much has changed in terms of who does domestic labor, and this is typically as true when both partners are employed as it is when the mother stays home (Drakich 1989). Women can give up the hope for equality or they can hire other women at (typically) meager wages to carry the burdens of dependency for them. In either case, it is some woman's labor that is appropriated for necessary caretaking and goes unpaid or undercompensated even within the charade of the egalitarian marriage. Caregiving remains invisible because the law thinks of family care as matter of love and obligation, not personal choice or an arms' length transaction (Estin 1993: 776; Siegel 1994: 1214; Davis n.d.: 16–17).

In instances where it is necessary that one career be temporarily compro-mised for caretaking, strong economic incentives guide the choice between marital partners. Equality fictions in the family may abound, but the reality of continuing market inequalities typically makes the efficient selection the lesser earning woman when there is a need for a family member to accommodate caretaking by forgoing market time, wages, and career opportunities (Estin 1993: 780; Starnes 1993; Oldham 1992).

In addition to this gross economic channeling, centuries of social and cultural conditioning operate to shape the ways women understand and exercise their "choices" in defining their own family role (Carbone 1994: 363–72; Siegel 1994). Family failures in regard to children, evidenced in even minor deviations from an unattainable ideal, are most likely to be placed at a mother's feet (Stark 1991). It is mothers in the workplace that elicit fears of generations of children abandoned to neglect and the horrors of day care regimentation and potential abuses. The social assignment of dependency is even more pronounced (and less challenged) when it comes to care for the elderly or ill. It is daughters (or daughters-in-law) to whom elderly parents look for expected accommodations (Nelson and Nelson 1992).

In the case of single mothers, whether they are divorced or never married, the inadequacies of the private family are not capable of resolution by pretenses toward equality within the natural or nuclear unit. These families are too far outside that paradigm and as a result they are stigmatized and demonized. Single-mother families are consistently referred to as "deviant" and "pathological." Ignoring evidence that indicates it is poverty, not family form, that causes harms, single mothers are represented as the cause of crime, poverty, and general societal decline. This language is used of both types of single mother, although it is most vicious when applied to never-married mothers (Fineman 1991b: 280–82).

On a policy level, the tragedy is that the rhetoric currently surrounding never-married mothers obscures the magnitude and dimensions of the economic deprivations which make it difficult for any women outside of the patriarchal family (and many within) to raise their children. There is a great deal of evidence that reliance on the private solution of child support is inadequate and insufficient. Out of ten million women living with children under twenty-one years of age whose father is not living in the household, only 58 percent were awarded child support payments. Of these, about half received the full amount of payments they were due, leaving 32 percent of all such families below the poverty level (Lugaila 1992: 41). Of the 4.2 million women who were never awarded child support payments, 64 percent wanted an award but did not obtain one (Lester 1991: 10).

Furthermore, there is significant doubt as to whether the provisions of the reforms are effective measures for increasing child support payments from absent fathers. The detailed requirements for wage withholding call for accurate records; when the reforms were enacted, states were faced with large backlogs of delinquent cases.[4] Delays in states' institution of wage withholding, in approval of federal funding for the automation of child support systems, and in the issuing of federal guidelines for the systems have contributed to a low rate of collection of payment under the reforms. Eighty-one percent of advocates questioned indicated that enforcement of payment through use of liens was "poor" and used phrases like "never done," "nonexistent," and "refuses to do this" when commenting on these provisions. In one case, an advocate was told by the enforcement agency that personnel did not know the procedure for enforcing payment through liens.[5] Rather than addressing the needs of existing caretakers, legislators compete to concoct disincentives, punishing women for reproducing or promoting incentives designed to push mothers to create a nuclear family.

B. A CLAIM FOR JUSTICE

The approach in this country must change, and women who are caretakers must be given a right to resources that enables them to perform the tasks we demand of them. The concept of justice must be reformulated so that punitive and mean-spirited laws designed to discipline women and children into patriarchy are not seen as appropriate. Transforming justice requires an attack on the underlying ideology that valorizes the nuclear family. A reformulated vision of justice would relate to the empirical needs of society, accepting and accommodating the inevitability of dependency and recognizing the claim of caretakers for resources necessary to accomplish their nurturing tasks.

For too long, and to too great an extent, family policy in this country has been fashioned and formulated on the nuclear family ideal. Policy based on this entity fosters the assumption that the maintenance of intimacy (everything from contraception to responsibility for the day-to-day care of children) is primarily a "private" task.

It is essential for feminists to point out consistently that without substantial rethinking of the concepts underlying patriarchy, such as that of the private-natural family, the condition of women is unlikely to improve significantly. Without such rethinking it will be a bleak future for women and those inevitable dependents for whom we typically care.

NOTES

1. For a multicultural economic study of households past and present, see Becker 1991.

2. These include UTAH CODE 30-1-2(5)(1994); ARIZ. RE. STATS. ANN. §25-125; FLA. STAT. ANN. §741.04 (1993); GA. STAT. ANN. 19-3-30 (1994), IDAHO CODE 32-412A.

3. For an extensive discussion of this point regarding the reform of divorce and property division laws, see Fineman 1983: 851–52.

4. See Hearings 1987: 134–43, statement of Robert C. Harris, Associate Deputy Director, Family Support Administrator, Office of Child Support Enforcement, U.S. Department of Health and Human Services.

5. See Hearings 1987: 162–72, statement of G. Diane Dodson, Special Counsel for Family Law and Policy, Women's Legal Defense Fund.

BIBLIOGRAPHY

Anderson, Sherry Ruth, and Patricia Hopkins. 1991. *The Feminine Face of God: The Unfolding of the Sacred in Women*. New York: Bantam.

Bachu, Amaru. 1993. *Fertility of American Women*. Bureau of the Census Current Population Report. U.S. Department of Commerce. June. Publication Number P20-470.

Bane, Mary Jo, Laura Lein, Lydia O'Donnell, C. Anne Stueve, and Barbara Wells. 1979. Child Care Arrangements of Working Parents. 102 *Monthly Labor Review* (Oct.), 50.

Bartlett, Katharine T. 1984. Rethinking Parenthood as an Exclusive Status: The Need for Legal Alternatives When the Premise of the Nuclear Family Has Failed. 70 *Virginia Law Rev.*, 879.

Beck, Joan. 1993. Nation Must Stem the Tide of Births Out of Wedlock. *The Times-Picayune*, Mar. 6, p. B7.

Becker, Gary. 1991. *A Treatise on the Family*. Enlarged ed. Cambridge, MA: Harvard Univ. Press.

Benson, Lynn. 1995. Letter to the Editor. *Minneapolis/St. Paul Star Tribune*, Feb. 4, p. 16A.

Blackstone, William. 1862. *Commentaries on the Laws of England*. Vol. 1, 3d ed. London: J. Murray.

Brophy, Julia, and Carol Smart, eds. 1985. *Women-in-Law: Explorations in Law, Family and Sexuality*. London and Boston: Routledge and Kegan Paul.

Carbone, June. 1994. Income Sharing: Redefining the Family in Terms of Community. 31 *Houston Law Rev.*, 359.

Casper, Lynne M., Sara S. McLanahan, and Irwin Garfinkel. 1994. The Gender-Poverty Gap: What We Can Learn from Other Countries. 59 *American Sociological Rev.*, 594.

Cohen, Richard. 1993. Judging Single Mothers. *Washington Post*, July 16, p. A19.

Collins, Patricia Hill. 1987. The Meaning of Motherhood in Black Culture and Black Mother/Daughter Relationships. 4 *Sage*, 2.

Coontz, Stephanie. 1993. Family Values: Dan Quayle Is Still Wrong. *Washington Post*, May 11, p. 5B.

Cott, Nancy F. 1977. *The Bonds of Womanhood: "Women's Spheres" in New England, 1780–1835*. New Haven, CT: Yale Univ. Press.

Davis, Joyce. n.d. *Enhanced Earning Capacity/Human Capital: The Reluctance to Call It Property*. Manuscript on file with author.

Dean, Jenny. 1995. The Modern Orphan. *St. Petersburg Times*, Jan. 29, p. 1A.

DeParle, Jason. 1993. Big Rise in Births Outside Wedlock. *New York Times*, July 14, p. A1.

Drakich, Janice. 1989. In Search of the Better Parent: The Social Construction of Ideologies of Fatherhood. 3 *Canadian Journal of Women and the Law*, 69.

Eisenberg, Melvin Aron. 1988. *The Nature of the Common Law*. Cambridge, MA: Harvard Univ. Press.

Estin, Ann Laquer. 1993. Maintenance, Alimony, and the Rehabilitation of Family Care. 71 *North Carolina Law Rev.*, 721.

Fineman, Martha Albertson. 1983. Implementing Equality: Ideology, Contradiction and Social Change: A Study of Rhetoric and Results in the Regulation of the Consequences of Divorce. 1983 *Wisconsin Law Rev.*, 789.

————. 1991a. *The Illusion of Equality: The Rhetoric and Reality of Divorce Reform.* Chicago: Univ. of Chicago Press.

————. 1991b. Images of Mothers in Poverty Discourses. 1991 *Duke Law Journal*, 274.

————. 1991c. Intimacy Outside of the Natural Family: The Limits of Privacy. 23 *Connecticut Law Rev.*, 955.

————. 1992a. Feminist Theory in Law: The Difference It Makes. 1 *Columbia Journal of Gender and Law*, 21.

————. 1992b. Legal Stories, Change and Incentives—Reinforcing the Law of the Father. 37 *NYU Law Rev.*, 227.

————. 1995. *The Neutered Mother, The Sexual Family and Other Twentieth-Century Tragedies.* New York and London: Routledge.

Fineman, Martha Albertson, and Anne Opie. 1987. The Uses of Social Science Data in Legal Policymaking: Custody Determinations at Divorce. 1987 *Wisconsin Law Rev.*, 107.

Fuchs, Victor R. 1986. Sex Differences in Economic Well-Being. 232 *Science*, 459–64.

Goldscheider, Frances K., and Linda J. Waite. 1991. *New Families, No Families?: The Transformation of the American Home.* Berkeley: Univ. of California Press.

Hearings. 1987. Family Welfare Reform Act: Hearings on H.R. 1720 before the Subcommittee on Public Assistance and Unemployment Compensation of the House Committee on Ways and Means, 100th Congress, 1st Session.

Jameson, Fredric. 1991. *Postmodernism.* Durham, NC: Duke Univ. Press.

Jones, Rachel L. 1994. Talk of Orphanages Collides with Grim Realities. *Pittsburgh Post-Gazette*, Dec. 25, p. A10.

Kolb, David. 1986. *The Critique of Pure Modernity: Hegel, Heidegger, and After.* Chicago: Univ. of Chicago Press.

Labor Conference. 1993. *Workers with Family Responsibilities.* International Labor Conference, 80th Session. Report III (Part 4B).

Labor Report. 1992. *Report of the International Labor Organization.* Sept. 6.

Lamott, Anne. 1993. When Going It Alone Turns Out to Be Not So Alone at All. In "Single But Mothers by Choice," *New York Times*, Aug. 5, pp. C1, C10.

Law, Sylvia A. 1984. Rethinking Sex and the Constitution. 132 *University of Pennsylvania Law Rev.*, 955.

Lawson, Carol. 1993. "Who Is My Daddy?" Can Be Answered in Different Ways. In "Single But Mothers by Choice," *New York Times*, Aug. 5, pp. C1, C10.

Lester, Gordon H. 1991. *Child Support and Alimony: 1989.* Bureau of the Census Consumer Income Series. U.S. Department of Commerce. Publication Number P60-173.

Lewin, Tamar. 1994. Poll of Teenagers: Battle of the Sexes on Roles in Family. *New York Times*, July 11, pp. A1, B7.

Lipton, Eric. 1995. Officials Ask: What Price More Spending Authority: GOP Reform of U.S. Programs Has Fans, Foes. *Washington Post*, Feb. 20, p. DO1.

Lugaila, Terry. 1992. *Households, Families and Children: A Thirty-Year Perspective.* Bureau of the Census Current Population Report. U.S. Department of Commerce. November. Publication Number P23-181.

Maccoby, Eleanor E., and Robert H. Mnookin. 1992. *Dividing the Child: Social and Legal Dilemmas of Custody.* Cambridge, MA: Harvard Univ. Press.

Mitchell, Alison. 1996. Banking on Family Issues, Clinton Seeks Parents' Votes. *New York Times,* June 25, p. A19.

Murray, Charles. 1993. The Coming White Underclass. *Wall Street Journal,* Oct. 29, p. A14.

Nelson, Hilde Lindemann and James Lindemann Nelson. 1992. Frail Parents, Robust Duties. 1992 *Utah Law Rev.,* 747.

News. 1995. Center of Social Welfare Policy and Law, Ways and Means Committee Backs Block Grants. Welfare Reform News. March: 1.

Norton, Arthur J., and Louisa F. Miller. 1992. *Marriage, Divorce, and Remarriage in the 1990's.* Bureau of the Census Current Population Report. U.S. Department of Commerce. October. Publication Number P23-180.

Okin, Susan Moller. 1989. *Justice, Gender and the Family.* New York: Basic Books.

Oldham, J. Thomas. 1992. Putting Asunder in the 1990s. 80 *California Law Rev.,* 1091. Review of *Divorce Reform at the Crossroads* (1990), ed. Stephen D. Sugarman and Herma Hill Kay.

Olsen, Frances E. 1983. The Family and the Market: A Study of Ideology and Legal Reform. 96 *Harvard Law Rev.,* 1497.

Pear, Robert. 1996a. Clinton Endorses the Most Radical of Welfare Trials. *New York Times,* May 18, p. A1.

———. 1996b. Clinton Waivers after Backing Welfare Plan. *New York Times,* June 14, p. A1.

Pollitt, Katha. 1993. Bothered and Bewildered. *New York Times,* July 22, p. A23.

Project. 1982. Law Firms and Lawyers with Children: An Empirical Analysis of Family/Work Conflict. 34 *Stanford Law Rev.,* 1263.

Report. 1993. *How We're Changing: Demographic State of the Nation: 1993.* Bureau of the Census Current Population Report. Special Studies Series. U.S. Department of Commerce. February. Publication Number P23-184.

Report. 1994. *How We're Changing: Child Care by Fathers Has Sharply Increased.* Bureau of the Census Current Population Report. U.S. Department of Commerce. January. Publication Number P23-187.

Rhode, Deborah L. 1991. The "No-Problem" Problem: Feminist Challenges and Cultural Change. 100 *Yale Law Journal,* 1731.

Rhodes, Erik. 1995. Letter: Sweden's Social Policies Put Us to Shame. *New York Times,* Feb. 10, p. A28.

Roberts, David J., and Mark J. Sullivan. 1992. The Federal Income Tax: Where Are the Family Values? 57 *Tax Notes* (Oct. 26), 547.

Roddy, Dennis B. 1995. The War on Welfare; Legislators Sing the Praises of Orphanages, Foster Homes, with Little Mention of the Cost. *Pittsburgh Post-Gazette,* Jan. 29, p. A1.

Sanger, Carol. 1989. Seasoned to the Use. 87 *Michigan Law Rev.,* 1338. Review of Scott Turow, *Presumed Innocent* (1987), and Sue Miller, *The Good Mother* (1986).

Sawhill, Isabel V., and Demetra S. Nightingale. 1995. Real Reform or a Shift of Responsibilities? *Washington Post,* Op-Ed, Feb. 20, p. A29.

Schwinn, Elizabeth. 1996. Gay Unions Bill Advances in House; Judiciary Panel OKs Limit on Marriages. *San Francisco Examiner,* June 13, p. A11.

Siegel, Reva. 1992. Reasoning from the Body: A Historical Perspective on Abortion Regulation and Questions of Equal Protection. 44 *Stanford Law Rev.*, 261.

———. 1994. Home as Work: The First Women's Rights Claims Concerning Wives' Household Labor, 1850–1880. 103 *Yale Law Journal*, 1073.

Simon, William H. 1983. Legality, Bureaucracy, and Class in the Welfare System. 92 *Yale Law Journal*, 1198.

Sorrentino, Constance. 1990. The Changing Family in International Perspective. 113 *Monthly Labor Rev.*, 41.

Stack, Carol B. 1974. *All Our Kin: Strategies for Survival in a Black Community.* New York: Harper and Row.

Stark, Barbara. 1991. Divorce Law, Feminism, and Psychoanalysis: In Dreams Begin Responsibilities. 38 *UCLA Law Rev.*, 1483.

Starnes, Cynthia. 1993. Applications of a Contemporary Partnership Model for Divorce. 8 *Brigham Young University Journal of Public Law*, 107.

Stevenson, Richard W. 1995. A Deficit Reins in Sweden's Welfare State. *New York Times*, Feb. 2, p. A1.

Swerdlow, Amy, Renata Bridenthal, Joan Kelly, and Phyllis Vine. 1989. *Families in Flux.* 2d ed. New York: Feminist Press.

Taub, Nadine, and Elizabeth M. Schneider. 1982. Perspectives on Women's Subordination and the Role of Law. In *The Politics of Law: A Progressive Critique*, ed. David Kairys. New York: Pantheon.

Taylor, Paul. 1991. Welfare Policy's "New Paternalism" Uses Benefits to Alter Recipients' Behavior. *Washington Post*, June 8, p. A3.

Thomas, Richard M. 1991. Milton and Mass Culture: Toward a Post-Modernist Theory of Tolerance. 62 *University of Colorado Law Rev.*, 525.

Treuthart, Mary Pat. 1991. Adopting a More Realistic Definition of "Family." 26 *Gonzaga Law Rev.*, 91.

Unger, Roberto M. 1976. *Law in Modern Society: Toward a Criticism of Social Theory.* New York: Free Press.

Van Reijen, Willem, and Dick Veerman. 1988. An Interview with Jean François Lyotard. 5 *Theory, Culture and Society*, 277.

Weston, Kath. 1991. *Families We Choose: Lesbians, Gays, Kinship.* New York: Columbia Univ. Press.

White, Keith. 1996. Committee OKs Bill That Would Deny Spouses Benefits in Same-Sex Marriages. *Gannett News Service*, May 30.

Whitehead, Barbara Defoe. 1993. Dan Quayle Was Right. *The Atlantic Monthly*, Apr., p. 47.

Whitmire, Richard. 1993. Number of Never-Married Moms Stretches across Income Lines. *Gannett-News Service*, July 13.

Wicke, Jennifer. 1989. Postmodern Identity and the Legal Subject. 62 *University of Colorado Law Rev.*, 455.

Yang, John E., and Ann Devroy. 1992. "Hollywood Doesn't Get It" Administration Struggles to Explain Attack on TV's Murphy Brown. *Washington Post*, May 21, p. A1.

STATUTES

ARIZ. REVIEW STATS. ANN. Section 25-125

CAL. WELFARE AND INST. CODE, ANN. Section 11477 (West 1995)

FLA. STAT. ANN. Section 741.04 (1993)

GA. STAT. ANN. Section 19-3-30 (1994)

GA. STAT. Section 49-4-115 (1993)

1994 HAW. SESS. LAWS, Act 217 Sections 1, 6, and 8

IDAHO CODE Section 32-412A(1994)

N. J. STAT. ANN. Sections 44.10, et seq., especially Section 10-3.5 (West 1993)

TENN. STAT. Section 71-5-133 (1993)

UTAH CODE Section 30-1-2(5)(1994)

WI. STAT. ANN. Sections 49.50(7)(a)4(am)(1993) and 7(f)

WI. STAT. ANN. Sections 49.19(1)(a)3, (1)(c)2

WI. STAT. Sections 49.50(7)(g) and (h) (1993)

WI. STAT. ANN. Section 767.45(6m)(1994)

26 USC 2056, 2523 (West Supp. 1993)

41 USC Section 602(a)(26)(B)(1988)

43 C.F.R. Sections 232.42 (a)(1)(i)–(iii)(1990)

CASES

Allen v. Eichler. No. 89A-Fe-4 (1990 WL 582230) (Del.Super.Ct.).

Baehr v. Lewin. 1993. 852 P.2d 44 (Haw.).

Franz v. United States. 1983. 712 F.2d 1428. (D.C. Cir.).

Lester v. Lester. 1949. 87 N.Y.S.2d 517 (N.Y. Family Court, 1949).

Loving v. Virginia. 1967. 388 U.S. 1.

Meyer v. Nebraska. 1923. 262 U.S. 390, 434 S.Ct. 625, 67 L.Ed. 1042.

Maynard v. Hill. 1888. 125 U.S. 190, 8 S.Ct. 723, 31 L.Ed. 654.

Reynolds v. United States. 1878. 98 U.S. 145.

Turner v. Safley. 1987. 482 U.S. 78.

Waller v. Carlton County Human Servs. Dep't. No 06-89-1116 (1989 WL 145393) (Minn. App. 1989).

FIGURING THE FUTURE: ISSUES OF TIME, POWER, AND AGENCY IN ETHNOGRAPHIC PROBLEMS OF SCALE

❖

CAROL J. GREENHOUSE

I. INTRODUCTION: ETHNOGRAPHY BETWEEN THE LOCAL AND GLOBAL

The globalization of culture, technologies, markets, politics, and law has engaged anthropologists and others at the borders of the social sciences and humanities for several years now. Given the intellectual and historical context of these engagements, it is not surprising that most of the attention has focused on the "global."[1] Now, a growing body of ethnographic literature confirms that globalization and modernization do not spell homogenization (Hannerz 1992: 232–39). Locales may be swept up in global politics, markets, and cultural practices, but they are not swept away by them. In this essay, I focus on the implications of this realization for ethnography. Over the past decade, some of contemporary sociocultural anthropology's most compelling questions have arisen from the interpretive, reflexive, and reformist challenges of rethinking the local from more global perspectives.

In this spirit, and in a variety of ways, several anthropologists recently have called for some ethnographic reassessment of the "local" in the context of globalization. For some, this means exploring the local as a potential site of retrenchment against the broadening reaches of globalization and its seeming imperatives with respect to political, economic, and cultural expression. For others, the local is the site of confrontations with modernity that make "the 'global' thinkable in the first place" (Comaroff and Comaroff 1993: xiii; see, e.g., Ferguson 1993; Lomnitz 1994; Malkki 1993; Nash 1994; Smith 1992: 497; Varenne 1993: 111). Beyond anthropology, too—particularly at the intersections of sociolegal studies, cultural studies, feminism, and political theory—theorists from the right, left, and center envision a range of communitarian responses to globalization, rethinking the local as scholars and citizens.[2]

The issue I take up here is a methodological one—in the conviction that ethnography's methodological conundrums arise directly from the conditions and crossed purposes in the world we study. Where is the *ethnographic* ground between, or under a distinction between, the local and the global? It is one thing to acknowledge the local importance of globalization as a matter of theory, but quite another to bring some precision to the question of *what* is global about the local. In what follows, I will suggest that it is our conventions of scale that are most challenged by the condition of the local in "the global ecumene" (Hannerz 1992: chap. 7). Rethinking the local in current world conditions invites us to rethink what scale means—and does not mean. In that regard, I will anticipate my argument with a paraphrase of Latour (1993): "we have never been local."

When I refer to ethnography's "conventions of scale," I mean the methodological habit that treats the local as a space contained or encompassed by larger spaces. It might seem obvious that this should be the case; however, as Benedict argued thirty years ago, scale is not the same as size. Scale has to do with the presence or absence, and relative efficacy, of overarching institutions, not geographic or demographic extent (Benedict 1966). Moore's (1973) concept of the semi-autonomous social field provided a means and a rationale for ethnographic investigation of such lateral and vertical linkages and their social effects on the ground. Notwithstanding these influential formulations, anthropologists still tend to practice their craft as if the "local" were a social unit, and as if there *is* a "local" *apart from* or *at another level* from the "global." These are not everyone's assumptions, but they are integral to the poetics (though not necessarily the politics) of the communitarian appeals I referred to above. It is assumptions and metaphors such as these that globalization specifically challenges us to rethink as ethnographic questions.

Importantly, social anthropology's conventions of scale are not its own, but derive from the bureaucratic organization of Anglo-American law and its geometries of scale. Villages, towns, cities, states, and countries—these are legal entities basic to the common law. The self-legitimating mythos of the common law anchors legality to custom and moral consensus, and moral consensus to place. In this mythos, "local" is always smaller scale, relatively speaking, since the myth stipulates that communities are capable of self-regulation on the basis of their moral consensus. From this perspective, the law's networks of jurisdictional boundaries and hierarchies are not merely an apparatus of bureaucratic administration, but, in theory, a moral geography.

That moral geography makes the "local" small scale, and correspondingly defines the need for law in the heterogeneity of the larger scale society.

While few anthropologists would defend these mythic meanings of law as current theory, the common law's moral geography reinforces and is reinforced by anthropological traditions that conflate society with governmentality and make culture the attribute of social wholes (Strathern 1988; Thomas 1994: 43; see also Herzfeld 1987). Strathern (1988, 1995) and others have made penetrating reflexive critiques of these assumptions, particularly as they bear on issues of comparison and relativism in ethnography.[3] I would only add that the distorting effect of incorporating state law into ethnographic practice in this way is a very specific one, in addition to the obvious ethnocentrism. This particular occidentalism (to borrow Carrier's [1995] term) not only distorts *other* people's knowledge practices and legalities, it also misrepresents the way state law operates in its *own* domains. I will explain what I mean, briefly here and at length in my ethnographic discussion.

State legal organization is not a fixed reality, except in its own theory. As cultural practice anywhere, jurisdictional boundaries involve a host of implicit and explicit claims about identity, place, time, agency, and, of course, social order. In practice, when the differentiation of jurisdictions (e.g., local, state, or federal in the United States) has social reality, that reality is contingent on the significance (and signification) of "difference" in specific conflict situations. In the United States, people understand their legal order in the same terms with which they understand the parties and stakes in the real-world struggles that they have experienced directly or indirectly.

But "difference" is not a classificatory template, either. To say that cultural practice builds *legal orders* out of more broadly circulating signs of difference also underscores a relationship between cultural questions of difference and contests involving the state. The conventional geometries of scale (whether in law or ethnography) encode taken-for-granted notions about the significance of difference and the power of law, in practical circumstances. If we are concerned nowadays to find the global in the local, I suggest that one way to begin is by taking a fresh look at the sorts of circumstances that instantiate these conventions of scale. That is what I propose to do here, with a pair of illustrative examples.

I begin with some comparative points of orientation before moving onto ethnographic ground.

2. TIME, SPACE, AND SOCIAL ORDER

Conventions of scale make the local conceptually and pragmatically counterposed to the global in at least two ways—one spatial, the other temporal (Appadurai 1990; Baker 1993; Harvey [1973] 1988; Sassen 1991: 323). As spatial referents, "local" and "global" imply *directions of transfer* of new combinations and commercializations of people, things, and expressivities.

As temporal referents, the terms imply a certain *present* vulnerability of people and practices in relation to the oncoming traffic of change. Given new worldwide "flows" (in this context, the term is Appadurai's) of capital and immigrants, globalization readily lends itself to analyses that stress its spatial dimensions—thus heightening the illusion that the local and the global inevitably involve differences of scale. But this is a view from above. Viewed from the ground, some of the spatial and temporal effects of globalization are already encoded in the meanings of difference (especially race and ethnicity) and social order.[4]

The time-space implications of the local arise not only in opposition to the global, but also in relation to the varied formulations of postmodernity that construe postmodernity as overwhelming former, more intimate worlds of interaction and meaning.[5] The opposition of a fragile but meaningful "local" and an uncontainable "global" is inscribed in much current theorizing about postmodernity (e.g., Giddens 1991; Harvey 1989). In particular, where "the global" suggests spatial complementarity with "the local," "postmodernity" implies a temporal complementarity between local and global socialities and sensibilities. Again, such constructions of time and space are built on a platform of assumptions about locale and the ways diversity affects the functioning of social orders.

Giddens (1991) links the acceleration of late modern social processes and institutions at the global level to the marked *de*acceleration of allowable affirmative expressions of difference (as if community did not break down, but grew to monstrous proportions). His core image is that of a "colonising of the future" (e.g., Giddens 1991: 111). The phrase refers to the politics of late modernity which, in his view, characteristically involves a pitched contest for control over the rhetorical meanings of the future. The very fact that the rhetorical power of the future is an object of open competition is defining the relationship between "self and society in the late modern age," as Giddens calls it in his subtitle. In the late modern age, he suggests, time and space are unhinged from each other, and community is lost under the crushing pressure of a global mass culture with complex effects on the subjective experience of self.

In that context, Giddens refers to the "end of nature," but it would probably be more accurate to envision the "end of sociology" in this passage: "The 'emptying' of time and space set in motion processes that established a single 'world' where none existed previously. . . . [L]ate modernity produces a situation in which humankind in some respects becomes a 'we', facing problems and opportunities where there are no 'others' " (Giddens 1991: 27). This otherless "we" is not a utopia, but rather one against which no rival first person plurals have breath enough to make their voices heard, no legitimate discourse for pressing distinctive demands in public political arenas.[6]

My general point at this juncture is to suggest how globalization and postmodernity can be enlisted in the provisioning of a "myth of community" to the extent that conventions of scale and temporality make diversity at the local level seem exceptional. The myth of community in this sense is a pastoral myth that has always existed in relation to its antithesis (the myth of the slum)—even before the world was "global" (Stallybrass and White 1986: 125–48; Williams 1985).[7] One implication of my ethnographic discussion is that postmodernity is not about the end-state of history or the loss of "community's" social forms, but about markets and currencies in which specific configurations of law, community, and difference are being valued anew.

3. PLURALISM AND PARADOX IN THE UNITED STATES

In the United States, the contemporary anthropological interest in retheorizing the local in relation to globalization evokes older civic republican notions regarding the significance of community within the nation.[8] From these republican roots, "community" has had a long and distinctive career in public discourses as a synonym for self-regulating social orders of almost any scale in the United States (Varenne 1977, 1986). Moreover, though one can refer to "community" and "nation" as if they were separate entities, for my purposes it is the opposition between the terms that conveys their sense. Related oppositions with broad currency and legibility would be between the community and the city or, indeed, between local and global. American usages of "community" are always potentially polysemic, as a call for both inclusion and exclusion, and as both hegemonic and counterhegemonic. Correspondingly, U.S. institutions are highly porous with respect to discourses of community.[9] It is this polysemy—more than any particular community (there *is* no "itself")—that accounts for much of "community's" importance in U.S. political debate as well as in the organization and practice of many civic institutions (Greenhouse 1992; Greenhouse, Yngvesson, and Engel 1994; Yngvesson 1993). Thus, "community" is crucial to the everyday practice of life in the United States, even though the field of potential, actual communal practices is regulated and granted only very selective acknowledgment under U.S. law (Minow 1990; for a related discussion of Thatcher-era Britain, see Strathern 1992: esp. 128–98).

The myth of community tends to associate communities presumptively with civility, solidarity, and the democratization of social space, but "community" is not just about human feeling; it is also about political and legal organization. Republican notions of pluralism make law central to community as the legitimate mediator of alterity in the public sphere; "community" fuses with the "local" to the extent that community values are taken to be the means and ends of face-to-face deliberative processes—the common law mythos enacted. Yet this ideal has an obverse, in that law's theoretical role is predicated on the assumption that certain forms of diversity are intrinsically disruptive to the civic order; in practice, race and class diversity are paradigmatically cast in this negative relation to civility. This is a self-fulfilling assumption, in that urban forms built on this principle exact highly uneven costs from populations conceived in these terms (Feldman 1991; Gilroy 1982; Harvey [1973] 1988; Perin 1977). The case studies below show with particular clarity how "community" is apt to be built over and even *against* the very diversity whose defense some communitarians might take as their goal.[10]

In the United States, the popular assumption that "community" is the historically authentic or original basis of local, regional, or national life adds to "community's" moral value (Greenhouse, Yngvesson, and Engel 1994).[11] There might be many reasons why the past confers moral value on people who successfully claim to be its conservators. In the ethnographic context of my own work, people who celebrated the past in this way are in effect imagining *the present* but with specific omissions. Their identification of their town's history as their own families' past provided a tacit though telling contrast with their perception of the present town as virtually overwhelmed by "newcomers"—their generic figuration of big government, multinational capital, racial minorities, among other unwelcome presences they deemed unsettling. A concept of community framed in terms such as these enlists "the other" into the deictics of the time and space of modern life by making "the other" a hypothetical nonpresence in the past, and a hypothetical nonabsence in the present.[12] Erasure and marginalization tidy up the categories of past and present, then and now; indeed, time and place *are* categorical (and moral) only by dint of such selective notice and reinscription.

Such spatial and temporal sleight of hand allows people to refer to "community" and "diversity" as if they were opposites even when (and this is key) local demographics are and always have been mixed. In effect, this makes the "local" a simultaneously double form: the authentic "community" (unmixed) and the modern "community" (diverse) are twins. These twins are held together (or lost to each other) in the variously inclusive and exclusive meanings of "community," "belonging," "not belonging," "order," and "disorder"— and similar terms, which are always provisional and contingent. In practice, race and class diversity, the icons of the imaginary slum, are implicit in the contemporary myth of community *as absences.*

These points are illustrated in the case studies. In different situations, race and class diversity are made out to be consistent with "community" only to the extent that the state intervenes actively through social control measures, either as police action and/or judicial intervention. In the case studies, the visualization of "community" within the nation—or, in other terms, of a civil society as separate from the state—appears to be the symbolic and institutional architecture within which the state's centrality in the social management of collective identities becomes the correlate of liberal democracy. An antinomy of "diversity" and "community" *necessitates* the conceptual separation of state and civil society—to leave space, as it were, for both the normal, negative meanings of diversity (as disorder) and their transformed, positive meanings as the canvas of the state's agency ("law and order"). In the United States, conventional usage makes active social control (through the civil or criminal process) the automatic corollary of "community." Such safeguards, including the safeguards of rights, might be necessary in fact; however, defending civil rights and law enforcement is not the same as conceding an a priori association of a heterogeneous population with a heightened need for state control of persons, relationships, and social space.

This returns us to the point that there is something to be gained in rethinking the conventions of scale that derive from the state's jurisdictional organization—as a way of rethinking the "local" as an element in ethnographic practice. Let us turn now to two illustrative case studies. Both are from the United States and involve highly public contexts. I have chosen them deliberately for this reason, as well as for their superficially extreme differences. Together they suggest how and why the "local" in the United States both confirms and confounds the myth of community and, with it, the conventions of scale that tend to render the distinction between the local and the global in spatial and temporal terms.

The first case is an examination of the press coverage of the events following the violence in Los Angeles in the spring of 1992.[13] I pick up this story at the point when the violence was over, and the newspapers became a forum for debating the question of how the violence should be understood.

Next, in the second case, I review a selection of major civil rights texts, judicial opinions, and legislation from recent times that struck down racial segregation and affirmed equal rights for all citizens. Thus, the first case involves massive disruption and violence; the second involves the legal poetics of equality.

Comparing the two cases, I argue that from a certain standpoint, the two cases' differences are superficial. In fact, they *both* associate diversity axiomatically with violence, and both associate diversity with a corollary need for active legal intervention. The interventions differ in form—police action in Los Angeles and judicial and legislative action in the civil rights context—but not in their operative premise that diversity is intrinsically uncivil without the intervention of the law. Thus, in the first case, commentators assess "Los Angeles" as the result of a latent potential for violence that becomes manifest; in the legal texts, such violence is claimed to be held back by the law's preemption of it. I return to the question of rethinking the local in the conclusions.

4. COMMUNITY AS THE LOCUS OF CIVIL UNREST

In an unplanned, though I will not say unwitting, anticipation of events in Los Angeles in April, 1992, Toni Morrison wrote that:

> Race has become metaphorical—a way of referring to and disguising forces, events, classes, and expressions of social decay and economic division far more

threatening to the body politic than biological "race" ever was. . . . It seems that [racism] has a utility far beyond economy, beyond the sequestering of classes from one another, and has assumed a metaphorical life so completely embedded in daily discourse that it is perhaps more necessary and more on display than ever before. (Morrison 1992: 63)

Within days of the violence in Los Angeles, public discussion of the violence itself seems to have settled into just the sort of metaphorizing and display that Morrison evokes here. The very term "Los Angeles" quickly became a synonym for a confusing and volatile amalgam of race, class, ethnicity, law, and lawlessness; it became a genre. One heard media reports and conversations about other places becoming or not becoming "*a* Los Angeles." Los Angeles had already captured the "diversity" genre with futuristic overtones (Rieff 1991); the new usage only switched the meanings of diversity from positive or neutral to negative, and of the future from dominating to vulnerable.

In what follows, I draw on the *New York Times* and the *Los Angeles Times* from roughly two weeks following the violence, as the stories of the violence themselves gave way to other related headlines in news and feature sections.[14] I do not pretend to know how to sum up these accounts; they are diffuse and immensely complex. I focus on just a few patterns that seem to bear directly on the ways in which the "local" and "community" can become a canvas on which to portray, juxtapose, and assess the related possibilities of alterity, order, and disorder.

Once "the riots" had passed as an event, they lingered in a confusing temporal discourse that called the actuality of Los Angeles as a community into question. By this I mean that the violence seems to have unsettled everyday uses of chronology in the reporting of events. Certainly, the starting point of "the riots" became increasingly ambiguous: Was it the court verdict? the beating of King? the growth and poverty of the city's minority populations? Drawing on American histories of race and class, commentators described Los Angeles or, sometimes, the nation itself, as exposed, as if the riots revealed something underlying, latent or festering, beyond and before the King verdict.

Nor did the media portray "the riots" as being conclusively over; for example, a Los Angeles poll revealed that most people expected renewed violence, although they felt safe at present. In this sense, the riots seemed to pool both the past and the future together into the present. One essayist for the *Los Angeles Times* wrote of the "long overdue" "death" of the city's image as "THE city of the 21st century" (May 13, 1992: T3).[15] To borrow Giddens's (1991: 17) language here, the commentaries contained vivid images of the past and future emptying their contents into the present. The future in particular was represented as empty; hopelessness was a recurring theme in the commentaries.

Once "the riots" were no longer discussed purely as an event, but as a sign of something latent in the city, nation, or world, Los Angeles similarly became the name of a place and a type of place. The coverage unsettled the ordinary meanings of place—as commentators portrayed Los Angeles as a situation (rather than a place). Again, drawing on larger issues of race and class, commentators questioned whether the causes and meanings of the violence were to be found in Los Angeles, specific L.A. neighborhoods, "cities" in general, or the nation as a whole. There was great variation along these lines.

On the one extreme, the *Los Angeles Times* eventually seemed to settle on an approach that reclaimed both time and place in very specific ways, looking to specific gangs, gang members, and their histories of violence in particular neighborhoods as the root cause of what were commonly referred to as the "King riots." On the other extreme, syndicated columnist Andrew Hacker looked generally to "white America" and its control of a zero-sum race-based competition for the future for the causes of the riots. In the same vein (although from a very different perspective), then Vice President Dan Quayle asserted a cause in what he implied were African Americans' abdications of self-control, referring to the "poverty of values" in the "inner city" (reprinted in the *New York Times*, May 20, 1992).[16]

Importantly, the media assessment of the violence as the breakdown of community gave commentators a variety of idioms with which to articulate connections between social diversity (ethnicity, race, and class) and violence. Race and class provided the figurative ground from which the actual time and place of the violence could be rhetorically transformed into some more generic object lesson for the nation as a whole.

What did they take that lesson to be? To some extent, it was that some groups are volatile; however, I believe the clearer lesson was supposed to be that groups become volatile when they mix, for example, as neighbors. That is, it is not so much *difference* that is disorderly (to borrow the phrase of Sarat and Berkowitz 1994), but *diversity.* Furthermore, by identifying the riots as racial and class conflicts, the riots lost their particularity and became signs of more global social relationships in terms of which diversity acquires its modern referents.

In committing themselves to a view of the violence as literally significant (i.e., a sign of something beyond itself), commentators repeatedly used the figures of race and class to move discussion away from times and places where violence occurred. I understand the oft-repeated references to the "reality" of Los Angeles (as opposed to the television or Hollywood images of the city) in this way, as gestures toward the unspecified significance of the event. Vice President Quayle's reference to the television character Murphy Brown (in the controversial speech cited above) also played on the contrast between reality and television.[17]

Quayle's speech also represented the culmination of another pattern in the media reporting and commentary, which heightened distinctions of gender in print and in photographs. Descriptions of violence focused on men of color; women were represented as alarmed or bereaved bystanders. African-American women in particular were presented in the role of commentators on the events. For example, the *New York Times* ran a news feature on

Representative Maxine Waters, complete with a boxed insert offering a capsule description of her career and hobbies, while the *Los Angeles Times* found women on the street to share their accounts of what they had seen. Quayle's focus on female and male roles only made these same distinctions more generic by presenting them in a highly moralistic sociological discourse.

The feature stories on African-American women's sensibilities seemed part of an effort to balance the news development at the same time, involving the arrest of four young black men in connection with the beating of a truck driver at a city intersection. The Los Angeles police introduced these men to a press conference from their photographs, commenting on each one's part in the "visuals" from the videotape of the attack on a truck driver in the early hours of the riots.[18] At the time, the arrest of four black gang members (made notorious by the videotape) seemed to parallel the arrest of the four white policemen (also made notorious by videotape).[19]

Palumbo-Liu (1994: 380) stresses the importance of news photographs of the violence in Los Angeles as images that focused the narratives of the event: "[T]he narratives set into motion by these text/images implicate . . . the mechanisms by which the dominant ideology comes to account for, pacify, and use to its own advantage a seemingly inexplicable event, while apparently standing outside and beyond violence." While Palumbo-Liu makes this point as prologue to a detailed examination of a single photograph, his point that the photographs generally served to "[solidify] structures of feeling around the issues of race, ethnicity, class, capital, and human justice" (1994: 380) appears to hold true for the broader demographics of the photographic images. Out of the several photographs accompanying the daily stories on developments, I found only two photographs that mixed genders.[20] Only a small number of photographs mixed races or ages. Of these, most involved multiracial groups of children engaged in some activity of good will. In general, the photographs seemed to reestablish—indeed, to excess—the separate "identities" that comprised Los Angeles's "diversity."

The resegregation of the urban visual field was only one sign of the evident strain with which the newspapers approached the problem of illustrating the racial dimensions that were implicit or explicit in the print stories. The definition of the racial dimension of the violence emerged somewhat differently in the two newspapers, as one photographic miscasting made clear. For the *New York Times,* the issue appeared to be one of black versus white, most vividly in a front-page news account with the headline, "Riots Shook Affluent Blacks Trying to Balance Two Worlds" (May 10, 1992). Although there were several photographs of affluent black men on the inside continuation of the story, the front page photograph accompanying the lead showed two young white women cleaning graffiti from a mailbox in Los Angeles. For the *Los Angeles Times,* the issue seemed to be diversity of a more complicated sort, one story referring directly to "Anglos," "Blacks," "Hispanics," and "Asians" (although without quotation marks in the original text) and repeatedly reviewing the ethnic geography of the violence.

Not surprisingly, the law figured frequently in the news and commentary, particularly in the *Los Angeles Times*'s reports of local arrests and prosecutions. I leave aside the presentation of the jury verdict itself, which was universally cited as the precipitating event (if not the cause of the violence). In the aftermath, coverage of the arrest of the gang members, prosecution of individuals arrested for looting, and the arraignment of Laurence Powell (one of the four police officers charged for beating Rodney King) for retrial provided occasions for reiterating descriptions of the legal process as arbitrary and vulnerable.

Additional law-related themes involved the literal and figurative displacement of law. In a literal appeal for displacement, Powell's attorneys asserted that their client could not hope for a fair trial anywhere in or near Los Angeles, or even in the state of California. Meanwhile, the *New York Times* reported a 50 percent increase in the sale of guns in California. In another more figurative vein, the violence was attributed to *people* who were out of place, as presidential candidate Pat Buchanan linked looters to patrol problems at the California-Mexico border. In addition, stories on the history of Los Angeles noted increases in U.S. and foreign-born immigrants to that city, as if these demographics stood in self-evident contradiction to a viable community life.

5. COMMUNITY AS THE LOCUS OF CIVIL RIGHTS

In contrast to the deeply troubled images of community with which commentators interpreted the implications of racial and class diversity in Los Angeles, the language of recent civil rights law offers very different images of the positive potential in human associations. The legal developments I consider here were aimed at protecting citizens from the negative meanings of difference. They did this by defining the public space—community—as the meeting ground of a diverse population. The law represents its own part in these efforts as constitutive of the new relationships on that public ground. Federal civil rights law is by definition national in its scope, as permitted and delimited by the Constitution. In practice, this means that the government's claims (through any of the three branches) to the constitutional power to make, adjudicate, or enforce civil rights law must always be explicit—and it is often contestable. For these reasons, the law's rhetoric is highly performative in that it addresses these contests, and in so doing, alters their terms.

My focus in the four examples below is on the figuration of "race" in the Supreme Court's and Congress's efforts to defend federal interventions in the cause of civil rights. In effect, this meant reinventing the "local" in relation to federal powers, primarily as the object of its powers. In all four examples, commerce features as a diffuse sign of the federal (translocal) dimensions of "American society" and the nation's social health. *Brown* refers to the future productivity of Negro citizens, the Acts of 1964 and 1965 refer more directly to interstate trade, and the Civil Rights Act of 1991 is focused directly on employment in various business contexts. (Later, I will return to the theme of commerce and its proximity to the the cultural construction of legal power.) My examples come from four legal texts: *Brown v. Board of Education of Topeka,* the Civil Rights Act of 1964, the Voting Rights Act of 1965, and the Civil Rights Act of 1991.

In *Brown v. Board* (347 U.S. 483), the U.S. Supreme Court referred to "races" and racial distinctions in a general way, although the sole named racial distinction is the one between "Negroes" and "whites." This was consistent with a prevalent view at that time of two "races" or "castes" (the term in this context is Lloyd Warner's [Warner 1962]). The *Brown* court referred repeatedly to the education of children, and the education of "white" children, but never to "Negro" children. The plaintiffs' argument had made African American children relevant to the American public at large as future adults, and, accordingly, the court made reference to the education of Negroes—linking the plaintiff's cause of action to a rhetorical strategy that invited readers to imagine present children's futures as adults.[21]

The Brown court wrote of a divided society, even a caste society—where people "are" either Negro or white. At the same time, the substance of the opinion evoked a collective society in which such distinctions are not determinative of well-being. The court envisions "[removing] all legal distinctions among 'all persons born or naturalized in the United States' " (347 U.S. 489). The collectivity—a United States without legal racial distinctions—is elaborated in a discussion of the central importance of education to the future of the United States. Though the opinion contains extensive references to the history of public education in the United States, and, in particular, the social advances of African Americans, the rhetorical purpose of these references is to anchor the constitutional issue firmly in the present:

> In approaching this problem, we cannot turn the clock back to 1868 when the Amendment was adopted, or even to 1896 when Plessy v. Ferguson was written. We must consider public education in the light of its full development and its present place in American life throughout the Nation. Only in this way can it be determined if segregation in public schools deprives these plaintiffs of the equal protection of the laws. (347 U.S. 492)

The opinion configures the past, present and future in its evocations of children, the benefits of education, and the fruits of citizenship.

The Supreme Court in *Brown* justified federal powers in relation to public school desegregation with a discussion of the vulnerability of children, the importance of education, and the prospect of a productive citizenry. Subsequent civil rights developments concretized and tightened the relationship between the justifications for federal power and the imperatives of economic growth. In the 1960s, as Congress labored over the Civil Rights Act of 1964, civil rights advocates defended the federal powers with an invocation of the commerce clause of the Constitution. Although the sociological reality behind federal intervention might have involved local grievances of citizens pleading for legal relief, its legal reality was made to be the constitutional mandate to protect interstate commerce. Only by constructing the local as both a site of discrimination *and* commerce were civil rights advocates, in practice, able to secure federal power, bring it (in effect) over state lines, and apply it at the local "level." As in Los Angeles, but even more directly, translocal commerce can be read (and, I believe, is read by the commentators) as a materialization of the state's power to protect and enforce civility at the local level. Indeed, in some respects, the conceptual separation between local and federal that is essential to modern civil rights law is a metaphorical spatialization based on the real geography of interstate commerce. For example, a segregated lunch counter may be the sign of the "local," and an integrated one the sign of the "federal," but they are the same place under different legal circumstances.

The Civil Rights Act of 1964 (Public Law 88-352; 78 Stat. 241) uses a somewhat different range of figures in guaranteeing new rights in the areas of voting, public accommodations, and other public facilities, education, and so forth. In Title I, the reference is neutral and collective in its singularity; it refers to "any individual"; later, the reference is to "any person." In Title II, difference is offered as the "ground" of "discrimination or segregation": these grounds are enumerated as "race, color, religion, or national origin." These terms are modified for the specific contexts of their relevance: for example, Title IV, on education, introduces "parents" and "minor children" as potential complainants; Title VII, on equal employment opportunity, defines a person as: "one or more individuals, labor unions, partnerships, associations, corporations, legal representatives, mutual companies, joint-stock companies, trusts, unincorporated organizations, trustees, trustees in bankruptcy, or receivers." In short, the Civil Rights Act of 1964 abandons the caste language of *Brown v. Board,* and maintains the reality of race in an entirely different way. In the act, there is no reference to "whites," "Negroes," or any population marked by race. Instead, race figures entirely as practice, that is, as intrinsic to patterns of social experience.

In other words, the act envisions people who are selectively aggrieved by enumerated acts of discrimination—literacy tests, denials of access to public places, and so on—but whose identities are not limited to those experiences. In the act, race is the name of an experience, not a "kind" of person. Furthermore, race figures as one among several grounds of illegal discrimination. Although there are timetables attached to specific legal procedures in the act, there is no explicit reference to the past, present, or future; its prohibitions of discriminations are immediate, categorical, functional, and timeless.

The Voting Rights Act of 1965 (Public Law 89-110; 79 Stat. 437) collectivizes "any citizen" and "persons" in its guarantee of protection against denials and abridgments of voting rights "on account of race or color." As in the Civil Rights Act of 1964, this act evokes racial groups only by implication, as a social construction, that is, as people who have experienced the illegal discriminations enumerated in the text. As above, the temporality of the Voting Rights Act is immediate and timeless; the focus is the immediate need for legislation. The future does not feature in the act, which is preoccupied with "now." Again, the act makes no direct or indirect reference to race as a classifier of populations; the relevance of race is entirely social, never biological, in the act.

The Civil Rights Act of 1991 (Public Law 102-166; 105 Stat. 1071) offers additional remedies and some modifications of existing protections in the workplace. Its constructions of protected classes and its enumerations of prohibited practices are, again, markedly different from the other texts we have been considering. There are virtually no references to "persons" or "individuals," as in the older texts. Here, we read of "entities," "parties," and "employers."

In Title II, called the "Glass Ceiling Act of 1991," the protected population is named as a category, as "women and minorities." (White men are not mentioned.) The naming of these categorical distinctions stands in marked contrast to the *social* constructions of victims of discrimination by experience in the acts of 1964 and 1965. Here, the figurative language is defined, at least in part, by the institutional contexts of conflict.

This is a text that suggests a more complicated world than the earlier ones. Rather than identifying the federal courts firmly with the contexts in which the law provides remedies, the act gestures toward other venues— negotiation, alternative dispute resolution, and foreign legal systems. The public space is more crowded in this act, not only with categories of people but also with sources of authority. In the earlier acts, the federal government rhetorically claimed to monopolize the constitutive power of civil rights; here, that monopoly has been to some extent redistributed to additional agencies and practices.

The temporality of this act is also somewhat different from the relative immediacy of the others. The act evokes a diffuse connection across past, present, and future, unlike the evocations of timeless justice in the earlier acts. The Glass Ceiling Act is particularly distinctive vis-à-vis the earlier acts in adopting a temporal language that draws continuities between the past and the present (as in "despite a dramatically growing presence in the workplace, women and minorities remain underrepresented in management"), where the other acts emphasized discontinuities. In terms of its evocations of the future, it refers to the "desirability" and "importance" of "eliminating artificial barriers" to opportunity, casting the purpose of this part of the act in terms of preferences rather than guarantees.

Taken together, the most significant parallel among these four legal documents is in their construction of community as the literal and figurative ground where the significance of difference is to be forged through law. Explicit references to the future are associated with direct references to racial and other protected categories (e.g., in *Brown* and the Civil Rights Act of 1991). Conversely, where the texts make law timeless, they also make identity faceless (as in the legislation from the 1960s). The acts of 1964 and 1965 name no subgroups of citizens, no forms of agency beyond the law, and no temporality (e.g., no timetables). I read these patterns of variation as indications of the extent to which the law contends simultaneously with the relationship of difference, constructions of the future, and the nature, functions, and limits of its own powers—as related issues. Elsewhere, I have argued that this is what social time is: a symbolic repertoire for bridging agencies, identities, and social forms within a single regime of accountability (Greenhouse 1996).

In these law texts, the law positions "itself" at a juncture where the "social order"—that is, dominant institutions of power and their practices—is both timeless and timely (in its own constructions). The temporal element is (literally) essential. The texts imply that time—as law—is the history of justice, and that justice will be the ultimate triumph of law over humans' "natures" (as racial, gendered, violent, weak, and so forth). More explicitly, the texts create the law's power at precisely the place where differences are volatile: taking over, as it were, from the forces of "nature" that made race (see Wade 1993) and made race matter.[22] Law, in other words, constructs its own power as an agency capable of suspending the negative consequences of "diversity," claiming the power to transform diversity into civility.[23]

6. THE TWO CASES COMPARED

In some ways, the newspaper accounts of life in Los Angeles and the civil rights law texts reveal different images of law, society, and the future — indeed, textual apples and oranges. In other ways, though, they are similar in their construction of the public space as a site of engagement among "groups," and the law as having a central role in mediating those engagements. These are crucial parallels between the current commentaries on Los Angeles and the legal texts. In Los Angeles, the engagement of "groups" is violent, and the centrality of "law" means local police. The civil rights texts feature the federal judiciary as the agent of an orderly "diversity." Either way, the transformation of diversity into civility is the state's business, offering protection from the consequences of difference through law (civil rights) or through law enforcement (policing).

There is also an economic side to the state's efficacy in social control. In 1963, some rights advocates in Congress and the executive branch (including Attorney General Robert F. Kennedy) invoked the Constitution's commerce clause (the federal obligation to protect interstate commerce) as the constitutional basis for legislation guaranteeing the right to vote and access to public accommodations (the Civil Rights Act of 1964) (for excerpts from the Senate hearings, and commentary, see Gunther 1985: 159–91, esp. 159–62). The fact of federal civil rights legislation was controversial, since it applied federal powers to what many people saw as state and local matters. The bill's advocates required a constitutional basis for applying federal power over state lines, and argued among themselves as to whether the stronger basis was in the 14th amendment (guaranteeing due process) or the commerce clause.

In his testimony before the Senate Committee on Commerce, Kennedy (and subsequently, Assistant Attorney General Burke Marshall) worried aloud that the Fourteenth Amendment, though more directly addressed to issues of discrimination, might not stand a court test if states challenged it as a basis for the federal legislative powers he and other rights advocates sought:

> [We] base this on the commerce clause which I think makes it clearly constitutional. In my personal judgment, basing it on the 14th amendment would also be constitutional. [I] think that there is argument about the 14th amendment basis—going back to the 1883 Supreme Court decision . . . , and the fact that this is not State action—that therefore Congress would not have the right under the 14th amendment to pass any legislation dealing with it. [Senator], I think that there is an injustice that needs to be remedied. We have to find the tools with which to remedy that injustice. [There] cannot be any legitimate question about the commerce clause. That is clearly constitutional. We need to obtain a remedy. The commerce clause will obtain a remedy and there won't be a problem about the [constitutionality]. (quoted in Gunther 1985: 159; brackets in Gunther text)

The debate that ensued focused on the definition of interstate commerce—did it mean only national chains, or also local establishments that used goods that had moved across state lines? was there a minimum percentage of a business's trade that made it interstate commerce? was proximity to airports a factor? Some senators took the position that protection from discrimination on the basis of race was a moral issue (covered by the Fourteenth Amendment), not an economic issue. Kennedy and Marshall emphasized the negative impact of racial discrimination on local business and the viability of community life, especially in the South, by (in Marshall's words) discrimination's "artificially restrict[ing] the market available for interstate goods and services" (quoted in Gunther 1985: 162).

Kennedy and Marshall eventually prevailed, drawing the outlines of federal civil rights powers on the canvas of the nation's expanding economy. Critics at the time (including advocates of the legislation) argued that the commerce clause basis created unlimited federal powers to regulate at the local level (cf. Gunther 1985: 162). Today, civil rights debates continue to be waged in terms of economic competitiveness, though less optimistically, as rights are also assessed as potential business costs (as recent federal electoral politics has made abundantly clear). It is impossible to understand the contemporary crosscurrents of rights debates—and "diversity" itself—without understanding the very immediate relevance the shifting world economic order has in relation to them. This point had a particular salience in Los Angeles's "recovery."

Los Angeles's period of "recovery" was cast by commentators as a medical transition from distress to health, and this occasioned the explicit juxtaposition (in print) of positive and negative images of community. "Recovery" is thus interesting ethnographically since commentary isolated particular signs of community and traced their circulation around and across the former sites of violence.

Signs of the more positive meanings of community were taken (by the commentators) to be confirmed in the rapid commitment of public funds for relief and rebuilding, which won early bipartisan support. The need for literal rebuilding lent force to particular figurative images of reconstruction; rebuilding quickly took on vivid metaphorical meanings, as moral reconstruction. This was not the only aspect of the city's recovery that claimed attention, but, significantly, the commentary on investment made recovery contingent on the state's (regained) control of urban space.

In such figurative contexts, private space ("values," for example) was also turned inside out, commoditized and claimed as capital for use in the public domain. This particular inversion provided recurring imagery for politicians on both the left and the right. On the left, for example, Tom Hayden (*Los Angeles Times,* May 13, 1992) envisioned the possibilities of a moral reengagement of white businessmen with Los Angeles's problems, although he was skeptical of the Ueberroth commission (which was appointed to lead planning for the city's recovery). On the right, Vice President Quayle's equation of poverty with a poverty of values is a more generic inversion of the ordinary meanings of public and private.

Literally and figuratively, then, in Los Angeles and in the civil rights law (as we saw in the previous section) commerce emerges as an ongoing materialization of the state's agency that—more episodically—takes up its vigil over the public space through law enforcement. I want to stress that this is not a matter of foreground and background, or action and context, or simple means and ends. In the case studies discussed here, the discursive practice of "community" itself is predicated on the necessity and possibility of state interventions of various kinds, and *simultaneously* channels commerce and all that goes with it.

In terms of the case studies' respective visions of the future, they imply equally (though with different degrees of optimism) that the colonization of the future will be financed with capital borrowed from the meanings of difference. Some evidence within the case studies makes it seem unlikely that those loans of meanings will ever be repaid, given their association of difference with depletions of public resources. For example—and most vividly — in his analysis of what he called "lawless social anarchy," Quayle's rhetorical effort appeared to be aimed at excluding racism from public discussion of the causes of urban violence, on the grounds that the United States "faced racism squarely" in the 1960s. In his speech, the rhetorical proximity of the future heightened the negative and disruptive meanings of difference and, correspondingly, the demand for an otherless political discourse. Other examples of media coverage after the riots also conveyed the implication that difference should have no place in the civic arenas of the future.

To summarize these U.S. case studies, civil rights law and public under-standings of violence construct "community" around the central axis of the state's role in the management of diversity in physical space—literally and figuratively, the common ground. On that ground, the ordinary meanings of diversity are negative, inherently uncivil. To the extent that a community is *disorderly,* racial and class diversity normalize conditions of violence and call forth the law's coercive powers of physical social control. To the extent that a community is *orderly,* racial and class diversity confirm the controlling power of federal law. In both circumstances, the symbolic relationship of community and alterity is constructed the same way, in that both rights claims and urban violence invoke the state as mediator among groups whose lives as neighbors are implied as being ordinarily inimical to each other.

Thus, the image of civility is constructed around the *suspension* of the negative outcomes ordinarily associated (in this same worldview) with di-versity. The police are the icons (even when they are not the agents) of social order when diversity's ordinary meanings prevail. Similarly, federal civil rights law is the icon of social order when those meanings can be seen to be actively suspended, as citizens merit (and this term is crucial) protection from the negative consequences of their "identities." The cases also suggest how and where "local" and "global" intersect in practice, in various connections between "law and order," "the economy," and the meanings of difference.

7. CONCLUSIONS

There are undoubtedly distinctively American dimensions to my argument—not only in the events and ethnographic contours reported here, but also in the particular history of U.S. immigration, including internal immigrations. The constitutional structure of government in the United States is discursively (and distinctively) welded to local semantics of identity and community. There is a reflexive dimension to the argument as well, in that U.S. ethnography's attention to racial and ethnic communities since the 1960s is especially resonant with the liberal pluralist legal discourse that peaked during the civil rights era of the 1950s and 1960s. This discourse still tends to give American monographs about the United States their prevailing tone of optimism and, increasingly (judging from prefaces and epilogues), their irony and paradox.

At the same time, given the state of the world, this cannot be just a local discussion. The U.S. cases might be distinctive, but they are not unique. For example, Gilroy (1982) explores at length the connection between economic health and "law and order" as a growing political issue in Great Britain during the 1970s. Hockenos (1993) reviews related recent developments in Eastern Europe in his survey of the rise of the racist right. In another vein, Comaroff and Comaroff (1992: 7) identify the present climate of paradox in anthropology as arising in part from our discipline's status as a "liberalizing" discourse vis-à-vis other disciplines:

> [T]he current status of ethnography in the human sciences is something of a paradox. On the one hand, its authority has been, and is being, seriously challenged from both within anthropology and outside; on the other, it is being widely appropriated as a liberalizing method in fields other than our own— among them, cultural and legal studies, sociology, social history, and political science. . . . Does [ethnography's] relativism bequeath it an enduring sense of its own limitation, its own irony?

To this, their answer seems to be yes. Indeed, in the United States, it *must* be yes, given that ethnography's relativizing concerns vis-à-vis racial and ethnic minorities are so directly tied historically and discursively to liberal pluralism, itself now on the wane, judging from media coverage of public debate.

The main ethnographic advantage of rethinking the local would be the possibility of reclaiming some of the questions that the conventions of scale ordinarily preclude: in this essay, such questions are about the commoditization of race and the materialization of law in particular social forms.[24] My main ethnographic argument here has been that in both legal theory and local practice the law's relationship to commerce is not just an aspect of "race relations," but is integral to the meaning of "race" itself. Thinking of "local" and "global" as inevitably involving differences of scale only obscures the way the meanings of "race" in fact collapse the distinctions of scale that governments maintain as if they were articulations of natural social formations.

Specifically, as the case studies show, "race" accounts for the telescopings of scale that complicate anthropological discussions of the local in the global and, *in the very same terms,* legal discussions of the local in relation to state and federal jurisdictions. In Los Angeles, for example, the meanings of race and class "diversity" were such that the very presence of African Americans and other non-"Anglos" made the city's situation generic. To be sure, poverty and racism are not just of local manufacture, but this observation only underscores the extent to which the idea of community requires constant maintenance and manipulation. This is not just a semiotic point, but also a highly pragmatic one.

In the civil rights texts, too, the reformulation of the "local" was explicit in that federal law enforcement agents "stepped in" to protect citizens' rights where the agents of municipal and state law had failed or refused to do so. In order to intervene within the terms of the Constitution's protections of states' rights, federal agents had to somehow redefine the "local" as "national." The means was found in the commerce clause, as noted above, and in the figuration of African Americans (and other minorities) as *national* citizens. This cultural reallocation of agency is part of the dynamic of the "twinning" effect raised earlier in the discussion of the mythical distinction between community's authentic and modern forms. Perhaps this rhetorical effect can now can be seen more clearly as a product of the ways nonwhite individuals are denied substantial agency of their own at the local "level," and recast as permanent "outsiders." One element of this social distancing seems to be a semiotics that makes "minorities" into icons of the state's agency; the state's agency is by (semiotic) definition marshaled elsewhere and deployed "locally." The colloquialism involves the government "stepping in." But again, this is not just a semiotic point.

More generally, the flexible applicability of the term "community" should not be taken for granted as mere metaphor. Rather, the polysemy of "community" is sometimes deliberately reworked as legal and political strategies by architects and adversaries of change. Again, separating the "local" and the "global" into "levels" or as differences of scale tends to conceal these strategic maneuvers as well as their practical reference to race. For all of these reasons, I take the conventions of scale that divide the local and the global as a trompe l'oeil—a visual trick—of the spatial metaphors associated with state social control, translocal commerce, and public moral economies of private individuals' bodies and virtue.[25]

In the case studies, the state's centrality in the public management of "diversity," the materialization of that agency in investment and commerce, and the commoditization of identity emerge as inextricably linked ideas and social processes. Again, in practice, they do not define actual persons individually or even collectively, and they do not necessarily preclude alternative formulations of community. Still, they are powerful ideas in that, in practice, they tend to weld issues of identity and solidarity to present probabilities. This brings us back to the methodological question with which the essay began: Where is the ethnographic ground under the distinction between the local and the global?

To some extent, rethinking the local under conditions of globalization means rethinking what it has always been, at least in modern times. In the United States, "local" and "global" trace older lines on the map: the lines of community and nation, or local and federal—except when these maps are drawn from below. From below, one can see more clearly where these lines have been crossed, crossed out, erased, and unevenly redrawn many times over, by many different hands, even within this generation.

An ethnographic distinction between global and local can perhaps be most usefully read as a shorthand acknowledgment of the multiple currencies and markets now simultaneously in play within on-the-ground struggles over the value of difference, including the question of whether that value is material or not. A reference to local and global also acknowledges the countervailing pressures that keep these currencies and markets in play, in spite of their potentially rending incommensurabilities. As we have seen in the case studies, these pressures do not necessarily align along an axis defined by a relationship *between* a dominant modernist group and a more traditional "other," but by relationships *among* multiple groups—in the United States, relationships complicated by changes in the economy, demography, and democracy. As opportunities and rights contract, and the "ethnic census" expands, the accelerating circulation of signs of difference highlights the extent to which they are signs of contested social hierarchy rather than of settled human collectivities. In other words, over the long term, the significance of social categories is more stable than their association with actual people; people can change their status, but the status remains for other "tenants." This should not be surprising, given that signs of difference are signs of the law's power and its domains of control, at least as much as they are also signs of any one group's social reality. To refer to signs in this way takes us directly back to considering how the pragmatics of people's life chances are categorically fused to the materiality of state power, for better and for worse.

The case studies suggest that from an ethnographic standpoint, the play of forces "between" the local and the global are not first questions of scale, but questions of power and communication. I have suggested that one way of keeping the local and the global within the same ethnographic frame is to keep in view the semiotic and material connections between "diversity," "community," and law—as well as the projections and substitutions of agency that these entail. This is not to dismiss questions of structure and scale as unimportant, but to suggest that from an ethnographic point of view, their context is within actual contests over human possibility, not the other way around.

NOTES

The original version of this paper was prepared for a session on law and temporality at the annual meeting of the Law and Society Association in 1992. I am grateful to Phil Parnell for his invitation to participate in that session and for his comments. In recasting the paper for the Law and Society Association's Summer Institute, I benefited from critical readings by Bryant Garth, Davydd Greenwood, Stephanie Kane, Felice Levine, Elizabeth Lucas, Takyiwaa Manuh, Austin Sarat, Beverly Stoeltje, Paula Wagoner, Susan Williams, and Dvora Yanow, as well as anonymous reviewers.

1. For example, by Appadurai 1990; Hannerz 1992; and Robertson 1992.

2. For overviews and examples, see Benhabib and Cornell 1987; Frazer and Lacey 1993; Ginsburg and Tsing 1990; Nicholson 1990; Rhode 1989; Young 1990. The case studies in this essay point to some of the real-world processes and struggles that instantiate these elisions.

3. Strathern (1995) also discusses anthropological conventions of scale as a comparative ethnographic question. Somewhat earlier, Simon Roberts's (1978) reflexive critique of legal anthropology specifically focused on the embeddedness of officialized concepts of Western state law in ethnographic practice.

4. While the history of globalization in the 1980s may have involved technological and personal reconfigurations of time, space, and scale, the primary ethnographic dimensions of globalization are in the social significance of cultural difference—for reasons explained in the text.

5. I take "discourse" to refer to language as well as the activities in which language has (or might have) meaning. For a useful untangling of postmodernisms, see Hebdige 1988: 181–207.

6. In modern times, the myth of community has been no less punishing of the categorical "others" whose presence seems always (though not always in the same way) implied as the symbolic rupture (and literal disruption) of community. Color and class have always been implicit in the corollary that the myth of community draws between consensus and belonging. Indeed, invocations of community provide avenues by which specific propositions about the positive or negative meanings of race and class can be imported into the analysis of social situations, and materialized in social space, without seeming to be (Harvey 1988 [1973]; Lawrence 1982a, 1982b). This is not to say that it cannot be inclusive, but the invocation of community does not settle this question by itself.

7. Jameson (1991: ix), e.g., opens his book on postmodernism with the claim that "It is safest to grasp the concept of the postmodern as an attempt to think the present historically in an age that has forgotten how to think historically in the first place." My own view is that the neglect (if that is what it is) of history is only the corollary of an even more entrenched refusal to think ethnographically, that is, to take difference seriously and affirmatively. Balibar (1991) links "neoracism"—the view that diversity exceeds the limits of the state—to postmodernity. For fuller discussion of postmodernity as legitimacy crisis, see Bauman 1987, 1992.

8. The discussion in this section draws on Greenhouse 1986a, 1986b, 1989, 1992, 1994 and Greenhouse, Yngvesson, and Engel 1994.

9. In my earlier ethnographic work in "Hopewell," Georgia, I found that ordinary people, a variety of professionals (in the church and the courts, e.g.), social anthropologists, and other academics easily shared a vocabulary of sociological description. This confounded the problem of ethnographic description—and made the reflexive questions associated with "community" and related terms (e.g., "the individual," "society," "insiders/outsiders") quite pressing. For examples, discussion, and analysis, see Greenhouse 1994 and Greenhouse, Yngvesson, and Engel 1994.

10. As others have also noted (most recently, Wolf 1994: 2), anthropological and public idioms of race, ethnicity, and culture borrow readily from each other's lexicons and funds of meaning; they also suffer from the same embarrassing deficits when it comes to "attempting to account for the post-melting pot period of American history" (de la Campa 1994: 313).

11. I do not mean to claim this as a universal American view, by any means, but still, the association of "community" with moral ends rather than pragmatic ones is standard usage, if not belief (see Varenne 1986).

12. Local situations might involve different processes of marginalization, erasure, or highlighting, but the widespread popular images of the modern diasporas as quintessentially urban and of native Americans as quintessentially premodern offer illustrations of this point.

13. For readers who might not have been following American news at the time, the violence followed the acquittal of four white police officers accused of excessive force in apprehending an African-American man named Rodney King. The trial galvanized national attention. Although the violence was quickly labeled the "King riots," this was a misnomer for the immediate context, which was the verdict in the policemen's trial. Indeed, the question of what to call the violence—riots? uprising? civil unrest?—remains analytically and politically highly charged, as the editor's introduction to a collection of articles on the "L.A. disturbances" notes (in *Contention*, Spring 1994). For source material and cultural analyses of the violence in Los Angeles, in addition to the *Contention* essays (Jackson, Johnson, and Farrell 1994; Sonenshein 1994; and Miles 1994), see contributions to Gooding-Williams 1993.

14. *Los Angeles Times*, May 10–17, 1992; *New York Times*, May 10–21, 1992.

15. Stallybrass and White (1986), too, write of the proximity of desire and revulsion in the urban landscape of nineteenth-century London. For discussion of class, caste, and the polarities of self-control and conflict, see Greenhouse 1992; Greenhouse, Yngvesson, and Engel 1994; and Yngvesson 1993.

16. Quayle's image linking poverty to poverty of values has older parallels in the classic anthropological literature on American concepts of race and class; see Greenhouse 1992 for a review of this literature for its implications about the relationship between diversity and violence.

17. Murphy Brown is the protagonist in a television sitcom of the same name. Shortly before "Los Angeles," the series plotline had unwed Brown give birth to a son. The vice-president alluded to the episode, in aid of his argument that Hollywood glorifications of single parenting were in part to blame for the condition of the inner city.

18. Denny was a truck driver who was hauled from the cab of his truck and nearly beaten to death by four men on the street. He was rescued by civilian witnesses to the attack. Some witnesses said that Denny provoked the beating by shouting racist insults at the crowd; others said the beating was unprovoked. The videotapes of the beating from a news heliocopter were replayed very frequently during and after the riots.

19. In his essay on the so-called King trial (i.e., the trial of the police officers who apprehended King) and Desert Storm, Feldman (1994: 411) refers to the violence inflicted on King and the repetition and refinement of that violence through replays of the videotape as the "territorialization of King's body." The phrase refers to Feldman's analysis of the trial as the state's assertion of the meaning of the event—both to King and to history—via its claims of monopoly over King's sensory experience.

20. One of these showed Representative Waters with a male Congressional colleague, and another showed the family of the one person killed by the National Guard grieving at his coffin. The man was an unregistered immigrant, a refugee from El Salvador, who—evidently fearing deportation if he were to be apprehended without proper papers—attempted to escape in his vehicle from a Guard roadblock. Guardsmen interpreted his sudden change of direction as an attempt to run them down and shot him.

21. This implicit portrayal of children as future adults was the inverse of the L.A. photographs, which invited readers to think of today's adult "others" as former children by photographing children of mixed races/ethnicities together—of course, the children were also a palpable sign of the hope for a better future.

22. In the United States, public discourse makes all "differences" generic within the race paradigm; see Greenhouse 1992.

23. I borrow this term from Harding's (1984) analysis of the civil rights movement in the American South as involving two phases, white civility and white supremacy. Her thesis is that the civil rights movement involved a renegotiation of the terms of white hegemony.

24. Such meanings of race are not necessarily oppressive in material terms—though they might be. And, in practice, as the second case study shows, civil rights guarantees might depend on them. Thus, when I suggest that *for these very reasons* the structural opposition of local/global (or community/nation) fails as an ethnographic concept, it is not to imply that it fails as a concept for activists, who do indeed have to organize their struggles in relation to established jurisdictional "maps." The ambiguous definitions of conflict and the ambiguities of outcomes in the real struggles within the "communities" in these case studies are precisely what complicate anthropological discussions of ethnographic terms and vantage points. To the extent that ethnography might yield some counterdiscourse to the racial and cultural essentializings at the heart of contemporary (and dominant) public discourses of "community" and "nation" (and, most recently, "American civilization"),

this project will be aided by maintaining within the ethnographic frame the question of how and where the self-legitimations of particular state agencies rest on manipulations of the concept of culture and cultural diversity.

25. The temporal metaphors (as discussed above) are also implicated here, but in this context, primarily in the service of the metaphorical spatializations of social distance and control. The "visual trick" I refer to is not just a matter of metaphors; the topics listed here correspond easily to different university departments and agencies in the public sector.

BIBLIOGRAPHY

Appadurai, Arjun. 1990. Disjuncture and Difference in the Global Cultural Economy. 2 *Public Culture*, 1.

Baker, Houston. 1993. *Black Studies, Rap, and the Academy*. Chicago: Univ. of Chicago Press.

Balibar, Etienne. 1991. Is There a "Neo-racism"? In *Race, Nation, Class: Ambiguous Identities*, ed. E. Balibar and I. Wallerstein, 17–28. London: Verso.

Bauman, Zygmunt. 1987. *Legislators and Interpreters: On Modernity, Post-Modernity and Intellectuals*. Cambridge: Polity Press.

———. 1992. *Intimations of Postmodernity*. London: Routledge.

Benedict, Burton. 1966. Sociological Characteristics of Small Territories and Their Implications for Economic Development. In *The Social Anthropology of Complex Societies*, ASA Monographs 4, ed. Michael Banton, 23–35. London: Tavistock.

Benhabib, Seyla, and Drucilla Cornell, eds. 1987. *Feminism as Critique: Essays on the Politics of Gender in Late-Capitalist Societies*. Cambridge: Polity Press.

Carrier, James G. 1995. *Occidentalism: Images of the West*. Oxford: Oxford Univ. Press.

Centre for Contemporary Cultural Studies. 1982. *The Empire Strikes Back: Race and Racism in 70s Britain*. London: Hutchinson.

Chock, Phyllis P. 1987. The Irony of Stereotypes: Toward an Anthropology of Ethnicity. 2 *Cultural Anthropology*, 347–68.

Chock, Phyllis P. 1991. "Illegal Aliens" and "Opportunity" Myth-making in Congressional Testimony. 18 *American Ethnologist*, 279–94.

Comaroff, Jean. 1985. *Body of Power, Spirit of Resistance: The Culture and History of a South African People*. Chicago: Univ. of Chicago Press.

Comaroff, Jean, and John L. Comaroff. 1993. *Modernity and Its Malcontents*. Chicago: Univ. of Chicago Press.

Comaroff, John L., and Jean Comaroff. 1992. *Ethnography and the Historical Imagination*. Boulder, CO: Westview.

de la Campa, Ramón. 1994. The Latino Diaspora in the United States: Sojourns from a Cuban Past. 6 *Public Culture*, 293–317.

Feldman, Allen. 1991. *Formations of Violence*. Chicago: Univ. of Chicago Press.

———. 1994. On Cultural Anesthesia: From Desert Storm to Rodney King. 21 *American Ethnologist*, 418.

Ferguson, James. 1993. De-moralizing Economies: African Socialism, Scientific Capitalism and the Moral Politics of "Structural Adjustment." In *Moralizing States and the*

Ethnography of the Present, ed. S. F. Moore, 78–92. Washington, DC: American Anthropological Association.

Frazer, Elizabeth, and Nicola Lacey. 1993. *The Politics of Community: A Feminist Critique of the Liberal-Communitarian Debate*. New York: Harvester/Wheatsheaf.

Giddens, Anthony. 1991. *Modernity and Self-Identity: Self and Society in the Late Modern Age*. Stanford, CA: Stanford Univ. Press.

Gilroy, Paul. 1982. Police and Thieves. In *The Empire Strikes Back*, Centre for Contemporary Cultural Studies, 143–82. London: Hutchinson.

Ginsburg, Faye. 1989. *Contested Lives: The Abortion Debate in an American Community*. Berkeley: Univ. of California Press.

Ginsburg, Faye, and Anna Lowenhaupt Tsing, eds. 1990. *Uncertain Terms: Negotiating Gender in American Culture*. Boston: Beacon.

Gooding-Williams, Robert, ed. 1993. *Reading Rodney King/Reading Urban Uprising*. New York: Routledge.

Greenhouse, Carol J. 1986a. *Praying for Justice: Faith, Order and Community in an American Town*. Ithaca, NY: Cornell Univ. Press.

———. 1986b. History, Faith and Avoidance. In *Symbolizing America*, ed. Hervé Varenne. Lincoln: Univ. of Nebraska Press.

———. 1989. Interpreting American Litigiousness. In *History and Power in the Study of Law*, ed. June Starr and Jane Collier. Ithaca, NY: Cornell Univ. Press.

———. 1992. Signs of Quality: Individualism and Hierarchy in American Culture. 19 *American Ethnologist*, 233–54.

———. 1994. Revisiting Hopewell: A Reply to Neal Milner. 17 *Law and Social Inquiry*, 335.

———. 1996. *A Moment's Notice: Time Politics across Cultures*. Ithaca, NY: Cornell Univ. Press.

Greenhouse, Carol, Barbara Yngvesson, and David Engel. 1994. *Law and Community in Three American Towns*. Ithaca, NY: Cornell Univ. Press.

Gunther, Gerald. 1985. *Constitutional Law*. 11th ed. Mineola, NY: Foundation.

Hale, Charles R. 1994. Between Che Guevara and the Pachamama: Mestizos, Indians and Identity Politics in the Anti-Quincentenary Campaign. 14 *Critique of Anthropology*, 9–39.

Hannerz, Ulf. 1992. *Cultural Complexity: Studies in the Social Organization of Meaning*. New York: Columbia Univ. Press.

Harding, Susan. 1984. Reconstructing Order through Action: Jim Crow and the Southern Civil Rights Movement. In *Statemaking and Social Movements: Essays in History and Theory*, ed. Charles Bright and Susan Harding, 378–402. Ann Arbor: Univ. of Michigan Press.

Harvey, David. 1988 [1973]. *Social Justice and the City*. Oxford: Blackwell.

———. 1989. *The Condition of Postmodernity*. Oxford: Blackwell.

Hebdige, Dick. 1988. *Hiding in the Light*. London: Routledge.

Herzfeld, Michael. 1987. *Anthropology through the Looking-Glass: Critical Ethnography in the Margins of Europe*, Cambridge: Cambridge Univ. Press.

Hockenos, Paul. 1993. *Free to Hate*. New York: Routledge.

Huntington, Samuel P. 1993. The Clash of Civilizations? 72 *Foreign Affairs*, 22–49.

Jackson, M-R., J. H. Johnson, Jr., and W. C. Farrell. 1994. An Analysis of Selected Responses to the Los Angeles Civil Unrest of 1992. 3 *Contention*, 3:3–21.

Jameson, Fredric. 1991. *Postmodernism: or, the Cultural Logic of Late Capitalism*. Durham, NC: Duke Univ. Press.

Kristeva, Julia. 1988. *Etrangers à nous-mêmes*. Paris: Fayard.

Lamphere, Louise, ed. 1992. *Structuring Diversity*. Chicago: Univ. of Chicago Press.

Latour, Bruno. 1993. *We Have Never Been Modern*. Cambridge, MA: Harvard Univ. Press.

Lawrence, Errol. 1982a. Just Plain Common Sense: the "Roots" of Racism. In *The Empire Strikes Back*, Centre for Contemporary Cultural Studies, 47–94. London: Hutchinson.

———. 1982b. In the Abundance of Water the Fool is Thirsty: Sociology and Black "Pathology." In *The Empire Strikes Back*, Centre for Contemporary Cultural Studies, 95–142. London: Hutchinson.

Lomnitz, Claudio. 1994. Decadence in Times of Globalization. 9 *Cultural Anthropology*, 257–67.

Malkki, Liisa. 1993. A Global Affair: Nationalism and Internationalism as Cultural and Moral Practices. In *Moralizing States and the Ethnography of the Present*, ed. S. F. Moore, 119–37. Washington, DC: American Anthropological Association.

Michelman, Frank I. 1986. Foreword: Traces of Self-Government. 100 *Harvard Law Rev.*, 3.

Miles, Jack. 1994. The Alternative to Anarchy: A Response to Maria-Rosario Jackson, James H. Johnson, Jr., and Walter C. Farrell, Jr. 3 *Contention*, 3:30–37.

Minow, Martha. 1990. *Making All the Difference: Inclusion, Exclusion and American Law*. Ithaca, NY: Cornell Univ. Press.

Moore, Sally Falk. 1973. Law and Social Change: The Semi-Autonomous Social Field as an Appropriate Subject of Study. 8 *Law and Society Rev.*, 719.

Morrison, Toni. 1992. *Playing in the Dark*. Cambridge, MA: Harvard Univ. Press.

Nash, June. 1994. Global Integration and Subsistence Insecurity. 96 *American Anthropologist*, 7–30.

Nicholson, Linda, ed. 1990. *Feminism/Postmodernism*. New York: Routledge, Chapman, and Hall.

Palumbo-Liu, David. 1994. "Los Angeles, Asians, and Perverse Ventriloquisms: On the Functions of Asian America in the Recent American Imaginary. 6 *Public Culture*, 365–81.

Perin, Constance. 1977. *Everything in Its Place*. Princeton, NJ: Princeton Univ. Press.

Rhode, Deborah. 1989. *Justice and Gender: Sex Discrimination and the Law*. Cambridge, MA: Harvard Univ. Press.

Rieff, David. 1991. *Los Angeles: Capital of the Third World*. New York: Simon and Schuster.

Roberts, Simon. 1978. Do We Need an Anthropology of Law? 25 *Royal Anthropological Institute News (RAIN)*, 4.

Robertson, Roland. 1992. *Globalization: Social Theory and Global Culture*. London: Sage.

Sanjek, Roger. 1990. Urban Anthropology in the 1980s: A World View. 19 *Annual Review of Anthropology*, 151–86.

Sarat, Austin, and Roger Berkowitz. 1994. Disorderly Differences: Recognition, Accommodation, and American Law. 6 *Yale Journal of Law and Humanities*, 285.

Sassen, Saskia. 1988. *The Mobility of Labor and Capital*. Cambridge: Cambridge Univ. Press.

———. 1991. *The Global City: New York, London, Tokyo*. Princeton, NJ: Princeton Univ. Press.

Smith, Michael Peter. 1992. Postmodernism, Urban Ethnography, and the New Social Space of Ethnic Identity. 21 *Theory and Society*, 493–531.

Sonenshein, Raphael J. 1994. What about Politics? 3 *Contention*, 3:23–27.

Stallybrass, Peter, and Allon White. 1986. *The Politics and Poetics of Transgression*. Ithaca, NY: Cornell Univ. Press.

Strathern, Marilyn. 1987. Introduction. In *Dealing with Inequality: Analysing Gender Relations in Melanesia and Beyond*, ed. M. Strathern, 1–32. Cambridge: Cambridge Univ. Press.

———. 1988. *The Gender of the Gift: Problems with Women and Problems with Society in Melanesia*. Berkeley: Univ. of California Press.

———. 1992. *After Nature: English Kinship in the Late Twentieth Century*. Cambridge: Cambridge Univ. Press.

———, ed. 1995. *Shifting Contexts: Transformations in Anthropological Knowledge*. London and New York: Routledge.

Sunstein, Cass R.. 1985. Interest Groups in American Public Law. 38 *Stanford Law Rev.*, 29.

Thomas, Nicolas. 1994. *Colonialism's Culture: Anthropology, Travel and Government*. Cambridge: Polity Press.

Varenne, Hervé. 1977. *American Together: Structured Diversity in a Midwestern Town*. New York: Teachers College Press.

———. 1984. Collective Representation in American Anthropological Conversations: Individual and Culture. 25 *Current Anthropology*, 389–94.

———. 1986. Drop in Anytime: Community and Authenticity in American Everyday Life. In *Symbolizing America*, ed. H. Varenne, 209–28. Lincoln: Univ. of Nebraska Press.

———. 1993. Dublin 16: Accounts of Suburban Lives. In *Irish Urban Cultures*, ed. C. Curtin, H. Donnan, and T. Wilson, 99–121. Belfast: Queen's University, Institute of Irish Studies.

———. n.d. Cultural Diversity as an American Cultural Category. Paper presented to the annual meeting of the American Anthropological Association, Washington, DC, 1993.

Vidich, Peter, 1993, "Race," Nature and Culture. 28 *Man* (n.s.), 17–34.

Warner, W. Lloyd. 1962. *American Life, Dream and Reality*. Chicago: Univ. of Chicago Press.

Williams, Patricia. 1991. *The Alchemy of Race and Rights: Diary of a Law Professor*. Cambridge, MA: Harvard Univ. Press.

Williams, Raymond. 1985. *The Country and the City*. London: Hogarth.

Wolf, Eric R. 1994. Perilous Ideas: Race, Culture, People. 35 *Current Anthropology*, 1–12.

Yngvesson, Barbara. 1993. *Virtuous Citizens, Disruptive Subjects*. New York: Routledge.

Young, Iris Marion. 1990. The Ideal of Community and the Politics of Difference. In *Feminism/Postmodernism*, ed. L. J. Nicholson, 300–323. New York: Routledge, Chapman, and Hall.

PUBLIC DOCUMENTS

347 U.S. 483 (74 S. Ct. 686).

Public Law 88-352.

Public Law 89-110.

Public Law 102-166.

POVERTY, DEPENDENCY, AND SOCIAL WELFARE: PROCEDURAL JUSTICE FOR THE POOR

❖

JOEL F. HANDLER

I. INTRODUCTION

Contemporary interest in procedural justice for the poor can probably be dated from Charles Reich's article "The New Property" (1964). Reich canvassed the various ways in which ordinary people were becoming increasingly dependent in their relationships with government. The evil was that important individual interests were subject to arbitrary, discretionary decisions by government without the restraints or protections of law. In order to protect people from arbitrary government action, these relationships should be considered legal entitlements—The New Property. Analogizing to traditional property relationships, the holders of these entitlements would be protected from government either by clear substantive rules or procedural due process.

"The New Property," of course, was of a piece with the civil rights movement and the War on Poverty. Legal Services, part of the Office of Economic Opportunity's Community Action program, was based on the assumption that if the poor were properly represented, the law could be changed and become an instrument for the poor instead of against them.[1] The United States Supreme Court, in *Goldberg v. Kelly*, encoded Reich's theory: statutory welfare grants were legal entitlements subject to due process of law. The court explicitly rejected the prior law that welfare was a mere privilege entitled to no protection for government acts. Now, a welfare recipient was entitled to a fair hearing before benefits could be terminated.

At one level, the program that Reich and others called for succeeded. There were vast changes in legislation and administrative codes recognizing the new legal status of minorities, women, the ill, and the poor. Many social harms were converted into protectable legal rights. There were significant changes in our legal culture, our ways of looking at the citizen and the state. "Rights" talk became commonplace. The period has been aptly called the "legal rights revolution" (Handler, Hollingsworth, and Erlanger 1978).

On closer examination, however, the reforms did not work at least in terms of protecting dependent people. When relations were governed by clear rules, the rules turned out to be oppressive; in the political process, the more powerful interests usually prevail. When relations were subject to official discretion, clients were unable to use due process remedies. Despite the changes in procedural law, most dependent people most of the time are not able to take advantage of their rights (Handler 1986: c. 2).

In order for the due process remedy to work, there has to be a *complaining client*. Our legal system is not proactive. People have to know that they have been harmed, they have to blame someone other than themselves, they have to know how to pursue a remedy, they have to have the resources to pursue that remedy, and the benefits that they expect to gain from winning have to outweigh the expected costs. The important point is that if *any* of these conditions fail, the due process remedy will fail. And, in reality, most of these conditions present formidable obstacles to dependent people most of the time. This is especially true for dependent people in their dealings with government bureaucracies. The result is that in the overwhelming majority of ordinary citizen-agency encounters, complaints are just not made, and when they are made, citizens rarely prevail.[2]

The reasons for the failure of due process remedies lie in the nature of bureaucratic discretionary power. The problem of the relationship of poor people with bureaucracy is often stated in terms of discretion. Discretion is ubiquitous, hence difficult to define.[3] Basically, it involves the existence of choice, as contrasted with decisions purportedly being dictated by rules. A common and useful example is criminal law enforcement. The police officer, in assessing an event, exercises choice as to whether to invoke authority and how much authority; the prosecutor, after weighing the evidence, decides whether to prosecute or not. Similar kinds of choices are available to many regulatory agencies—whether to cite violations or institute other kinds of actions. The opposite would be situations where the officer feels that there is no choice, that the rules dictate a particular decision. This is a theoretical distinction, and it should not be exaggerated. While it is probably true that in a great many situations, officers do feel that they are bound by rules, many important decisions are made by low-level eligibility workers, tax auditors, licensing officials, and other kinds of bureaucrats (Kagan 1984). Discretion is everywhere in the bureaucracy (Smith 1981; Winkler 1986). Choice has been exercised in the framing of the rules and, quite often, more often than we would like to acknowledge, officials conceal their choices behind the excuse of a rule (Lipsky 1980). In any event, in the relationships that I will be discussing—those involving social service agencies—the distinction is not important. The officials—doctors, social workers, teachers, mental health workers—have lots of choice.

Discretion, especially in its contemporary manifestations, has been attacked on both substantive and procedural grounds. As compared to the idealized version of the rule of law, where parties have equal access and the court applies neutral rules evenhandedly, it is argued that discretion allows for the bargaining away of publicly defined normative standards and may further disadvantage the weak and the powerless. With regulation, for example, negotiated resolutions will fall short of substantive goals; without procedural protections and the applicability of substantive rights, the poor and weak will be even more victimized by employers, landlords, merchants, and bureaucrats. Bargaining takes place within a normative framework. How are the rules of the game to be maintained? If one party can exploit the rules, there will be an unfair advantage.[4]

Choice, at least normatively, should be based on a careful weighing of the interests and needs of the client in relation to public considerations. Should this child be placed in this particular special education program? Does this particular applicant qualify for social benefits, and if so, under what conditions? Discretion contemplates a conversation within a normative framework, but dependent people—the poor, minorities, the uneducated, and unsophisticated—are often at a serious disadvantage. They lack the information, the skills, and the power to persuade. The official has the unfair advantage. It is for these reasons that the advocates for the poor and the weak have been so opposed to discretion.

As stated, generally speaking, law has taken two approaches to the problem of discretion. The first is strict or narrowly drawn substantive legal rights which would minimize discretion. The paradigmatic example is the Social Security retirement program. The applicant presents documentation, basically as to age and work history, and benefits are computed by formula. The program doesn't exactly work like this, but this is the idea.[5] The second approach is to grant applicants and recipients procedural rights to challenge the exercise of official discretion. There is also a third approach which is difficult to label. It views people in social rather than legal relations. It seeks to foster communication, the exploration of needs rather than rights, it looks to cooperative rather than zero-sum solutions. We can call this *communitarian* or *participatory*. In philosophy, this approach would be dialogism (Bernstein 1985); in law, alternative dispute resolution, bargaining, and negotiation; in social welfare, a revitalized professional social work practice (Simon 1986).

I will argue that none of these remedies work for most of the poor most of the time. On the other hand, I think that there are ways in which improvements can be made. But first, we have to consider more systematically just how the poor are denied procedural justice, how they are disempowered, before we can consider proposals for empowerment.

2. THE MANIFESTATIONS OF POWER

What is power, and how is it manifested? Why do clients submit to agency power? Power is not always direct and observable; it is often subtle and manipulative. The standard definition of power is: A has power over B to the extent that he can get B to do something that B would not otherwise do.[6] At first blush, the definition seems unproblematic, especially in the context of the dependent bureaucratic client. The client, as the price of receiving something that is needed, has to do something that the official insists upon—participate in a work program, reveal a matter of privacy, or engage in other kinds of behaviors. The model assumes an objective conflict of interests; there is a direct exercise of power and a knowing albeit unwilling submission. Suppose, however, that the client willingly submits? Has there been an exercise of power if B *appears* to do what A wants? Now the situation becomes more problematic. What does consent mean in a hierarchical relationship? Can we take the client's position at face value? What other choice do we have? Steven Lukes, in *Power: A Radical View* (1974), addressed the problem of power and quiescence. Lukes argued that there are three dimensions of power. The one-dimensional approach is the example given above where A gets B to do something he otherwise would not have done. This dimension focuses on observable behavior—"who participates, who gains and loses, and who prevails in decision-making" (Gamson 1968: 3; Polsby 1963: 55). As such, it assumes that grievances and conflicts are recognized and acted upon, that participation occurs within decision-making arenas which are assumed to be more or less open, at least to organized groups, and that leaders or decision makers can be studied as representatives of these groups. Nonparticipation or inaction, then, is not a political problem; "the empirical relationship of low socio-economic status to low participation gets explained away as the apathy, political inefficacy, cynicism or alienation of the impoverished" (Gaventa 1980: 7). As Gamson puts it, inactivity can be seen as confidence (consent), alienation, or irrelevance (1968: 46). Quiescence lies in the characteristics of the victims; it is not constrained by power.

The two-dimensional view of power seeks to meet this last point. Bachrach and Baratz argued that power has a "second face" by which it is not only exercised upon the participants within the decision-making arenas but also operates to exclude participants and issues altogether; that is, power not only involves who gets what, when, and how, but also who gets left out and how (Bachrach and Baratz 1962, 1970; Bachrach and Botwinick 1992). Some issues never get on the political agenda—for example, the issue of pollution in a company-dominated town, or the failure of southern Blacks to register and vote prior to the 1965 Voting Rights Act. Apparent inaction is not the result of the lack of grievances. The study of power has to also include barriers to the expression of grievances.

Lukes argues that the two-dimensional view, while a considerable advance, does not go far enough; it fails to account for how power may effect even the *conception* of grievances. The absence of grievances may be due to a manipulated consensus. Furthermore, the dominant group may be so secure that they are oblivious to anyone challenging their position—"the most effective and insidious use of power is to prevent . . . conflict from arising in the first place" (Lukes 1974: 23). This is the third dimension of power. A exercises power over B not only by getting him to do what he does not want to do, but "he also exercises power over him by influencing, shaping or determining his very wants" (Lukes 1974: 23). This may happen in the absence of observable conflict even though there is a latent conflict between the interests of A and the "real interests" of excluded B.

An important characteristic of the third-dimensional view is that it is not confined to looking at the exercise of power in an individualistic, behavioral framework; rather, it focuses on the various ways, whether individual or institutional, by which potential conflicts are excluded. It is much more sociological than either the one- or perhaps the two-dimensional views. Under the third dimension, two theoretical approaches are combined—the hegemonic social and historical patterns identified by Gramsci (1971) and the subjective effects of power identified by Edelman.[7] The two- and three-dimensional approaches promise to be particularly relevant when considering dependent or relatively powerless people: "In the two-dimensional approach is the suggestion of barriers that prevent issues from emerging into political arenas—i.e., that constrain conflict. In the three-dimensional approach is the suggestion of the use of power to pre-empt manifest conflict at all, through the shaping of patterns or conceptions of non-conflict" (Gaventa 1980: 13).

What are the mechanisms of power in the three dimensions? In the first dimension are the conventional political resources used by political actors—votes, influence, jobs. The second dimension adds what Bachrach and Baratz call the "mobilization of bias." These are the rules of the game—values, beliefs, rituals, as well as institutional procedures—which systematically benefit certain groups at the expense of others. The mobilization of bias operates not only in the decision-making arenas but also, in fact primarily, through "nondecisions" whereby demands are "suffocated before they are voiced, or kept covert; or killed before they gain access to the relevant decision-making arena; or failing all of these things, maimed or destroyed in the decision-implementing stage of the policy process" (Bachrach and Baratz 1970: 43). Quiescence can be the product of force or its threat, cooptation, symbolic manipulation, or the silent effects of incremental decisions or institutional inaction (Gaventa 1980: 15). The mechanisms of power in the third dimension are the least understood. Here is where

> power influences, shapes or determines conceptions of the necessities, possibilities, and strategies of challenge in situations of latent conflict. This may include

the study of social myths, language, and symbols, and how they are shaped or manipulated in power processes. It may involve the study of communication of information—both of what is communicated and how it is done. It may involve a focus upon the means by which social legitimations are developed around the dominant, and instilled as beliefs or roles in the dominated. It may involve, in short, locating the power processes behind the social construction of meanings and patterns that serve to get B to act and believe in a manner in which B otherwise might not, to A's benefit and B's detriment." (Gaventa 1980: 15–16)

Third-dimensional mechanisms of power not only include the control of information and socialization processes, but also fatalism, self-deprecation, apathy, and the internalization of dominant values and beliefs—the psychological adaptations of the oppressed to escape the subjective sense of powerlessness. Voices become echoes rather than grievances and demands. Behaviors and beliefs intertwine. Political consciousness and participation are reciprocal and reinforcing; those who are denied participation will not develop political consciousness. As Paulo Freire puts it, because dependent societies are prevented from either participation or reflection, they are denied the very experience necessary for the development of a critical consciousness; instead, they develop a "culture of silence." Moreover, it is the culture of silence which may lend legitimation to the dominant order. Finally, if their voices do emerge, they are especially vulnerable to manipulation by the powerful (Freire 1985; Gaventa 1980: 15–16).

Gaventa argues that the various mechanisms of power as well as the attributes of powerlessness, in all three dimensions, are interrelated and cumulative; they serve to reinforce each other. Repeated defeats lead to quiescence which give the dominant group more opportunity to create barriers of exclusion. The maintenance of power becomes "self-propelled"; thus, "power relationships can be understood only with reference to their prior development and their impact comprehended only in light of their own momentum" (Gaventa 1980: 23).

While Lukes's three faces of power has been very influential, it has been criticized as presenting a view of power that is overly monolithic, sovereign, top-down—in short, hegemonic. It emphasizes negative, prohibitory power, the denial of sovereignty to sovereign individuals. Stewart Clegg, taking a poststructuralist approach, argues that power is never that complete, that there is always a dialectic between agents (Clegg 1989). Rather than a "single all-encompassing strategy," power is a "shifting, inherently unstable expression in networks and alliances" (1989: 154). Rather than a sovereign view, power is a " 'capillary form' which 'reaches into the very grain of individuals' " (1989: 155).

Power, according to the post-structuralist view, is

neither in specific individuals (Lukes) nor in concrete practices (Foucault) but in the way in which agents and practices are articulated in a particular fixed ensemble of representations. There is only representation; there is no fixed, real, hidden or excluded term or dimension. To the extent that meanings become fixed or reified in certain forms, which then articulate particular practices, agents and relations, this fixity is power. . . . Power is textual, semiotic, and inherent in the very possibility of textuality, meaning and signification in the social world. (Clegg 1989: 184; Honneth 1991: 112)

Power, then, is not a "thing," rather it is a "property of relations" (Clegg 1989: 189). Networks of interest are constituted and reproduced both through conscious strategies and unwitting practices. The study of power is how agents constitute interests, how they attempt to enroll others to their strategies. Power is relational. When these relational interests are reproduced, when they become fixed or reified, then power tends to be regarded as thinglike, material, concrete. This means that despite theoretical instability, in practice, power can be "as 'objective' as the policeman's power to arrest" because of the "fixity of stabilized disciplinary powers and discursive practices" (Clegg 1989: 177).

Agents—which can be either individuals or collectivities—exercise power. Existing social relations constitute the identities of agents. Agents possess varying control of resources and varying means of producing outcomes. Power will automatically reproduce the existing configurations of rules and domination; transformation comes about only when existing practices are challenged. Domination, however, is not challenged that often because agents are embedded within organizations controlled by others and thus lack the collective organization to resist. They may not know about the existence of other resources—they may not know the rules of the game or even recognize the game. Often they are unaware of potential allies; in which case, resistance is isolated and easily defeated. Or there may be conflicts within potential allies. Or they may be aware, but the cost of resistance is too high. Clegg also says that conditions of the agents may be such as to render whatever knowledge they have useless. He uses as an example labor's need to earn a living and the deadening effect of ceaseless, routine activity as a form of discipline. "Routine," he says, "takes on the form of ritual; myth and ceremony serve to reinforce and make meaningful the routines of everyday subordination" (Clegg 1989: 222).

Rules of meaning and membership in organizations are fixed by institutional isomorphism (Powell and DiMaggio 1991). Certain meanings are privileged and certain membership categories are aligned with these meanings. Organizational fields develop when other organizations and agencies are enrolled, producing a stabilizing network of alliances and coalitions. Agencies in the field are reflexively aware of their constitution as a field. Clegg adopts the views of Meyer, Rowan, DiMaggio, and Powell as to the sources of organizational stability and change. Transformation is most likely to occur when there is a lack of fit between the core institutional order and the material substructure, where there is a "strain" arising from the functional incompatibility between the institutional order and the material base (Clegg

1989: 233). The tendencies toward contradiction are contingent on relations of meanings and membership. With higher degrees of isomorphism, there is more of an equilibrium of power (" 'thought-control' and 'hegemony' "; 1989: 237). The dialectic of power and structure is "our irremediable entrapment within webs of meaning together with our organizational capacity to transform these" (1989: 239–40).

In sum, there appears to be a high degree of convergence as to the characteristics or manifestations of power.[8] Depending on the situation, power can be objectively observed as A getting B to do what B would not ordinarily desire, as the subtle manipulations of the agenda, or as the construction of ideologies and meaning so that B is not aware of alternatives. From the perspective of the bottom, B may be able to negotiate all the conditions of the due process remedy and successfully fight back, or be aware of what is happening but, for a variety of reasons, not able to resist, or may be able to resist in nonconventional ways (Ewick and Silbey 1992), or be socialized into accepting dominant interests.

Not surprisingly, concepts of citizen empowerment mirror the multiple meanings of power. Power or empowerment is "the ability to act effectively" (Bachrach and Botwinick 1992: 57). Empowerment is both psychological and behavioral. It involves a sense of perceived control, of competence, a critical awareness of one's environment, and involvement in activities that, in fact, exert control (Zimmerman 1993). Empowerment is more than an absence of alienation or sense of helplessness. It involves a sense of connectedness (Zimmerman and Rappaport 1988). Charles Keiffer, in his study of participants in grassroots organizations, argues that empowerment is a long-term process of learning and development (1984). He emphasizes the importance of the connections between the experiences of daily life and perceptions of personal efficacy. The contrast is powerlessness. Building on the ideas of Freire—where the individual becomes powerless when he or she assumes the role of object rather than subject—powerlessness is a sense of loss of control over social relations, "a construction of continuous interaction between the person and his/her environment. It combines an attitude of self-blame, a sense of generalized distrust, a feeling of alienation from resources for social influence, an experience of disenfranchisement and economic vulnerability, and a sense of hopelessness in socio-political struggle" (Keiffer 1984: 16). Keiffer quotes one of his respondents: "It would never have occurred to me to have expressed an opinion on anything. . . . It was *inconceivable* that my opinion had any value" (1984: 16).

How then do individuals move "beyond . . . situations of powerlessness and oppression"? Keiffer argues that the process must be specific; generalized feelings of injustice or consciousness-raising are not sufficient. According to his participants, tangible and direct threats to individual or familial self-interests were necessary to provoke responses that would eventually lead to empowerment. There must be a "personally experienced sense of outrage or confrontation" (1984: 19). Examples include a woman being assaulted, or the betrayal of trust on the part of a landlord toward a tenant farmer. The next phase is what Keiffer calls the emergence of "participatory competence." By this he means getting over being scared, demystifying the symbols of power and authority, that is, coming to realize that officials do not know everything, and that ordinary people can change things. The process continues with the help of more experienced allies (role models, mentors, instructors, friends), supportive peer relationships, and a more critical understanding of social and political relations. Action must be reflective. Direct experience is used not only to gain skills but also to increase understanding and confidence, which, in turn, increases motivation. Eventually, the participants achieve an "increasingly self-conscious awareness of self as a visible and effective actor in the community," and they use their skills to integrate their "new personal knowledge . . . into the reality and structure of their everyday life-worlds" (1984: 23–24).

In discussing the relationship between thought and action, Keiffer is careful to point out that his respondents are not talking about theoretical concep-tualization. Rather, thought is used to inform action, to make future activity more effective. There has to be both thought and experience, extending over a period of time. "Empowerment is not a commodity to be acquired, but a transforming process constructed through action" (1984: 27). Empower-ment is a "long-term and continuing *process* of adult development" (1984: 31). Empowerment as "participatory competence" involves the development of a sense of self-competence, a more critical or analytical understanding of one's social and political environment, and individual and collective resources for social and political activity (1984: 31). Keiffer argues that this definition of empowerment "places the notion of competence and coping within an explicitly political context" (1984: 32).

Subsequent research confirms Keiffer's conception. Thus, Zimmerman and Rappaport report that studies of participants in a wide variety of settings and organizations suggest that empowerment is a combination of personal beliefs about control, involvement in activities to exert control, and a critical awareness of one's environment. They, too, emphasize experience—behaviors designed to exercise control (Zimmerman 1993; Zimmerman and Rappaport 1988).

We now illustrate the three faces of power in human service agencies.

3. POWER IN HUMAN SERVICES AGENCIES

Social work practice theory recognizes that there are natural unequal power relationships between the worker and the client but that, in most relationships, the power advantages will be neutralized through the voluntary mutuality of interests. This is because, according to the traditional view of social work prac-tice theory, the client-caseworker relationship is voluntary, mutual, reciprocal, and trusting.

Hasenfeld challenges this view; he describes the exercise of power from a political economy perspective (1992). The principal source of social worker power derives from the resources and services controlled by the agency. Workers are members of organizations, and it is the organizations that determine how their resources are to be allocated. If the clients want these resources, then they must yield at least some control over their fate. In addition to control over resources, workers have other sources of power: expertise, persuasion, and legitimacy. They have specialized knowledge and interpersonal skills. All of these sources of power are used in various combinations to exercise control over clients.

Much organizational power is exercised through its standard operative procedures—the type of information that is processed, the range of available alternatives, the decision rules. The agency is concerned with maintaining and strengthening its core activity—the delivery of services. The environment matters; goals represent the interests of those who control the key resources of the agency, which may or may not incorporate professional norms and/or the interests of the client. In public agencies, which chronically lack the resources to meet demand, social workers are relatively powerless to change the situation; thus, they develop various personal coping mechanisms such as withdrawal and client victimization.

Hasenfeld rejects the concept of mutuality of interests—that agencies and clients share the common goal of helping the client—in favor of a transactional approach. The interests of the client and the agency are determined by their respective systems. Each wants to maximize its own resources while minimizing costs. A person becomes a client to obtain needed resources but tries to do so with a minimum of costs; the social worker needs the resources controlled by the client while minimizing his or her and the agency's costs. The relationship is governed, then, by the power that each person has over their own interests. Thus, the amount of power that A has over B is a direct function of the resources that A controls and B needs and the inverse function of the ability of B to obtain those resources elsewhere. Agencies which have a monopoly of services exercise considerable power over clients. On the other hand, clients can exercise considerable power if they possess desirable characteristics. Thus, the exchange relationship between the client and the agency can be voluntary or involuntary depending on the degree of choice that each possesses. However, even in situations where social workers possess considerable power, that power may not necessarily be used. There are rules and regulations, and workers, in varying degrees, are influenced by professional norms and values. But, in any event, the traditional social work practice theory assumption of client self-determination is largely untrue for vulnerable groups. There, relationships tend to be involuntary. The agency is not dependent on the client for its resources. Demand exceeds resources, and most agencies are in monopoly positions. The agencies have the resources that the clients need. The clients usually have no alternatives. The asymmetrical power relationship between the agency and the client, and hence between the worker and the client, is maintained throughout the structure of social services. Social workers increase the power advantage through their monopoly of expertise, limiting client access to other workers, making the offer of services conditional on compliance, and limiting options for alternatives.

Agency processes reflect the evaluative criteria of the external funding and legitimating sources. The more powerful the agency, the more it will use its advantages to maintain its position; it will maintain a superior practice and select the more desirable clients. Within the agency, the more powerful workers are better able to control the conditions of their work. In this way, the dynamics of power perpetuate the unequal distribution of quality practice. Poor clients tend to receive poor services. This results not only in an inequality of practice but, Hasenfeld argues, the practice of inequality.

The exercise of power becomes more subtle when one considers agency technology. Human service agencies are designed to change people; thus, the technology not only requires knowledge of the complexities of human behavior, but it is also a *moral* system. Clients are invested with moral and cultural values that define their status. The processes of the organization—intake, intervention, and termination—are crucially shaped by the workers' moral evaluation of the client. Moreover, as clients progress within the system, moral and social attributes change. The technology is based on a conception of human nature, and this conception is reinforced through the selection, processing, and evaluation of the clients.

Because of the inherent uncertainties of the technologies and the pressure to respond to demands, the workers develop what Hasenfeld calls "practice ideologies"—sets of ideas or ideologies which seek confirmation in self-fulfilling prophecies by screening incompatible information and resisting change or reappraisal. The workers select and deal with those clients that will serve their interests—either to confirm their ideologies or comport with the demands of their working conditions, or both. Since technologies and resources are limited, the attributes of the clients who enter are important to organizational success. Thus, organizations seek to attract desirable clients and screen out the undesirable. Although public agencies are often limited in their ability to pick and choose, they employ other mechanisms for acceptance and rejection.

Hasenfeld describes the selection and processing of clients as "typification," which is a pervasive feature in the exercise of field-level discretion. The organization identifies client characteristics in terms of diagnostic labels which then determine the service response. Agency perceptions of the client's moral character are often determinative. Is the client responsible for his or her condition and is the client amenable to change? Is the client morally capable of making decisions? Is the client a subject or an object? The answers to these questions, in turn, determine the workers' moral responsibility to the client. The social construction of the client's moral character will have a decisive impact on the treatment that the client receives; thus, the constructed moral character becomes reinforcing.

Hasenfeld's description of power in human service agencies tracks the three dimensions of power. The first dimension is the objective observation of an exercise of power. A dependent person applies for welfare; a condition of aid is a behavioral change—for example, a work assignment—which the person would prefer not to do, but feels that she has to as the price of receiving assistance. The agency is acting either legally or illegally. In either case, it is a direct, observable exercise of power.

Assume that the agency is acting illegally—the woman may be legally exempt from the work requirements, the agency failed to follow required procedures (e.g., evaluation, offers of training, etc.), or adequate day care was not available. The client knows of the illegality but needs the aid, has no other adequate alternative, but lacks the resources to challenge the agency. Or the client has available competent legal services and does challenge the agency. This is the first-dimension of power—there is an objective event—individualized conflict and empirical evidence as to who won what under what circumstances. Power can be defined and measured.

Suppose, however, that the client acquiesces in the condition. Why is there quiescence? Assume that the client is of the same frame of mind—that is, she would prefer not to work. It may be that the agency is acting legally; in this case, the decision has been made legislatively and the agency is not exercising its discretion but is following a rule. The client is now precluded from voicing her grievance, certainly in this forum, but probably in any other arena as well. This would be a case of the second dimension. There is a grievance—the woman feels that she unjustly has to pay a price for the aid—but she has been effectively precluded from contesting the decision. There are other ways in which the second dimension of power can also operate. The agency may be operating illegally, the woman feels her grievance, but lacks the resources with which to pursue her remedy or for some other reason feels that it would be either useless or even counterproductive to pursue her remedy. She may, for example, fear retaliation. These are examples of the second dimension of power because, even though there is no objectively observed conflict, there is a grievance. Moreover, one could empirically verify not only the grievance but also the reasons for quiescence. Different client behaviors could be empirically established.

Postmodernists would look more closely at what appears to be acquiescence. Power, argues Clegg, is rarely that complete. There is room for resistance other than direct confrontation—manipulating the rules, offering excuses, shirking, or otherwise gaming the system. In many situations, it is burdensome to agencies to enforce formal sanctions, and clients know this. Most regulatory requirements in welfare are not systematically enforced. Most welfare recipients, somehow or other, get excused from work requirements (Handler and Hasenfeld 1991).

There are also several variations on the third dimension of power—where the absence of conflict is due to the manipulation of consensus, where A shapes and determines the very wants of B. The very idea of welfare as an *entitlement* is of recent vintage. Prior to the legal rights revolution of the 1960s, welfare was considered a gratuity, something that was offered on the terms and conditions of the grantor, much as private charity is given today. Given the extremely low level of legal challenges in social welfare programs, one questions even now how far the concept of entitlement has penetrated the consciousness of the disadvantaged. The work requirement is deeply ingrained in American public values—witness the astonishing consensus on work-for-relief today; many think it perfectly normal and appropriate that an applicant for public assistance should work at a public job as the price of the grant; there is very little support for the idea that one is *entitled* to a minimum level of support without any corresponding obligations.[9] To the extent that the applicant for assistance has internalized these values—the obligations of work, responsibility, and welfare—then the dominant group has prevented even the conception of the grievance.

The social and historical patterns and the subjective effects are, of course, much more deeply rooted, much more pervasive than even the complex example of the work obligation. They are manifest in many of the relationships between the dependent citizen seeking services or trying to avoid sanctions and the officer who controls the resources. Both the powerful and the powerless carry into the relationship their respective characters and self-conceptions, their root values, nurtured through immediate as well as past social relationships. Who they are and where they come from—class, race, childhood, education, employment, relations with others, the everyday structures of their lives, their very different social locations—crucially affect their languages, social myths, beliefs, and symbols—how they view themselves, their world, and others, which produce vastly different meanings and patterns in their encounters. How does the staff professional view herself in her full, deep context, and how does she view the person sitting across the desk? How does the client view herself, in her context, and the person sitting across from her? The structures of their social lives shape their identities and direct their behavior (Molotch and Boden 1985).[10] While in theory there is no agreement as to how hegemonic these power relationships are, in practice it is no surprise that social welfare clients either fail to pursue their grievances or even to conceptualize a grievance.[11]

Thus, power vs. empowerment is usually looked at in zero-sum terms—a contest between the agency and the client; what the client gains the agency has to give up. This is not necessarily true, even in the human service agencies that Hasenfeld describes. The zero-sum assumption does not sufficiently take into account the many situations where organizations bargain rather than rely strictly on commands. The various contemporary theories of organizations described organizations as collections of competing units and individuals, more or less vying with each other for the command over resources. In this struggle, organizational actors seek legitimacy, power, and resources from the environment. Legitimacy is acquired through conformity to dominant cultural norms and belief systems. The institutionalists argue that these norms are very powerful; they are the essence of organizational behavior. They determine an organization's rules and practices. Organizations that conform are more successful in commanding productive resources from the environment—money, legal authority, and desirable clients (Powell and DiMaggio 1991).

Both the political economy and the institutional perspective emphasize the importance of the organizational environment. Organizational fields are rarely static, especially since there are conflicts and contradictions among many of our basic institutions. Organizations both shape and are constrained by environmental influences. In many situations, organizations are proactive, seeking to strengthen and expand their influence by expanding the power of their interest group constituencies. In other situations, existing organizations seek to defend themselves from newcomers.

In a world of competition and unstable environments, there can be many reasons why organizations will find it in their self-interest to strike deals, to bargain, rather than attempt to secure their position by will. Bargaining, of course, occurs where the regulated subject has something that the agency needs but lacks the ability to command. Regulatory agency bargains with regulated industries are well known. But bargaining also occurs in situations which are not so obvious. A great many police encounters on the street are bargains; cooperation can leave both parties better off. Hasenfeld notes that human service agencies will bargain if clients have desirable characteristics. Organizations may bargain to save scarce resources, to gain a more favorable solution, to acquire resources that the client controls (for example, information). Imposing formal sanctions is often time-consuming and expensive. It is often easier to make a deal.

In sum, power and empowerment is a relational process, a dynamic process. It has both psychological and material or substantive aspects. Relationships are not stable. Resources and perceptions change; power changes as well. Specifically, all else being equal, we can expect that over time power will gradually shift to the more powerful agency. The agency has the surer command over resources; it has the staying power. This means that empowered clients have to keep struggling to maintain their position. There has to be a continuous structure of incentives; otherwise, energy will dissipate, and clients will become passive and coopted.

It is now easy to see why all three approaches to procedural justice are extremely problematic. All, in one way or another, require a proactive, complaining client—a person who is aware of what is going on, has resources, and is willing to take risks. With the dependent poor facing bureaucracies, these conditions present formidable obstacles. With rare exceptions, they have no bargaining power with the agencies. While agencies need clients, they can pick and choose, and the clients have no alternatives. Consequently, there is a pervasive failure of procedural justice. Legal rights are not invoked. When consultation or bargaining is required, it is usually a sham (Handler 1986).

4. EXCEPTIONS

Substantive Rights. There are, of course, exceptions. As far as I am aware, the substantive legal rights approach of the Social Security retirement program works reasonably well. However, to what extent is the recipient empowered? It could be argued that the recipient is a mere passive recipient of public largesse; there is no participation or sharing of control in the relationship with the government office. I think that this is too narrow a view. The recipient is a member of a long-standing, politically powerful social movement that created, maintained, strengthened, and continues to protect a large government benefit program. The aged are very active politically in defense of Social Security and there is no reason to assume that individual recipients are not aware of their rights and benefits. To the extent that the structure of the program continues to grant benefits under a minimum of discretion, each recipient as a member of a collective movement has exercised power. Returning to the second face of power, Social Security recipients have been listened to in the legislative process. Social Security is considered to be an insurance contract. Even though the insurance idea is considerably attenuated, recipients think of themselves as "rights bearing citizens." My guess is that an aggrieved Social Security recipient speaks a very different language than poor people confronting other social welfare programs.

Last, but not least, Social Security recipients get resources. The U.S. Social Security retirement program doesn't make anyone rich, but it compares favorably with Western European systems, and it has substantially reduced poverty among the elderly (Myles 1988). For these reasons, then, I would consider the Social Security retirement program empowering—rights have been granted, discretion (power of officials) has been minimized, and resources have been secured (Goodin 1988).

There are also some exceptions in discretionary social welfare programs. For a time, welfare recipients were very active in challenging public programs. From time to time, there are adversarial challenges in mental health, health, and education. But these are rare.

In the third approach to procedural justice—the communitarian or cooperative model—it is possible to restructure the relationships so that dependent people can be empowered. Empowerment in a cooperative relationship is not only a matter of good intentions. It depends on a careful analysis of what trust entails in a hierarchical relationship; a reconceptualization of professional goals and tasks; an appropriate technology; and an exchange of concrete, material resources.

5. TRUST AND EMPOWERMENT: SOME CASE STUDIES

Dependency and Trust. Trust is as ubiquitous as discretion. As a form of social organization, it is used whenever there are principals and agents, whenever we invest resources, responsibility, or authority in others (Shapiro 1987; Barber 1983). We trust strangers as well as intimates; trust, it is said, is necessary to reduce the complexities of life (Luhmann 1980: 4). Annette Baier (1986) draws a distinction between merely relying on the dependable habits of others and trusting; the latter relies on good will. When one relies on another's good will, one becomes vulnerable; but while there is the opportunity to do harm, one does not expect this to happen. We place ourselves in this vulnerable position because we need the help of agents to achieve or maintain things that we value—our lives, our health, our children, our property. Trust also involves discretion; we trust our agents to use their competence in our best interests, which also means that they have the ability to conceal their mistakes or their ill will under the pretense of honest judgment. Trust can be unconscious or cultivated.

Baier distinguishes trust from contract. Making contracts and promises includes trust, but contract does not capture the full variety and moral dimensions of trust. Contracts are mainly used by adults who are more or less equal in power; Baier is interested in trust relations with dependent people—children, servants, wives, and slaves.

Baier argues that trusting relationships are not necessarily morally decent; they can also be morally rotten. How can one tell the difference? Baier proposes a moral test in terms of expressibility—can the trust relationship survive the knowledge the parties are relying on to continue the relationship? The example she uses is an old-fashioned husband and wife where the wife is entrusted to care for the child. As long as there are not radical disagreements as to child-rearing practices, the husband can trust the wife to use her discretion. The trust, however, would be undermined if there were serious conflicts in values and the husband knew that the wife was willing to sacrifice his interests for hers. Trusting is rational. If the husband knew that the wife is only conforming to avoid sanctions, then he would rely on threats rather than trust. Similarly, the wife would only conform as long as she thought that keeping the trust would produce more of the benefits that she and the child were interested in than breaking the trust. In other words, rational trust can exist in a variety of situations where the parties are, in fact, quite suspicious of each other; threats and concealments would keep the trust going. This would be a "morally rotten" trust. Under the expressibility test, knowledge of what the other is relying on weakens the relationship. Conversely, with a moral trust, knowledge would strengthen the relationship—"the other's love, or concern for some common good or professional pride in competent discharge of responsibility" (Baier 1986: 256).[12]

Trust, under Baier's more expansive concept, alters power relationships. The most basic, elemental trust is between the infant and the parent; it is trust that does not have to be won but can be destroyed. Even though this is an example of extreme dependency and unequal vulnerability, Baier argues that it is still to some extent mutual; the parent is "vulnerable to the child's at first insignificant but ever-increasing power, including power as one trusted by the parent" (Baier 1986: 242).[13] The goods that the parent supplies are nutrition, shelter, clothing, health, and love. The child can expect the parent to keep supplying these goods because the goods that the parent supplies are also goods to the parents—they are *common goods*. Harm to these goods would be self-harm. Trust and vulnerabilities between the parent and child become more mutual over time and, eventually, adult children may become responsible for their parents; but this latter relationship, however contractual or not it may be, does not transform the initial trust into a contractual exchange. The childhood relation may be a moral reason, says Baier, for taking care of one's parents, but it is not consideration. Trust, then, between unequal participants does not necessarily have equality as its goal; what it does have, under the expressibility test, is equal moral agency.[14]

Baier's expressibility test connects with the empirical problems of the third dimension of power. The empirical problem involves the issue of what appears to be manipulated consent that suffocates even the conception of a grievance. There are situations where expressibility meets both objections; if the true reasons for the relationship are disclosed and the relationship is thereby strengthened, then consent seems more genuine and less manipulated.

Some Case Studies. There are examples where powerful officials enter into conversations with dependent people, where information and decision-making authority are shared, where dependent people become partners, in effect, in the exercise of discretion. There is an alteration in power relations.[15]

Most of the time informed consent in health care is a fiction: it is a legal, bureaucratic hurdle that the physician has to negotiate. The task of the physician is to get the patient to sign the form to avoid malpractice liability. There is no real communication. Power has not changed. The paradigmatic example is the surgeon presenting the consent form the night before surgery (Katz 1984). Informed consent works differently with the chronically ill. There, the task of the physician is to get the patient to come to *understand* and *accept* the chronic condition and to *participate* in the therapy. A prominent example is renal dialysis patients. Here, patients become knowledgeable; they become very active in their treatment; they often speak in jargon and diagnose their own problems; and doctors listen. Patients are encouraged to learn about alternatives and are given real choice. Physicians, in these circumstances, are more successful than when patients only passively comply (Lidz and Meisel 1983).

Another example involves special education. Many handicapped children were either excluded from schools, or were improperly classified and seg-regated, and their lives were wasted. The Education for All Handicapped Children Act (1972) granted all handicapped children the right to an "ap-propriate" public education but left it to the local participants to decide what the content of that education was to be. Schools would decide on the specific programs, but parents were given the right of informed consent before a child was to be selected for diagnosis, evaluation, and placement in a special education program. Evaluation and the placement decision had to take place in a conference in which the parents had the right to attend and participate. If the parent disagreed with any decision, there were two administrative appeals (the district and the state) with the right of judicial review.

In most jurisdictions, the procedural innovations do not work. There are strong incentives to routinize the process and place and keep a child in available slots. Most parents, especially those from lower socioeconomic classes, lack the ability to participate. In addition to psychological burdens, the parents lack the necessary information and resources. The result is that participation and consent are formalities only. School officials decide cases beforehand, parents are presented with the staff recommendations, the consent forms are ritualistically signed. What we have is the classic case of either the second or third dimension of power. There is the subtle implication that the child or the parent is at fault. Parents who have grievances are overpowered; many have no idea that there are alternatives; doubts as to the wisdom of the powerful are not even raised (Heller, Holtzman, and Messick 1982; Handler 1986: c. 3).

The Madison, Wisconsin School District has a vastly different relationship with the parents—one that is based on trust (in Baier's sense), that treats parents as subjects, where power relations are altered, and where consent appears to be genuine. The district made three moves that serve as the foundation for their approach. The first was ideological; the parents had to be part of the solution to the task of educating handicapped students; if students were to be successful in school and in life outside and after school, then the parents had to be both knowledgeable and active participants; the school could not do it alone. Second, the technology was uncertain; therefore, diagnosis and treatment had to be flexible and experimental. By taking uncertainty seriously, the district lowered the level of potential conflict; participants can feel comfortable in agreeing to a course of action knowing that it will be open to renegotiation. Parents are given the opportunity to participate, but they lack the resources. The third move was to supply parent advocates—lay people who were experienced in the process (usually they were parents of handicapped children)—to help the parents. The parent advocates were to advise the parents as to the range of alternative services and programs, and that the parents could get independent evaluations; they would counsel them, accompany them to the meetings, and help them in the negotiations with the school people. The parent advocates were to deliberately introduce conflict, to ask questions that parents were afraid to ask or didn't know how to ask. A genuine dialogue involves questioning, listening, and openness. The parents not only had to feel comfortable with the decisions; they also had to be active participants in the plan. Quiescence—the standard practice in other school districts—was not enough. There were other things necessary to make the Madison approach work: social movement activity: parent groups, training sessions, and outings, all designed to decrease alienation and share information. The parents had access to independent experts who were welcome in the conferences.

In this system, the parents are considered subjects, not objects, the foundation of the relationship is reciprocal trust, power relationships have been altered, and consent appears to be genuine. The school has to get the parent involved; they would not do this unless they had confidence in the parent—that the parent understood what was expected, was capable, and would be active. The parent would not agree to this and perform in the manner that the school system considered necessary unless she understood and trusted the school people. Moreover, since the plans were tentative and experimental, always subject to renegotiation, the conversations had to continue. The teachers needed the active, understanding participation of the parent through the school life of the child.[16]

The parents were still parents and the teachers were still teachers; there were no redistributions of income and changes in social class. In real life, there were still great imbalances of power. Each brought with them their vast cultural differences. Yet, in this relationship, the parents approached equal moral agency. Trust based on good will, where Baier's test of expressibility would strengthen the trust relationship, altered power relations. The parent was given information and responsibility; she was empowered.

The parent was not only changed vis-à-vis the teacher, she herself was also changed. The ability to take more control over her life and the fate of her child means that there was a change in her self-conception, in her views about herself. Changes in practices necessarily mean a change in one's ideologies. Ideology defines experiences and constructs reality. Events become socially meaningful when they are interpreted.[17] The empowerment of the parent, in this transaction, was both transformative and constitutive.

Another example may be found in some demonstration programs providing community-based care programs for the frail, elderly poor. These programs are designed to provide cheaper, more effective care to people who are at risk of becoming nursing home residents. The clients are typically very old, single women who need help in a variety of activities of daily life—transportation, chore services, nutrition, bathing, toileting, and health needs. For most of the elderly in this situation, home care is provided by spouses or other family, but for those without such supports or where the support is having great difficulty in helping, then unless this care is provided, there will be rapid deterioration and the client will have to be institutionalized.

I examined several voluntary and for-profit agencies in the Los Angeles area that are operating community-based care programs (Handler 1989). While the programs vary, basically the agencies recruit clients, provide case management, and contract for services according to need. Most of the services are for the routine, mundane tasks of daily living—the most popular service is home help. If available, the agencies work with family. For a variety of reasons, the agencies have to enlist the active cooperation of the clients. Those who are familiar with the elderly know that it is no small matter to get the elderly to participate in service programs; not infrequently, they are fearful, confused, or have a determined, sometimes counterproductive, sense of independence.

These agencies, however, have to do more than get the clients merely to accept the services that are offered. The clients have to be engaged—for example, they have to interview the home help aides, supervise their work, and report to the agencies on the quality of the performance and, if necessary, discharge the workers. The agencies assist in various ways, but they simply do not have the resources to provide this kind of close supervision. They rely on the clients, and where available, family members, to provide the necessary information. As a result, instead of being passive recipients of services, the clients become active participants in the selection and supervision of a variety of services. They become part of the solution. This is often a difficult transition. It is accomplished through careful, patient conversations; clients (and family) are slowly brought along; confidences are established; gradually, agency staff and clients and family begin to rely on each other. There is cooperation based on understanding and trust.

These are examples where consent appears to meet the objections raised in the third dimension of power. In order for the dominant person—physician (of the chronically ill), teacher, or case manager—to perform the professional task, the dependent person has to become an active, understanding participant. I stress the word understanding because the professional relies on the dependent person for accurate information and judgment. To get this kind of participation, the dependent person has to have discretion, the ability to consider alternatives. At least in some respects, this satisfies the empirical concerns about the third dimension of power. Here, potential conflicts (alternatives) are considered. We also have the kind of trust that Baier is talking about; under the expressibility test, if the reasons for the relationship are disclosed, the relationship would be strengthened. Power has been altered both instrumentally and constitutively. The self-conceptions, the ideologies, of the empowered persons have been changed. As equal moral agents, the dependent person has a different conception of herself, the professional, and the relationship. This is the developmental process that Keiffer, Rappaport, and Zimmerman describe.

These examples may be contrasted with instrumental cooperation. There are many cooperative relations which are strictly instrumental, where expressibility is used to clarify the benefits and costs of dealing rather than fighting. Knowledge here is not of *common goods* such as mutual respect, love, good will, and professional pride. Cooperation is not the common good; it is only instrumental to reducing costs; if the costs to one of the parties begins to exceed benefits, then cooperation ceases. Cooperation can be based on trust or fear—as long as there is clear information. In these situations, power relations are not altered. Cooperation is neither constitutive nor transformative (Hawkins 1984; Handler 1990). With the chronically ill, the parents of handicapped children, and the frail, elderly poor, while there was no change in economic and social positions, power was altered; the patient or the client moved from a dependent person to an equal moral agent. The change on the part of the dependent people was constitutive in the sense that their ideologies changed—their conception of themselves and their relationships with the professionals.

How much change, and how significant? The transformative empowerment that occurs in these situations is partial in that it may only apply to the particular transactions between the clients or patients and the professionals. Further, it may not apply to the full range of alternatives; the clients (as well as the professionals) may be constrained within an unduly limited set of alternatives. The middle-class professionals work within bureaucracy; the clients are still dependent people. Even though they seemed to do well in their associations with the agencies, they are still dependent people. One would hope that the moral values developed in these relationships would have effects in other arenas—that doctors, teachers, and social workers would be more responsive to dependent people who come their way, and, similarly, that dependent people would use their enhanced self-conception in their other relationships, but this is uncertain. So we are talking about meeting the objections of the third dimension of power in an important, but nevertheless, selected area; in other areas, in other relationships between agencies and clients, and in other relations with these very same people, power may still be exercised in the conventional manner. The participatory examples are enclaves, alternative practices, within larger, hierarchical structures.

Moreover, the relationships may also be transitory. In the medical area, it has been verified that when the chronically ill become acute care patients, they and their physicians revert to the traditional role. With both the parents of handicapped children and the frail, elderly poor, the professionals have to constantly work to maintain active, understanding participation.

These limitations should not be surprising. Lawyers especially put too much faith in the relevance and durability of process, but process is always molded by substantive events. Partial relationships may be necessary for autonomy; even communitarian philosophers worry about social distance (Unger 1975: 279; MacIntyre 1984: 142–43). The task is to discover the conditions which will facilitate the creation and nurturing of empowerment in discretionary dependent relationships, not to search for some magical procedural formula.

6. CONCLUSION: STRUCTURING EMPOWERMENT

There are three conditions for the empowerment of dependent people in the discretionary relationships that I have identified. First, there must be changes in professional norms. In Baier's examples, dependent people become equal moral agents through love, mutual respect, altruism, and professional pride. Many have argued for such values in client-bureaucracy relations, such as informed consent in health care (Katz 1984) and social work (Simon 1986). In the examples that I used there were the humanistic values of mutual respect and professional pride. Patients, parents, and clients were reconceived as subjects rather than objects.

Second, the technology must lend itself to shared decision making. In human service agencies, it must be recognized that professional judgments are contextual, experimental, and not fixed, determinate rules. Clients are individuals, and their special circumstances and needs must be considered.

Participation is usually justified in process terms—autonomy, dignity, and respect. These are values in and of themselves. But I think that something more is necessary; there have to be substantive benefits from cooperation. This is the third condition—what I call reciprocal, concrete incentives. In the three examples, the professional could not perform her task unless the patient or client participated as an equal moral agent, that is, actively cooperated on the basis of understanding and trust. Although I distinguished these examples from instrumental cooperation, these examples also had strong instrumental elements. While they were more than instrumentalist, I want to emphasize that instrumentalism is at their base. Because the power relationship is so unequal when dependent people are dealing with large-scale public agencies, unless there are strong, reciprocal, concrete incentives, including financial incentives,[18] I don't believe that the humanistic values of mutual respect, love, altruism, and professional pride would be enough to sustain equal moral agency, at least in the long run. In the examples that I used, active, understanding participation was necessary if the physician or case manager were to perform satisfactorily their own professional task. More than reciprocal incentives are required—they are a necessary but not sufficient condition— but they are required. Power must serve the interests of the powerful; that is not disputed (Lukes 1986: 5). But in these examples, the interests are even better served by empowering the client.

The idea of reciprocal incentives increases the client's value to the worker and thereby encourages change in the power relationship. With reciprocal incentives, if the client fails, the worker fails; thus, the worker has a professional stake in empowerment. This is not inconsistent with changes in professional norms and ideologies; but since professional norms and ideologies are often used to manipulate or suffocate grievances, the presence of reciprocal concrete incentives gives one more confidence about the meaning of consent.

Dependent clients, too, need resources. Psychological burdens, of course, will vary; some clients will be able to take advantage of the opportunities being offered, but others will not. Although in my examples the professionals provided information and support, it would seem that in many other situations, social movement groups would be necessary. This would be a fourth condition. Groups provide solidarity, encouragement, and information. They show the clients that they are not alone, that others share their burdens; they can collectivize grievances. Groups can provide training and experts. Clients need groups in order to be able to participate. This means that the bureaucracy also needs the groups if it is to get the kind of client participation that it wants. The professional task is reconceptualized so that clients are part of the solution, but in order for clients to participate, client groups have to part of the solution as well.

The fact of discretion is inevitable in the modern social welfare state, and as long as government and large-scale agencies are serving and regulating the disadvantaged, then the consequences of unfair power in the exercise of discretion must be addressed. The solutions of the legal system—the reduction of discretion through the application of tightly drawn legal rules, and the enforcement of those rules through procedural due process, that is, the assertion of the rule of law—have limited application, especially since procedural due process protections are such a problematic remedy for the vast majority of dependent people. Instead, discretion must be addressed more positively, more creatively; ways have to be explored that will restructure relationships to empower dependent clients. This requires changes in professional ideologies, redesigning reciprocal incentives, and providing resources to clients so that they can participate. Still, one must proceed cautiously. The examples that I have outlined are special and fragile. While they may indicate beginnings, it must not be forgotten that they exist in small corners of large-scale, hierarchical structures.

Within the large-scale welfare bureaucracies, I think that the approach should move in the opposite direction—more toward the substantive justice model of Social Security retirement where procedural justice is the by-product. Space does not permit an extended discussion of reforms in social welfare programs, but let me sketch a few major points. Technology—what programs are trying to accomplish in light of resources and client characteristics—is the starting point because, as stated, unless the frontline technology is enhanced through client participation, then I think procedural justice for seriously dependent people is very problematic. If the major goal of social welfare programs is to move people from dependency,[19] then this requires both income-maintenance and strategies to connect recipients to decently paying jobs. However, as long as these programs are (1) large-scale, dealing with massive numbers of clients by overworked, understaffed, undertrained bureaucrats; (2) the clients vary greatly in terms of need, family circumstances, and employability deficits; (3) public attitudes toward welfare remain hostile; and (4) funding for people-changing programs, such as education, work, and training, remain very small, then procedural justice within the structures of the programs themselves is a chimera.

Rather, the approach should be in terms of substantive justice and market-based incentives. This can be done, primarily, by making work in the regular economy pay. At the present time, neither welfare (AFDC) nor work nor the combination are sufficient to lift most single-mother families out of poverty (Jencks 1992). It is estimated that the great majority of AFDC mothers have to work, mostly illegally, in order to survive. However, employment is so low-paying that they also have to stay on welfare. Employment can be made more attractive by expanding the Earned Income Tax Credit, and providing better health care benefits, child support, and housing subsidies. Depending on the levels of support, these measures could substantially reduce welfare rolls (Ellwood 1988). This would be something like the approach of Social Security retirement. Programs would be routinely administered, discretion would be minimized, and clients would be empowered through voluntarily acquiring resources. It is possible that stigma and hostility would be reduced. The principal income support would be rewarding work effort. Child support and in-kind benefits, such as health and housing, do not carry the same burdens as welfare.

More difficult problems arise for those programs whose technologies do not allow for a routinized, market-based approach. Many people still need special help—health services, substance abuse treatment, mental health services, education, training, supported work, and so forth. To the extent that these people remain within welfare programs, they are vulnerable to the additional reproach of failing where others seem to succeed. It would seem here that the approach should be to separate all of the people-changing programs out of the welfare system into something like separate, multipurpose agencies serving a wide range of people who need specialized, individually based programs, some of whom are poor but many of whom are not. There are many examples of these kinds of programs. Customers and clients pay fees according to income. Hopefully, in new, multipurpose family service agencies there would be room to experiment with local, community-based programs staffed by professionals who have internalized participatory norms and with local social movement groups that can participate in governance. There have been some remarkable programs in social services (Schorr 1988) and radically decentralized schools in very deprived areas.

NOTES

1. For a history of legal services, see Handler, Hollingsworth, and Erlanger 1978; Weisbrod, Handler, and Komesar 1978.

2. There is an extensive literature documenting the failure of due process remedies for dependent people in a variety of bureaucratic settings; see Handler 1986, 1990a.

3. For discussions of discretion, see Brodkin 1987; Adler and Asquith 1981.

4. There is also a considerable literature attacking discretion in informal justice. See, e.g., Abel 1982, 1985; Delgado 1985.

5. This description does not, of course, apply to Social Security Disability, which is a very troublesome program (Stone 1984).

6. While this may be a common, and for our purposes useful, definition of power, there is, in fact, no agreement on the various meanings of power. According to Talcott Parsons, "Power is one of the key concepts in the great Western tradition about political phenomena. It is at the same time a concept on which, in spite of its long history, there is, on analytical levels, a notable lack of agreement both about its specific definition, and about many features of the conceptual context in which it should be placed. There is,

however, a core complex of its meaning having to do with the capacity of persons or collectivities 'to get things done' effectively, in particular when their goals are obstructed by some kind of human resistance or opposition." Talcott Parsons, "Power and the Social System," in Lukes 1986: 94. The Lukes volume contains a series of essays on various approaches to power. At the end of the introduction, Lukes says: "[I]n our ordinary unreflective judgments and comparisons of power, we normally know what we mean and have little difficulty in understanding one another, yet every attempt at a single general answer to the question has failed and seems likely to fail" (1986: 17). For further discussion of power, see, e.g., Clegg 1989; Honneth 1991.

7. "Political actions chiefly arouse or satisfy people not by granting or withholding their stable, substantive demands but rather by changing their demands and expectations" (Edelman 1971: 8; Gaventa 1980: 13).

8. In describing the evolution of Foucault's theory of power, Honneth says: "Accordingly, he no longer regards individual actors or social groups as the subjects of this developed form of the exercise of power, but instead social institutions such as the school, the prison, or the factory—institutions that he himself must comprehend as highly complex structures of solidified positions of social power. The frame of reference for the concept of power has, therefore, secretly been shifted from a theory of action to an analysis of institutions" (1991: 173).

9. See, e.g., Hartmann 1987 and Mead 1986. For a discussion of the current consensus on work and welfare reform, see Handler and Hasenfeld 1991.

10. There is a vast theoretical and empirical literature dealing with the problems of lack of rights consciousness. See, e.g., Felstiner, Abel, and Sarat 1980–81; Bumiller 1988; Handler 1986.

11. It must be noted that the three-dimensional view of power does pose significant methodological problems. A major challenge raised to the two-dimensional view was the empirical difficulty of observing a "nonevent." With the third dimension, "how can one study what does not happen?" (Gaventa 1980: 25) How can one tell whether B would have *thought* and *acted* differently? There is a real issue of imputing interests and values to the voiceless. An even more difficult problem comes in empirically verifying the third dimension. When there is quiescence, how do we know whether the consent is genuine or manipulated? How does the researcher (the dominant group) avoid imputing her values, the social construction of meaning, to the quiescent?

   In real life, however, the methodological issues may not, in fact, be that severe in many situations. If there are major inequalities in social relations, at least as a first step, one should not assume that quiescence is natural but seek other explanations. In less obvious situations, Gaventa suggests a number of steps to try to explain the inaction. He would look to the historical development of the apparent consensus to see how the situation was arrived at and how the consensus has been maintained. He would look at the processes of communication and socialization and the relationship between the ideologies and beliefs. There may be comparative examples with different power relationships. However, "if . . . no mechanisms of power can be identified and no relevant counterfactuals can be found, then the researcher must conclude that the quiescence of a given deprived group is, in fact, based upon consensus of that group to their condition, owing for instance, to differing values from those initially posited by the observer" (Gaventa 1980: 25).

12. Baier's definition of trust is as follows: "trust is morally decent only if, in addition to whatever else is entrusted, knowledge of each party's reasons for confident reliance on the other to continue the relationship could in principle also be entrusted—since mutual knowledge would be itself a good, not a threat to the other goods. To the extent that mutual reliance can be accomplished by mutual knowledge of the conditions of that

reliance, trust is above suspicion, and trustworthiness a nonsuspect virtue" (Baier 1986: 259–60).

13. This conception of reciprocal power relations within an example of extreme dependency seems to fit Foucault's conception of the nature of power: "Power must be analyzed as something which circulates, or rather as something which only functions in the form of a chain. It is never localized here or there, never in anybody's hands, never appropriated as a commodity or piece of wealth. Power is employed and exercised through a net-like organization. And not only do individuals circulate between its threads; they are always in the position of simultaneously undergoing and exercising this power. They are not only its inert or consenting target; they are always also the elements of its articulation. In other words, individuals are the vehicles of power, not its points of application" (Foucault 1986: 234).

14. Baier's view of trust seems very close to Hannah Arendt's conception of power, which is the ability to agree upon a common course of action in unconstrained communication. See Arendt 1986 and Habermas 1986: 59–74, 75–93.

15. The examples are more fully discussed in Handler 1986, 1990a.

16. Consider the following quote from a lower-class parent: "Our family has never been criticized, they've never said, 'you're failing him.' They've encouraged us to allow him to do more and try more, and not to be afraid. They've convinced us he can do more than we think he can do" (Handler 1986: 79).

17. "There is no social world except as it is lived and experienced, and events become socially meaningful only when they are interpreted. . . . [Thus] ideology is constitutive, in that ideas about an event or relationship defined that activity, much as the rules about a game define a move or a victory in that game" (Merry 1986: 254).

18. In all three examples, the patient, parent, and client shared the work. Cooperation and trust would be much more difficult if financial incentives were perverse. Surgeons, most of the time, are not paid to talk.

19. This assumption, of course, is questionable. It can be argued that the goals of these programs are to maintain poverty and dependency—that the programs are designed to fail (Handler and Hasenfeld 1991).

BIBLIOGRAPHY

Abel, Richard, ed. 1982. *The Politics of Informal Justice*, Vols. 1, 2. New York: Academic Press.

Abel, Richard. 1985. Risk as an Area of Struggle. 83 *Michigan Law Rev.*, 772.

Adler, Michael, and Stewart Asquith, eds. 1981. *Discretion and Welfare*. London: Heinemann.

Arendt, Hannah. 1986. Communicative Power. In *Power*, ed. S. Lukes, 59–74. New York: New York Univ. Press.

Bachrach, Peter, and Morton Baratz. 1962. The Two Faces of Power. 56 *American Political Science Rev.*, 947–52.

———. 1970. *Power and Poverty: Theory and Practice*. New York: Oxford Univ. Press.

Bachrach, Peter, and Aryeh Botwinick. 1992. *Power and Empowerment: A Radical Theory of Participatory Democracy*. Philadelphia: Temple Univ. Press.

Baier, Annette. 1986. Trust and Antitrust. 96 *Ethics*, 231–60.

Barber, Bernard. 1983. *The Logic and Limits of Trust*. New Brunswick, NJ: Rutgers Univ. Press.

Bardach, Eugene, and Robert Kagan. 1982. *Going by the Book: The Problem of Regulatory Unreasonableness*. Philadelphia: Temple Univ. Press.

Bernstein, Richard. 1985. *Beyond Objectivism and Relativism: Science, Hermaneutics, and Praxis*. Philadelphia: Univ. of Pennsylvania Press.

Brodkin, Evelyn. 1987. Policy Politics: If We Can't Govern, Can We Manage? 102 *Political Science Quarterly*, 571.

Bumiller, Kristin. 1988. *The Civil Rights Society: The Social Construction of Victims*. Baltimore: Johns Hopkins Univ. Press.

Clegg, Stewart. 1989. *Frameworks of Power*. Newbury Park, CA: Sage.

Dahl, Robert. 1986. Power as the Control of Behavior. In *Power*, ed. S. Lukes, 37–58. New York: New York Univ. Press.

Delgado, Richard. 1985. Fairness and Formality: Minimizing the Risk of Prejudice in Alternative Dispute Resolution. 1985 *Wisconsin Law Rev.*, 1359.

Edelman, Murray. 1971. *Politics as Symbolic Action: Mass Arousal and Quiescence*. Chicago: Markham Publishing.

———. 1988. *Constructing the Political Spectacle*. Chicago: Univ. of Chicago Press.

Ellwood, David. 1988. *Poor Support*. New York: Basic Books.

Ewick, Patricia, and Susan Silbey. 1992. Conformity, Contestation, and Resistance: An Account of Legal Consciousness. 26 *New England Law Rev.*, 73.

Felstiner, William, Richard Abel, and Austin Sarat. 1980–81. The Emergence and Transformation of Disputes: Naming, Blaming, Claiming. 15 *Law and Society Rev.*, 631.

Foucault, Michel. 1986. Disciplinary Power and Subjection. In *Power*, ed. S. Lukes. New York: New York Univ. Press.

Freire, Paulo. 1985. *Pedagogy of the Oppressed*. New York: Continuum.

Gamson, William. 1968. *Power and Discontent*. Homewood, IL: Dorsey.

Garfinkel, Irwin, and Sara S. McLanahan. 1986. *Single Mothers and Their Children: A New American Dilemma*. Washington, DC: Urban Institute.

Gaventa, John. 1980. *Power and Powerlessness: Quiescence and Rebellion in an Appalachian Valley*. Urbana: Univ. of Illinois Press.

Goodin, Robert. 1988. *Reasons for Welfare: The Political Theory of the Welfare State*. Princeton, NJ: Princeton Univ. Press.

Gramsci, Antonio. 1971. *Selections from the Prison Notebooks*. New York: International.

Habermas, Jürgen. 1986. Hannah Arendt's Communications Concept of Power. In *Power*, ed. S. Lukes. New York: New York Univ. Press.

Handler, Joel. 1986. *The Conditions of Discretion: Autonomy, Community, Bureaucracy*. New York: Russell Sage.

———. 1989. Community Care for the Frail Elderly: A Theory of Empowerment. 50 *Ohio State Law Journal*, 541.

———. 1990a. *Law and the Search for Community*. Philadelphia: Univ. of Pennsylvania Press.

————. 1990b. Constructing the Political Spectacle: The Interpretation of Entitlements, Legalization, and Obligations in Social Welfare History. 56 *Brooklyn Law Rev.*, 899.

Handler, Joel, and Yeheskel Hasenfeld. 1991. *The Moral Construction of Poverty: American Welfare Reform.* London: Sage.

Handler, Joel, Ellen Hollingsworth, and Howard Erlanger. 1978. *Lawyers and the Pursuit of Legal Rights.* New York: Academic Press.

Hartmann, Heidi. 1987. Changes in Women's Economic and Family in Beneria. In *Women, Households, and the Economy*, ed. Lourdes and Stimpson, 33–58. New Brunswick, NJ: Rutgers Univ. Press.

Hasenfeld, Yeshekel. 1987. Power in Social Work Practice. *Social Service Review* (Sept.), 469–83.

————. 1992. *Human Services as Complex Organizations.* Englewood Cliffs, NJ: Prentice-Hall.

Hawkins, Keith. 1984. *Environment and Enforcement: Regulation and the Social Definition of Pollution.* Oxford: Clarendon Press.

Heller, Kirby, Wayne Holtzman, and Samuel Messick, eds. 1982. *Placing Children in Special Education: A Strategy for Equity.* Washington, DC: National Academy Press.

Himmelfarb, Gertrude. 1984. *The Idea of Poverty: England in the Early Industrial Age.* New York: Knopf.

Honneth, Axel. 1991. *The Critique of Power: Reflective Stages in a Critical Social Theory.* Boston: MIT Press.

Jencks, Christopher. 1992. *Rethinking Social Policy: Race, Poverty, and the Underclass.* Cambridge, MA: Harvard Univ. Press.

Kagan, Robert. 1984. Book Review: Inside Administrative Law. 84 *Columbia Law Rev.*, 816.

Katz, Jay. 1984. *The Silent World of Doctor and Patient.* New York: Free Press.

Keiffer, Charles. 1984. Citizen Empowerment: A Developmental Perspective. In President's Commission, *Prevention in Human Services*, vol. 3, pp. 9–36.

Lidz, Charles, and Alan Meisel. 1983. Informed Consent and the Structure of Medical Care. In President's Commission, *Making Health Care Decisions*, vol. 2, pp. 349–53.

Lipsky, Michael. 1980. *Street-Level Bureaucracy: Dilemmas of the Individual Public Services.* New York: Russell Sage.

Luhmann, Niklas. 1980. *Trust and Power.* New York: John Wiley.

————. 1986. The Self-Reproduction of Law and Its Limits. In *Dilemmas of Law in the Welfare State*, ed. G. Teubner, 111–27. Berlin: Walter de Gruyter.

Lukes, Steven. 1974. *Power: A Radical View.* London: Macmillan.

Lukes, Steven, ed. 1986. *Power.* New York: New York Univ. Press.

MacIntyre, Alasdair. 1984. The Virtues, the Unity of a Human Life and the Concept of a Tradition. In *Liberalism and Its Critics*, ed. M. Sandel, 125, 142–43. Oxford: Blackwell.

Mead, Lawrence. 1986. *Beyond Entitlement: The Social Obligations of Citizenship.* New York: Free Press.

————. 1992. *The New Politics of Poverty.* New York: Basic Books.

Menkel-Meadow, Carrie. 1984. Toward Another View of Legal Negotiation: The Structure of Problem Solving. 31 *UCLA Law Rev.*, 754.

Merry, Sally. 1986. Everyday Understandings of the Law in Working Class America. 13 *American Ethnologist*, 254.

Molotch, Harvey, and Deirdre Boden. 1985. Talking Social Structures: Discourse, Domination and the Watergate Hearings. 50 *American Sociological Rev.*, 273–88.

Myles, John. 1988. Postwar Capitalism and the Extension of Social Security into a Retirement Wage. In *The Politics of Social Policy in the United States*, ed. M. Weir, A. Orloff, and T. Skocpol, 265–92. Princeton, NJ: Princeton Univ. Press.

Nozick, Robert. 1974. *Anarchy, State, and Utopia*. New York: Basic Books.

Nussbaum, Martha. 1992. Justice for Women. *New York Review of Books*, Oct. 8, pp. 43–48.

Okin, Susan. 1991. *Justice, Gender, and the Family*. New York: Basic Books.

Parsons, Talcott. 1986. Power and the Social System. In *Power*, ed. S. Lukes. New York: New York Univ. Press.

Polsby, Nelson. 1963. *Community Power and Political Theory*. New Haven, CT: Yale Univ. Press.

Powell, Walter, and Paul DiMaggio, eds. 1991. *The New Institutionalism in Organizational Analysis*. Chicago: Univ. of Chicago Press.

President's Commission for the Study of Ethical Problems in Medicine and Biomedical and Behavioral Research (1983). *Making Health Care Decisions*, vols. 1, 2, 3. Washington, DC: Government Printing Office.

Rawls, John. 1985. Justice as Fairness: Political Not Metaphysical. 14 *Philosophy and Public Affairs*, 223–51.

Reich, Charles. 1964. The New Property. 73 *Yale Law Journal*, 733.

Schorr, Lisbeth. 1988. *Within Our Reach: Breaking the Cycle of Disadvantage*. New York: Doubleday.

Sen, Amartya. 1982. *Choice, Welfare, and Measurement*. London: Blackwell.

Shapiro, Susan. 1987. The Social Control of Impersonal Trust. 93 *American Journal of Sociology*, 623–58.

Simon, William. 1986. Rights and Redistribution in the Welfare System. 38 *Stanford Law Rev.*, 1431.

Smith, Gilbert. 1981. Discretionary Decision-Making in Social Work. In *Discretion and Welfare*, ed. M. Adler and S. Asquith, 47–68. London: Heinemann.

Stone, Deborah. 1984. *The Disabled State*. Philadelphia: Temple Univ. Press.

Unger, Roberto. 1975. *Knowledge and Politics*. New York: Free Press.

Weisbrod, Burton, with Joel Handler and Neil Komesar. 1978. *Public Interest Law: An Economic and Institutional Analysis*. Berkeley: Univ. of California Press.

White, Lucie. 1990. Subordination, Rhetorical Survival Skills, and Sunday Shoes: Notes on the Hearing of Mrs. G. 38 *Buffalo Law Rev.*, 1.

Wilson, William. 1987. *The Truly Disadvantaged*. Chicago: Univ. of Chicago Press.

Winkler, J. T. 1986. The Political Economy of Administrative Discretion. In *Discretion and Welfare*, ed. M. Adler and S. Asquith, 82–134. London: Heinemann.

Zimmerman, Marc. 1993. Empowerment Theory: Psychological, Organizational and Community Levels of Analysis. In *Handbook of Community Psychology*, ed. J. Rappaport and E. Seidman. New York: Plenum.

Zimmerman, Marc, and J. Rappaport. 1988. Citizen Participation, Perceived Control, and Psychological Empowerment. 16 *American Journal of Community Psychology*, 725–50.

Zimmerman, Joseph. 1990. Regulating Intergovernmental Relations in the 1990s. 509 *Annals of the AAPS* (May), 48–59.

JOHN BARRY'S CUSTODIAL RIGHTS: OF POWER, JUSTICE, AND COVERTURE

HENDRIK HARTOG

I. INTRODUCTION

What does legal history offer to the study of law and society? In particular, is there a legal historical "take" on power and justice? One could draw any of a number of approaches out of historical scholarship. Among them:

- A grand narrative about the evolution of legalized power and/or its restraint; or one about the coming to consciousness of moral sensibilities of justice and oppression.

- Alternatively, one might read history to capture decline: including a loss of faith in reason and an emergent bankruptcy of moral vision; history may demonstrate the drift away from justice, the subversion or corruption of moral aspirations.

- Or, perhaps a reading of history will reveal "justice" itself as a flawed aspiration, one that has substituted inadequately and incompletely for more satisfying, more democratic, more human aspirations.

- Or, history challenges grand narratives, undermines the plausibility of conventionally held beliefs in historical evolution. Historians often insist on the inherent and inevitable historicity—the time-boundedness—of apparently timeless concepts like power and justice, and they frequently reduce the apparently "meta" to any number of local struggles over and about power.

The community of legal historians could supply any of these. Seek and ye shall find.

But not here.

All I offer is a case study. In it I reveal a historian's characteristic interest in how particular individuals—dead people—attempted to confront and to exercise power and to do justice. Along the way, I exemplify the historian's characteristic exercise of power over his or her subjects. Some voices are emphasized; others are suppressed. I choose, perhaps I even construct, my subjects.

Two perspectives on justice animate this essay. Both are rooted in the workaday practices of history as a discipline.

The first perspective is framed by the claim of injustice. The evidence of legal history, what survives in past legal records, is often the voice of those who believed they had been treated unjustly, within the terms of their own legal world. One business of legal history, in its contextual and sociohistorical modes, has been to imagine and to describe the contexts for the experience of injustice.[1] What were the structures of values and belief that offered support for the worldviews of the unjustly treated? Where did they find the means—institutional, moral, religious—to resist injustice? Or, in the alternative, what powers worked to persuade them to accept injustice as legitimate or natural or inescapable? Can we, as historians, as persons inevitably located at a temporal remove from our subjects, come to understand past structures of power in all their contradictory grandeur, so that we can see our subjects as creative improvisers within the limits of their world, as creatures of habit and as transformative agents? Can we understand injustices that make no sense in our present-day world?

The second perspective flows out from the humanistic goals of historical practice. To want to write history means to want to treat others—dead people—justly, empathetically, to give voice to their coherence and their confusions, to recognize the sense they found in their lives, and to portray it. Those who left markings in the historical record often appeared unattractive to contemporaries. They may seem very like people we know and hate. Yet, as a discipline, in several senses of the word, history demands that we do justice to them, whether or not they received or deserved to receive justice in their own time. As historians, we listen quietly to people we might hide from if we met them today.

2. AN UNHAPPY MARRIAGE

John A. Barry was a widower when he married Eliza Ann Mercein in the spring of 1835. She was the daughter of a prominent New Yorker, Thomas

Mercein, a former labor leader then the head of the Equitable Insurance Company. Barry was a businessman from Nova Scotia. She was not young, at least twenty-five or twenty-six, perhaps older, and strongly attached to her parents' home in New York. He was forty-three.[2]

Their marriage represented the conclusion of protracted negotiations and a relatively long courtship. They had entered into an engagement in November 1834, including an informal antenuptial agreement that he would move his family to New York within one year after their marriage. The meaning of that promise would later be much litigated and debated. He assumed that after spending time in New York, he was free to go where he pleased, and that he had a right to expect his wife to follow and to obey. Legally, he was right, but he ought not to have assumed her acquiescence. In a number of anguished prenuptial letters she had told him of the conflicts she felt between her attachment to her father's home and to her personal identity and her desire to be with Barry. In one, she asked rhetorically, "Why our republican ceremonies should retain that monarchical word OBEY to trammel our free-born citizens." She could not, she wrote Barry in January 1835, imagine a lasting separation from "home," yet she wanted to "unite" her destiny with Barry's, and truly loved him.[3]

I don't really know much about either of them. Neither retains a place in history, aside from the custody suit to which they gave their names.[4] To our eyes he appears a bit rigid in his insistence on patriarchal prerogatives. Some of his contemporaries, including several judges, agreed with that judgment. Everyone regarded her as nervous and odd in her insistence that she had to live in her father's house.[5]

There were conflicts from the beginning of their marriage. He, according to one judge's reconstruction of their life together, had supposed that "all was to be authority with him"; she had assumed that "all was to be accommodation to her." Instead, they both were "led to the irresistible conclusion that there is no perfection short of Heaven" (8 Paige's Ch. 57).

They moved back to New York in May 1836 as agreed, after having spent exactly one year in Liverpool, Nova Scotia. Thomas Mercein provided capital to help Barry open a store selling lamps, glass, and china on Broadway, which within a year went bankrupt during the Panic of 1837. Barry then proposed that he and his wife return to Liverpool, where he had been a prominent merchant and a member of the provincial assembly. In the spring of 1838 he returned to Nova Scotia with the four children from his first marriage to start anew in business, while she remained in New York with their two infants. He visited New York a few weeks later to arrange Eliza's move to Nova Scotia and, evidently, to try to gain some financial assistance from his father-in-law. She refused to help him talk to her father and announced that she would not leave New York.

A few days later, on June 7, 1838, they both signed a "separation agreement," one he later claimed he had drafted knowing that it was unenforceable and "illegal."[6] The agreement declared that neither party then wished for a final separation. He "agreed" that in the event of a final separation he would relinquish his parental rights over their infant daughter, Mary, while retaining sole custodial rights over their four-year-old son. He then returned to Nova Scotia, still hoping that she would soon follow.

Later in the year, Barry came again to New York and picked up his son who was then with Eliza Barry at the Mercein residence. In a long pamphlet he wrote in 1839 to defend his actions, Barry explained that he took the child in order to convince his wife to follow him to Nova Scotia. To those who challenged the propriety of using the child as bait, he responded: "[T]he child was mine. I had a right to take it [*sic*], and no one had any right to complain" (Barry 1839: 50). And evidently his wife and father-in-law agreed, for they gave the older child up without a struggle.

But when, a few months later, he demanded the return of Mary, the baby, Eliza Barry and Thomas Mercein resisted. And in the summer of 1839 John Barry brought the first of a series of habeas corpus writs in the New York courts for the return of wife and infant child to his custody. These writs were uniformly directed at Thomas Mercein, who, Barry alleged, was unlawfully detaining his dependents and interfering with his rights. Early on, Chancellor Reuben Walworth ruled against Barry, in an elaborate opinion including a detailed narrative of the marriage. Although the New York Supreme Court, by legal repute the leading common law court in the United States, twice upheld Barry's rights, each time their decision was overruled by the New York Court for the Correction of Errors. In all, Barry sued out seven writs, all of which eventually failed.[7]

The last failure, of a writ brought in federal district court for the return of the daughter, was ratified by the United States Supreme Court in 1846. According to Chief Justice Taney, the court lacked authority to review the district court's decision. The dispute, he wrote, was about the "custody, care, and society" of a child. The Judiciary Act of 1789 granted appellate jurisdiction only where "rights of property" were involved, "where the matter in dispute" had "a known and certain value, which can be proved and calculated, in the ordinary mode of a business transaction." Yet, in this instance the matter in dispute was "evidently utterly incapable of being reduced to any pecuniary standard of value," as it rose "superior to money considerations." A child was not to be reduced to a cash value. It could never be property (5 How. 120).

John Barry's custody case has come down to us as the leading child custody case of the nineteenth century, as authority for the then new proposition that children are not property. It is still cited for the notion of *parens patriae*, the idea that public authorities have the right, independent of parental rights, to make decisions in the best interest of a child. It is one of a small number of early cases which are seen as undoing a previous regime of father's rights.[8]

Close examination of this (to twentieth-century eyes) ordinary story of marital discord, together with a reading of the large number of judicial opinions which the conflict generated, advances and complicates an ongoing inquiry by legal historians, social historians, and academic lawyers into the historical emergence of a vision of children as not-property. This inquiry has been driven by our perception of the overwhelming rightness of seeing child custody as different than custody over things. The distinction between custody rights and property rights has been a constitutive feature of modern American family law. The conventional wisdom of family law incorporates an optimistic history. That history declares that, once upon a time, fathers ruled, but that by the time of *Mercein* children ceased to be seen as the legal possession of their fathers. Courts learned to dispose of children according to their understanding of the child's best interests, which usually meant vesting custody in mothers. The most important historical study of American family law, Michael Grossberg's *Governing the Hearth* (1985), has modified that history significantly. It demonstrates that the "best interest of the child" standard and the "tender years" rule of thumb, both used by nineteenth-century courts to justify mother's custody, were viewed as extensions of the "patriarchal" power of American courts. Judges did not transfer rights and powers from fathers to mothers; they asserted power in themselves over traditional patriarchal prerogatives, and then allowed mothers to receive children contingent on their meeting judicially defined standards of maternal conduct. Yet Grossberg, like his predecessors, takes the undoing of a father's possessory rights over his children as the significant result of the era of *Mercein,* a result determinative of modern understandings of family law.[9]

Little in this chapter detracts much from that overarching history. Indeed, I want to stress my indebtedness to Grossberg in particular. My concerns here are different. What does the Barry case tell us about the received regime of legal expectations that surrounded nineteenth-century domestic life? In particular, what did it mean to be a father who could not sustain his identity as parent?

At the heart of the case was John Barry's obsession with his rights.[10] He felt slandered by Chancellor Walworth's 1839 decision refusing his writ and wrote a sixty-five page self-defense of his character and legal rights. He felt personally affronted by the chancellor's judgment, shamed before a larger community. Although he was not a lawyer, he immersed himself in the minutiae of the old law of baron and feme and habeas corpus law and, thereafter, argued his own cases and wrote his own briefs. Was he a nut? Did he have a fool for a client?

Today, divorce lawyers "know" that mothers are frequently willing to give up various rights to which they may be entitled in order to ensure that they will retain custody over their children. This is a "fact" husbands' lawyers exploit and wives' lawyers try to mitigate in negotiating a divorce settlement. All understand that many mothers take threats to their custody as challenges to their personal identities. They regard custody as nonnegotiable (which means, of course, that it forces them to bargain from a position of weakness on other negotiable issues). Without custody, a mother may feel shamed, "lost," no longer a "real" mother.

I am not suggesting that John Barry's passionate involvement in his case was the same as that of modern mothers. Indeed, his actual relationship to his child was quite irrelevant to the issues at stake, as he viewed them. The comparison to modern maternal identity is worth raising, however, because it helps us understand the challenge to his identity posed by judicial attacks on "his" rights as the custodial parent. He should have been recognized as being a responsible adult, meaning a man who kept and cared for dependents under his legal control. Yet the courts denied him the recognition he deserved. Wives, all men agreed, moved with and obeyed their husbands; yet his wife did neither, although there was no basis for a legal separation. Fathers were the natural guardians and custodians of their children; yet his youngest child was kept from him. If those events were legal, what sort of a father and husband was he? Who was he?

Like Barry, all the judges who tried to resolve the substantive conflicts in the case knew that a custody case—meaning an attempt by a father to enforce a habeas corpus writ for the return of his child—concerned the identity of the father as a rights bearer within an ongoing marriage.[11] It was taken as given that the question of which parent was entitled to custody was intertwined with Mrs. Barry's claimed right to live apart from her husband. In fact, all but one of those judges saw it as raising precisely the issues that obsessed Barry. They understood that questions about the *parens patriae* jurisdiction of a court—of its equitable authority to settle custody in terms of the best interests of the child—arose within a context shaped by the settled priority of a married father's legal rights (rights drawn from the law of coverture).

The Barry case, which has been cited as a foundation of modern family law, remains a case comprehensible only within a traditional structure of marital rights and duties. Much had changed; much more was changing. Yet, the structure of traditional marriage still survived.

A. FATHER AGAINST FATHER

It is important to note what the case was not about. It was not about a mother's right to custody over her children. Indeed, it would still have been virtually impossible for a married woman to claim custody of her child as a matter of mother's rights.[12] Rather, the case was about a husband and father's legal capacity to maintain custodial control over his wife and children.

The case began, over and over again, with the return of a writ of habeas corpus ad subjiciendum.[13] The writ was always directed to Mercein, initially commanding him to bring both Eliza Barry and her infant daughter before the court, later only the daughter. Each time, Mercein would respond that he was not holding Mrs. Barry against her will, that she was free to come and go as she pleased, that there was, therefore, no unlawful imprisonment, no constraint on her personal liberty. If a writ of habeas corpus were to be directed against anyone, it should, according to Mercein, be made to Mrs. Barry herself, since the child was within her custody.

To this defense, Barry responded that his father-in-law's correspondence proved that Mercein was unlawfully restraining Eliza Barry and her daughter.[14] Because of him Eliza Barry remained inaccessible to her husband (as well as subject to her father's patriarchal control over his family). And that was the point, not her ostensible freedom to come and go as she pleased. Indeed, talk of her freedom to come and go as she pleased, talk of her legal right to stay at her father's, was all a form of non sequitur. Questions of her freedom and of her legal rights—more properly, questions of her status—depended, as Esek Cowen of the New York Supreme Court wrote in 1842, "upon a rule too elementary to require the adduction of authority; and too obvious to have been denied in the whole course of this particular controversy. . . . The principle is thus stated in *1 Black. Com. 468:* 'The very being or legal existence of the woman is suspended during the marriage, or, at least, is incorporated and consolidated into that of the husband.'" A father who kept wife and child away from her husband was interfering with the husband's rights, a wrongdoer, a tortfeasor. The rules of marriage, regarded as equivalent to coverture, meant that only Barry's will, his freedom, and his rights ought to be relevant to the question of the legal responsibility of his father-in-law for keeping his wife away from him (3 Hill 407).

Barry was legally mistaken in asking a court to enforce a writ of habeas corpus for the return of a wife against the wife's father. Even Cowen reluctantly conceded the point. In 1816, the New York Supreme Court had already held that a father did no legal wrong in taking in his married daughter.[15] John Barry might possess a theoretical right to Eliza Barry's custody, but American courts would uniformly deny a husband's right (or power) to invoke habeas corpus to compel an absent wife to return to him. No American court, according to Chancellor Walworth, had "any jurisdiction or authority, upon habeas corpus or otherwise, to compel a wife to return to the bed and board of her husband and to the performance of her conjugal duties, where she voluntarily absents herself from him, either with or without justifiable cause." No American court ever enforced a suit for restitution of conjugal rights, of the sort which was still theoretically available in the English ecclesiastical courts. The law required that Mrs. Barry be at "perfect liberty . . . to return to her husband, or to seek the protection of any other relative or friend who may think proper to assume the legal responsibility of affording her a shelter," in opposition to Barry's marital rights. Courts could not compel her to return; she was left "only responsible to her own conscience and to her God, for such a violation of her conjugal duties."[16]

Barry learned his legal lesson. After his writ for the return of Eliza was rejected by Chancellor Walworth in 1839, later writs only claimed the court's assistance in regaining the custody of his daughter. And yet, there was enough ambiguity in the law that Barry could be forgiven for having assumed that he had a right to the writ for his wife.[17]

In any event, the fact that courts refused to enforce the writ against Mr. Mercein for the return of Mrs. Barry did not mean that judges thought

Mercein was not the appropriate person to be sued for the return of Barry's child. The question was not, according to Justice Bronson, whether the child was actually suffering under imprisonment, but whether there was "that kind of restraint which defeats the right of the [infant's] father." Mercein had made it impossible for his son-in-law, John Barry, to see his child, except on terms "which a proper self respect made inadmissible." He could see Mary, but he could not take her under his care and protection. Such a restraint defeated "the right of the father to the custody of his child" and laid "a proper foundation for asking redress by habeas corpus." Cowen was characteristically blunt in explaining why Mercein—not Mrs. Barry—was the proper recipient of the writ: "It is impossible to avoid seeing that, if Mr. Barry is entitled to the custody of his child, Mr. Mercein is, in fact, the principal offender. Had his hand been withdrawn, it is morally certain that the relator [Barry] would have been put to encounter no serious difficulty in reclaiming the custody of his child without a law suit." Without her father's help and protection, economic necessity would have driven Mrs. Barry back into her husband's household, and with her would have come their daughter (25 Wend. 80; 3 Hill 406–7; see Barry 1839: 8).[18]

B. JUDGES' VERSIONS

The legal right of Eliza Barry to live apart from her husband remained the central issue for courts deciding who should have custody of their daughter. According to Chancellor Walworth, "if [John Barry's] misconduct toward the partner of his bed and his bosom," had "furnished her with good cause for seeking again the protection of the paternal roof," no law, "either human or divine," required the judge "to remove this infant from her arms, or from the same friendly shelter." The judges of the New York Supreme Court posed the problem more narrowly and more legalistically: only a finding that she had effectively established a right to a legal separation could possibly justify her claimed right to the custody of her child.

How could she establish her right to live apart from her husband? The received law gave her only two related options: either demonstrate Barry's mistreatment and abuse of her or a clearly stated and legally binding separation agreement (usually known as a separate maintenance agreement). In effect, a contest over custody became a contest over the legal right of a wife to separate from her husband. And that depended entirely on his conduct. Unless Mrs. Barry and her father could prove that John Barry had acted to divest himself of his rightful authority over wife and child—either through misconduct or contractual agreement—the child was presumptively his.[19]

It is important to understand that, from the very beginning of the nineteenth-century, wives had been awarded custody of their children in New York and in other American jurisdictions.[20] The received legal culture of early nineteenth-century America did not grant husbands unfettered or unquestioned custodial rights over their children. Bad husbands could lose custody rights, along with other rights. Even a patriarchal conservative like Greene C. Bronson of the New York Supreme Court acknowledged that father's rights were not absolute and inalienable.[21]

And yet, courts took custody over dependents as a central attribute of a husbandly identity.[22] A father could lose his rights, but in a just legal order he should not be required to subject his rights to the vagaries of judicial sentiments about appropriate child care, about the "best interests of the child," about who was the better parent. Bronson, reflecting the orthodox view, assumed that the goal of the court was to provide for the welfare of the child, but "knew" that the law had already settled that the father was preferred by that standard, absent proof of such "grossly immoral conduct, as shows him plainly disqualified for the proper discharge of parental duties" (25 Wend. 72–73).

The child was Barry's, absent a demonstration of limited circumstances that justified divesting him and transferring what was his to others. The theory of a writ of habeas corpus for the return of a child implicitly paralleled that of an action in ejectment, the typical form of action to settle questions of possessory rights in real estate. In ejectment, the plaintiff (through an elaborate structure of fictions) puts before the court his title in the land, forcing the defendant—who is characterized as having wrongfully ejected the plaintiff—to challenge the quality of the plaintiff's title, rather than putting into evidence the defendant's competing claim. The plaintiff can lose because of misuse or nonuse, or because his title had never been perfected. He should not lose because of a comparative judgment about whose title is preferred.[23]

And yet, Chancellor Walworth's opinion, the most famous and most quoted of the many opinions contributed, began by insisting on his equitable obligation to conduct a "summary inquiry" into the "relative merits or demerits" of the conduct of each separated spouse. According to Walworth, a writ of habeas corpus was not the proper instrument to test the "legal right" of a party to guardianship or custody (that is to say, the property right in the child). All the court could do under the writ was decide whether the child was being held under unlawful restraint. In making that determination, the court ought to exercise its discretion and its moral judgment. Walworth was at pains to emphasize his disproval of informal separations by couples. It was, he wrote, "contrary to public policy to allow the husband or the wife to withdraw from the duty of matrimonial cohabitation for any slight causes, which do not endanger the personal safety of the party: as such withdrawal is wholly repugnant to good morals and to the injunctions of the divine lawgiver." And he resolved to "set" his "face" against any attempt on the part of married persons to throw off the duties of the marriage contract. Still, where, as in this case, parents were already living apart from each other, an inquiry into the circumstances of their separation was inevitable (8 Paige's Ch. 55–56).

Walworth's version of the story of their marriage began with John Barry's agreement that the couple would return within one year after the wedding to live in New York City "for the future." The chancellor understood that this was not a legally enforceable agreement, since it would have changed a fundamental term of the marital contract, that is, the husband's right to decide where the marital home should be. Yet, it was evident that neither Eliza nor her parents would have gone through with the marriage absent his agreement, and the chancellor regarded it as constituting something of a moral obligation on John Barry. More importantly, it evidenced her extraordinarily strong and "uncontrollable" attachment to her parental home, something John Barry should have understood when he married her (8 Paige's Ch. 57–58).

Chancellor Walworth proceeded to give a highly colored and romantic picture of the marriage of John and Eliza, an account designed to show how both were "at fault" in the failure of their marriage. At first, Eliza had loved her husband, "as few have ever loved before." Her letters to and about him revealed "the strong and convincing language of nature and of truth—the natural language of a heart which must have been perfectly satisfied." John too loved his wife intensely, although the chancellor thought that he detected from the beginning some harshness towards his wife, a hasty temper, explained, in part, by his financial difficulties. Such a temperament would not necessarily make him an unkind husband, although it would "naturally" require "more prudence and circumspection on the part of the wife" (8 Paige's Ch. 60).

Three events dominated Walworth's narration, all of them events about which Eliza had testified. Each of them revealed what the chancellor termed John Barry's "unworthy desire to enforce implicit obedience to an unreasonable command, with the view of triumphing over her."

The first occurred while they were still living in Liverpool, in February 1836. Eliza had accidently swallowed a peach pit. John thought her life was in danger, and he consulted a doctor, who prescribed cream of tartar and sulfur mixed with honey. She refused to take the medicine, as she hated sulfur. John regarded her refusal as "a mere whim." The feelings of both became "too much excited," and it became a matter of principle on John's part, as to which of them should give way:

> For the husband does not appear then to have learned that the relinquishment of his legal right to enforce obedience, on the part of a most devoted and affectionate wife, could not have detracted in the least from his true dignity, under the circumstances in which she was placed, even if he was fully satisfied that her refusal was the result of mere caprice. (8 Paige's Ch. 61–62)

He did not do anything to make her take the medicine, but he declared, indiscreetly, that he would leave their bedroom until she complied.

That night he slept on the sofa in another room,[24] and he stayed away until the following afternoon, when she agreed to take the medicine. "[U]pon which he immediately took her in his arms and kissed her, said she was a good girl, and carried her to her room." Yet, the chancellor noted, it was evident that she was not reconciled to her situation, for she had said, in front of a servant, that his and her happiness was now at an end. She, wrote the chancellor, had yet to learn "that the true dignity of a wife cannot be violated by submission to her husband" (8 Paige's Ch. 62).

The second and third "difficulties" were ones in which John Barry was, according to the chancellor, more "clearly" in the wrong. Both occurred in the months after their return to New York City. The second took place shortly after the birth of their first child, while Eliza was still bedridden. Her mother, who was acting as nurse, had been called back to her home. John had promised to take the mother's place, but he, apparently angered that Eliza had spent two dollars for a cot without his permission, left her alone with her infant. The third, a few months later, involved an argument between the two of them after their servant Dolly gave notice. John, who thought her "the best servant that ever lived," evidently blamed Eliza. After their quarrel, he went away and stayed at his offices for ten days, until she came and "sued for peace." To the chancellor, who tried to make "every allowance for the necessary coloring which a party to such a contest would be likely to give it," John's conduct was "overbearing and cruel" (8 Paige's Ch. 63–64).

None of these events were sufficient to "sever the strong cord of affection" that bound her to him. Yet, they had led her to the unwarranted suspicion that he was unfaithful and no longer loved her. And she fell into what we (looking behind the chancellor's ornate language) can only assume was a period of emotional depression.[25]

Then John Barry's business failed, and he began to look around for new employment. Nothing was found in the New York area. So in the spring of 1838 he arranged for Eliza and their two infant children to remain with her father, while he went to Nova Scotia with his four elder daughters, to look for work. According to the chancellor, John was probably not aware at the time of Eliza's unwillingness to return to Nova Scotia, "or of the half formed resolution which then existed in her mind that she would not again leave the immediate neighborhood of her father's residence." Thus his surprise when he returned to New York a few weeks later and found her unwilling to accompany him back. He, irritated, took his baggage to a boarding house, where he received a letter from her stating her reliance on their "antenuptial" agreement. He then wrote her "the fatal answer" renouncing her forever (a declaration that he soon retracted). And on June 7, 1838, he prepared a document called a separation agreement.

If, wrote the chancellor, John Barry "had always treated his wife with kindness, I am not prepared to say that it would not have been her duty, notwithstanding the ante-nuptial agreement and her strong filial attachments, to have followed him any part of the world where he had a reasonable prospect of bettering his condition." But, given what had transpired, he had no right to insist on her consent. Walworth did not believe that grounds existed to justify a "final" or formal separation of John from Eliza. In particular, the agreement was void, on the grounds that it was a contract for a future separation, rather than an agreement determining the consequences of a present separation.[26]

Still, it no longer was her duty to go with him to a foreign land to reside. Enough had occurred to justify her "both legally and morally," to refuse "for the present to place herself under his entire control, in a land of strangers" (8 Paige's Ch. 68).

John Barry's various acts of unkindness and authoritarianism played a part in this decision, as perhaps did some judicial parochialism.[27] But above all else was John Barry's adamant (and perhaps, neurotic) insistence on his rights. He had never learned what the sentimental chancellor regarded as the crucial lesson for success in marriage. Instead, he endangered "his former high standing, both as a gentleman and a christian, by an indiscreet attempt to enforce what he believed to be his marital and paternal rights" (8 Paige's Ch. 61, 65–68).

Thus, Eliza Barry was "equitably" justified in her refusal to accompany John to Nova Scotia, and thus, she was not living in a state of separation which should be regarded as illegal and immoral. Thus, her child was not in the custody of persons of such a legal character as would require her removal for her best interests, and thus, according to the chancellor, it was within his discretion to deny the writ of habeas corpus. Since a mother, "all other things being equal, is the most proper person to be entrusted with such a charge in relation to an infant of this tender age. And where no sufficient reasons exist for depriving her of the care and nurture of her child, it would not be a proper exercise of discretion in any court to violate the law of nature in this respect." The child was not improperly restrained (8 Paige's Ch. 69–70).

The judges of the New York Supreme Court, who reviewed the chancellor's decision on appeal in 1840, thought the chancellor had misconceived the nature of legal or equitable discretion. And they reversed him unanimously. That decision was then reversed by the ostensibly democratic Court for the Correction of Errors, which reinstated the chancellor's holding.[28] But Greene Bronson's opinion for the New York Supreme Court remained for a generation a significant source of child custody doctrine. The issue was not open, he thought. The New York Supreme Court had recently decided a number of cases on consistent principles, from which it had never wavered. In controversies between husband and wife, the husband had the better title to the custody of minor children:

> The law regards him as the head of the family; obliges him to provide for its wants; and commits the children to his charge, in preference to the claims of the mother or any other person. . . . Whatever sympathy we may feel for this lady, or however strongly we may wish that the relator [Barry] had relinquished his claim to one of the two children, we have no choice but to administer the law as we find it. (25 Wend. 72–73)

The judges of the New York Supreme Court agreed with John Barry that Eliza Barry had not established her legal right to a separation, and therefore had not succeeded in challenging Barry's custodial rights. According to Bronson, Barry was not foreclosed from asserting his custodial rights by the agreement he had drafted in June 1838. He agreed with Walworth that such an agreement, to provide for a future separation, while the parties were in a state of marriage, was presumptively void. The narrative of the marriage (laid out in the chancellor's opinion) revealed a number of incidents of anger and unkindness on Barry's part, incidents indicative of what we today might consider mental cruelty. Barry was unceasing in his insistence on his legal rights and rightful authority as a husband and father. Yet, as even the chancellor had reluctantly conceded, nothing had occurred by the summer of 1838 legally sufficient to authorize a decree of separation. Even if Mrs. Barry had been able to charge her husband with those "grossly immoral acts which authorize a divorce," wrote Justice Bronson, it did not necessarily follow that she would be entitled to the child. But she had "no such heavy accusations to bring against her husband." Instead, she relied "on a highly wrought picture of their family jars," in which surely "there were faults upon both sides," and which, "in any point of view," did not "form a proper subject for judicial inquiry." They were merely part of "the many little things which go to make up the happiness or misery of married life" (25 Wend. 75).

In 1842, on a renewed application by John Barry for a writ of habeas corpus, the New York Supreme Court again voted in Barry's favor.[29] The child ought to be delivered to John Barry. Again, the New York Court of Errors reversed, holding against John Barry. But again, the opinions of the New York Supreme Court in 1842 remained significant authority on the developing law of child custody, even though the New York Court of Errors had the final word on the case.[30]

In 1842, Cowen, in particular, used the issue of the purported separation agreement as an opportunity to vent his general disgust with the liberal trends he saw around him. To Cowen, coverture meant that a man could not grant anything to his wife, "for the grant would be to suppose her separate existence; and to covenant with her would be only to covenant with himself." Even if imagined as a legal delegation of power, such an agreement was inherently revocable (and, obviously, in this case had been actually revoked) (3 Hill 408, quoting Blackstone).[31] More important still, children were a special kind of property (like property held in trusteeship or property affected with a public interest). A father was obligated, because of the "character and condition which by law results from the state of marriage," to provide and to care for them, and he should not be able to evade his responsibility by contracting away their custody. Private agreements should not be used to avoid public duties (3 Hill 411).[32]

Cowen's 1842 opinion directly challenged the chancellor's efforts, as Cowen put it, "to oppose the supposed necessities of nurture to the demands of law." In 1839 and 1840, when the child was just weaned, perhaps a temporary denial of the relator's rights had been justified. But in 1842, "Why should this child be longer withheld?" Barry had a right to train his child "to serve him affectionately in the business of his household," and he had a right to see her "properly educated." Indeed, such training was, according to Cowen, "essential to the child's welfare."

Conversely, the claim that a daughter should be left under the control of a mother who voluntarily separated herself from her husband, would, according to Cowen, "if allowed, work an entire subversion of his right." For one thing, legal recognition of her claim would teach the child an immoral lesson about the capacity of dependents (like wife and daughters) to escape from their rightful obligations to their superiors. For another, such recognition would confirm the mother, Mrs. Barry, in her wrongful course of action, in refusing to return to her husband. The claim, in any event, was unjustified in fact. Whatever may have been his situation earlier, in 1842 Barry commanded "a comfortable home with adequate means for supporting the child." He was "at the head of an interesting family, mostly I believe daughters, . . . bred under his care in the best manner; some of them from childhood to age." That he was "qualified, and eminently so, for the moral and mental instruction of this child" was "clear" (3 Hill 414–15).

C. JOHN BARRY'S VERSION

Barry himself found every element of the chancellor's 1839 opinion outrageous and personally offensive and wrote a long and chaotic pamphlet to explain the threat it posed to his character and public identity. Only danger to the child—a charge not made—or immoral character—a charge refuted—would justify denying his right to custody of his daughter. He was not one of those "foul characters" contemplated by the law. He was, rather, a kindly, admittedly imperfect, husband, who had tried "to conciliate, and to bring to something like reasonable terms, in a peaceful and private manner, one of the most unreasonable—and inexorable, because one of the most romantic of women" (Barry 1839: 27, 44).[33]

The chancellor's judgment had been twisted by Eliza Barry's "female artfulness," which overwhelmed his "moral courage." Walworth had seen her as "a very angel," as "all love, affection, and forgiveness." But she wasn't. And in allowing her to retain the custody of their daughter, in declaring that Eliza was, all things being equal, the proper person to be entrusted with this charge, the chancellor was denying "unpalatable scriptural truth" and violating "natural" laws. The chancellor had done more, Barry noted, than even Fanny Wright might imagine could be done to "break down the bulwarks, and loosen all the foundations of social and domestic life, and consequently of all civil society." And in denying John Barry the legal guardianship and protection of his children, he had imposed on Barry a "thralldom," a form of bondage, and inflicted on him "a suffering and an anguish which only the Almighty himself possesses the prerogative to impose" (Barry 1839: 13–14, 33).[34]

Much in Barry's polemic imagined him as victimized by the dangerous powers of women. Behind John Barry's misogyny, however, was the question of his rights. Barry believed that he had rights, and, he wrote, "I am well advised that this belief is correct. This sustains me in my endeavors for their attainment." If he did have rights in his child, and even the chancellor seemed to concede the point, then how could the chancellor deny their enforcement? In hearing the writ of habeas corpus, the chancellor was acting as a law judge, not as a court in equity. There was no foundation for the kind of equitable discretion that the chancellor claimed as his. Barry quoted from the opinion of the antislavery northern judge who had enforced the rights of slaveholders in the famous case of the Amistad: "Whatever private motives the Court may have, or whatever may be their feelings on this subject," they were "not to be brought into view, in deciding on this subject." It was "the province and the duty of the Court, to determine what the laws are, and not what it is desirable that they should be" (Barry 1839: 47, 9).

The chancellor had written that he was not settling a question of guardianship or of legal right. He was only deciding whether the child was being held under such restraint as to justify the intervention of the court. Yet, the writ of habeas corpus was the means by which a father's legal rights were tested. If the writ were refused it must be because of proven misconduct on the father's part, as a husband. When the chancellor held that Barry was not entitled to enforce the writ, he held, according to Barry, that he was an unfit husband and father, that he was a bad man, dishonored, lacking in virtue. Otherwise the writ would have been enforced.

Worse yet, the chancellor entrusted the child to a mother who the chancellor acknowledged did not have grounds for a legal separation, a wife who had left her husband because of what the chancellor himself labeled a monomania about staying close to her father's family. Thus the decision granted rights to a wife who was committing a legal and moral wrong, a woman who was by definition unfit to have custody over a child.

Barry identified a number of mistakes in Walworth's narration of his married life. In the first place, Walworth wrote as if the antenuptial "agreement" that the couple would move to and live in New York City had some sort of legal effect. Barry, following standard doctrine, insisted that such an agreement was clearly unenforceable because it changed a fundamental term of marriage. Further, even if it were theoretically enforceable, it had been complied with when John and Eliza moved back to New York City one year after their marriage. He was under no legal or moral obligation to remain in New York in perpetuity. Indeed, no just legal order would ever compel such a reading. He had a right to move where he chose in pursuit of his livelihood, and he had a right to expect his wife to accompany him.[35]

In the second place, the chancellor gave inordinate weight to small and inconsequential conflicts, conflicts that Barry himself had forgotten. Such conflicts occurred within the private sphere of marriage. "For sound reasons of public policy," they should never become grounds for separation. These conflicts were, according to Eliza's own testimony, quickly resolved. If so, how could such petty stories become the foundation for her right to live apart? In any event, these stories hardly demonstrated misconduct on his part. For example, when Eliza Barry recounted the tale of their argument over the servant Dolly, John Barry had "thought his Honor might possibly conclude . . . that there had probably been manifested, on her part, rather too much pertinacity and obstinacy, in maintaining her asserted claim to equality." She had testified that he had responded to her claim with the assertion that there can be "no more two equals in one house than two Gods Almighty in the universe." He did not think that that was anything he would ever have said. It was not his style of address. But even if it were, it did not sound like a man "drunk or demoniac." Rather, it appeared merely a statement of God's truth. And it was certainly not an expression of violence (Barry 1839: 31).

Barry particularly resented the chancellor's notion that his very insistence on his patriarchal rights justified her separation. That insistence was not at all inconsistent with a course of conduct toward Eliza Barry marked by "liberality and generosity." He never intended to violate anyone else's rights, nor to deal with them on any basis other than that of fairness and kindness. But in the prosecution of his rights, he would not be intimidated or sidetracked by the chancellor's "bugbear" (Barry 1839: 51).

Most of all, Barry's pamphlet screams his dismay at the challenge the chancellor's holding posed to his constitutional identity as a husband and father. Any right-thinking man, faced with a like situation, would have done as he had. "Show me then a father, who looks at the associations by which his child is surrounded,—the relative situation of himself too, and discovers them to be like mine, and if he do not feel as I do, I would not own him a brother of the species." He continued:

> Where is the man—having the spirit of a man—deserving the name of a man, who would yield his child! I confess I am not he. . . . No, it cannot, must not, shall not be done. The object now is, to keep it from me in New-York during its tender years:—bring it up of course in hatred of its father, and ignorant of its brother and sisters. Then, at some future day, when I have to leave the other extended interests of my family, and come for the sixth time to the city and ask again for my child, I shall be refused. I shall probably have to get two or three more writs of habeas corpus, or have again to take it by force, and be published as a Man-stealer, and a Robber. If I succeed in bringing it before the Recorder [city judge] again, his Honor it may be supposed will have it stood in Court, and enquire of itself, with whom it will reside? Can the answer be doubted? It knows its mother; the father is to it, but as any other stranger, and I may return whence I came, and be forever cut off from a darling child, having its inalienable claims on me, however, as every other of my children. No! I never will submit to this state of things, until I know, of a truth, that such is the law of this land; yes, to use no uncommon phrase, of this "land of law." But I know it is not—millions of other interests, similar to mine, are to be protected by the same laws, and, I am persuaded, will be solemnly protected. (Barry 1839: 47–48)

3. MODERN VERSIONS

John Barry was wrong. He lost. And, what is more, the law of child custody soon assumed that the decisions "who gets the child" and "who is the better parent" were theoretically independent from conclusions as to fault in marriage or rights to separation (or divorce). In Michael Grossberg's well-known image, the patriarchal authority of husband-fathers was assumed by judges, who became judicial patriarchs in control of the custody decision. Thus the dominant story of American family law—like the accepted story of family history—has been of a regime of patriarchal rights soon overwhelmed by the power of child-centered public officials.[36] Judges, like other child savers, drew on a liberal critique of parental power rooted in eighteenth-century educational theory, as well as a vague but potent analogy between wrongful power within the institution of the family and the institution of slavery. Particularly after the Civil War, it became important to say that children were "not property."[37]

We can see important elements of this "modern" point of view in one published opinion in the Mercein proceedings. This is Senator Paige's opinion as a member of the Court of Errors in 1840, which reversed the decision of the Supreme Court in John Barry's favor. The "great principle," which Paige alone at that time found running through American and English cases, was that judicial attention ought principally to be directed to "the benefit and welfare of the infant." The necessary result of this principle was that questions of custody required the exercise of judicial discretion.

Like the chancellor, he believed "the mother is the most proper person to be entrusted with the custody of a child of this tender age." He also shared the chancellor's sense that a good father would not press his claims to custody, if inconsistent with the child's best interests (25 Wend. 105–6). Yet he rooted those judgments in a broader statement of judicial authority and in a different political vision of the nature of parental rights. "By the law of nature," Paige began, a father has no rights superior to those of a mother. All he has is the power he may be able to arrogate to himself over others in his family. With the coming of civil society, the power of the "chief of a family" was transferred to the government of a nation, which then delegated to parents "such portion of the sovereign power . . . , subject to such restrictions and limitations" as was thought "proper to prescribe." No parental power existed independent of the state. And when civil authority deprived a father of parental authority, the decision did not "come in conflict with or subvert any of the principles of the natural law." A child was, first of all, a citizen of the country of its birth, "entitled to the protection of that government." And thus, in custody decisions the "welfare, comfort and interests" of the child should be determinative (25 Wend. 103).[38]

Did Paige's opinion signal victory over an older, property-centered conception of child custody? Perhaps. Yet, I want to caution against reading that opinion as the "right" answer, in light of a familiar trajectory of legal or constitutional change.

Contemporaries read the opinions as leaving the law of child custody in a deeply confused state. In 1841, Judge Oakley gratefully denied a new writ of habeas corpus brought by John Barry, on grounds of *res judicata*. If he had to decide the substantive issues, he wrote, he would have had a difficult time of it, because "The legal principles . . . have not been rendered more certain than they were by the elaborate but apparently conflicting opinions" of the high court judges. "[W]hat might at one period have been considered settled law has been thrown so far into serious doubt."[39] In his 1845 treatise, Edward Mansfield characterized the traditional rule of father's rights as barbaric and described *People v. Mercein* as unsettling and overturning that rule. To Mansfield, the case was "stronger" than ones involving divorce because Eliza Barry had concededly separated "voluntarily and purposely" from her husband (and thus could be regarded as having violated her marital vows). Nor was the child, at least in 1842, so young as to "need" the care of her mother. Yet, Mansfield's statement of the holding of the case was quite narrow: "where the mother *was not morally guilty,* and a separation took place between the parents," courts would give the custody of *daughters* to the mother.[40]

Throughout the rest of the nineteenth century (indeed, into the twentieth century), litigants and judges constantly claimed the various opinions in *People v. Mercein* as authority—for every side and position. The case was authority for the state's interest in child care. It was also authority for parental autonomy and authority. It was relied on by numbers of women asserting the propriety and legality of a court determination that child custody should be given to them. It was also cited by courts and lawyers that wished to reaffirm father's rights.[41] In his *Treatise on the Constitutional Limitations,* Thomas Cooley concluded a short discussion of the use of the writ of habeas corpus in domestic relations by noting that, on the one hand, father's right was "generally recognized as best." That right, however, was not absolute and had to "yield to what appears to be for the interest of the child." Courts had great discretionary authority, and "the tendency of modern decisions" was to expand that authority. "Barry's case" was then cited as primary authority, since it exhausted "all the law on the subject" (Cooley 1868: 348).[42]

Specialized treatises agreed on the significance of the case. To Rollin Hurd, it embodied the "spirit of the American cases" that attempted to resolve conflicting claims of parents for the custody of their children, although he also recognized that it was more "remarkable for great research and ability displayed in the discussion of the questions involved," and for the "exceeding pertinacity with which it was pursued by the relator [John Barry]," than for the legal issues it settled (Hurd 1876: 511–17). Other treatise writers used it to establish sharply conflicting points. In the seventh edition of Story's 1857 treatise on equity, *Mercein* stood for the proposition that as "between husband

and wife, the custody of the children generally belongs to the husband; and the latter cannot, by an agreement with his wife, . . . alienate to her the right to the custody and care of the children."[43] Some writers saw it as limiting the father's authority; others saw it as establishing the mother's rights, particularly if the child were of "tender years." It stood as confirmation of the inability of the courts to compel a wife to reside with her husband. It also established that a custody determination (through habeas corpus) would be conclusive (*res judicata*), while the circumstances of the parties remained unchanged, a bar to subsequent writs of habeas corpus by the noncustodial parent.

The future of *People v. Mercein* as legal authority was immensely confused, irreducible to a simple trajectory. One could plausibly regard *Mercein* as an ink blot capable of being relied on as support for any of a number of positions: father's rights, mother's rights, judicial discretion, contractual freedom, and contractual constraint, all depending on which portion of which opinion was being relied on as authority. Indeed, I decided to write this chapter when I read the trial judge's opinion in the Baby M case, where the chancellor's opinion is cited as authority for the judge's discretionary capacity under *parens patriae* to give the child to the father and to terminate all the birth mother's rights.[44]

Yet another demonstration of indeterminacy is not my goal in conducting this reading of the case, however. Rather, it seems to me that a close reading of *Mercein* should focus us on husband's legal rights—as an aspect of coverture— as a constitutive and continuing feature of nineteenth-century family life. These rights were not simply atavisms from a rejected past. They were part of the emotional reality of family law and life for both men and women. Remember, Eliza Barry never challenged her husband's continuing custody rights over their young son. Nor was her defense of her custody over their daughter framed, at least at first, in terms of her natural rights, or even her daughter's needs. Rather, she (or, rather, her lawyer) framed her case around John Barry's express alienation of his rights to his infant daughter, through the separation agreement. Her defense might be read as a concession of his legal rights.

For men like John Barry, protection of those rights was a fundamental obligation of a legitimate legal order. For women like Eliza Barry, some male legal rights constituted wrongs that a legitimate constitutional order ought to overcome. But the structure of traditional marriage remained a presence in both their lives, the foundation for their legal improvisations.

Those judges who worked to develop the notion of *parens patriae*—the notion of the state's responsibility for the best interests of the child—saw that notion as of a piece with conceptions of the police power. *Parens patriae* justified the regulation of private (property) rights, but it, like the police power, would not have made sense to most judges without the prior existence of private marital rights. *Parens patriae* epitomized the public values of a legitimate public sphere, of the state's growing responsibility to assure "the best interests of the child." As such, it would take precedence over traditional parental (patriarchal) rights. It was not, however, understood as an abrogation of those rights.[45]

Unless we understand the received emotional power of the structure of male domestic rights, we will never fully appreciate the courage and ingenuity of the women—and their lawyers—who worked to undo coverture and father's rights. To many early feminists, the image of marriage implicit in the continuing reality of father's legal rights made marriage law into an exact parallel of slave law and made any defense of traditional marital obligations equivalent to a defense of the morally corrupt slaveholders' constitution. They knew that change would require a fundamental social and constitutional reconstruction.[46] Women like Eliza Barry pursued, of necessity, a different strategy. Their goal had to be to persuade male judges and other public decision makers both that there were socially and legally accepted reasons for denying husbands' particular vested claims and, as well, that the exercise of judicial discretion in such situations was part of the judges' constitutional role. They had to make fathers' rights appear less vested—less certain of enforcement—than they were (in the process reconstructing judges as benevolent patriarchs), in order to create the legal conditions for the undoing of those rights.

And along the way, women like Eliza Barry made men like John Barry recognize that a structure of rights and entitlements that they had taken as given, that they had assumed provided the foundation for a just society, no longer provided that foundation, no longer could be taken as given. Once, only a few years earlier, a husband's custodial rights over his dependents were so much a part of the natural order as to be unchallengeable, even in the case of a husband who had violated—had destroyed—his identity as legitimate husband.[47] To John Barry, by way of contrast, the fact that he had always been a "good" husband, in all the ways that the legal order ordinarily recognized, was not enough to secure him his rights.

A structure of understandings that had once been hegemonic—tacit and presumptively true—was on its way to becoming ideological—contested, challenged, and recognizably partial.[48]

NOTES

1. For law and society scholars, legal history means sociolegal history. See, for programmatic statements, all focused on American legal history, Gordon 1975, 1984; Forbath, Hartog, and Minow 1985; Hartog 1987. Friedman 1985 remains the best American survey. Sociolegal history was once contrasted to doctrinal history (Gordon 1975). The recent shift in historical work to intellectual legal history, sometimes called the history of legal thought or the history of legal consciousness, has complicated that contrast; see Kennedy 1980.

2. There are two main sources for this sketch of the story of their marriage: the Chancellor's opinion in *People ex rel. Barry v. Mercein*, 8 Paige's Ch. 47 (1839), and John A. Barry (1839). On Mercein, see Wilentz 1984.

3. He thought quixotically that the latter sentiments justified him in his assurance that the November agreement was a dead letter (Barry 1839: 16–20).

4. Was Eliza Barry an early feminist? Probably not. Anne Boylan of the University of Delaware has been kind enough to share with me her research (1984) on New York City's female benevolent organizations. In the records of those organizations, notably the Female Union Society for the Promotion of Sabbath Schools, the Methodist Episcopal Sunday School Union, and the New York Female Assistance Society, there are scattered references to a Miss Mercein (who may as likely be Eliza's sister). Yet, Boylan has demonstrated that the women who belonged to benevolent organizations typically did not join more radical reform organizations, such as moral reform societies or antislavery societies, that would have put them in contact with the early woman's rights movement.

5. At the same time, my reading of other marital disputes suggests that many nineteenth-century women feared leaving their parental home, as Eliza Barry did. In *Democracy in America*, Tocqueville had noted that an American woman found her father's house "a home of freedom and pleasure," in contrast to her husband's where she must live as if it were a "cloister." "In America a woman loses her independence forever in the bonds of matrimony" (1969: 592). See, likewise, Ellen Rothman's study of American courtship (1987). Mary Ryan's (1981) study of the family in Utica, New York, argues that middle-class women experienced something like an oedipal crisis in their later twenties when the majority of them married (as did Eliza Barry). That crisis was not always resolved, and it often left them with a sense of separation from a truer home (1981: 194–95).

6. On the uncertain legality of most separation agreements, see Hartog 1991.

7. A summary of the procedural history of the case would look as follows:
    1. Writ of habeas corpus brought by John A. Barry in the New York Court of Common Pleas, for the return of wife and daughter—1839. Denied.
    2. Writ of habeas corpus brought by Barry before Chancellor Walworth, for the return of wife and daughter—1839. Denied, 8 Paige's Ch. 45 (NY, 1839).
    3. Writ of habeas corpus brought by Barry before New York Court of Common Pleas, for the return of daughter—1839. Denied.
       New York Supreme Court reversed (writ reinstated and sustained)—1840. 25 Wend. 64, 73 (NY, 1840).
       New York Court for the Correction of Errors reversed New York Supreme Court (writ denied)—1840. 25 Wend. 83 (NY, 1840).
    4. Writ of habeas corpus brought by Barry before New York Superior Court, for the return of daughter—1840. Denied, 1841 (A copy of Judge Oakley's unpublished order can be found in the Luther Bradish Papers, uncarded correspondence, New York Historical Society [NYHS]).
    5. Writ of habeas corpus brought by Barry before New York Supreme Court—1842. Sustained, 3 Hill 399 (NY, 1842).
       New York Court for the Correction of Errors reversed (writ denied)—1843 (unpublished holding).
       [Mrs. Barry filed with vice chancellor to establish validity of separation agreement and to ask for an injunction to stop Barry from filing writs of habeas corpus—1844. Denied, 3 Saratoga Chancery Sentinel 13 (1844).]
    6. Writ of habeas corpus brought by Barry before the United States Supreme Court—1844. Denied, 2 Howard 65 (43 U.S. 65)(1844).
    7. Writ of habeas corpus brought by Barry in United States District Court—1844. Denied, 42 F. 113 (1844).
       United States Supreme Court affirms district court decision—1846. 4 Howard 574 (1846); 5 Howard 103 (1846).

8. Jamil Zainaldin, in his essay on child custody and adoption law (1979), treats some of the opinions in the case as momentary conservative reactions on the way to a modern family law. The other "great" nineteenth century custody case was the D'Hauteville case decided in Philadelphia in 1840. Unlike *Mercein*, this case was never appealed and thus did not have *Mercein*'s doctrinal significance. Michael Grossberg's wonderful new study (1996) of that case traces as well the complex interactions between the litigants and lawyers involved in both cases.

9. See Grossberg 1983, 1985. Martha Fineman (1988) has challenged modern versions of the evolutionary story. Family lawyers sometimes draw the optimistic story out of historical works, like Stone 1976, that relied on a modernization hypothesis.

10. While I take Barry's obsessions as representative of the concerns of many other (male) Americans, as did nineteenth-century treatise writers in discussing the case, it is important to remember that Barry was not an American citizen and had spent most of his life in Nova Scotia.

11. This statement ignores the federal judges who saw the case solely as a problem of federal jurisdiction.

12. Note that Mrs Barry never challenged her husband's right to take her young son away from her. She and her father only resisted when Barry tried to take her infant daughter away, in spite of his ostensible agreement to leave the daughter with his wife and father-in-law. On the other hand, see Grossberg 1996. By the early nineteenth-century, cultural expectations that women had rights as well as duties as mothers had become common (see Kerber 1980). And the wrongness of the law in denying women custody rights was a constant feature of early feminist rhetoric:

> The question in regard to the right of property, however, sinks into insignificance, when compared with that of the right in children. The laws, as we have said before, do not recognize any natural right of a woman to her children. She may bring them into the world with terrible suffering, she may watch over their infancy and youth with the most tender, faithful care, esteeming her own ease or individual gratification as nothing in comparison with their welfare; and yet, if her husband prove to be so bad a man that she cannot live with him, or that he chooses, by way of tormenting her, to separate her children from her, or order their lives in a manner that she conceives to be detrimental to them, she has no redress. Even if he is unfaithful to her, unless she can prove his infidelity (and if he have the adroitness which commonly attends knavery and wickedness, he will be sure not to put any proof within her reach), the children belong to him as a matter of course, and the mother is for ever deprived of them. . . .
>
> If the law were to do its duty, by admitting that the mother has an equal right to the children with the father, the parties would arrange between themselves, either that each should have the children half the time—the father, if necessary, continuing to provide for their support—or, that each should take a part of them. (Anonymous 1844: 482–83)

At the same time, the statement in the text should not be read as assuming an unchanging common law regime in which fathers had automatic and unquestioned custodial rights. Danaya Wright's ongoing research (1996) into the longer history of English custody law reveals the development of absolute paternal custody rights as an eighteenth-century novelty. Earlier, mothers who separated could have often expected to retain custody over their children. More importantly, separations were both relatively rare and informal (that is, beneath the contemplation of legal authorities) until the eighteenth century, so that there was little doctrine available to build an absolute right on.

13. In 1844, Eliza Barry brought an action before the chancellor asking for an injunction to keep her husband from bringing more actions in habeas corpus. The bill attempted to establish the validity of the separation agreement and her attendant right to the custody of the infant, as provided by the agreement. The chancellor, however, considered it "doubtful whether the court had jurisdiction upon a bill filed by the wife, to protect her mere personal rights, or her right to the care and custody of her children depending upon such an agreement alone," and refused to grant the injunction. Thus, John Barry could continue to test his claim to custody through renewed writs of habeas corpus (3 Saratoga Chancery Sentinel 13 [1844]).

14. In a letter dated May 19, 1838, Mercein had written that he was "determined to resist every effort to change their position, and to keep them where they now are." And a week later he wrote that he forbade any further communication with Barry by any member of his household, except in negotiating terms for a permanent separation between John and Eliza (Barry 1839, 7).

15. In re Waldron, 13 Johns Ch. 418 (1816).

16. The chancellor continued: "I will therefore only say here, as I have before said, that a christian wife and mother should suffer long and much before she can be justified in resorting to the doubtful and dangerous expedient of separating herself permanently from him whom she has once chosen for the partner of her bed and bosom, thereby placing both herself and him in the 'undefined and dangerous situations of a husband without a wife, and a wife without a husband'" (8 Paige's Ch. 45, 54). My reading of the early nineteenth-century case law suggests that Walworth was right that husbands lacked a remedy to force absent wives to return to their households, although it is very difficult to prove an absence. A famous series of eighteenth-century English cases, decided by Lord Mansfield, were taken as establishing that, in habeas corpus proceedings by a husband for his wife, courts need only ensure that the wife was set free from improper restraints, and need not require her to return to her husband. Ex Parte Sandilands, 12 Eng. Law and Eq. 463; Rex v. Lister, 8 Mod. 22; Rex v. Wiseman, 2 Smith 617, Anne Gregory's case, 4 Burr. 1991, Rex v. Clarke, 1 Burr. 606, Rex v. Mary Mead (John Wilkes), 1 Burrow's 542. In England, these cases were overturned in the late eighteenth century. A famous decision, In re Cochrane, 8 Dowl., P.C. 630 (1840), decided at the same time as the Mercein dispute, held that a wife could be recaptured and held in physical custody by her husband, if he had reason to believe that her conduct apart from him would lead to embarrassment. In America, the doctrinal authority of Mansfield's decisions remained, although always contested. Some state court judges complained about the absence of legislation to give courts the power to order restitution of conjugal rights. See *Coverdill v. Coverdill*, 3 Harrington 13 (Del., 1844). But no legislature ever responded.

17. Throughout the nineteenth-century, the operative question remained what the courts should recognize as a wife's autonomous will. The leading nineteenth-century American treatise on habeas corpus law, after noting that a husband was not entitled to a writ of habeas corpus where the wife "voluntarily leaves her husband and remains absent without any restraint," added in a footnote that a wife had no right to a writ to be released from the custody of her husband, "unless it appear that she is actually restrained of her liberty without good cause." If he stopped her from leaving because he feared she would live in an "improper" place, her writ should be refused (see Hurd 1858, 1876: 449, 452). At the very end of the nineteenth century, another treatise writer wrote that a husband had "the right to the custody of his wife so long as she is willing to submit to it, and if he is deprived of that right by another, who holds the wife in custody against her will, his remedy to recover her person is by habeas corpus" (Church, 1893: 659).

18. Other judges saw the question differently. For example, Judge Oakley of the New York Court of Common Pleas, who rejected Barry's renewed request for a writ of habeas

corpus in 1841, posed the question of the father's right to keep his daughter's husband out as a choice between the property rights of the father and the asserted custody rights of the son-in-law: "[The facts stated in this affidavit] show in substance, that the relator [Barry] was violently prevented from entering the house of Mercein whether he had gone to see his child. The right of Mercein to forbid the entrance of the relator into his house cannot be questioned. . . . [A]s long as the mother chooses to remain with the child under her father's roof, she being as has been decided, entitled to the present care and custody of it—a refusal on [the] part of her father to permit the relator to enter his house cannot strengthen the claim of the relator to the custody of the child" (Ms. Luther Bradish papers, uncarded correspondence, NYHS). Note that even Oakley seemed to concede that if Barry's right to immediate custody were established (or, rather, if Eliza Barry's custody were overturned), his father-in-law's legal position would be much weaker.

19. The two options were related because the legality of a separate maintenance agreement often rested on a demonstration of husband's wrongdoing

20. In *Barrère v. Barrère*, decided by Chancellor Kent in 1819, a wife was granted a divorce *à mensa et thoro* because of her husband's extreme brutality. Kent's order included an award of custody to the wife, in part because the husband's employment as the keeper of an ice cream garden was inappropriate as an "influence upon the habits and manners of his son," but mostly because the husband had been responsible for the separation, was in the wrong, and therefore had lost his rights as a husband. *Barrère v. Barrère*, 4 Johns. Ch. 187, 197 (1819). See also *Codd v. Codd*, 2 Johns. Ch. 141 (1816); *Pawling v. Bird's Executors*, 13 Johns. 192 (Sup. Ct., 1816); *Graves v. Graves*, 2 Paige 62 (1830); In the Matter of Rachel Hansen, 1 Edmunds' Select Cases 9 (1834). See, generally, Grossberg 1985. On the complexity of the English background to these American developments, see Wright 1996.

21. *People ex rel Ordronaux v. Chegaray*, 18 Wend. 637, 642–43 (1836).

22. In 1810, John Deming was convicted of forgery. Conviction of a felony was understood as a form of civil death. In 1811, his wife married someone else who became the guardian of Deming's children. In 1812, the governor of New York pardoned Deming. Deming then sued in habeas corpus for the return of his children. Did the pardon restore his parental rights? Yes. The effect of the pardon was to return him, insofar as possible, to his status before the conviction. According to the New York Supreme Court, that did not challenge the validity of the second marriage of his "former" wife. The pardon would not divest any person of rights or interests acquired in reliance on the conviction. But the pardon did restore Deming to the condition of father. And his children were ordered returned to his care. In the matter of Deming, 10 Johns. 232, 483 (Sup. Ct., 1813).

23. See the discussion in Donahue, Kauper, and Martin 1973: 57–74.

24. He did so, "to the manifest danger of his own health; for she says 'it was bitter cold weather'" (8 Paige's Ch. 62).

25. "The occasional sallies of passion that occurred . . . would not of themselves, I think, have rendered the continuance of life entirely indifferent to her, while her first born child, then but a few months old, stood so much in need of a mother's care. But the distracting thought that one whom she had loved with such deep devotion was wholly worthless and degraded, would indeed be madness; and might render even life itself a burthen" (8 Paige's Ch. 64).

26. While sitting as a member of the Court for the Correction of Errors in 1840, reviewing the appeal from the decision of the New York Supreme Court, Walworth later changed his mind and decided that this was an agreement founded upon a present separation, and therefore valid (25 Wend. 96).

27. Judicial parochialism, a preference for the local parent over the parent from another jurisdiction, remains to the present an important part of American child custody practice, the bane of those law reformers who have worked since the early nineteenth century to create a uniform national law.

28. The vote in 1840 within the Court of Errors was 19–3. Two opinions were published at that time, both arguing against enforcement of Barry's writ of habeas corpus. One, by the chancellor, defended his earlier holding and was marked by his new insistence that the separation agreement between the Barrys was valid and binding. The second, by Senator Paige, to be discussed below, laid out a strikingly different analysis of the preferred resolution of child custody disputes (25 Wend. 63, 73, 83 [1840]). The struggle between the Supreme Court and the Court of Errors, the popular name for this court of review made up primarily of senators, was continuous throughout the late 1830s and early 1840s, resulting in a constitutional crisis (built around conflicting interpretations of the constitutional authority of the legislature to pass a general incorporation statute) that was only resolved by the abolition of both courts and the creation of the new Court of Appeals in the New York Constitution of 1846.

29. This time Samuel Nelson dissented, on the ground that the earlier reversal by the New York Court of Errors had settled the law for this case. The conflict was *res judicata*. But both Esek Cowen and Greene Bronson held to their original judgments.

30. The decision of the Court of Errors in 1842 was unreported. It is mentioned in the summary of the case history made to the United States Supreme Court. This case was, I suspect, a small skirmish in the ongoing struggle for legal authority between the Court of Errors and the New York Supreme Court. That struggle, whose major battles were fought over issues connected to the legal import of general incorporation statutes and banking laws, was not settled until 1846, when the new state constitution abolished both courts and set up the New York Court of Appeals as the highest court in the state. See Hartog 1983: 212–16 for another piece of the story. The struggle as a whole still awaits its historian.

31. Cowen knew that many separation agreements (for maintenance and support) had been held valid by courts in both England and in the United States, but he inveighed against extension of the trend, as inconsistent with sound public morals. "Husbands and wives with feelings and appetites already too violent for the restraints of duty or of shame, are thrown into the highway of temptation. . . . If the husband has a right to transfer the marriage bed to his wife, I deny that he has, therefore, the right still farther to violate his duty by selling his children, with or without it" (3 Hill 409–10).

32. Cowen, of course, knew that fathers were permitted to bind out their children in apprenticeship agreements, but he insisted "Those countries in which the father has a general power to dispose of his children, have always been considered barbarous."

33. Only the gross wrongfulness of the chancellor's opinion forced Barry to write a public response, he explained, for he considered himself "one of those who think that the sanctity alone of the domestic hearth—the domestic altar—should ever shield all its minor difficulties from the intrusive, and unhallowed gaze of impertinent curiosity" (Barry 1839: iii).

34. "Such a thing [the mother's claim to a natural right to custody] between man and wife cannot be supposed. In such a case, she invades a province not hers; and shows her want of good, sound, discriminating common sense: a quality not inferior in value, in a wife, to the most highly wrought accomplishments." Moreover, in deciding that Eliza's separation from John was neither immoral nor illegal, the chancellor was producing a legal situation "calculated to bring into the most sovereign contempt, all the doctrines he has so elaborately advanced and asserted for the sanctity and indissolubility of the marriage

relation" (Barry 1839: 13–14, 33). In my continuing research on marital conflicts in nineteenth-century America, I have noticed repeated mobilization of the image of Fanny Wright, the early nineteenth-century activist and divorce reformer, as a symbolic threat.

35. He also argued that the agreement had been canceled by the later language of his wife in a letter.

36. Useful sources for this story are casebooks in family law published from the end of the nineteenth century through the 1950s. Typically, their coverage of child custody law would begin with one of the "bad" English cases from the early nineteenth century, involving an immoral, intemperate, and abusive husband who still would have received custody of the child. The cases that followed this principal case recited the basic "rule" that father's rights were primary and paramount, but then found one or another reason to transfer custody to mother, to kindly relatives, or to child welfare agencies. The pedagogical lesson was of a legal rule deluged by its exceptions. See Jeremiah Smith, *Cases on the Law of Persons* (Boston, 1899); William Edward McCurdy, *Cases on the Law of Persons and Domestic Relations.* 4th Ed. (Chicago, 1952) (other editions in 1926, 1927, 1933, 1939).

37. See In re O'Neil, 3 *American Law Rev.* 578 (Mass., 1869), and *Chapsky v. Wood*, 26 Kansas 650 (1881). On the transformative features of eighteenth-century educational thought, see Fliegelman 1984.

38. The contemporary notes of future Supreme Court Justice Joseph Bradley describe the overall "spirit" of the holdings in the various *People v. Mercein* cases in terms very like Paige's. The father has no absolute right to custody. "The real question is what are the rights of the child; and those rights are, to be protected in the enjoyment of its personal liberty, according to its own choice, if arrived at the age of discretion, and if not, to have its personal safety and interests guarded and secured by the law acting through the agency of those who are called upon to administer it" (Joseph P. Bradley Papers, New Jersey Historical Society [NJHS], Law Notes, Folder 9). Dan Ernst was kind enough to share this with me.

39. Ms. Luther Bradish papers, uncarded correspondence, NYHS.

40. Mansfield 1845: 336–44. Bradley gave the opinions a somewhat broader reading. He found the "Spirit" of the decisions as tending to "the exercise of a sound discretion . . . having reference solely to the present interests of the child" (Law Notes, Folder 9, Joseph P. Bradley Papers, NJHS).

41. This generalization is founded on a reading of post–Civil War custody cases and an exhaustive Shephardization of the various opinions in the Mercein/Barry cases.

42. See, likewise, an 1853 article on "The Rights and Liabilities of Parents in Respect of Their Minor Children," in the *American Law Register.* The author of the article devoted two paragraphs to conflicts between husbands and wives over custody. The first paragraph describes American law as following English common law in protecting father's rights (citing the 1842 opinions of the New York Supreme Court in *Mercein*). The paragraph goes on to note that courts have "at times" deviated from this rule (citing the chancellor's 1838 opinion). But then the author indicates the "high discretionary power," assumed by courts, resulting in decisions, "although far from disregarding the abstract right of the father, compel this right to give way when the public good and the best interests of the child absolutely demand it" (citing the 1840 decision of the Court of Errors).

43. Story 1857: 703.

44. In re Baby M, 217 NJ. Super. 313, 525 A.2d 1128 (1987). The trial judge's opinion was, of course, reversed.

45. On the history of the police power, see Novak 1996.

46. See Clark 1987; DuBois 1987.

47. See Hartog 1993.

48. See Susan Silbey, in this volume.

BIBLIOGRAPHY

Anonymous. 1844. The Legal Wrongs of Women. 14 *Democratic Review*, 477–83.

Barry, John A. 1839. *The Barry Case. A Review of, and Strictures on the Opinion of His Honor the Chancellor of the State of New York, Delivered 26th August, 1839, in the Late Case of the People, ex relatione John A. Barry, versus Thomas R. Mercein. Affording Also, a Correct View of the Circumstances of the Case, and the Persecutions of the Reviewer by His Wife's Father and Family, and Others Their Partisans, up to the Present Time.* New York.

Boylan, Anne M. 1984. Women in Groups: An Analysis of Women's Benevolent Organizations in New York and Boston, 1797–1840. 71 *Journal of American History*, 497–523.

Church, William S. 1893. *A Treatise on the Writ of Habeas Corpus Including Jurisdiction, False Imprisonment, Writ of Error, Extradition, Mandamus, Certiorari, Judgements, etc. with Practice and Forms.* San Francisco: Bancroft-Whitney Co.

Clark, Elizabeth. 1987. Religion, Rights, and Difference in the Early Woman's Rights Movement. 3 *Wisconsin Women's Law Journal*, 29.

Cooley, Thomas. 1868. *Treatise on the Constitutional Limitations which Rest upon the Legislative Power of the States of the American Union.* Boston: Little, Brown.

De Tocqueville, Alexis. 1969. *Democracy in America.* Vol. 2. New York: Doubleday.

Donahue, Charles, Thomas Kauper, and Peter Martin. 1973. *Property.* St. Paul: West.

DuBois, Ellen. 1987. Outgrowing the Compact of the Fathers: Equal Rights, Woman Suffrage, and the United States Constitution, 1820–1878. 74 *Journal of American History*, 836–62.

Fineman, Martha. 1988. Dominant Discourse, Professional Language, and Legal Change in Child Custody Decisionmaking. 101 *Harvard Law Rev.*, 727.

Fliegelman, Jay. 1982. *Prodigals and Pilgrims: The American Revolution against Patriarchal Authority, 1750–1800.* Cambridge and New York: Cambridge Univ. Press.

Forbath, William, Hendrik Hartog, and Martha Minow. 1985. Introduction: Legal Histories from Below. 1985 *Wisconsin Law Rev.*, 759.

Friedman, Lawrence M. 1985. *A History of American Law.* 2d ed. New York: Simon and Schuster.

Gordon, Robert W. 1975. J. Willard Hurst and the Common Law Tradition in American Legal Historiography. 10 *Law and Society Rev.*, 9.

———. 1984. Critical Legal Histories. 36 *Stanford Law Rev.*, 57.

Grossberg, Michael. 1983. Who Gets the Child? Custody, Guardianship, and the Rise of a Judicial Patriarchy in Nineteenth-Century America. 9 *Feminist Studies*, 235–60.

———. 1985. *Governing the Hearth: Law and the Family in Nineteenth-Century America.* Chapel Hill: Univ. of North Carolina Press.

———. 1996. *A Judgment for Solomon: The d'Hauteville Case and Legal Experience in Antebellum America.* Cambridge and New York: Cambridge Univ. Press.

Hartog, Hendrik. 1983. *Public Property and Private Power: The Corporation of the City of New York in American Law, 1730–1870.* Chapel Hill: Univ. of North Carolina Press.

———. 1987. The Constitution of Aspiration and "The Rights That Belong to Us All." 74 *Journal of American History*, 1013–34.

———. 1991. Marital Exits and Marital Expectations in Nineteenth-Century America. 95 *Georgetown Law Journal*, 95.

———. 1993. Abigail Bailey's Coverture. In *Law in Everyday Life*, ed. Austin Sarat and Thomas R. Kearns, 63–108. Ann Arbor: Univ. of Michigan Press.

Hurd, Rollin C. 1858, 1876. *A Treatise on the Right of Personal Liberty and on the Writ of Habeas Corpus and the Practice Connected with It: With a View of the Law of Extradition of Fugitives.* Albany, NY: W. C. Little.

Kennedy, Duncan. 1980. Toward an Historical Understanding of Legal Consciousness: The Case of Classical Legal Thought in America, 1850–1940. 3 *Research in Law and Sociology*, 3.

Kerber, Linda. 1980. *Women of the Republic: Intellect and Ideology in Revolutionary America.* Chapel Hill: Univ. of North Carolina Press.

Mansfield, Edward. 1845. *The Legal Rights, Liabilities and Duties of Women: With an Introductory History of Their Legal Condition in the Hebrew, Roman and Feudal Civil Systems.* Salem, MA: John Jewett.

McCurdy, William Edward. 1952. *Cases on the Law of Persons and Domestic Relations.* 4th ed. Chicago: Callaghan (other editions in 1926, 1927, 1933, 1939).

Novak, William. 1996. *The People's Welfare.* Chapel Hill: Univ. of North Carolina Press.

Rothman, Ellen. 1987. *Hands and Hearts.* Cambridge, MA: Harvard Univ. Press.

Ryan, Mary. 1981. *Cradle of the Middle Class: The Family in Oneida County, New York, 1790–1865.* Cambridge and New York: Cambridge Univ. Press.

Smith, Jeremiah. 1899. *Cases on the Law of Persons.* Boston.

Stone, Lawrence. 1976. *The Family, Sex and Marriage in England.* New York: Harper and Row.

Story, Joseph. 1857. *Commentaries on Equity Jurisprudence as Administrated in England and America.* 7th ed. Boston: Little, Brown.

Wilentz, Sean. 1984. *Chants Democratic: New York City and the Rise of the American Working Class, 1788–1850.* New York: Oxford Univ. Press.

Wright, Danaya. 1996. The DeManneville Case and English Custody Law. Ph.D. diss., Johns Hopkins Univ.

Zainaldin, Jamil. 1979. The Emergence of a Modern American Family Law: Child Custody, Adoption, and the Courts, 1796–1851. 73 *Northwestern Law Rev.*, 1038.

JUSTICE AND POWER IN
STUDIES OF LEGAL PLURALISM

❖

ROBERT L. KIDDER

I. INTRODUCTION

It would be difficult to present a discussion of legal pluralism without focusing on issues of justice and power. From its earliest manifestations, legal pluralism has been a concept and a project driven by a concern that its opposite, legal centralism, is not only a distortion of reality, but one which reproduces injustice and reinforces unequal power relationships.

Even the attempt to define legal pluralism draws one into these issues. A simple dictionary definition would not convey the meaning which the term has acquired with its introduction into law and society literature. John Griffiths defined legal pluralism as "that state of affairs, for any social field, in which behavior pursuant to more than one legal order occurs" (1986: 2). Earlier Friedman had defined it as "the existence of distinct legal systems or cultures within a single political community" (1975: 196–97).

Neither of these definitions, however, conveys fully the range of phenomena with which Griffiths, and most others who have applied the term to their own research interests, are concerned. What they do study is the existence of "legal orders" within legal orders, "nonstate law" in contrast with "state law," "informal law" in contrast with "formal law." A central point of the whole enterprise has been to discover, examine, explain (and sometimes to advocate the virtues of) activity systems which in some way (functional, structural, ideological) resemble state legal systems but which operate within the gaps of injustice, neglect, and powerlessness either created and reinforced by state legal systems or unaddressed by those systems.

There is advocacy in Griffiths's definition, as there would be in most attempts to define legal pluralism, because he consecrates these other activity systems by deeming them to be *legal* orders. I could make the same point by saying that he consecrates the words "law" and "legal" by associating them with these other nonstate activity systems. With either of these perspectives on Griffiths's definition, the point is that the legal pluralism project itself obliterates most distinctions between state legal order and orders created by other structures and groups. It emphasizes what all legal orders have in common rather than differences between them. Where it discovers differences, it resists the assumption that one way is better than another. It puts the question of evaluation in the context of the needs of the actors involved rather than the abstract features of the system itself. All legal orders, whether state-supported or not, thus become not only analytically equal, but bestowed with whatever legitimacy the term "legal" can support. Or we can say that Griffiths's definition dethrones state law from the top of a system of legal centralism and puts all "legal" systems in the same social scientific petri dish for scrutiny.

I will argue in this paper that the intellectual basis of the movement for legal pluralism, both as an intellectual movement and as a political project, shares a common perspective and set of values with the original movement for legal centralism and with those who more recently have stepped in to criticize legal pluralism, particularly as it has taken concrete shape in specific policies. I will argue, moreover, that the fact that these different movements share both perspective and values creates a particular dilemma for legal pluralism. It poses an unresolved contradiction between two features which have clearly been fundamental to this movement's development: the empowerment of ordinary people versus the taken-for-granted endorsement of universal principles of justice. I will begin with a review of the roots of legal pluralism in order to show how its history is rooted in the shared perspectives and values. Then I will discuss the intellectual challenges to legal pluralism in order to show how opponents share the same perspectives and values. I will then discuss a very recent attempt to reframe the entire debate by fracturing the usual idea of a state/society dichotomy that has served as a fundamental framework for legal centralists, legal pluralists, and critics of legal pluralism alike. Then I will conclude by arguing that none of these efforts breaks successfully from the basic notions of universalized justice which have contributed so effectively to the rise of the institutions of formal law.

2. LEGAL CENTRALISM AND ITS DISCONTENTS

Legal pluralism, as a separate analytical category, has its roots in several converging trends that can be summarized as a crisis in theories of legal centralism. The main trends include changes in legal scholarship, legal anthropology, alternative dispute resolution, the sociology of law, and studies of development.

A . L E G A L S C H O L A R S H I P

The phenomenon to which legal pluralism is a reaction, legal centralism, includes a view of law as a special achievement of higher forms of civilization. Law, in this picture, is a triumph of progress toward universalism. It is based on reason rather than superstition, favoritism, nepotism, or emotion. It wins support because it relies on due process and is therefore accepted as fair. It reigns supreme also because it replaces all previous and more parochial forms of authority with a principle of universalism. As a secular ideal it is above not only narrow particularistic interests of limited groups, but also above other universalistic codes such as world religions because it embraces all without regard to "race, creed, color, or national origin." It is a seamless web able to rectify existing social problems, and, as a method, able to address all future problems in society. Its ability to live up to its ideals rests on the creation and maintenance of a class of professionals whose education and social position insulate them from the forces of particularism.

This view of law (also sometimes known as the Austinian model) began to unravel even as it was being constructed. The sociological jurisprudence of legal scholars such as Roscoe Pound (1921, 1943) challenged the ability of any authority to achieve justice while ignoring sociological facts that moved thinking toward particulars rather than universals. Legal realists such as Holmes (1968), Frank (1950), and Llewellyn (1960, 1962) went even further, claiming that the facts most relevant to an understanding of the law were those concerning the actual operation of the legal system itself and its real, not merely imagined or prescribed, impact in society.

Thus, within the relatively cloistered environment of legal academe, issues of justice and power were pressing scholars to reject the Austinian model of law in favor of research into the multiplicity of social influences on it. They did not reject the link between universalism and justice. Rather their belief was that the universalism of social science research would rectify the real failures of universalism in the everyday operations of legal institutions. Social justice for all was still the goal. Failures to achieve universalistic standards were the material on which the promotion of justice would proceed.

B . L E G A L A N T H R O P O L O G Y

These legal theorists were guided in part by a concurrent move within anthropology to challenge the dominant colonialistic ideology which said that "savages" and "natives" in "less civilized" cultures did not have law. The research of Malinowski (1926, 1961), Hoebel (1954), Gluckman (1963), Bohannan (1965), and Nader (e.g., 1969) all expressed the view that "primitive" or nonmodern peoples did indeed have a wide range of legal tools which they had developed to deal quite effectively with problems of conflict and order, and that these systems existed even under conditions of colonial rule and should not be summarily dismissed as either inferior or irrelevant. Their message was that indigenous legal orders made sense as rational, often effective, responses to conditions facing these peoples. Justice could be produced without all the trappings of state authority. In other words, indigenous peoples deserved the respect of Westernized outsiders, including legal scholars, because they were capable of producing justice as it was understood in the West.

Although the tradition of anthropological studies of law developed as an exercise in scientific ethnography, it was driven by concerns about justice and power. These anthropologists saw attempts to relegate indigenous law to the realm of mere primitive custom as expressions of imperialistic strategies to expand central control over native populations. As such, the anthropological evidence was a call to resist both ethnocentrism and colonial power. Justice was not to be viewed as something which only "The Law" of the state could produce. Rather we are to find it wherever indigenous groups maintain their own substate orders. Failure to protect indigenous legal orders would produce unjust consequences even if the "better" law of the West were "given" to indigenous populations because the Western law would be part of a process of disempowering the indigenous peoples.

C. ALTERNATIVE DISPUTE RESOLUTION (ADR)

A development related to legal anthropology's thrust, but with other sources of input, contributed to the further development of legal pluralism by bringing it "home" to "developed" societies. Nader (1980) and others began by focusing on the injustice and powerlessness implied in the idea of "access to justice" being denied to the poor and powerless in industrial and postindustrial societies. Because of the expense, formality, and complexity of modern legal systems such as that in the United States, "access" critics charged that justice was available only to the rich, the "repeat players" (Galanter 1974), the insiders who could afford to play the law game.

This insight accompanied research which began showing that people in modern urban settings, like "natives" in colonial territories who practiced their own alternatives to colonial law, had already developed or were in the process of developing community-level alternatives to formal law. These discoveries of alternatives, of informal law, when examined in the context of anthropological descriptions of practices in Africa, Asia, and Latin America, contributed to a growing movement to promote access as part of government policy. Researchers, along with policy advocates, argued that informal legal systems should be encouraged as a substitute for formal law because they would provide greater access to justice. Informal alternatives such as neighborhood mediation councils, ombudspersons, and nonjudicial arbitration panels would be cheaper, faster, more comprehensible, and closer to people's values and would therefore spread justice and empower people to control their own lives in much the way neighborhood clinics, midwives, and holistic medicine would make good health more accessible to ordinary people. Now dubbed Alternative Dispute Resolution, many of these ideas have been incorporated into the activities of the formal legal system itself.[1] But the entire vocabulary and theoretical thrust of the access to justice movement has been to emphasize the capacity of other, or alternative, legal systems within modern industrial societies to deliver justice and empowerment.

D. THE SOCIOLOGY OF LAW

In a sense, we come full circle when we look at the predominant research agenda of the sociological movement in law (Hunt 1978). A substantial majority of studies usually identified with the sociology of law (since the inception of the *Law and Society Review* in 1966) delve into the actual operations of legal institutions as opposed to the "law on the books." Many of these studies can be described as the fulfillment of the research agenda called for by the legal realists mentioned above. In these studies, a kind of legal pluralism is implied in the discovery that police officers, prosecutors, judges, courts, lawyers, and government regulators construct a whole variety of informal procedures, legal categories, networks of relationships, and so on, which produce legal impacts not foreseeable from a knowledge of the law alone. In other words, not only is there pluralism outside the realm of state law, but state law itself is far from the monolithic doctrine or process which its theorists and apologists present. Justice and power are to be found, lost, attacked, or defended within a rich ecology of "normal crimes" (Sudnow 1965); courtroom working groups (Eisenstein and Jacob 1977); non-contractual relations (Macaulay 1963); relations between "haves and have nots" (Galanter 1974); and activities done within "the shadow of the law" (Mnookin and Kornhauser 1979).

Taken together with the other trends mentioned above, this sociological research on the inner workings of the legal institutions of state law contributes to a tantalizing but elusive search for the essence of what is legal, what is law. The deal making, the negotiation, the compromising, the exertion of pressure through resources both rule-bound and not rule-bound, and the mobilization and use of political support which occurs within these institutions are found to differ so little from those "informal," nonstate social orders that state law is supposed to supplant, that it becomes increasingly difficult to distinguish them sociologically. Sociolegal studies, therefore, have produced at least partial obliteration of distinctions between legal and nonlegal modes of social order. Running throughout this literature is a message about power and justice: either the informal reality of the legal system allows for the perpetuation of inequality and injustice, or it achieves greater equality and justice than anything that formal legal orders can produce.

E. THE CRITIQUE OF "DEVELOPMENT" THEORY

One other source of ideas on legal pluralism has been the criticism leveled against efforts within American government and academic circles to export American legal concepts and institutions to Third World countries as a means of promoting economic and political development. Trubek and Galanter (1974) typify this criticism by focusing specifically on efforts of the Ford Foundation to sponsor legal development projects which were supposed to create the kinds of business environments in which investment could thrive.

These projects were part of a broader American development aid strategy based on theories of economic "takeoff" within individual Third World nation states. Development strategists took it as given that development was only likely to occur following Western patterns. They therefore placed law in the center as a necessary tool of organization. Implied by this theory was a model of law as a system of professionals who would preside over the crafting of written laws, and the creation of institutions to administer those laws. These professionals would then assume responsibility for administering the systems thus created. This model of development also presumed a political context of participatory, representative democracy. In other words, the entire project was based on a vision of individual nation states gradually accruing all of the characteristics of "modern" industrialized states in the West.

Within this vision, indigenous or "native" legal systems were viewed as examples of the old which must be replaced with the new. They were not understood as being potential models for the new nor as institutions that would inevitably coexist with the new. Industrialization would render them irrelevant. Hence they were also not understood as institutions which would have to be taken into consideration in constructing nation-building legal systems. Moreover, since aid givers were operating with a liberal democratic model of law, they perceived their recommendations and creations as agents of justice and equality without analyzing the differing patterns of indigenous order and conflict which would inevitably intersect with the institutions they were constructing.

The diversity of social structures, and the variety of broadly based inequalities and conflicts deep in each of these Third World nations could, according to development theory, be ignored because these were relics of a past being abandoned by progressive-minded classes in developing societies. Such relics were only to be taken seriously if they offered resistance to modernization. The pluralism of indigenous institutions dealing with conflict was, as with other indigenous institutions, either relegated to the relic pile of other "irrelevant" social phenomena, or strategists sought to enlist those institutions as "lower," or "entry-level," opportunities for involving the populace in the "real" legal systems of development-oriented governments. India's post-independence panchayat system was a good example of this policy and attitude (see Galanter 1985).

With regard to the issues of justice and power, the vision of liberal democratic institutions produced a paradox. In the name of the goals of greater equality through the "rule of law," development strategists were collaborating with Third World governments in either contesting or coopting the power of indigenous legal institutions. The "justice" of national courts was being inserted as a rival to the justice of indigenous practices, and the inequalities of free-market capitalism were being offered as more practical, and therefore ultimately more just, than the inequalities of "underdeveloped" socioeconomic systems.

Thus the legal forms of Third World nations were lumped together with all other social forms as backward and incapable of sustaining the kind of social system it would take to rise out of antiquity and poverty. Like other versions of legal centralism, the development model advanced Western forms of professionalized, institutionalized law to the exclusion of indigenous forms, rendering them, by definition, "informal," and projecting their obsolescence.

3. JUSTICE AND POWER IN THE CHALLENGE TO PLURALISM

Just as the attack on legal centralism was gaining momentum, its alternative, legal pluralism, began receiving critical scrutiny because of issues of justice and power. In a collection entitled *The Politics of Informal Justice,* Abel (1982) and others called into question the entire intellectual project of legal pluralism on the grounds that "informal" justice, ADR, and programs to increase access to justice could weaken or destroy legal rights that had been won through political struggle. Fascist governments in prewar Germany and Japan demonstrated this threat most clearly with their emphasis on the "informal" maintenance of social harmony (Reifner 1982: 81; Haley 1982: 125). Even governments in precapitalist societies such as India (Meschievitz and Galanter 1982: 47) demonstrated the lack of fit between socially embedded conflict-resolution practices and their reincarnation as agents of social control within development-driven government planning schemes. And Garth (1982: 183) warned that professional paternalism within the welfare states of North America and Western Europe could transform access to justice reforms into measures that trample on the rights of the "have-nots": "the profession has tended to emphasize 'access' . . . or at most the ideal of 'let the tribunal fit the case'. [S]uch institutions may turn out to be inconsistent with, or at least irrelevant to the enforcement of rights" (Garth 1982: 203).

In the case of revolutionary socialist situations, the significance of popular tribunals was not their provision of some permanent alternative to central control, but rather their role in challenging presocialist institutions of control (Santos 1982: 251).

The pendulum has thus swung between discoveries and praises of nonformal, indigenous "law," on the one hand, to condemnation of legal pluralism as disempowerment via social fragmentation, on the other. Left at this point, the research agenda consisted of trying to measure the relative levels of justice and empowerment being provided by either centralized law based on enforceable rights or by decentered law based on more communal processes and protections:

> This suggests that the enforcement of rights through informal procedures and institutions can succeed only if it overcomes the limitations inherent in the lack of a political constituency and builds organizations that will strengthen those who stand to benefit from those rights . . . if constituencies are not built, then procedural informalism, even when consistent with the enforcement of rights, is likely to resemble conciliation or diversion. (Garth 1982: 205–6)

4. INTERPRETATION AND ``CRITICAL EMPIRICISM'': JUSTICE AND POWER AS SMOKE AND MIRRORS

Several approaches have since emerged to challenge this "either/or" conception of law, justice, and power. One answer, or cluster of answers, is most closely identified with the work of some members of the Amherst seminar. This is the approach which Trubek and Esser (1989) dubbed "critical empiricism." Its relevance to discussions of legal pluralism comes in the concept of ideological production.

From this perspective, legal pluralism is a body of thought based on a language which privileges "law," the modern state-centered institutions associated with that term, as the primary point of reference. Law in this sense is just one ideological system, produced by a historically specific ideological project. Its terms, concepts, and social forms are therefore just one among multiple possible and actual projects.

Looked at this way, legal pluralism becomes another of those ideological production projects (Harrington and Yngvesson 1990). Ideologies need to be understood as evolving products of conflict. No single center, whether it be contestants advocating "rights" under "the law" or other contestants advocating social integration through "indigenous law" or "alternative dispute resolution," for example, should be recognized as having sole possession of the vocabulary or means for producing justice and empowering people. No scientific justification can be given for privileging the terms, propositions, or "realities" of any of the competing ideologies. Research becomes advocacy whenever it adopts any of these vocabularies as descriptors.

Even the language of justice and power begins to vanish within this sea of relativity. Justice can no longer be easily centered in one conception of right outcomes. It is understood differently from different perspectives in a given niche of competitive or conflictful relationships. In some contexts, the vocabulary of the ideology producers even eliminates justice entirely from discourses about right outcomes, as in the case of some Southern Baptists (Greenhouse 1986). As with the Amish and the Japanese (Kidder and Hostetler 1990: 895), the Baptists in Greenhouse's study settle on "harmony" as the controlling concept, and harmony means the suppression of conflict through the personal project of suppressing selfish desire rather than pursuing justice.

Even as justice performs this vanishing act, power becomes a process of conducting relations rather than a variable controlling those relations. The powerful, those with official titles and/or "dominant roles," are found to be limited within the ebbs, flows, and changes in relationships. Control over state law, while sometimes associated with power, is no automatic guarantee of it, and continued research on this relationship seems to contribute to an increasing gap between law and power as law becomes demystified.

5. RETHINKING LAW AND SOCIAL CONTROL

Some recent thought has moved in the direction of establishing new conceptual categories that obliterate many of the issues discussed above. One such approach is that taken by Santos (1985). Pointing to the dilemmas raised by the concept of legal pluralism, Santos argues that these are symptoms of a greater failure of social theory. That failure centers on repeated futile attempts to establish a simple distinction between the state and society, and to treat the nation/state as the primary unit of analysis. The model nation/state in these analyses is a hypothetical composite of the "core" societies of advanced capitalism. This leaves weaknesses in analyzing both substate entities and global developments which are beyond the limits of states. Specifically for the issue of legal pluralism, this model provides inadequate concepts for making the kinds of comparisons that legal pluralists have attempted. Yet legal pluralism has relied on the conceptual universe of state law as the basis of its criticism of that universe. The relativist confusion into which legal pluralism has plunged stems from this conceptual inadequacy.

The primary conceptual villain is the state/civil society distinction. The pervasiveness and persistence of this distinction in the face of its obvious flaws is, according to Santos, no accident. It serves a hegemonic function by dividing economy from politics so that the exploitative relations of production within capitalism can be disguised ("naturalized," Santos 1985: 306) and separated from their politically transformative potential. Political progress in social relationships (the rise of liberal democratic political institutions) has been the "happy face" side of a two-faced process that has also produced economic regression or degradation in social relationships. This process required the hegemonic conceptual divorce of economics from politics. Hence the research agenda of the legal pluralists—to shine a bright light of discovery on the coexistence of law and state politics (with their liberal, liberative ideals) on the one hand and a host of "contrasting forms of law and politics" (what we have been calling "legal pluralism") on the other—actually compounds the hegemonic failure to merge the social relations of capitalism with the relations of production.

Santos proposes that questions addressed in debates such as we have considered under the rubric of legal pluralism can be resolved successfully only if we understand structures of social relations correctly. He proposes a four-tiered system of structurally autonomous "places": "the householdplace, the workplace, the citizenplace, and the worldplace." Their autonomy, a feature which enables us to see them as separate places, is a unique product of capitalist social formation. With respect to law, its characteristics and the changes in its significance within a given nation/state will be determined by structures and changes of relationships within and between each of the four interrelated place systems.

For example, deregulation is actually "reregulation" based on "delegation and proliferation" of authority as the line between state and civil society dissolves into new structures of relationships among the four places. It does not mean fewer rules or less restriction. It simply means a change in the location of authority and control. Though not addressed directly by Santos, the legal pluralism "movement," in his scheme, would be the discovery and repackaging of what was there all along—a variety of modes of law within the four places—as the relations among those four places are transformed by postmodern changes, including the evolving relationships between core and peripheral societies within a world economic and political system.

If issues of justice and power are to be pursued at all in the study of law, they must be examined within the broader context of these four places. The dichotomy (law vs. nonlaw) merely distracts from these questions. State law, as only one of many forms of law "circulating in society" (Santos 1991: 114), will follow the trend of law in general toward particularism and complexity as power becomes more evenly distributed in society, because negotiations among equals produce narrower reforms in law than those that can be imposed by a centralized state authority. This reverses the trend Weber saw as leading to justice—the move toward universalistic legal standards—because democracy in practice, says Santos, will produce particularism. Or it might be more accurate to say that this process negates the concept of justice that Weber put forward: that justice comes most reliably out of universalistic procedures and rules.

Santos's message, while impressive in its scope and detail, may be missing an essential characteristic of state-related law and legal systems. Modern state systems of law, including the courts, legal scholars, practitioners, and legislators, operate within an ideological framework of universalism even when specific policies appear to be particularizing. The universalistic ideology of states (that allocation decisions, decisions about crime and punishment, decisions about procedure, decisions about enforcing private contracts, etc., should be based on abstract, codified principles of rights and duties because these produce justice) is precisely the idea that has accompanied law in its rise to hegemony and has perhaps been a major source of the state's power. Even when state legal systems appear to fragment into pluralized forms such as those that have arisen from the movement for legal pluralism, the involvement of the state in those various spin-offs is conducted by actors who use the theme of universal justice as justification for tolerating pluralistic structures. Such structures must "pay their way" by producing, or at least appearing to produce, demonstrable levels of justice. If they don't produce, they may be subjected to further reform or elimination. Only a change in this basic ideology would eliminate the potential for centralizing tendencies under the banner of law.

Is there something inevitable, as Santos seems to suggest, about the equal-izing of relationships as state institutions become submerged in globalization? If there was power to be gained previously by building states based on an appeal to universal justice, why should we expect that power to dry up? Does the growing influence of suprastate structures signify the decline of everything associated with the state, including the ideologies on which states were built? Why would the universalistic ideologies of law not, for example, emerge in new forms at more global levels of organization? On what other power base are those global entities growing? Not appeals to ethnic purity. Not tribal loyalty. Not even mass-based religion. If the answer be "whatever is good for business," then why would we expect the very ideology on which businesses flourished at state levels to dissolve into something more particularistic?

It would appear that the kind of universalism on which state legal forms grew is very much a part of emerging social forms. After all, even the academi-cians of legal pluralism have sung its praises (the wisdom of local custom as a tool for justice, the efficiencies of down-scaled justice, etc.) largely in terms of universalistic values that can be appreciated by those who are outsiders to the groups in question. If they were to evaluate particularistic procedures and outcomes in terms most meaningful to insiders, their analyses would either be incomprehensible to the outsider, or they might portray a landscape which, to the outsider, would appear composed of venality, viciousness, hypocrisy, and arbitrary power. "Why should we men of the tribe give power to women?" "Why let outsiders come and live in our community?" "Of course he deserved to be murdered. He insulted our chief." "We must have ethnic cleansing." And so on. Only by serving as an "interpreter" of local customs can legal pluralists turn particularized local relationships into ammunition in the battle against law's hegemony. Local autonomies do not speak for themselves—just ask the Bosnian Serbs or the Somali "warlords" or the Haitian "strongman" of 1993. In other words, legal pluralism as an academic enterprise has been built on the bedrock of universalism even as it celebrates particularism. And the universals that pluralists use are the same as those on which the legal forms of the state were built.

Moreover, even the recent critics of legal pluralism, those who charge it with threatening the hard-won rights of the weak, express their criticism in the language of the same universals which characterize both the law and the analyses of the legal pluralists. As mentioned above, Abel, Harrington, and others emphasize the disempowering effects of particularization, its tendency to give free reign to localized tyrannies. Their yardstick of social justice, like the yardstick of the legal pluralists, is essentially the same as that which forms the basis of the state legal institutions in question.

Therefore one wonders about Santos's projection about growing equalization and particularization when the predominant thrust of three major academic discourses is based on a shared vision of universal justice. Even if the significance of the state/society dichotomy is broken down and we begin thinking of the world in terms of Santos's four places, will not the attractions, strengths, or seductions of the ideas of universal justice, which have driven both the development of legal centralism and the attack on it, continue to serve as a basis on which legal activities are organized? Is particularism the future, or is it universalism disguised in the fact that individual advocates of universal justice do not agree on what that is in any particular case?

NOTES

1. For a comprehensive critique of this position, see Yngvesson's (1988) critique of Goldberg, Green, and Sander 1985.

BIBLIOGRAPHY

Abel, Richard, ed. 1982. *The Politics of Informal Justice*. Vols. 1 and 2. New York: Academic Press.

Bohannan, Paul. 1965. The Differing Realms of Law. *The Ethnography of Law*. Supplement to 67 *American Anthropologist*, 2:33–42.

Eisenstein, James, and Herbert Jacob. 1977. *Felony Justice: An Organizational Analysis of Criminal Courts*. Boston: Little, Brown.

Frank, Jerome. 1950. *Courts on Trial: Myth and Reality in American Justice*. Princeton, NJ: Princeton Univ. Press.

Friedman, Lawrence M. 1975. *The Legal System: A Social Science Perspective*. New York: Russell Sage.

Galanter, Marc. 1974. Why the "Haves" Come Out Ahead. 9 *Law and Society Rev.*, 95.

———. 1985. *Competing Equalities: Law and the Backward Classes in India*. Berkeley: Univ. of California Press.

Garth, Bryant. 1982. The Movement toward Procedural Informalism in North America and Western Europe: A Critical Survey. In *The Politics of Informal Justice*, vol. 2, ed. Richard Abel. New York: Academic Press.

Gluckman, Max. 1963. *Order and Rebellion in Tribal Africa*. New York: Free Press.

Goldberg, S. B., E. D. Green, and F. E. A. Sander. 1985. *Dispute Resolution*. Boston: Little, Brown.

Greenhouse, Carol. 1986. *Praying for Justice: Faith, Order, and Community in an American Town*. Ithaca, NY: Cornell Univ. Press.

Griffiths, John. 1986. What Is Legal Pluralism? 24 *Journal of Legal Pluralism and Unofficial Law,* 1.

Haley, John. 1982. The Politics of Informal Justice: The Japanese Experience, 1922–1942. In *The Politics of Informal Justice,* vol. 2, ed. Richard Abel. New York: Academic Press.

Harrington, Christine, and Barbara Yngvesson. 1990. Interpretive Sociolegal Research. 15 *Law and Social Inquiry,* 135.

Hoebel, E. Adamson. 1954. *The Law of Primitive Man: A Study in Comparative Legal Dynamics.* Cambridge, MA: Harvard Univ. Press.

Holmes, O. W. 1968. *The Common Law.* London: Macmillan.

Hunt, Alan. 1978. *The Sociological Movement in Law.* Philadelphia: Temple Univ. Press.

Kidder, Robert, and John Hostetler. 1990. Managing Ideologies: Harmony as Ideology in Amish and Japanese Societies. 24 *Law and Society Rev.,* 895.

Llewellyn, Karl. 1960. *The Common Law Tradition: Deciding Appeals.* Boston: Little, Brown.

———. 1962. *Jurisprudence: Realism in Theory and Practice.* Chicago: Univ. of Chicago Press.

Macaulay, Stewart. 1963. Non-Contractual Relations in Business: A Preliminary Study. 28 *American Sociological Rev.,* 55–67.

Malinowski, Bronislaw. 1926, 1961. *Crime and Custom in Savage Society.* London: Routledge.

Meschievitz, Catherine, and Marc Galanter. 1982. In Search of Nyaya Pachayats: The Politics of a Moribund Institution. In *The Politics of Informal Justice,* vol. 2, ed. Richard Abel. New York: Academic Press.

Mnookin, Robert, and Lewis Kornhauser. 1979. Bargaining in the Shadow of the Law: The Case of Divorce. 88 *Yale Law Journal,* 950.

Nader, Laura. 1980. *No Access to Law: Alternatives to the American Judicial System.* New York: Academic Press.

Nader, Laura, ed. 1969. *Law in Culture and Society.* Chicago: Aldine.

Pound, Roscoe. 1921. *The Spirit of the Common Law.* Boston: Marshall, Jones.

———. 1943. Sociology or Law and Sociological Jurisprudence. 5 *University of Toronto Law Journal,* 1.

Reifner, Udo. 1982. Individualistic and Collective Legalization: The Theory and Practice of Legal Advice for Workers in Prefascist Germany. In *The Politics of Informal Justice,* vol. 2, ed. Richard Abel. New York: Academic Press.

Santos, Boaventura de Sousa. 1982. Law and Revolution in Portugal: The Experiences of Popular Justice after the 25th of April 1974. In *The Politics of Informal Justice,* vol. 2, ed. Richard Abel. New York: Academic Press.

———. 1985. On Modes of Production of Law and Social Power. 13 *International Journal of the Sociology of Law.* 299.

———. 1991. The Postmodern Transition: Law and Politics. In *The Fate of Law,* ed. Austin Sarat and Thomas Kearns. Ann Arbor: Univ. of Michigan Press.

Sudnow, David. 1965. Normal Crimes: Sociological Features of the Penal Code in a Public Defender Office. 12 *Social Problems,* 255–76.

Trubek, David, and John Esser. 1989. "Critical Empiricism" in American Legal Studies: Paradox, Program, or Pandora's Box? 14 *Law and Social Inquiry,* 3.

Trubek, David, and Marc Galanter. 1974. Scholars in Self-Estrangement: Some Reflections on the Crisis in Law and Development Studies in the United States. 1974 *Wisconsin Law Rev.*, 1062.

Yngvesson, Barbara. 1988. Disputing Alternatives: Settlement as Science and as Politics. 13 *Law and Social Inquiry*, 113.

INTEREST, COMMITMENT, AND OBLIGATION: HOW LAW INFLUENCES BEHAVIOR

❖

LEWIS A. KORNHAUSER

I. INTRODUCTION

Law often claims a normative preeminence; whatever obligations an individual faces must, in case of conflict, yield to those imposed by law. Occasionally law makes a more encompassing claim of normative exclusivity: an individual faces *only* those obligations imposed by law. In a monolithic society, law might succeed in realizing these imperial claims. Society, though, is rarely, if ever, monolithic. Individuals within a society often have multiple normative commitments that arise from their membership either in smaller communities within the larger society as a whole or in communities that extend beyond the larger society. A resident of the United States, for example, though subject to its laws, has other, occasionally conflicting, commitments and loyalties: to her religion, to her workplace or her union, to her family and to her friends.

This multiplicity of normative systems poses several questions for the study of law and society. A central question of the philosophy of law, for instance, concerns the relation between legal and moral obligation: Must a legal obligation necessarily be moral as well? Does law define "conventional morality?" Or does "conventional morality" determine which behaviors the law will condemn? Analogous questions arise with respect to every other source of obligation; what, for instance, is the relation between legal obligation and the informal obligations that arise among neighbors? Does the law simply embody the "customary" practices of individuals? Or does it form these practices?

A second set of questions concerns the role that these various normative systems play in the determination of individual action. This question has both theoretical and practical import as it lies at the center of much debate about civil disobedience: When the law requires what one's god or one's conscience prohibits, how does one act? The question, however, arises in more mundane contexts as well because the law's requirements may conflict not only with one's obligations but also with one's interest. Studies of criminality must untangle the effects that norms within particular communities play in the determination of legitimate behavior from the economic incentives that individuals have to engage in that behavior. Similarly, the study of settlements in the "shadow of the law" must consider both the role of self-interest and of notions of equitable treatment and fair play.

In the law and society literature, these questions concerning the interaction of multiple systems of norms recur in various guises. The literature on legal pluralism, for instance, began with the observation that conquest resulted not in the replacement of indigenous law with imperial law but in a complex interaction between them. The literature (surveyed in Griffiths 1986 and Merry 1988) then expanded to include the study of the relation among legal and nonlegal normative systems. While this literature has provided much insight into the role of law in society, it has not paid sufficient attention to how an individual acts when she is subject (or committed) to multiple normative systems. This oversight derives in part from a failure adequately to distinguish between the expressed content of norms and the institutional arrangements that create, interpret, and enforce them.

The literature on private governance (surveyed in Macauley 1986) has also broached these issues either through the explicit comparison of legal and alternative methods of dispute resolution or through extended studies of nonlegal but formal systems of governance. This literature has tended to see nonlegal normative systems as placing a limit on the extent of social control that the law may exert. This perspective ignores other ways that systems of private governance might influence the content of the legal order.

In this essay, I outline a framework for understanding the relation among normative systems and how an individual, faced with the demands of multiple normative systems, might act. Section 2 begins with a simple distinction between the "textual" and "institutional" aspects of any normative system and concludes with a crude classification of types of normative systems. Section 3 sketches some different ways in which law may accommodate (or fail to accommodate) other normative systems. Section 4, the core of the essay, distinguishes preference theories of action from obligation theories of action; these two classes of theories resolve the conflicts among normative systems and between normative systems and individual interest differently. Section 5 briefly considers the possibility that self-interest might explain the content of a normative order. Section 6 extends the argument by suggesting how the prior analysis applies to the study of actors within a normative regime. Section 7 discusses some implications of the multiplicity of normative systems for the analysis of power. Section 8 addresses the implications of normative pluralism for the evaluation of legal institutions. Section 9 offers some concluding remarks.

2. NORMATIVE ORDERS AND NORMATIVE REGIMES

A. ORDERS AND REGIMES DISTINGUISHED

Law, as noted in the introduction, is merely one of many sources of individual obligation, albeit a highly elaborated and articulated one. Legal sophistication has two aspects. First, law announces a complex, interrelated, and comprehensive set of requirements, permissions, and prohibitions. Second, an equally complex set of institutions has emerged to create and implement this complex system of norms.

Every normative system displays to some extent these twin faces which I shall call the "normative order" and the "normative regime." "Normative order" refers to the system of requirements, permissions, and prohibitions that, in many normative systems, are embodied, or more correctly, expressed in texts. The legal order of the United States, for example, is expressed in the Constitution, federal and state statutes, administrative regulations, and judicial opinions. The normative order of Judaism is expressed in the five books of Moses and in the millennia of commentary that have succeeded it. In other normative systems, no clear or even conscious expression of the normative order may exist. Rules of syntax, for example, are largely applied unconsciously by native speakers.

"Normative regime" refers to the institutional aspect of a normative system. Again, normative systems differ greatly in the extent and manner of institutional elaboration. "Advanced" legal systems exhibit a complex institutional structure with distinct legislatures, courts, administrative agencies, police, and, often, a professional bar. Many of these features recur in other formal systems of norms. A study, for example, of the governance of a large corporation would attend to the different bureaucratic structures that create, implement, and adjudicate rules within the organization. Informal social norms (and norms of language use), by contrast, have no differentiated structures at all.

The distinction between normative orders and normative regimes of course has fuzzy borders. A constitutional norm mandating separation of powers, for example, may determine in part the normative regime and may express a commitment to a normative order protective of individual rights. Moreover, two normative systems that share, initially, a normative order but differ in their normative regimes will almost surely evolve quite differently. Finally, because a normative system modulates its requirements through an institutional structure, a gap may arise between the behaviors explicitly required by the normative order and the behaviors actually observed.

For much of this essay, I shall assume that normative regimes in general and legal institutions in particular conscientiously implement the requirements expressed in the system's normative order. This assumption, though counterfactual, permits a clear articulation of the way in which normative systems interact with individual interests to yield action. In section 6 below, I suggest how this assumption may be relaxed.

B. A Crude Classification of Normative Systems

Two crude and often problematic distinctions that appear in the literature on private governance help classify normative systems.[1] The first, embodied in the idea of private governance, distinguishes between public and private systems. The two differ in the size of the scope of the normative order and the nature of their coercive power. The scope of a normative order, the primary component of this distinction, has two components. A public system governs an entire political community, broadly defined, while a private system generally governs a group within this wider community. This group may be as small as two, as in a contract or a marriage, or quite vast, as in a religious order. In addition, a public order generally has broader scope in the sense that it seeks to govern a wider range of conduct. State law, for example, often claims the authority to regulate all types of conduct though it may not always exercise this authority. The normative orders associated with private institutions such as corporations or labor unions, by contrast, generally claim a narrower authority.[2] A second, less significant component of the public/private distinction points to an element of the normative regime: the extent to which sanctions for the violation of the normative order rely on coercion.

The second distinction points to the degree of formality of the normative regime within the normative system. Two different, but overlapping, criteria are used. In one instance, greater formality arises from greater division of labor. State law in industrialized countries, for example, exhibits a high degree of division of labor with well-articulated legislative, executive, and adjudicatory agencies. Smaller, more pastoral, political communities often exhibit much less formal division of labor. In the limit, "custom" governs.

The second criterion of formality relies on a distinction between spontaneous and planned organization. Changes in linguistic meaning (and often syntax) emerge spontaneously from linguistic practice without any central guidance, planning, or control.[3] These linguistic norms are clearly both strong and informal. In most legal systems, by contrast, articulation of norms arises from more planned behaviors.[4]

These two distinctions suggest the following 2×2 classification of normative systems:

TABLE 1   CLASSIFICATION OF NORMATIVE SYSTEMS

	FORMAL	INFORMAL
Public	Law (Direct Regulation)	Custom
Private	Contract/ Organization	Markets/ Cooperation

In complex social systems, these categories may overlap and relate in complex ways. Private, informal orders such as markets, for instance, may depend on various legal rules, such as those guaranteeing security of the person and of property, for their successful operation. Similarly, many organizational governance schemes ultimately rely on state enforcement of these private arrangements. The next section discusses various forms in which these interactions among normative systems may occur.

3. THE RELATION OF LEGAL AND NONLEGAL NORMATIVE ORDERS

The legal order may have a variety of complex positions relative to other normative orders and to behavior. I shall describe three relations: subordinate, semi-autonomous, and autonomous.

A. PRIVATE ORDER SUBORDINATE TO LEGAL ORDER

Law often encourages or, less positively, permits (or tolerates) private ordering of affairs. This permission arises in two ways. First, and most important, certain legal rules are enabling. The law of contract, the law of wills, and the law of corporations, for example, impose few, if any, substantive obligations on individuals. Rather, they permit individuals privately to create obligations that the state will then enforce.

In some instances, these enabling regimes give rise to complex normative orders distinct from the law. The Wagner Act, the Norris-LaGuardia Act, and subsequent federal legislation enabled the creation of labor unions. The law of labor relations in the United States is in large part private, created through collective bargaining agreements and the day-to-day interaction of labor and management. These systems of private governance have their own institutions of legislation, enforcement, and dispute resolution. Indeed, federal law authorizes the independence of these arbitration proceedings.[5]

Second, even when a legal regime does not explicitly enable private ordering, it often permits it. In most states, for example, marital law requires a court decree that grants a divorce and allocates property and parental rights and responsibility. In fact, a court decree generally ratifies the private agreement of the spouses. Bankruptcy proceedings operate in a similar manner. Indeed, in almost every dispute governed by some legal rule, the parties can resolve that dispute by private contract.

Private order in these instances is subordinate to law in two senses. Law both authorizes this order and, to a greater or lesser extent, shapes the private order.

B. Autonomous and Semi-Autonomous Private Orders

Many normative orders stand in a more complex relation to state law than those created pursuant to legal permission. Religious orders, ethnic subcultures within a larger political community, and other groups often subscribe to norms distinct from and possibly in conflict with legal norms. Some of these orders may be largely parasitic on legal order, but others may have a high degree of independence from the law.

How ought we to measure the relative autonomy of two normative orders? One might begin with a determination of the extent to which the two normative orders cover the same behavior. In the event that the realms of application overlap, one might examine the extent to which, in principle, the norms of one system prevail over the norms of the other in event of conflict. Alternatively, we might ask to what extent the norms of each system in fact govern behavior when the norms conflict. Finally, one might consider the causal relations between the norms. The content of one normative order may depend in part on the content of the other.

4. PREFERENCE VS. OBLIGATION AS A THEORY OF CHOICE

Social order depends not only on normative order(s) but also on individual action in light of the relevant norms. A normative order divides our options in three: what we *must* do, what we *may* do, and what we *must not* do. Individuals choose in light of this tripartite division of their options; obviously their choices do not always correspond to the requirements (and proscriptions) of a normative order. Our understanding of and explanation for social order will therefore include a theory of choice among actions classified by norms.

I shall outline two broad classes of such theories of practical reason. One class, preference theories, include standard economic models of "rational" action. As a consequence, the structure of these theories is clearly elaborated and highly articulated. Given the relevant data, economic models identify a clear choice. Preference theories can also accommodate various conceptions of socialization and internalization of norms and conceptions of ideology. The other class, obligation theories, has received less formal attention and no exemplary or paradigmatic model of this theory exists. What such theories may dictate in specific circumstances is less clear. Obligation theories are important nonetheless for two reasons. First, their assumptions often underlie much implicit discussion about law and legal policy. Second, the contrast with preference theories illuminates some of the gaps and inadequacies of them.

The discussion that follows focuses on the role that a normative order plays in choice under each theory. I do not offer a complete account or criticism of either theory.[6]

A. PREFERENCE THEORIES OF CHOICE

In preference theories, choice depends on the individual's preferences, beliefs, and set of options. An individual's preferences satisfy two conditions. First, they are complete in the sense that, presented with any pair of possible options A and B, the individual either prefers A to B, prefers B to A, or is indifferent between them. Second, her preferences are transitive; presented with three options A, B, and C, if she prefers A to B and B to C then she must prefer A to C as well.[7] Beliefs are about the world. In most economic models, beliefs enter in theories of decision making under uncertainty in which they are beliefs about the likelihoods that particular states of the world will obtain.[8]

Consider, for example, an individual X who allocates a fixed income Y between two commodities fish (f) and meat (m). Her set of options is defined by her income Y and the prices p_f and p_m of fish and meat respectively. Assume to begin that X has preferences directly over the composition (f,m) of her diet. In a preference theory, X will first identify the combination of fish and meat (f,m) that she can buy, given her income Y and the prices p_f and p_m. Among these available options, she will choose the combination (f,m) of fish and meat that most satisfies her preferences. Beliefs play no role here because, as yet, the description of the world faced by X does not include uncertainty.

Suppose that X lives in a society S that has a norm against the eating of meat. This norm might affect X's decision under the preference theory in three distinct (but not mutually exclusive) ways: the norm might alter X's set of alternatives, her beliefs, or her preferences.

Recall that X's set of options depends on her income and on the prices p_f and p_m of fish and meat. While the norm does not directly influence her income, it may directly alter the prices she faces. The violation of a norm usually results in a sanction which we may regard as an additional component. If, for example, society fines an individual for each (detected) instance of meat eating, the price of meat rises by the amount of the fine (discounted by the likelihood of detection). Alternatively, an eater of meat may simply face social disapprobation or ostracism both of which also impose (nonpecuniary) costs on X. X will then see her purchase of meat as carrying a cost additional to its price.[9] This version of preference theory, which I shall call the theory of norms as incentives, is the version prevalent in economic analysis of law.[10]

Economic analysis of law generally adopts this understanding of the influence of legal rules on action: legal rules, like prices, provide incentives for choice. The sanction imposed determines the size of the incentive. Certainly, as a first approximation, this theory has an inherent plausibility. Sanctions do generally follow the violation of legal (and other) norms; these sanctions surely have some influence on individual decisions. They may not, however, be the exclusive influence.

Norms, for example, might also alter an individual's beliefs. The norm against meat eating might alter X's belief about how healthy meat is relative to fish. If X's preferences depend in part on how healthy her diet is, then altering beliefs about the health effects of meat will influence her decisions.[11]

Health and safety regulation may work to some degree in this way; the regulations inform individuals of various ill effects of their activities. Some theories about law assert that other legal rules also have this consequence. Most ideological theories of law contend that legal categories affect the beliefs of individuals concerning what is possible or "natural" (Unger 1987). (Call this form of preference theory, the theory of norms as information.)

Finally, norms may alter an individual's preferences. Economists have often considered indirect influences on preferences. For instance, wealth generally influences preferences indirectly in one of two ways. Thus, in a classic example, the consumption of potatoes in Ireland in the nineteenth century fell as income rose because the Irish substituted other foods for potatoes.[12] Similarly, the preference for environmental quality is often said to increase with income.[13] Alternatively, the allocation of a property right increases the wealth of the person to whom the right is assigned. The assignment of rights to impose risks to life, for example, may have this effect.[14]

On some accounts, however, norms have a more direct influence on preferences. People come to prefer what norms require of them. Put differently, norms cause preferences or, more cautiously, are embodied in them. For example, a norm against meat eating might be embodied in a preference for fish. Often the causal process (or process of embodiment) is not specified.[15] Many social norms are transmitted through processes of socialization which one might understand as processes which shape preferences in a specific way. On this account, legal norms either assist in this process of socialization or they result from the same forces that socialize. (Call this form of preference theory, a theory of norms as creating value.)

B. OBLIGATION THEORIES OF CHOICE

Obligation theories of choice describe a process of practical reasoning that differs in several respects from that which underlies preference theories. In a preference theory, the individual's preference ordering summarizes the process of reasoning in all possible decision circumstances. Specifically, it weighs the various reasons, whether self-interested, altruistic, or moral, that impinge on the actor's decisions. According to preference theories, the individual can always resolve these conflicting reasons into a complete, transitive ordering of actions.

Obligation theories, in contrast, distinguish between two types of reasons: first-order and second-order ones. First-order reasons correspond generally to the reasons weighed in constructing the preference ordering. Second-order reasons, however, indicate what weights should be given to first-order reasons in particular circumstances. In this catalog, norms are *exclusionary* reasons, reasons which provide an individual with both a first-order reason for action and a second-order reason to exclude a particular set of first-order reasons.[16]

Consider a simple example in which Henry asks Liza to help him organize a conference. Liza will consider various first-order reasons for action: she enjoys working with Henry; she will receive a reasonable wage; the conference will address an important topic; she dislikes administrative work; the work with Henry will complicate her relations with Freddy; she will have less time to devote to her own projects; and so on. In addition, some exclusionary reasons might also bear on her decision. For instance, Liza may have promised to spend the week necessary for organization with Doolittle. The promise functions as an exclusionary reason. It provides a first-order reason for her to refuse Henry's offer. But it also directs her to ignore various of her other first-order reasons, for example, the enjoyment she derives from work with Henry, the wage, or her dislike of administrative work.[17]

Norms in obligation theories thus play a different role than they play in preference theories. In our example, they do not alter Liza's beliefs. They do not alter the set of options available to her. They do not alter her preferences.[18] Instead, they describe a different process of analysis with different consequences for private ordering.[19]

Consider a legal example in which a state enacts rules prohibiting sulfur dioxide emissions above a certain level. Violation of this rule results in a per unit fine of some amount. Corporation C must decide how much sulfur dioxide to emit in its production process. Specifically, it must decide by how much, if at all, it will exceed the permissible level. Various first-order reasons bear on this question: the cost of compliance both in terms of higher costs of production and lower sales (because of higher price), the likelihood a violation will be detected, the size of the fine, and the loss in public good will it would suffer as a convicted polluter. On an economic theory, C weighs the costs and benefits of compliance and then acts. On an obligation theory, the rule requiring compliance excludes consideration of the other reasons and C would comply.[20]

C. Preference and Obligation Theories Briefly Compared

The theory of norms as incentives has received much more elaboration than either the theory of norms as exclusionary reasons or the preference theories of norms as information and as induced value. Consequently, the virtues and demerits of the theory of norms as incentives are most evident, and it provides a useful benchmark against which to compare the other three theories.

The greatest strength of the theory of norms as incentives derives from its predictions of action in the face of conflicting norms. Suppose an individual faces (or is committed to) competing norms. Under the incentive theory, the competition is easily resolved. A sanction attaches to the violation of each norm and these sanctions alter the prices and hence the set of options that the individual faces. Consider, for example, the owner O of a small factory that emits sulfur dioxide. In the absence of any norms, O's interests dictate that she disregard the extent of her emissions of sulfur dioxide as she wishes to maximize her profits. If the law prohibits emissions of sulfur dioxide above a certain level, then, on the incentive theory, O will consider this norm by weighing the costs of noncompliance (in terms of fines or other penalties) against the benefits of noncompliance (in terms of lower costs of production). If, in addition, O has religious or moral beliefs that proscribe emissions, then, under the incentive theory, these beliefs will influence her decision on the level of emissions to produce in the same way: she will weigh the costs of noncompliance with this moral norm with the costs of noncompliance with the legal norms and with its effects on her profits.

None of the other theories has received sufficient elaboration to offer any predictions in these cases. Consider first the preference theory of norms as information. The resolution of conflicts among norms will depend upon the specification of the way in which norms influence an individual's beliefs. If the norms operate through beliefs or preferences, however, it is less clear how this conflict should be resolved. The theory of norms as information may present some simple cases of application in which the norm conveys information about what state of the world prevails, and the actor follows some rational procedure for revising her beliefs about the world. In the case of the polluter O, for example, the legal rule may carry information about the extent of harm caused by sulfur dioxide emissions. If O cares not only about her profits but also this harm, she might update her beliefs about the harm in light of the information provided by the legal norm. Presumably a conflicting moral norm about the extent of emissions also carries information about the harms caused by O's actions, and O will follow a more complicated process of revision of her initial beliefs about harm.[21] When the actor believes that the information conveyed by the norm reflects the interests of the promulgator, the analysis will grow more complex.

Resolution of conflicts among norms under the preference theory of norms as induced values will depend on what process of value formation one postulates. Unfortunately, little systematic theorizing about these processes has occurred. In the example of the polluter O, both the legal norm and the moral norm might affect O's actual desire for clean air but, until some one specifies more precisely how these effects arise, little can be said.

Similarly, the obligation theory of norms as exclusionary reasons does not, without further elaboration, resolve conflicts among norms. In the pollution example, both the legal norm and the moral norm require O to exclude consideration of her self-interest. If one norm requires less emissions than the other, then no true conflict exists; O can simply meet the most restrictive requirements. In other instances, however, moral and legal norms may conflict. In the 1850s, for examples, federal judges in northern states confronted a legal norm that required them to return fugitive slaves to captivity in the South. Many of these judges also confronted a moral norm that abhorred slavery (Cover 1975). Each of these norms both required the judge to ignore the first-order reason for action provided by the other norm and to resolve the conflict of exclusionary reasons in its favor. Put differently, both the legal system and the moral system had rules for resolving conflicts of norms of different systems, but these conflict of norms provisions also conflicted.

Obligation theories acknowledge a discrepancy between an individual's normative commitments and her desires that preference theories ignore. This discrepancy implies that an obligation theory of action must have a more complex motivational structure than the one posited in preference theories. In a preference theory, one's normative commitments never conflict with one's interests because normative commitments are, in one way or another, reduced to interests. In an obligation theory, however, where no such reduction occurs, some structure for resolving such conflicts must be postulated; the absence of such structures renders obligation theories unusable for social analysis.[22]

On the other hand, this discrepancy between normative commitment and interest does capture an aspect of action that preference theories ignore. Return to the pollution example. We may imagine two distinct legal regimes which create identical incentives but differ in their normative consequences. In the criminal regime, the state imposes a criminal fine of $10,000 per unit (per day) of emission above a given standard. In the tax regime, the state imposes a tax of $10,000 per unit (per day) of emissions above the identical standard. Assume that the enforcement mechanisms in the two regimes are identical. As a consequence, the two regimes present O with identical costs and benefits for every action she might adopt. Yet, if O violates the standard in the criminal regime, she acts wrongly, while if she violates the standard in the tax regime, she acts legitimately. An obligation theory, therefore, predicts fewer emissions under the criminal regime.

Finally, each of the theories of action sketched is incomplete in at least one important way. None of the preference theories articulates the mechanism of preference formation and change. Analogously, the theory of norms as exclusionary reasons explains neither the interests of the actor nor the mechanism by which the actor commits herself to a norm.

5. NORMS AS SELF-INTERESTED BEHAVIOR

Self-interest may enter into the explanation of normative behavior in two distinct ways.[23] First, self-interest may explain the extent to which individuals violate norms. The theory of norms as incentives assumes that violation of norms provokes a "punishment"; the prospect of this sanction prompts individuals to conform to the norm. Second, self-interest might explain the content of the norm to which individuals adhere; that is, we have norms that encourage probity rather than corruption because such probity promotes individual interest.

To see norms, in the first way, as sanctions treats a normative system that governs a behavior or some set of behaviors as defining the rules of a game.[24] This view of norms as incentives underlies the perspective of economic analysis of law.

The second perspective views norms themselves as emergent from the incentive structures of particular games. On this account, norms do not define the rules of the games but rather define the expectations as to which equilibrium of a game will be played.[25] This approach is most commonly developed in the context of a "repeated game," one in which the same parties interact repeatedly with each other.

Consider the prisoner's dilemma in which two parties, Row and Column, each must choose one of two actions: cooperate or defect. The consequence to each party depends not only on her choice but on the act of her opponent. Matrix 1 presents the payoff (or valuation of the consequences) to each party for each of the four possible pairs of actions; the first number in each cell represents Row's valuation of that cell and the second number represents Column's valuation.[26] Suppose that Row and Column do not know each other, will play this game only once (and then not meet each other again), and cannot make any binding agreements about their play. How should each play this game? Because the game is symmetric, we need only consider the best play of one party, say Row. One principle of rationality, "dominance," argues that Row should defect. Dominance relies on the observation that, regardless of what Column does, Row does best if she plays Defect. So, if Column defects, Row gets 1 when she defects and −1 when she cooperates. Conversely, if Column cooperates, Row gets 3 from defection and only 2 from cooperation. Because Row and Column are symmetrically situated, dominance dictates that Column also defect. Both players thus evaluate that outcome at 1 though both would prefer that each cooperate and receive 2.

MATRIX 1 THE PRISONER'S DILEMMA

| | | COLUMN | |
		COOPERATE	DEFECT
Row	Cooperate	2,2	−1,3
	Defect	3,−1	1,1

Can a norm of cooperation resolve the dilemma? If norms operate only as sanctions, a norm of cooperation will succeed only if it alters the payoffs to defection; that is, if it changes the structure of the game.[27] If, however, Row and Column repeat the interaction summarized in matrix 1 indefinitely, then violation of a norm of cooperation in one period can be punished by refusal to cooperate in (some) subsequent periods.[28] A norm of cooperation would thus be self-enforcing in the sense that both Row and Column would find it to their advantage to adhere to a norm of cooperation (enforced by the appropriate sanction).

Of course, mutual defection forever is also self-enforcing in the same sense. Indeed many complex patterns of behavior will be self-enforcing in the indefinitely repeated game.[29] On this account, a norm of cooperation simply identifies which pattern of behavior will emerge by forming individual expectations about the behavior of others. Put differently, the account of norms as defining expectations does not reduce norms to self-interest; rather it uses norms to explain how one pattern of behavior of many consistent with self-interest emerges.

Some have offered evolutionary explanations for the emergence of norms. In these models, if individuals who cooperate interact differentially often with others who cooperate and if individuals who "do well" flourish more than those who do badly, then we would expect the population of cooperators to grow.[30]

6. THE STUDY OF NORMATIVE REGIMES

At the outset, I suggested that every normative system contained both a set of prescriptions, permissions, and proscriptions that I called a normative order and an institutional structure (which I called a normative regime) to create, implement, and adjudicate norms. The prior discussion has largely considered how multiple systems of norms impinge on the actions of individuals who are subject to, but not participants in, the normative regimes. Moreover,

I have assumed that the normative regime conscientiously implements the normative order with which it is charged. Both these assumptions are subject to challenge. Our polluter O, for example, does not simply confront a choice between meeting the emission standard or violating it; she may also attempt to alter the norm. Similarly, those individuals vested with the authority to implement a normative regime have interests and commitments that may be at odds with conscientious implementation of the normative order. Officials of the regulatory agency enforcing emissions standards, for example, may look forward to employment with O or with other businesses subject to enforcement. In this section, I suggest how the theoretical structure elaborated above applies to the analysis of normative regimes themselves when we relax each of these two assumptions.

A. OFFICIALS AS SELF-INTERESTED, COMMITTED AGENTS

We may view officials legislating, implementing, or adjudicating within a normative order in exactly the same fashion that we viewed individuals subject to that normative order: as individuals with both interests and commitments to multiple normative orders. We may then try to predict their actions within their official roles using one or another of the theories of action outlined in section 4.

Again consider officials within the agency enforcing the emissions standards that apply to O. I have already suggested that these officials might have private interests concerning future employment with those subject to regulation. Other interests and commitments may impinge on their enforcement of the regulatory rules. Some individuals may have joined the agency out of a prior commitment to preservation of the environment, a commitment that at times will be at odds with specific regulations. Officials not interested in private employment might instead have interests in perpetuating, and increasing the reach and power of, their own agency. The agency, like any bureaucracy, will have its own culture that influences individual behavior. The highest officials may have commitments to the political parties or individuals who appointed them or to their political platforms. Scientists, lawyers, and economists within the agency may have commitments to their professions that at times run counter to the explicit requirements of the agency.

Finally, the mission of an agency may itself contain conflicts. An agency charged with protection of the environment may also face pressure to minimize the costs of industrial compliance in order to promote economic growth. The criminal justice system, as another example, must protect the rights of defendants but do so on a limited budget. Two officials who conscientiously seek to implement a statutory regime may resolve these conflicting statutory or institutional goals differently.

B. Self-Interested, Committed Actors as Lawmakers

The situation of individuals who avail themselves of enabling regimes such as contract or corporate law suggests how one might begin to analyze normative orders which, though produced by the agents themselves, still constrain the actions of those who created the norms. Consider for example a client C and an architect A. C requires a new building for her business; she wishes to hire A to design the building (and to supervise the contractor during its construction). Any contract must overcome various impediments. First, C has a complex set of preferences over possible designs. Efficient operation of her business imposes various design requirements; but C may not know, prior to education by A, which designs will best meet these business requirements at a given cost. Further, C may have concerns about the environment or concerns about cash flows that make different designs more or less desirable. At the outset of the contract, of course, A will not know C's requirements or concerns. In addition, investigation of the site as design work proceeds may lead to reevaluation of the construction costs. C may fear that A will exploit her ignorance of design and cost features to commit her to an excessively costly project. By contrast, A may fear that C will abandon her project if her business prospects decline or if the costs grow too excessive. In these circumstances, A and C will attempt to design a contract that protects each of them from exploitation by the other.

Note that the optimal contract will not simply prohibit such exploitation because such bans may not be enforceable for at least two reasons. First, C may be unable to observe when A presents her with excessively costly designs to accomplish a given purpose. Barring such actions would not then prevent them. Second, even if C (or A) can observe when A (or similarly C) has breached a particular contractual clause, the costs of judicially enforcing the clause may exceed the benefit. A could then breach the clause with impunity. Thus, A and C will draft a contract that seeks to create incentives for both parties to adhere to their obligation and that minimizes the damage to each should the other breach. A, for example, might seek payment in installments to forestall C's cancellation of the project and refusal to pay. Similarly, C may contract to complete the project on the condition that the lowest contractor's bid on the final design not exceed some specified cost figure.

The creation of contract norms, of course, differs from the creation of legal and many informal norms. Contract norms arise from (unanimous) consent of the parties to the contract while legal norms arise either from legislation or adjudication. While, in each case, the law may impose obligations that some individual does not want, one would expect all parties affected by a legal rule to seek to formulate the rule consistent with their interests and commitments. Legislative and judicial institutions will constrain in several ways the ability of parties to formulate the rules as they see fit. First, the legislative process will identify those actions that (most) influence the outcome.

Different committee structures, for example, will identify different officials as key to the legislation. Rules of standing, mootness, and ripeness may, in some instances, foreclose a party from pursuing legal change through litigation. Second, different legislative processes will impose different costs of creating or altering legislation. Enacting legislation within a bicameral legislature may be more costly than enacting identical legislation in a unicameral legislature. In adjudication, complex procedural rules may raise the cost of litigation and thus make litigation as a route for legal change less desirable.

7. NORMATIVE PLURALISM AND THE ANALYSIS OF POWER

The prior discussion bears on two questions concerning power. First, the outline of the various preference and obligation theories of behavior suggest different conceptions of power. Second, the structure of the analysis suggests that the presence of multiple normative systems will affect both the exercise of and struggle for power. I briefly consider each question in turn.

A. THE CONCEPT OF POWER

The concept of power is one of the more elusive in social theory. In what follows, a naive definition of power as the ability of an individual, group, or institution to influence the behavior of another should suffice.[31] Note that, in this definition as in others, an exercise of power affects the actions of others. An analysis of power should then follow directly from a theory of individual action. Each of the theories of action sketched in section 4 should therefore correspond to some form of power.

This correspondence between a theory of action and a form of power is most easily elucidated, for the three distinct types of preference theories of action as they identify three parallel forms that power might take: coercive, persuasive, and evaluative.

Coercive power corresponds to the theory of norms as incentives; an institution may influence behavior by altering the consequences of an individual's actions. Persuasive power corresponds to the theory of norms as information; influence here acts through the beliefs that the actor has and which an individual or an institution may manipulate. Finally, evaluative power corresponds to the theory of norms as induced values; on this account, power alters the desires and motivations of an individual and thereby directs her action.

Each form of power will have limits determined in part by the nature of the institution exercising power and in part by the theory of behavior. The law's coercive power, for example, is limited by the set of sanctions the law may impose and the ability of legal institutions to identify and to prosecute successful violaters of its norms. The limits of persuasive and evaluative power are less clear because the mechanisms through which norms influence the beliefs and values of individuals are incompletely specified.

Notice that, in each version of the preference theory, we have identified a form of power that is divorced from the content of the norm. Suppose, for example, that a norm prohibits an action X. The coercive power of the norm might be fairly measured by the size of sanction imposed for violation of the norm; this measure will be independent of the nature of the action X.[32] Similarly, the persuasive and evaluative power of a norm may depend to a large extent on the mechanisms by which norms influence individual beliefs and preferences respectively. This observation suggests that, under each of these preference theories, two other forms of power also exist: the power to determine the content of the norms and the power to commit others to the normative system in question.

In highly elaborated normative systems such as legal systems, the power to create norms is delegated to a discrete set of individuals who occupy legislative and adjudicative roles. In more informal systems, however, such delegation may not be explicit. In the most spontaneous systems, such as language use, no identifiable individual or group of individuals may have the power to determine the content of a norm.

Notice that a complete obligation theory of action differs from preference theories in the forms of power to which it gives rise. Specifically, under an obligation theory of action there are no content-independent forms of power. Recall that, under an obligation theory, a norm influences individual action by altering the set of reasons that an individual committed to the norm considers when choosing among alternatives. The existence of the norm does not alter the individual's beliefs or values; nor does its violation lead to sanction. Rather, the norm (partially) dictates the individual's process of deliberation.

B. THE EXERCISE OF POWER

The manifestation of power depends not only on one's theory of individual action but also upon the social structure in which individuals act. In the study of normative systems, two structural questions assume particular importance: (a) Who determines the normative order and hence the content of norms? and (b) Who enforces the norms? Specific answers to these two questions distribute power among individuals and groups within a society.

A legislative choice between an enabling regime and a set of specific primary obligations amounts to an allocation of power to define the content of norms. The contrast is most clear if one compares creation of an enabling regime to delegation to an agency. In each case, the legislature has chosen to delegate the power to create norms, but the choice of delegatee may significantly influence the final distribution of benefits.

The delegation to an agency vests the power to create norms in a small body of individuals who will have their own interests and (often professional) commitments. Creation of an enabling regime, in contrast, delegates the power to make norms to private individuals. The interests and commitments of these individuals will undoubtedly differ from those of agency decision makers. Moreover, enabling regimes generally presume decentralized promulgation of norms so that different groups may adopt norms suitable to their individual circumstances. Within each group enabled by the delegation, some individuals may wield more power or authority and the enabling regime itself may validate this prior distribution of power.

Similar concerns arise when one examines the question of who enforces a given set of norms. Some normative regimes, such as the law of torts and some codes of honor, permit individuals to enforce the relevant norms. Other normative regimes, such as the criminal law and some collective bargaining systems, centralize enforcement in a single agent, such as the prosecutor or a union. Those authorized to enforce a normative order, of course, will make their enforcement decisions in light of their own preferences and commitments. An accident victim, for example, may choose not to enforce her right to recovery against her injurer. Similarly, a district attorney will choose which laws to enforce and which offenders to prosecute, or a union official will decide which grievances to pursue. The legitimacy of the official's discretion vests her with the power to grant or to withhold the grievance machinery. She may exercise this power for legitimate or illegitimate reasons.

These comments about the exercise of power, evident as they are, have much explanatory use, even in the analysis of a single, highly elaborate normative system. Control of one institution in a legal system, for example, may give a group sufficient leverage against other legal actors to procure change. John Reid (1977) has compared, for example, the roughly contemporaneous rebellions of the American colonies and the Irish against the British in the late eighteenth century. He argues that the American rebels succeeded while the Irish failed in part because the Americans controlled the jury while the Irish did not.

The presence of multiple normative systems greatly increases the bases for the exercise of power by different groups. In Moore's discussion of the effects of a change in the legal norms governing real property among the Chagga in Tanzania (Moore 1973), for example, the legal norms did not offer the only, or even the primary, claim on particular parcels. Nonlegal officials, such as senior members in the clan, had significant power to influence land allocations on the basis of nonlegal norms (and their own preferences). Similarly, in her description of the ostracism of a "deviant" member of the Chagga (Moore 1991), the operation of self-interest within the norms of the group are limited by the victim's legal power.

8. JUSTICE

This essay has focused primarily on one question raised by a multiplicity of normative systems: how do individuals act in the face of such multiplicity?

The previous section considered the implications that these various theories of action had for our understanding of power. This section asks what implications these theories of action have for an understanding of the equally contested and elusive concept of justice.

At the outset, one should note that neither preference nor obligation theories of action will bear directly on our conception of justice because justice, unlike power, is primarily an evaluative rather than a behavioral concept. Phrased differently, the ability to evaluate institutions against any theory of justice does not depend on which theory of action one accepts. Moreover, for each theory of action, there will be some just institutional arrangement under many differing conceptions of justice.

Nonetheless, the justice (or injustice) of particular arrangements might motivate some individuals to action, and this motivational story grows more complex in a normatively plural world. Section 8A identifies some of these complexities as well as discussing how multiplicity may complicate an individual's own sense of justice. Section 8B considers one implication that these various theories of action have for the evaluation of the justice of legal institutions.

A. INDIVIDUAL MOTIVATION AND THE SENSE OF JUSTICE

Each normative order within a society may embody conceptions of appropriate individual behavior, of fair process, and of just distribution. These conceptions may conflict, and their conflict gives rise to a variety of institutional and evaluative difficulties.

Consider a conflict between law and some moral conception to which an individual is committed. The law requires X and morality requires not-X. The individual must adjudicate between these two normative claims and the process of deliberation may lead her to alter her conception of justice. Of course, if she decides that justice requires her to violate the law, she may still do X for prudential reasons.

The "problem" of civil disobedience arises when individuals decide that morality requires them to disobey the law. Presumably their disobedience both acknowledges their commitment to the legal order and their desire to alter it. The challenge to the legal system is partial rather than complete as in rebellion.

Not all conflicts among conceptions of justice have such dramatic consequences. In some instances of normative conflict with the legal system, individuals may simply choose to avoid the legal system. Different circumstances might both cause and permit such avoidance of the legal system. Diamond traders in New York City have created their own system of contract largely because of the failings of the legal system; these failings both permit the creation of their own normative system and dictate its form.[33] Of course, successful evasion of the legal system requires that the social group not only have its own enforcement mechanisms but also a means to prevent individuals dissatisfied with the group's resolution of an issue from invoking the legal system.

B. The Evaluation of Legal Institutions

How should we evaluate legal institutions? A naive approach would assume, first, that the legal institution conscientiously enforced the relevant legal norms and, second, that those subject to the legal norm complied with it. The justice of the legal institution would then depend solely on the content of the relevant legal norms.[34] The argument of the previous sections contested both assumptions on which the naive approach to evaluation rests. This section suggests a more sophisticated approach to the evaluation of legal institutions: to evaluate the behavior "induced" by the legal institution, that is, the behavior that results from imperfect enforcement and the choices of individuals who respond in a complex way to the legal norms, self-interest, and other norms.

As an example, consider the rules governing the division of property (including future income) and custody to children upon dissolution of a marriage. A naive evaluation would, as noted, assume that the custodial arrangement and division of property dictated by the legal norms would in fact prevail. The best legal regime would then be the one the norms of which dictated the fairest (or most just or most utilitarian) custodial arrangement and division of property. Suppose, for example, that we thought the best outcome was joint custody and an equal division of property.[35]

The judicial announcement of a joint custody/equal division rule does not ensure that divorcing parties will implement such a rule. Rather, to the extent they are able, they will bargain in the shadow of this rule, understanding that a failure to agree will lead to the judicial imposition of joint custody and equal division of property. Most probably, such private agreements will be reached in the majority of cases; to evaluate the legal rule, then, we must assess the pattern of settlements (and the few court-enforced outcomes) induced by the legal rule, not the single outcome required by it.

Similar concerns arise when legal norms conflict with the requirements of other normative systems. As noted earlier, this conflict may result in a pattern of outcomes different from that dictated by the legal norm. Thus, both when the content of a norm conflicts with interest and when it conflicts with the content of a norm from another system, the evaluation of that norm requires one to "see through" the content of the norm to the pattern of behavior that actually occurs.

9. Concluding Remarks

An understanding of social behavior or of power relations within society as well as any evaluation of the justice of social institutions must begin with a recognition of the normative complexity of social life. Individuals have not only wants and desires but also multiple commitments and obligations.

In this essay, I have suggested how this perspective might inform the study of law and of private systems of norms. Much of the discussion focused on how one might understand individual behavior in the face of individual commitment to many normative systems. Section 6, however, argued that the same framework of analysis might also illuminate questions concerning the evolution of normative systems themselves. The complex commitments of today's officials within a normative regime may influence not only the application of today's norms but also the content of tomorrow's norms. This influence on the evolution of the norms, of course, may induce a contest for control of the normative regime.

The analytic framework offered in this essay represents only a beginning. Most significantly, it omits any discussion of the evolution of individual wants and commitments. What individuals desire undoubtedly depends on a process of socialization created and maintained by various normative systems, including law. This process of preference formation requires explication. Equally, an individual's commitments may depend on the social environment in which she lives; this process of evolution of one's normative commitments also merits attention.

NOTES

Chris Eisgruber, Howard Venable, and participants at the Law and Society Summer Workshop on Justice and Power provided helpful comments on earlier drafts.

1. The second distinction concerning division of labor is explicated in Griffiths 1984.

2. The criterion of scope captures the crude sense of the public/private distinction for most normative systems but it fails with respect to religion. Some religious communities are larger than any political community and the normative order of most religions seeks to regulate conduct at least as comprehensively as state legal systems.

3. Indeed, the change often emerges in spite of efforts to guide or control.

4. The common law system presents an interesting mixture of clear division of labor and a partially spontaneous order.

5. When no union exists, labor relations are governed by contract, another enabling regime. Again, state law understands the complex institutional structures in terms of this enabling regime. The parties, in some sense, create their own law though in many instances management and labor have unequal power in the formulation of the relevant rules.

6. Preference theories are often called "rational choice" theories, a term I have avoided because it suggests that obligation theories are not rational. The literature on preference theories is vast. Kreps (1990: chaps. 2–5) offers a clear introduction to that theory.
   My articulation of obligation theories follows Raz (1975). A shorter, clear introduction appears in Hart (1982).

7. Note that preferences are over all possible options and not just the set of available options. A third restriction on preferences is that they be context-independent in some relevant sense. For a discussion, see Broome 1991.

8. Note that this discussion of preference theories does not refer to "utility." In rational choice theories, "utility" is a construct, a convenient way to represent an individual's preferences, that has no independent meaning. Much of the articulation of rational choice theory identifies when an individual's preferences can be so represented. Thus the core of subjective expected utility theory consists of a representation theorem that states the conditions under which an individual's preferences over uncertain actions may be represented by an expected utility form which separates these preferences over uncertain actions into preferences (represented by a utility function) over outcomes and a set of beliefs, represented by a set of probabilities, about states of the world.

9. A norm against the eating of meat might be enforced by a ban on its production and sale. This, too, can be understood as affecting the price of meat. If, in the unlikely event, the ban is successful, it raises the price of meat to infinity. In the more likely event, however, the ban will induce a black market in meat in which prices will rise in response to the increased costs of supply faced by (illegal) producers and sellers. (Bans on the production and sale of narcotics and other drugs offer an obvious analogy.)

   Note that the norm against meat eating may also increase the price of fish by increasing the demand for fish. Indeed, if norms acted only through preferences (i.e., there were no sanction or it did not operate like a price), a norm against meat eating would decrease the price of meat and increase the price of fish.

10. Kornhauser (1989) discusses this view at greater length.

11. This example is consistent with the economic view that beliefs arise from uncertainty about states of the world. Here, the relation between diet and health is unknown.

12. Put differently, as the price of potatoes fell, the amount demanded also fell because a price decrease increased an individual's real wealth and as wealth increased she preferred more meat and fewer potatoes.

13. Baumol and Oates 1988.

14. In the welfare economics literature and in the controversy between economic analysis of law and critical legal studies, this problem goes under the name of the "offer/asking price" problem because, when a wealth effect exists, the highest price an individual is willing to pay (offer) for a good differs from the lowest price at which she is willing to sell it. One formulation of the "Coase theorem" is that asking price equals offer price when the value of the property right is small relative to the total wealth of the individuals.

15. This gap in the theory undercuts most claims that legal norms influence preferences. One difficulty arises because the content of legal norms often changes abruptly while preferences seem to change slowly. More generally, one must specify precisely what preferences norms influence. Socialization might induce a preference for specific behaviors, a preference for conformity, or a preference for compliance with appropriately announced norms. These are all very different.

16. Exclusionary reasons thus put a weight of 0 on those reasons that the decision maker should exclude.

17. In fact, it probably excludes all the reasons listed above. It might not, however, exclude all possible reasons. Suppose completion of the task that afternoon would provide enormous and otherwise unavailable benefits to humanity. If these benefits were sufficiently great they might override the promise.

18. One might argue that they alter her preferences because she has a preference not to break her promises which is more important (in a lexical sense) than her other reasons. When more than one exclusionary reason applies, however, this tactic may not succeed.

19. Two other differences merit comment. First, under obligation theories, the individual need not have a complete ordering. In some theories, individuals have incommensurable first-order reasons for action. Second, context plays a much larger role in these theories; consequently, the resulting "preference" may not be transitive.

20. Contrast this analysis with the situation that arises when the state imposes a tax rather than a fine on excess emissions. In this instance, C's calculation is permissible under an obligation theory.

21. O must, for example, decide which of the norms provides a more accurate appraisal of the actual harms.

22. The philosophers who have investigated obligation theories have not generally considered them as theories of action designed to explain social phenomena.

23. Elster (1989) discusses the various relations that norms may have to self-interest.

24. Thus, an individual committed to more than one normative system that governs a single behavior must then play many games simultaneously. How does the individual determine her strategy in this complex system? The various preference theories and obligation theories answer this question differently. The theory of norms as incentives resolves this question in a simple, direct manner: a player considers only the net costs and benefits of each action.

25. Note that, alternatively, the expectations might concern the extent to which a given player will act rationally. In the presence of multiple normative commitments, the problem for preference theories and obligation theories alike then becomes determining how conflicting expectations about the play of a single individual are resolved.

26. I have made no assumption about the nature of Row or Column's preferences. The numbers in the matrix simply represent the ordinal ranking of the outcomes of each player. (Row prefers one outcome to another if a higher number is associated with it.) Both players may be purely self-interested. Or they may have altruistic motives, for even altruists may differ somewhat in their evaluation of outcomes, and they too may face the problem of coordination embodied in the prisoner's dilemma.

27. This fact illustrates why the theory of norms as sanctions models norms as defining the rules of the game. Note that if norms only affect beliefs so that, when a norm of cooperation prevails, Row believes it more likely that Column will cooperate, then Row still does better to defect.

28. A sanction will only be successful if players value future payoffs sufficiently highly. Suppose, for example, that a norm of cooperation prevails and that both parties know that violation of the norm means the opponent will defect ever after. Column, contemplating defection in period t, sees a benefit of "1" to defection in period t (he gets 3 instead of 2), and a cost of "1" in periods t + 1, t + 2, and so on. If Column values one unit tomorrow as δ units today ($\delta < 1$), then Column defects as long as

$$1 > \delta + \delta^2 + \delta^3 + \ldots = \delta/(1 - \delta)$$

which is true as long as $\delta < \frac{1}{2}$.

On repeated prisoner's dilemmas see Fudenberg and Tirole 1991.

29. The "Folk Theorem" says that any pair of individually rational and feasible payoffs is supported by an equilibrium of some probably complex set of strategies in the infinitely repeated game (for sufficiently high discount rates) (Fudenberg and Tirole 1991).

30. See, e.g., Axelrod 1984, Axelrod and Dion 1988, and Hirschleifer and Coll 1988. On these accounts, "cooperating" individuals are not "pure cooperators"; they cooperate with other cooperators but not with those who defect. Ellickson (1991) adopts this approach to analyze the content of informal social norms. Some skepticism about these models is expressed in Kornhauser 1992.

31. For an extended discussion of the concept of power see Wrong (1979: 2) who elaborates the simple definition: "Power is the capacity to produce intended and foreseen effects on others."

32. Note that the efficacy of the norm, however, may well depend on its content. Compare two actions X and Y where action X generally confers very high benefits to the actor and action Y confers low benefits. Suppose a normative system contains both a norm proscribing X and norm proscribing Y and that the normative system imposes the same sanction D for violation of each norm. Then the normative system might deter action Y but not action X even though coercive power, in the sense of the text, is exercised to the same degree. As I discuss further in section 7B, normative pluralism may affect the efficacy of an exercise of power in other ways as well.

33. Bernstein (1992) argues that the legal system has two failings: it is too slow and it undercompensates for breach of contract.

34. We may evaluate legal institutions against many criteria, most prominently, against criteria of fairness, justice, and goodness.

35. Our identification of the best outcome may depend on our assumptions about the justice of other prevailing social arrangements. If other social structures differentially harm or disable women, for example, we may think that equal division on divorce is not sustainable.

BIBLIOGRAPHY

Axelrod, Robert. 1984. *The Evolution of Cooperation*. New York: Basic Books.

Axelrod, Robert, and Douglas Dion. 1988. The Further Evolution of Cooperation. 242 *Science*, 1385.

Baumol, William, and Wallace Oates. 1988. *The Theory of Environmental Policy*. 2d ed. New York: Cambridge Univ. Press.

Bernstein, Lisa. 1992. Opting Out of the Legal System: Extralegal Contractual Relations in the Diamond Industry. 21 *Journal of Legal Studies*, 115.

Broome, John. 1991. *Weighing Goods*. Oxford: Basil Blackwell.

Cover, Robert. 1975. *Justice Accused*. New Haven, CT: Yale Univ. Press.

Ellickson, Robert. 1991. *Order without Law*. Cambridge, MA: Harvard Univ. Press.

Elster, Jon. 1989. *The Cement of Society*. New York: Cambridge Univ. Press.

Fudenberg, Drew, and Jean Tirole. 1991. *Game Theory*. Cambridge, MA: MIT Press.

Griffiths, John A. 1984. The Division of Labor in Social Control. In *Toward a General Theory of Social Control*, ed. D. Black. New York: Academic Press.

———. 1986. What Is Legal Pluralism? 24 *Journal of Legal Pluralism*, 1.

Hart, H. L. A. 1982. Commands and Authoritative Reasons. Reprinted in Hart, *Essays on Bentham*. Oxford: Oxford Univ. Press.

Hirshleifer, Jack, and Juan Coll. 1988. What Strategies Can Support the Evolutionary Emergence of Cooperation? 32 *Journal of Conflict Resolution,* 367.

Kornhauser, Lewis A. 1989. The New Economic Analysis of Law: Legal Rules as Incentives. In *Law and Economics,* ed. N. Mercuro. Boston: Kluwer Academic.

———. 1992. Are There Cracks in the Foundations of Spontaneous Order? 67 *New York University Law Rev.,* 647.

Kreps, David. 1990. *A Course in Microeconomic Theory.* Princeton, NJ: Princeton Univ. Press.

Macauley, Stewart. 1986. Private Government. In *Law and the Social Sciences,* ed. L. Lipson and S. Wheeler. New York: Russell Sage.

Merry, Sally E. 1988. Legal Pluralism. 22 *Law and Society Rev.,* 869.

Moore, Sally Falk. 1973. Law and Social Change: The Semi-Autonomous Field as an Appropriate Subject of Study. 7 *Law and Society Rev.,* 719.

———. 1991. Inflicting Harm Righteously: Turning a Relative into a Stranger: An African Case. In *Fremde der Gesellschaft,* ed. M. T. Fogen. Frankfurt am Main: Vittorio Klostermann.

Raz, Joseph. 1975. *Practical Reason and Norms.* London: Hutchison.

Reid, John Philip. 1977. *In a Defiant Stance: The Conditions of Law in Massachusetts Bay, the Irish Comparison, and the Coming of the American Revolution.* University Park: Pennsylvania State Univ. Press.

Unger, Roberto M. 1987. *Social Theory.* New York: Cambridge Univ. Press.

Wrong, Dennis. 1979. *Power: Its Forms, Bases and Uses.* Oxford: Basil Blackwell.

POWER AND JUSTICE IN
SOCIOLEGAL STUDIES OF REGULATION

❖

NANCY REICHMAN

The regulation of business conjures up images of "special interests," political privilege, and social power.[1] This paper examines how sociolegal scholars understand the dynamics of power in regulatory processes and the conceptualization of justice that informs "power" analyses. The synthesis of regulation studies that I present does not fully represent the growing literature in this area. My more modest goal is to examine how the relationship between law and power developed and changed in the study of regulation and to consider how these changes correlate with changing perceptions of, and possibilities for, justice.

Regulatory rules develop in a number of different ways. Legislatures enact statutes that define broad regulatory mandates and establish agencies to carry them forward. Agency staff create rules to implement the regulatory objectives.[2] Regulatory law is made as administrative judges and civil court judges review regulatory rules and procedures.

To the sociolegal scholar interested in the behavior of law, law is made through its practice as legal actors grapple with and transform the rules that define their work. Law is intimately connected to its social context, including the relationships of social power that contextualize and inform regulatory decision making. In the following pages I argue that sociolegal scholars who study regulation have conceptualized this important relationship between law and power in two ways. In the first way, regulatory power is used to explain the limits of law or the gaps between the law on the books and law in action. Power is defined as the structural and cultural constraints that influence regulatory practice. As Kagan (1990: 35) argues, from this perspective "law is used as both weapon and shield." Importantly, this way of thinking about regulatory legal process assumes relatively little independent agency and agenda setting for the legal system. Although the research focus is the state and particularly the legal system, the driving force of social action lies outside.

In the second perspective (or way of thinking about regulation), law and power are more explicitly connected, each being shaped by one another. Law's power rests not only in the technologies of coercion and control that are invoked through it, but in the cultural frameworks for action that are created by regulatory policy. From this perspective, law constitutes power. Law shapes the structure of social arrangements, choices and contingencies that constrain action, and it is, in turn, shaped by the very arrangements it creates. Research in this tradition looks beyond the state and its legal apparatus to consider how those involved in a broadly defined regulatory field use and transform law through its practice.

Our understanding of justice and injustice correlates (and may be contingent upon) the dynamic of power that informs the analysis of regulatory behavior. When power is conditioned by position and circulates around the resources and authorities that interested parties bring to the regulatory arena, justice discourse is more likely to focus on the distributive nature of justice, for example, on how regulatory burdens ought to be shared, the fairness of its procedures, and its implementation. When power is negotiated or enacted through regulatory practice, questions of justice necessarily focus on the very foundations of social order. Questions about the frameworks of meaning that give purpose and structure to social action precede and inform structural concerns about who gets what and why.

The studies cited below were chosen to illustrate my argument about power and justice and, thus, do not cover the full range of important work in the field. I approach this paper as a sociologist of law, and the analysis reflects my own sociolegal perspective. There are also important literatures from political science, notably those that focus on the institutional conflicts between the branches of government and the political constraints on the power of administrative agencies (e.g., Shapiro 1988; Bryner 1987); from the traditions of public policy and public administration (e.g., Melnick 1983); and from the growing literature on law and economics, but they are not included here.

One further caveat. To illustrate my argument I have relied almost exclusively on the American and British regulatory experience. Some scholars, for example, Vogel (1986) and Kelman (1981), argue that legal culture affects a nation's regulatory enforcement practice. I am not prepared to comment on what a more comparative approach might yield for our understanding of power and justice in regulatory process other than to note that more comparative work by sociolegal scholars is very much needed.

I. REGULATION

> The idea of regulation as we understand it today implies a social world divided into state and economy, a world in which the state "intervenes" in the economy to achieve certain goals which the economy is not achieving on its own. (Meidinger 1989: 156)

The modern regulatory state developed alongside "big business" and the coordination of business interests at the turn of the twentieth century. The federal regulatory agency was certainly not the first nor only legal foray into state oversight of business practice. States and localities intervened with inspection laws, licensing laws, and laws about weights and measures, and established local commissions over industry (railroad and insurance commissions or boards, for example) well before the twentieth century. But as business grew in size and complexity, "traditional" agencies of government could no longer do the job of regulating business or "taming" its infrastructure. Courts were not effective regulators of the big business environment either. "When the states could not meet the demands of their constituents, these constituents embarked on federal adventures" (Friedman 1985: 441). Administrative agencies, authorities of government other than the executive, legislative, or judicial branches, were established to administer particular pieces of legislation enacted to manage the market. The Securities and Exchange Commission, for example, was established in 1934 by the Securities and Exchange Act after the 1929 stock market crash and subsequent Congressional investigations made clear that existing control mechanisms could no longer foster continued investment in the nation's stock market.[3]

It is hard to find a simple way to characterize the regulatory state, in part, because it has passed through distinct, overlapping, stages of development (McGraw 1975) and, in part, because the definition, goals, and purposes of regulatory programs are contested in scholarly debates. Scholars generally concede two phases of regulatory intervention, however, to which I will add a third. These phases are distinguished by how state intervention is structured.

A. ECONOMIC REGULATION

The first phase of regulatory intervention, corresponding roughly to regulatory agencies created in the first half of the twentieth century, is often referred to as economic regulation. The goal of economic regulation is to make markets work better, to control entry into the market, to monitor, if not control, prices, to prevent the formation of cartels, and, less often, to control unscrupulous and illegal behavior (i.e., to protect principal-agency relationships).[4] This stage in regulatory intervention is often called the New Deal era, reflecting the philosophy of progressive intervention and positive possibilities for government. The authority to regulate is located in expert agencies created to oversee a particular sector of the economy. As initially conceived, these expert commissions were subject to minimal legislative or executive interference.[5] Forty-two major regulatory agencies and programs were created by Congress during the 1930s (Bryner 1987: 13).

B. SOCIAL REGULATION

The second phase of regulatory intervention, referred to as social or protective regulation, began in the 1960s and peaked in the 1970s. In contrast to controlling specific market arenas, social regulation governs a particular problem across market sectors by setting production standards and monitoring business performance along specified criteria. The state intervenes to correct for negative externalities and/or lack of information in the market model (Manning 1989).[6] The implementing agency is often, although not always, headed by a single administrator. "In the 1960s, 53 new regulatory programs and agencies were formed. Between 1970 and 1980, 130 major regulatory laws were enacted" (Bryner 1987: 13). The Environmental Protection Agency (1970), the Occupational Health and Safety Administration (1970), and the Consumer Product Safety Commission (1972) illustrate this kind of problem-oriented regulation.

C. DISCIPLINARY REGULATION

There appears to be something of a third phase of regulatory intervention, disciplinary regulation. This new form of state intervention moves away from the command and control policies that typify the programs of economic and social regulation to include more theoretically collaborative and flexible[7] forms of social control, including what is often described as deregulation.[8] I call this form of regulation, disciplinary regulation, because it corresponds to Foucault's notion of disciplinary control. Rather than regulating through sovereign commands and constraints, disciplinary control regulates through procedure and surveillance. Disciplinary regulation is an "integrated system, linked from the inside to the economy and to the aims of the mechanism in which it was practiced" (Foucault 1977: 176).

One example of a disciplinary approach to regulation is to use markets as tools to meet regulatory objectives. The premise underlying market based regulatory controls is to structure incentives for regulated entities so that compliance with regulatory objectives is inversely related to its cost. The most direct approach is to tax unwanted outcomes, for example, taxing emissions (also see Huppes 1992.) Advocates of a carbon tax, for example, suggest that polluters pay for their carbon emissions. A second approach is to create direct monetary incentives and disincentives in ways that effectively create regulatory markets, such as markets in pollution rights. The basic objective is to develop a private system of resource allocation that encourages businesses to invest in technologies of compliance. Meidinger (1989) describes how the Environmental Protection Agency created a market for pollution permits: "Permits would be required for all emissions. Only a limited number of permits would be available. Therefore, those polluters for whom emissions controls are most expensive would buy up the permits, while those for whom controls are least expensive would reduce emissions." A similar market based system was designed by the EPA to control the use of chloroflorocarbons (Rabin 1989).

An increasing emphasis on self-regulation offers a second illustration of the shift to more disciplinary forms of social control.[9] Some projects bolster an already strong regulatory program by extending liability to cases where self-regulation is not performed. New securities laws regarding insider trading, for example, now require firms to establish, maintain, and enforce written policies and procedures reasonably designed to prevent the misuse of material, non-public information, and to face criminal and civil liability if they don't (ITSFA 1988). Other regulatory agencies attempt to build self-regulation into ongoing programs. Joseph Rees (1988) describes an experiment, the Cooperative Compliance Program (CCP) established by California's Occupational Safety and Health Administration in 1979, to officially mandate self-regulation. The CCP created a three-way arrangement involving union, management, and California OSHA to establish model job site safety committees to act as OSHA surrogates and to encourage voluntary compliance with OSHA rules. The committees were charged with conducting monthly OSHA-type inspections, documenting violations, conducting weekly meetings to discuss matters of compliance, and reviewing safety forms submitted to the Safety Department (Rees 1988: 139). Designated compliance officers were appointed by the deputy chief of CAL/OSHA to guide the job site committees through OSHA regulations and procedures. In 1982, federal OSHA announced the creation of its Voluntary Protection Program to encourage, if not mandate, self-regulation. Although some successful experiments developed out of these initiatives, they were never expanded into full programs, in part a reflection of OSHA's weak regulatory presence overall (Ayres and Braithwaite 1992).

A third important trend in regulation is the opening up of regulatory rule making and, to a lesser degree, enforcement to participation and surveillance by public interest groups (PIGs) and the use of private mediators to help negotiate or mediate a consensus about regulatory practices. Proponents of mediated regulation argue that agreements made though negotiations with affected parties will be faster and more likely to meet the needs of those affected than traditional methods of rule making (Susskind and Cruikshank 1987; Amy 1987).

The shift away from command and control that these regulatory initiatives encourage offers an empirical justification for rethinking the relationship between law and power in regulatory arenas. State intervention into markets has changed and continues to change in ways that challenge models of power informed by command and control. Indeed, I argue that these empirical trends require that we rethink our understandings and analyses of law and power. To reach that position we must first look at what scholars have taught us thus far and where we might head in the future.

2. POWER OUTSIDE LAW

Because they are delegated authorities with broad mandates, regulatory agencies are perhaps uniquely exposed to the vagaries of political, economic, and social power.[10] Scholars locate the limits of regulation in the institutional and structural constraints that bind regulatory actions. For Mashaw and Harfst (1990), regulatory agencies are constrained by the separation of powers that makes " 'administrative policymaking' an oxymoron" (1990: 226–27). Although the administrative agency is primarily responsible for making and enforcing the rules, including adjudicating complaints/violations of those rules, the power of these agencies is "checked" by the relative powers of legislatures, the executive, and the judiciary. Congress, for example, vetoes legislation, withdraws necessary funding, and alters the rules that enable regulators to act. Presidents issue executive orders that strengthen the role of the Office of Management and Budget to impose cost-benefit and other economic (efficiency) based requirements on agency decision making.[11] Commentators generally agree that judicial review of administrative agencies is becoming more common (see Shapiro 1988 and the discussion in Aman 1992).

Bryner (1987), following the argument of Shapiro (1988), locates the "paradox" of regulation in its attempt to satisfy rationalist policy objectives and pluralist governance—that is, the power of competing influence. Kagan (1990) describes the political struggle between those who want to encourage economic efficiency through the markets and others who want the state to regulate its externalities (largely an interest model). Scholars such as Mashaw (1983) and Lipsky (1980) locate regulatory struggles and conflicts in the constraints of modern bureaucracies and scarce resources. Power here is located in the organizational and situational resources that parties bring to the regulatory game.

Still others locate the limits of regulatory law in the structures of capitalist relations that mediate state action. Diver (1989) , Gunningham (1987), Yeager (1991) , and Calavita (1983, 1992), for example, locate power struggles in the symbiotic connections between law and the economy and the regulators' dependencies on those they regulate.

The following section examines the work of sociolegal scholars who consider how powerful interests shape the behavior of regulatory law, generally limiting its effect. Scholars utilizing this perspective locate law in a wide range of cultural, psychological, and social structural forces that influence legal outcomes. While this general perspective recognizes that legal rules and behavior may directly participate in their own corruption, power and more generally power structures are regarded as something outside of law that determines its outcome. Some scholars locate power in the politics of influence and the situational and organizational factors that predict outcomes. Others understand power in terms of the structural positions of regulatory actors and the general contradictions of capitalist development.

A. Power and the Politics of Influence: From Capture to Accommodation

One approach to understanding the relationship between power and law considers regulation as an outcome of politics, a consequence of how particular power structures are arranged to influence the legislative process. Studies from this perspective describe how factors traditionally thought of as "outside law" influence the construction of regulatory authority, agendas, and work.[12] The power structures that have been studied for their influence on regulatory authority and law include: large business interests, class politics, traditional political parties, the judiciary, unions, consumer groups, and the media.

Both regulatory policy and regulatory practice are susceptible to influence. At its best, sociolegal scholarship tries to break down some of the distinctions between policy and practice that too often define the disciplinary approaches to the study of regulatory behavior. Sociolegal scholars attempt to show that frontline decision makers, the street level bureaucrats in Lipsky's (1980) terms, bring substance and meaning to legal rules as they carry on their work; they establish policy through practice. Similarly, an agency's policy (legal) staff can be directly implicated in practice, when, for example, they draft a particular compliance agreement (see Meidinger 1989). Still, most scholars who study the extralegal factors that condition the regulatory response orient their work to either policy making or its implementation. This section of the paper reflects that particular organization of scholarship.

Capture and Accommodation in Regulatory Policymaking

Theories of regulatory capture by big business informed the early studies of power and influence in regulatory policy making.[13] Historian Gabriel Kolko is often credited with beginning an important tradition of scholarship that addresses why big business sought control of the regulatory agenda. While, on its face, regulation appears to be antithetical to business interests, Kolko's work (1963, 1965) suggests that large firms welcomed regulation and even influenced the drafting of regulatory rules at the federal level where they quite correctly believed they could exert powerful influence.[14] Big businesses embrace regulation because it provides the necessary legal and economic certainty for their development, because it favors larger business that can better afford the increased costs of compliance than their smaller counterparts, and because the higher unit costs of compliance imposed on smaller firms reduces competition from those firms. (For a more contemporary argument, see Barnett 1981.)

Bernstein's (1955) classic study of the independent regulatory commission provides an early model of agency capture. He suggests that agencies follow a particular life cycle. At first, they appear to be aggressive reformers. But as their agendas becomes institutionalized, political leaders become less interested in their work. Soon, the agency finds itself interacting only with the interested constituency it had originally targeted for control. And then, to secure support for its continued existence, the agency begins to accommodate and reflect the interests of the regulated.[15]

Scholars who seek to test the capture thesis empirically consider factors such as industry domination over regulatory appointments, "revolving door" career patterns where regulatory officials and corporate executives move in and out of the two spheres (Freitag 1983), and the corruption of regulatory officials (see the discussion in Noll 1985). Although empirical support for capture models is weak, the conceptual legacy lives on. More sophisticated models of influence grounded in pluralist and corporatist political relations were developed by Lowi (1979) and Wilson (1980) respectively. In their work they offer different understandings of how outside interests coalesce to influence regulatory policy and how the state responds to facilitate, thwart, or neutralize particular interests. In an important corrective to simple capture models, Lowi (1979) introduces the state as an interested and powerful party to the regulatory arena. He argues that the broad delegation of discretion away from the electorate to professional career administrators contributes to conditions of patronage that empower those administrators and their activities. "Discretion enables them [the regulatory agents] to convert regulatory or welfare policies into resources for group or individual patronage" (Lowi 1987: 322). Lowi considers the "tendency of organized groups to become privileged clients of key state administrative agencies and officials, thus squeezing out effective pluralistic interaction and policy innovation in important public sectors" (McCann 1988: 376, referring to Lowi's classic articulation). State administrative processes are important sources of power that mediate the effect of business and other group interests.

Wilson offers an organizational model of power and influence that considers how goals are determined, conflicts resolved or managed, standards set and policies enforced (1980: vi). He suggests that the distribution of costs and benefits unique to each regulatory program will determine the potential for and style of influence (e.g., whether entrepreneurial, majoritarian, and interest group coalitions prevail). In his conceptualization, the power to influence regulatory outcomes is associated with the relative resources that are mobilized by the unique configuration of interests that determine goals and objectives. How government organizes itself to accommodate those interests, he argues, will make a difference to regulatory efficacy (1985: 359).

Although most research that models patterns of influence examines state policy, self-regulation has been explained by political models of influence and conflict as well. Rees's (1988) study of the adoption of self-regulation over workplace safety locates policy emerging out of the conflict between industrial unionism that sought more government action against employers and construction unions that sought relief for them. According to his analysis, proposals for self-regulation are mediated by the competing interests that are affected by those rules.

Two notable efforts to challenge traditional models of influence are found in the models of radical pluralism and tripartism suggested by Michael McCann, and by Ian Ayres and John Braithwaite, respectively. Both suggest that public interest groups can provide important sources of countervailing power that effectively break apart the dyadic and corporatist relationships that typified regulatory politics in the past. McCann (1988) argues that public interest groups, while individually marginal, taken together represent an adversarial posture toward both business and government: "Far from encouraging trends toward quasicorporatist governmental accommodation of social groups, these reform groups actually have challenged corporate capture, clientelism, iron triangles, subgovernments and other manifestations of exclusive private control over public authority wherever they exist" (1988: 388).[16] Ayres and Braithwaite (1992) advocate a model that empowers a representative public interest group (PIG) to join as an equal player in the regulatory game. In their republican model of regulation, interests are structured in ways that allow them to become contingent and intertwined. They "conceive of capitalists as internalizing the interests in the law, PIGs as internalizing the interests of firms and regulators, and both as having their interests shaped by third and fourth structural factors" (1992: 96).[17] Possibilities of capture and cooptation are negated by the countervailing power of the institutionalized third party.[18]

Together, these studies of regulatory policy making and proposals for change suggest that regulatory law can be influenced by powerful group interests. How the interests coalesce to affect law depends in large measure on the degree (extent) of influence and the underlying theory of power (pluralist, class, power-elite, or even republicanism/communitarian models) that the researcher brings to her interest based analysis.

In the following section I consider studies that show how extralegal factors enter into the regulatory process itself to determine regulatory outcomes. Again, power is defined in terms of the resources that condition the legal response and affect the outcome of a particular regulatory interaction.

Accommodation in Regulatory Practice

Sociolegal scholars of regulatory work tend to distinguish between two dimensions of regulatory practice—compliance with regulatory rules and cooperation with regulators, on the one hand, or rule enforcement and sanctioning activities, on the other (Hawkins 1984; Reiss 1984; Manning 1987). Compliance oriented regulation tends to focus on the prevention of violations. It structures the organizational environment of regulated entities, sets standards, diverts conflicts, and neutralizes the source of violations. The purview of compliance is the technical, procedural violation that, left unchecked, might create opportunities for more serious violations in the future. Enforcement oriented regulation, by way of contrast, focuses on the detection of past violations and sanctioning of violators. It is oriented toward deterrence; violators are apprehended and sanctioned in order to discourage future violations.

Behavioral studies of regulatory policy examine factors that condition the regulatory response as oriented either to compliance or enforcement.[19] Bardach and Kagan's (1982) model of regulatory discretion and Hawkins's (1984) so-called bargain-bluff model of regulation represent two streams of research in this field. Although offering different explanations of outcome, both understand regulation as a negotiated response. The "street level work" of regulatory agencies is the research focus.

Bardach and Kagan (1982) show how politics, law, and bureaucracy combine to create "regulatory unreasonableness," a "stringency" (Kagan 1978) to law that discourages rather than encourages responsible behavior. Strict, legalistic rule enforcement, overregulation in their terms, creates a defensive, adversarial relationship to regulation that produces antithetical regulatory outcomes.[20] A regulator's forbearance,[21] or the decision not to enforce the law, can become an effective form of regulatory currency traded to accomplish meaningful compliance. The research by Bardach and Kagan has spawned a good deal of scholarship that examines the politics of regulatory work, that is, the bargains and negotiations that are struck by regulators as they manage the problem of "overinclusive rules"[22] and conflicting demands of legislatures, courts, and regulated entities.[23]

Keith Hawkins's (1984) work locates power in the interpretive perspectives that regulators bring to their discretionary decisions about when and how to enforce the rules. He suggests that regulatory outcomes depend on the orienting frameworks that regulators bring to and develop from their work. In his study of pollution control in Great Britain, he reminds readers that pollution is more than a physical residue; it is a human judgment about a harm, its cause, and the moral status of its creators. And because there are few objective measures and only vague political mandates, regulators create and act on their own interpretative frameworks which are refracted by political and organizational demands. Discretion is organizationally and politically contingent in this analysis.

I collapse these two models of regulatory implementation to show how regulatory research informed by one or the other, or both, attempts to isolate factors that influence the political or interpretative decisions of regulatory agents. Regulatory power is conceptualized as control over the rules, relationships, and resources that guide regulators' actions and ultimately regulatory (legal) outcomes.[24] Regulators and those they regulate bring power into the regulatory process through their control over the regulatory interaction.

Controlling Regulatory Relationships. Nearly all behavioral studies of regulatory behavior recognize that the interaction between regulators and the regulated entity influences regulatory outcomes. Regulatory power is associated with those who can exert the most control over the regulatory decision. According to Kagan (1978: 67), representatives of regulated firms are continually in positions to present their problems and to mount challenges. Substantive discretion is molded by the political, economic, technical, and legal resources that regulated entities bring to regulatory interactions. The ability to influence outcomes is not evenly distributed among industry representatives, however. Powerful—read economically strong—corporate actors are better able to thwart or neutralize regulatory action than their smaller counterparts (see Lynxwiller, Shover, and McClelland 1983).

The regulatory interaction itself can be structured in ways that more subtly privilege particular regulatory interests. Nader and Serber (1980) describe how meetings between state insurance regulators, typically midlevel civil servants, and relatively high status industry representatives, create a climate of cooperation and accommodation that serves the interests of the regulated industry. "Regulators feel a privileged and personal part of the social milieu of industry rather than a part of the public, thereby negating the motivation to make the agency function as a power-equalizing institution working in the interests of the people" (1980: 334).

But influence can be felt even prior to any direct meetings between regulators and those they regulate. Diver (1989) suggests that policy makers implicitly assess the application or compliance costs when making rules. He argues that regulatory policy accommodates business needs before they are even articulated. Gunningham (1987) similarly reports that regulators are sensitive to the wishes and power of the regulated group even during the enforcement process (see also Bardach and Kagan 1982).

Other public agencies and officials who monitor the activities of regulatory agencies can be a powerful, albeit more indirect, force in managing regulatory interactions. Gilboy's (1992) study of the Immigration and Naturalization Service (INS) inspectors demonstrates how public officials can indirectly affect how immigration law is implemented. She found that INS inspectors anticipate that public officials will make casework complaints, and, consequently, offer systematic preferential handling for the types of cases most likely to provoke this kind of political intervention. In the case of regulatory enforcement, regulatory agents frame their actions within their perceptions of how other legal actors, notably U.S. attorneys, are likely to evaluate their cases. Hawkins (1989) describes this kind of regulatory accommodation in terms of regulators' legal risks, the uncertainty of successful prosecution should official legal action be invoked.[25] At least part of the explanation for the relatively few eligible securities cases referred by the Securities and Exchange Commission to the Justice Department for criminal prosecution is the likelihood that the prosecutors would act (Shapiro 1984, 1985). And, as private enforcement continues as a strategy of choice, the preferences of the judiciary become an increasingly influential interest in implementation as well as policy making.

Controlling Regulatory Resources. Organizational scholars (e.g., Kanter 1977) often measure power in terms of the amount and type of resources that can be mobilized to achieve a desired end. Agency funding to implement a regulatory program or a regulated entity's resources to fight regulatory action can be an important determinant of regulatory outcomes. Hutter and Manning (1990) observed that periods of economic hardship increased pressure on the Health and Safety Inspectorate in Great Britain to be efficient and effective while at the same time reducing the resources available to do the job. The structure and meaning of regulatory work changed as a result. In short, money is a powerful resource in the mobilization of law.

But there are other important resources that affect the direction of law. Sociolegal scholars demonstrate that even with adequate funding and staff, regulatory outcomes are influenced by access to a key element of the regulatory program, information. Although regulatory agencies have power to issue subpoenas for information necessary to implement and enforce their rules, they are not well positioned to know what data exist nor how material they might be. Agencies are rarely staffed sufficiently to gather the necessary information; they must rely on the regulated entities to provide the data necessary for effective regulation. According to Clinard and Yeager (1980), these data are often incomplete for agency needs, but the agency rarely has the means or the power to augment or verify that which is provided. As an example, they note that the Department of Energy "finding" that the 1979 gasoline shortage was not contrived by the oil industry was based solely on data provided by the oil industry. Shapiro's (1984) study of the Securities and Exchange Commission enforcement shows the power of information (e.g., the strategies available for detecting rule breaking) in explaining regulatory policy—affecting which rules are enforced and which violators are sanctioned.

Organizational structures and cultures can be powerful determinants of how information that is made available is understood and used. Studies of criminal law enforcement demonstrate that implementation decisions are affected by knowledge about other cases. Over time, legal actors accumulate sufficient knowledge that allows them to "typify" cases into predefined categories that drive subsequent inquiry and disposition.[26] Emerson (1991) argues that this kind of typification has an organizational as well as a cognitive basis. Organizational demands and the practical problems of legal actors combine with what Emerson elsewhere (1992) refers to as organizational horizons[27] to shape the categorization of cases and their path to resolution. Gilboy (1991) applies Emerson's organizationally grounded model of decision making to the study of immigration inspectors. She finds that the distinctive task of primary inspectors and the concerns of the port of entry explain the persistence of "normal" categories and the differential handling procedures that follow from them.

Controlling Regulatory Rules. Commentators suggest that regulatory rules, because they must accommodate multiple constituencies and broad policy mandates, invite their own corruption. At the core of this critique is the power to interpret rules and facts in ways that suggest that the rules do not apply or do not apply in traditional ways to the conduct under investigation. As noted above, the relative status of the regulator may be determinative here. Powerful regulatory actors may be able to manage the interpretation of rules in ways that privilege their interpretation of facts and rules. At its most basic, the complexity of regulatory law makes it accessible only to the most sophisticated players (businesses, organized public interest groups) who have the resources to sort through it.

But rules can be limited by their substantive content as well. Yeager (1991) notes that environmental law is self-limiting because it controls pollution outside of the factory rather than directly regulating manufacturers' production practices. He suggests that the substance of regulatory rules "privileges the autonomy of industrial processes" over the interests of the environment. Edelman's (1991) analysis of equal employment opportunity/affirmative action law also illustrates how law is constrained by its substance. She argues that laws such as EEO/AA laws, that constrain procedure rather than substance, are effective at controlling only the most blatant kinds of discrimination. And she suggests that "procedural constraints enhance the potential for organizations to develop forms of compliance that appear to comply with the law but have little substantive effect" (1991: 1538).

B. POWER AND THE CONTRADICTION OF CAPITALIST DEVELOPMENT

A different model of power informs the work of sociolegal scholars who study the limits of law in terms of the contradictions of capitalist development. In these studies power is not a simple matter of influence or available resources. Power exists in broader based structures outside of law; that is, in the forces of production and the structural contradictions that limit the effect of the state as a mediating force.[28] Law and legal institutions are caught within the contradictory demands of capital to insure private growth and public harmony (Yeager 1991: 44; Chambliss 1986). Regulatory law fails because it must support innovation and profit at the same time that it promotes certainty, order, and stability.[29]

One way lawmakers resolve the contradictions they face is to write law in ways that make its effect nothing more than symbolic.[30] Calavita's studies of OSHA and the Immigration and Naturalization Service illustrate this approach. The Immigration Reform and Control Act, passed in 1986, included a provision that a "good faith" document check of potential employees provided employers with an affirmative defense that they had not knowingly hired illegal aliens. Calavita's (1990) analysis of INS enforcement shows how the law was written in such a way as to "label all but a handful of the most blatant violators as 'compliers,' thus not only shielding them from prosecution but holding them up as examples to be followed" (1990: 1045). She argues that "compliance with the paperwork requirement had come to stand in for compliance with the real heart of the employer sanctions law" (1990: 1059). Laws that are passed "without teeth" further illustrate the symbolic resolution of the need to promote capitalism and maintain harmony and certainty in productive relations. This occurs when, for example, Congress passes legislation but provides few sanctions for its violation or when strong legislation is enacted but only limited funds are provided for its implementation. Yet another way the state can resolve the contradictory demands it confronts is to socialize regulation by socializing its costs, that is, the "public sector pays for correcting social harms imposed by industry" (Barnett 1992: 105). This occurs when the state raises taxes or increases the debt to support the externalities of private accumulation. Using tax money to clean up superfund sites offers an illustration. And, of course, deregulation offers important possibilities here.[31]

Whatever interventions are adopted, they must not openly appear to privilege a particular interest, or they risk losing state legitimacy or the underlying bases of support. Regulatory law must at once "deny hierarchy and serve it" (Trubek et al. 1993: 13; see also O'Conner 1973: chap. 1 for a classic discussion of this dilemma).

> The state must provide for and protect the conditions for capital accumulation, but it must simultaneously appear to be class neutral. In other words, while it must often be class biased in providing optimum conditions for profit maximization, the capitalist state must maintain a semblance of impartiality if it is to retain its legitimacy and minimize social protest. (Calavita 1983: 438)[32]

Therein lie the limits of law. Law is constrained by the requirements of capital.[33]

Those who embrace the model of contradiction show that law, caught within the contradictory demands of capitalist economies, reproduces and exacerbates the inequities and externalities it was adopted to address. Yeager (1991) and Barnett (1981) have argued, for example, that environmental regulation burdens smaller companies disproportionately, increasing economic concentration and intensifying inequalities among market sectors. Regulation, according to these analyses, creates destabilizing consequences that will eventually require more regulation. Barnett (1981) goes further to argue that, caught within the contradiction of capitalist development, regulation may even reproduce the conditions for the conduct that was the original target of the regulatory law. Firms that view regulatory law as largely symbolic and not adequately enforced may choose to risk noncompliance. Gunningham (1987: 84) argues similarly that should regulatory agencies reject prosecution as a regulatory tool, "Regulated enterprises will often find it more profitable to break the law and hope that no inspection will take place." The pressure to violate the law for economic reasons may not be evenly distributed among firms. Smaller firms, burdened with the cost of regulation, may find themselves in financially precarious situations where noncompliance may be viewed as the only solution (see also Vaughan 1983).

Reichman's (1991) analysis of securities law suggests that securities regulations, wed to universalistic principles at the ideological level and then applied to the highly competitive and differentiated structures within the stock market, may actually intensify diverse, particularistic responses that undermine or at least work in opposition to the very principles on which the law was based. In competitive and rapidly changing business environments, those who can do so will move beyond the status-neutral regulations to seek out new arrangements for managing their investment risk to complement and in some cases usurp statutorily based risk management programs.

Sociolegal scholars use structural models of power to challenge the impact of increased participation in the regulatory arena. On its face regulation appears to be more accessible to a wide range of interests. Beginning in the 1970s, regulatory agencies included deliberation and participation by advocacy groups into virtually every phase of rulemaking and enforcement in the law (Yeager 1991: 18). The Freedom of Information Act, the Government in the Sunshine Act, and the Ethics in Government Act opened up regulatory processes to public scrutiny in ways that attempt to set important limits on regulatory power. In addition, Congress broadened standing-to-sue standards that allow advocacy groups to challenge administrative decisions that do not meet their regulatory objectives. As noted earlier, public interest groups have won some important regulatory battles through this process.

But, in what may be regarded as a corollary to Abel's (1982) contradiction of informal justice, regulatory scholars show that increasing access to the regulatory domain may do little to change the hierarchies of power that privilege interests and outcomes. Silbey's (1984) analysis of consumer complaint handling in the Massachusetts Consumer Protection Department found that regulation that was on its face responsive to consumer demands, in fact, more directly accommodated the interests of sellers. By "failing to make law general [i.e., requiring case by case complaint handling], consumer protection takes place in a sphere where one party is more powerful and where major advantages rest with business" (Silbey 1984: 162).

Similarly, Harrington (1988) demonstrates that efforts to open up the rule making process to accommodate different interests has served mostly to privilege and support the market system that is the target of regulatory control. Her work describes the rule making reform that brings private mediators ("neutral conveners") to the regulatory arena to identify interested parties and issues and to negotiate new rules. "Political legitimacy derives not from the accountability of public authorities or even from the publicness of the process; instead, the process of sharing in making the 'ultimate judgment' about the rules is said to provide legitimacy to regulatory negotiations" (1988: 307). Although the discourse is about communication and negotiation, the process privileges the conceptualization of a self balancing market system (1988: 306).

In short, she argues, negotiated regulation allows the state to withdraw from its regulatory role, leaving the most powerful interest in charge.

Together, Silbey and Harrington show that "responsive regulation" has worked mostly to silence the state—to support existing power (market) arrangements. Others, for example, Mashaw (1985) and Harris and Milkis (1989), suggest that the effort to be "responsive" may actually undermine traditional forms of democratic process. "Paradoxically, while the public lobby regime has 'opened up' the regulatory process, it also has sheltered regulatory policy from broader democratic influence such as the presidency or electoral politics" (Harris and Milkis 1989: 51).

C. POWER AS CONSTRAINT: THE MOBILIZATION OF BIAS

Whether power is understood as a matter of influence or a force of production, regulatory scholars traditionally view it to be an extralegal phenomenon. Law mobilizes biases that exist outside. (For a discussion of the faces of power and mobilization of bias, see Bachrach and Baratz 1970 and Schattschneider 1960.) While for some mobilization occurs through the use of political and economic resources (votes, jobs, influence), for others bias is mobilized through the structural hierarchies and associated values and beliefs that systematically benefit some at the expense of others. Law is the vehicle through which external power becomes effective. Law reacts to power.

There is another perspective on power (Gaventa 1980), a third face (Lukes 1974) that locates power in the shared systems of meanings that shape our consciousness, our identities, and preferences. From this perspective, power emerges from the social interactions that define legal practice. Power is a process that "moves through circuits in which rules, relations, and resources that are constitutive of power are translated, fixed, and reproduced/transformed" (Clegg 1989). The following section examines this conceptualization of law's power. Law shapes the meaning and structure of social life, defining the parameters of regulatory authority, the spheres of interest, and the structures of action.

3. POWER ENACTED THROUGH LAW

The past decade in sociolegal scholarship suggests a new orientation to power and its relationship to law and legal institutions. From this new perspective power is understood as an emerging dynamic of social control rather than an imposition of it. Law does not simply reflect or reconstruct power nor does it simply insert itself into regulatory interactions (Silbey 1992), but is instead "instantiated in action" (Giddens 1979: 9). Power emerges from legal interactions just as power shapes law.[34]

The shifting orientation to power owes an intellectual debt to Michel Foucault who, among other important insights, "decentered" the state though his contrast of sovereign and disciplinary power. Sovereign power (read, state power) is power above and outside society. "It operates by setting external limits to behavior, establishing negative prohibitions and laying down channels of proper conduct" (Mitchell 1991: 93—and of course see Foucault 1977). Sovereign power fits Weber's classic definition of law as somehow external to the social arrangements that gave rise to it. "Disciplinary power by contrast works not from the outside but from within, not at the level of an entire society but at the level of detail, and not by constraining individuals and their actions but by producing them" (Mitchell 1991: 93). Disciplinary power is power enacted through the structures and techniques of knowledge.

Contemporary legal scholars recognize law as a critical form of knowledge that structures and provides meaning for social arrangements. Law, through its practice, authenticates certain claims and experiences at the expense of other claims and experiences. The power of law is its local application to constrain and limit the choices and preferences of actors. This perspective on power has been applied to empirical work on disputing (Yngvesson 1993; Felstiner and Sarat 1992). Rather than viewing power in terms of the resources disputants bring to the dispute, these scholars understand power as continually enacted in the disputing process. Disputes "structure the definition and interpretation of trouble in families, neighborhoods, courts and in other 'private' and 'public' settings" (Yngvesson 1993: 10). The analysis of disputes is the analysis of power. Similarly, I would argue, the analysis of regulatory practice is an analysis of power.

To study law's power in terms of local or everyday practice does not deny the ideological importance of the state as a neutral arbiter of powerful interests. Law is most effective when it appears to be separate from the social arrangements it governs and when it is able to inscribe acts patterned by social power as natural or inevitable. As Silbey (1992: 48) notes, "the assertion of externality [and neutrality] itself is integral to the effects of power; this is evident when we speak of 'the law' or 'the state' as though it were somehow something external that shapes and determines people and things."[35] Timothy Mitchell (1991) argues that it is the appearance of state and society as separate entities that is the defining characteristic of modern capitalist states, the way a "given financial and economic order is maintained" (Mitchell 1991: 90).

The task for regulatory scholars is to articulate a reflexive relationship between law and power that challenges the assumption of the externality of power and recognizes regulatory law as an organizing framework that both shapes and responds to power. To understand law as a producer and product of social power does not deny the tendency for power to concentrate in predictable ways. The cumulative impact of local practice is systemic institutionalized power. Social structures, including social hierarchies, are quite "real." Law is directly implicated in the construction and maintenance of hierarchy and markets and can no longer be viewed as either "interference" with or "panacea" for (depending on your point of view) capital.

As our understanding of law shifts to include the structures of knowledge and action that are constructed through regulatory behavior ("action in the world"), our empirical attention moves away from state-centered, top-down command structures to the "complex webs of relational practices" (McCann 1992: 734; Jessup 1982) that organize regulatory practice. The shift in focus away from state command structures to local practices means that the study of regulation must extend to regulated entities and how they manage, mediate, and resist the legal frameworks that organize their lives.

To illustrate how regulatory scholarship can be transformed by thinking about power and legal institutions as enacted through legal practice, I borrow insights from a group of quite disparate regulatory studies that share a common theme if not a theoretical perspective. Each demonstrates how power emerges out of and is transformed by legal practice. The first illustration, supported by the work of "new institutionalists," demonstrates how law operates as an organizing framework for social action. Law constrains not by force but by creating the very categories of action that define social life. The second set of studies illustrates that frameworks of action are not "natural," "arbitrary," or randomly constructed. Regulatory studies that implicitly or explicitly incorporate Bourdieu's concept of legal fields are used to demonstrate how objective forces shape local predispositions to act. The power and justice implications of these regulatory productions are demonstrated by the construction of regulatory authority, the privileging of particular regulatory solutions, and the reestablishment of social hierarchies.

A. CREATING FRAMEWORKS FOR ACTION

The new institutionalism in sociology and political science reflects a turn toward more cognitive and cultural explanations of social patterns. The new institutionalism takes as its starting point the "homogeneity of practice," the "taken for granted" routines that provide individuals with their personal and collective identities and the vocabularies of motive that form the basis of their action. As described by DiMaggio and Powell (1991: 11), "the perspective emphasizes the ways in which action is structured and order made possible by shared systems of rules that both constrain the inclination and capacity of actors to optimize as well as privilege some groups whose interests are secured by prevailing rewards and sanctions." Institutional arrangements constrain choice not by coercion or force but by establishing the criteria by which people discover their preferences or shape their responses. Institutions do not merely reflect the preferences and powers of the units constituting them, the institution shapes those preferences and power. Thus, they have transformative potential.

Lauren Edelman's work on the development of workplace governance embraces the new institutionalism perspective directly. She argues that law (a pervasive and important institution surprisingly neglected by the new institutionalists in sociology, at least) creates and helps to constitute a normative environment to which organizations adapt (1991: 1402). This "legal environment" creates a lens through which organizational actors view the world and develop strategies for action. Edelman found that affirmative action law created an expectation that demanded an organizational response. Indeed, once antidiscrimination law was passed, organizations closest to the public sphere and, in that sense, most influenced by their legal environment, were relatively quick to adopt nonunion grievance procedures. Organizations further from public scrutiny were slower to change in response to a shifting normative frame. In later work, Edelman shows how the ambiguous and broad principles of employment law gave organizations affected by it a wide latitude of response. Those responses, locally constructed meanings for compliance, mediate the impact of law on society.

> At the level of individual organizations, the construction of compliance becomes a function of internal organizational politics tempered by industry norms and the standards of professional personnel. . . . At a broader level, organizations' structural responses to law help to shape legal and societal expectation about what constitutes compliance and good faith efforts to comply. (Edelman 1992: 1568)

Taken as a whole, Edelman shows how institutional arrangements (law) operate to shape organizational behavior and how, in turn, local choices about meaningful and substantive response transform the law itself.[36]

Burk's (1988) analysis of the institutionalization of the stock market demonstrates how the categories of action created by law enable new forms of power. In the case of securities markets, regulatory rules adopted in the 1930s and revised in the subsequent decades opened up the market to the public. Disclosure rules guaranteed that information would be made available so that all those who wanted to participate in the market could do so on the same terms as investment bankers and corporate issuers, the traditional insiders (1988: 55). Licensing requirements and trading rules were enacted to construct a relatively stable environment that offered less experienced individuals the chance to make "sound" and "reasoned" investment choices. In practice, the new regulations spawned a virtual industry of financial professionals who could provide expert interpretation of the new data and who could shepherd potential investors through the maze of regulatory rules that governed the market. Because legislators believed that the new market regulations and the technical, "scientific" knowledge they generated made it possible for professionals to safely invest monies held in public trust, managers began to invest pension funds, trust funds, and insurance funds in the market. Together, the change in information requirements, the professionalization of the industry, and the relaxation of the restraints on investments by trustee institutions changed the categories of action in the market and paved the way for the formation of increasing numbers of large, repeat players (institutional investors) in the market.

My own work extends Burk's analysis to show how the new forms of market power (institutional investor) create new risks that ultimately undermine the meaning and efficacy of regulatory rules. I show how changes in investor "demographics" led to new constellations of risk managers and risk management techniques. New investment philosophies (trading values replace asset values), new products (derivative instruments), and new trading strategies (program and index trading) were devised to meet the needs of these collective players with their increased capacity for assuming and redistributing risk. I suggest that these changing players and products challenge the very basis of market regulation (Reichman 1991). In short, regulations create structural arrangements that enable changing forms of agency and power that ultimately transform the rules themselves.

From a different perspective, Keith Hawkins's (1984) work on the social construction of pollution demonstrates how the authority of the state as a legitimate regulatory actor is constructed through local practice. He suggests that regulatory enforcement not only articulates behavior that is no longer socially acceptable (defining moral boundaries in the classical sense), it also serves to legitimate a particular regulatory regime. Hawkins argues that what is criminally enforced in regulatory regimes is not pollution per se, but deliberate or negligent law breaking that symbolically assaults the legitimacy of regulatory authority (1984: 205). In this way, regulatory action constructs and legitimates the state. In other work, I suggest that the energy expended to prosecute the scandalous instances of insider trading in the 1980s might be similarly regarded. Insider trading cases were scandalous in part because they threatened to expose the weaknesses of the regulatory system. The prosecution of these particular cases had as much to do with establishing the state as an independent and authoritative actor in the market as any kind of deterrence against future rule breaking (Reichman 1993).

Alfred Aman's (1992) analysis of shifts in judicial activism between the New Deal and the contemporary, global regulatory era demonstrates how legal doctrine shapes regulatory discourse and action. In the New Deal era, courts took a deferential approach to oversight. "On matters of policy the courts equated administration with legislatures. On matters pertaining to the application of law, courts allowed administrators the interpretive discretion normally reserved to judges" (1992: 22). Administrative agencies realized substantial regulatory authority to create change through their adjudicative powers. In the environmental era (largely 1960–80), the courts developed a "hard look doctrine," close judicial scrutiny of the reasoning and procedures agencies used to make their decisions. As judicial power over agency discretion grew, administrative discourse shifted to insuring procedural fairness through rule making and away from the more specific substantive decision making that defined the earlier eras. The global, deregulatory era seems to be increasingly marked by judicial deference to the executive (1992: 89). As the executive branch becomes more involved in the day-to-day affairs of regulatory agencies, Aman suggests we will see more abrupt changes rationalized in terms of political contingency and executive accountability rather than agency expertise (the New Deal Era) or reasoned agency deliberation (environmental era) (Aman 1992: 107–25). Legal doctrine, a historical and culturally contingent response, shapes the relative power of government agents and ultimately the substantive effect of regulation.

Mashaw and Harfst (1990) demonstrate how the larger legal culture, expressed through judicial review, the separation of powers, federalism, and associated checks and balances (1990: 9), conditions a response that limits regulations' substantive impact.[37] They describe the National Highway Traffic Safety Administration's reorientation from a rule-making agency established to force auto makers to create safe automobiles to an agency that administers the recall of motor vehicles that contain defects related to safety. They explain this shift in regulatory logic as the consequence of judicial review by generalist judges who construct the image of legitimate regulation "against the backdrop of the general remedial assumptions of products liability law . . . [when] the adequacy of the product design is at issue, the law generally gauges reasonableness in terms of current practice" (1990: 225). Recalls have a structural advantage for NHTSA regulators. They pass through far fewer decision points than administrative rules and are less carefully monitored by outsiders. But they also mean fewer efforts to use rules to force technology in new and safe directions and, ultimately, they protect the status quo. The logic of checks and balances and the separation of powers in their analysis do not support regulatory solutions that have measurable substantive impact.

B. Linking Meaning to Structure

While the new institutionalism stresses the importance of cognitive, normative frameworks for organizing social action, the work of Pierre Bourdieu reminds us that social structures and cognitive structures are recursively and structurally linked (Bourdieu and Wacquant 1992: 14; Bourdieu 1987). Bourdieu's theory of law argues that the social practices of law are in fact the product of the functioning of a field, a site of competition over the right to determine meaning. The logic of fields is determined by 1) power relations which give the field its structure and which order competitive action, and 2) the internal logic of a field which constrains the range of possible action and limits the realm of solutions.[38] Power emerges out of the interplay between structure and cognition; meaning is contested and informed by structure. The regulatory field is one site where such battles are fought.

The insights of sociolegal scholars who have examined the influence of experts might be reanalyzed using Bourdieu's conceptualization of fields. Kelman (1981), for example, argues that professional backgrounds of OSHA officials, trained in safety engineering and hygiene, explain preferences for particular solutions, for example, engineering solutions rather than equipment fixes. Similarly, Meidinger (1989) suggests that the move to emissions trading as a form of pollution control reflects the success of a new breed of technocrat oriented toward a form of social engineering based in economic decision theory. Stryker's (1990) analysis of the relationship between science and the growing welfare state shows how "state reliance on economists in drafting and implementing New Deal labor-relations and social-security legislation illustrates the capacity of social science to help 'steer' the economy, reproducing capitalism by helping to formulate policies that mitigate capitalism's destructive side effects for labor and other subordinate groups" (1990: 719). Each of these analyses shows regulation as a contested domain of professional meaning where structures of power influence the outcome. The winner is the expert or point of view that comes to dominate the regulatory agenda.

My own work (Reichman 1992) focuses on the contested domain of regulatory meaning in the securities industry and the structures of resistance and innovation that transform what law means and how it is practiced. I argue that the shape of regulatory policy, including the distribution of regulatory violations (the oughts and ought nots of securities practice), emerges out of the informal arrangements, tacit agreements, and pressures for conformity among professional groups that provide legal significance to behavior quite apart from regulatory action. Regulatory power, defined in terms of the authority to set the rules, to define the winners and losers, and to change the definitions of the regulation game (see also Meidinger 1987: 357), is enacted in the process of "doing deals," itself a complex competitive interaction that involves, among others, lawyers, accountants, and securities professionals. Regulatory power flows to those who can accumulate the greatest amount of financial, social, and cultural capital through the deal-making process. Regulatory power converts into business privilege when the norms, values, beliefs, and justifications associated with a particular regulatory culture become status indicators that authenticate the actions of some firms while marginalizing and discrediting the actions of others.

Again, from a different perspective, Yeager's (1991) empirical insights about how environmental law interacts with the logic of capitalist accumulation demonstrates the connections between structure and meaning. He describes how the use of cost-benefit logics in regulation "tends to reproduce the cultural perception that legally prohibited commercial conduct is morally ambivalent" (1991: 41)—a technical problem with a technical solution that benefits industry at the expense of the environment.

> Because the law concentrates on identifying and asserting the best pollution control technologies being utilized within industries, rather than on the environmental harm to receiving waters and human health, debates over the terms and application of standards tend to both disproportionately attract and favor the input of industry over the environmentalists. . . . Such regulatory exchanges necessarily favor the input of industry, which controls the technological information required for regulation. (1991: 199–200)

As regulators find themselves using the cost-benefit and technological logic offered by industry to set rules, issue permits, and grant variances or exceptions to the rules, they implicitly channel our understanding of environmental problems in terms of the logic of capitalist accumulation and private accumulation.

Yeager goes on to describe how these institutional logics in turn shape the legal response. He compares the regulatory approaches of the Clean Air Act to those of the Federal Water Pollution Control Act (FWPCA). The Clean Air Act used a media-quality based approach which mandates primary (health-related) and secondary (welfare-related) pollutant levels. In contrast, the water amendments focus on technology based standards. Yeager finds courts ruling in favor of industry challenges to water pollution law while upholding and even expanding the EPA's authority to control air pollution. He explains the different response in terms of the underlying logic of the regulation and the willingness of courts to challenge agency authority when terms are familiar economic and technological ones rather than when more uncertain measures of toxicology are used (1991: 198). Prosecutions of arguably criminal violations of water pollution were rare, in part, because of prosecutors' reluctance to bring criminal charges on the basis of technical, albeit legal, criteria absent that showing of environmental harm (Yeager 1991: 199). In sum, the use of technology based standards, theoretically rational and neutral, systematically protects the interests of polluters.

C. THE CONSTRUCTION AND CONTESTATION OF BIAS

While traditional law and society research in the area of regulation tackled the mobilization of bias, recent sociolegal scholarship suggests a new focus on the construction, affirmation, and contestation of bias through legal practice. This new perspective on power and law challenges the idea that power is something added to regulatory interactions. Instead, law and power are intertwined; power is both a given and emergent dimension of regulatory practice.

Although few studies have embraced this new understanding of law and power directly, the studies described above outline the utility of such an approach, particularly in understanding the limits of law. These studies demonstrate that law is a critical form of knowledge/power that channels our understanding of social phenomenon. In the case of environmental regulation, for example, law channels our understanding of what must be regarded as global problems (e.g., pollution) away from collective and innovative solutions. Why? A first answer would be that law is coopted and corrupted by powerful agents who thwart innovative solutions. A second answer might be that law constrains too much and does not allow innovative solutions to emerge. A third answer, consistent with this new notion of power, argues that legal practice defines the vocabularies by which solutions are found. As Yeager's analysis of environmental law suggests, law authenticates the experiences and solutions that maintain existing social hierarchies and categories of action. This is not necessarily a problem with rules, or law, but is an outcome of particular struggles over knowledge. One might imagine a different scenario, but not until power shifts occur that allow different kinds of knowledge to come to the fore.

4. QUESTIONS OF JUSTICE

While the notion of contest, if not explicitly power, has been a recurring current in sociolegal scholarship, discussions related to justice have been remarkably few. This is so despite the fact that Kagan's *Regulatory Justice* (1978) was one of the earliest sociolegal studies of regulatory behavior and *Bureaucratic Justice* (1983) by Jerry Mashaw followed shortly thereafter. When they do emerge, justice questions are related to questions of bias in enforcement or implementation.[39] In this section I explore the kinds of justice questions that have been raised by regulatory scholars. I consider "solutions" to the justice problem in light of the prevailing theories of power explored earlier. I suggest that while scholars have raised important questions about equity and fairness, they do not yet adequately address the "justice" of the underlying logic or character of the regulatory structure as a whole. The fundamental challenges to legal frameworks and social categories raised by feminist theory might be usefully appropriated to examine business regulation.

A. JUSTICE QUESTIONS

The following section distinguishes among the different kinds of justice articulated by Tyler (this volume) as central to law and society scholarship: distributive justice, procedural justice, and retributive justice. Mashaw (1983) offers a more specific set of justice criteria particular to regulation that equate legitimacy with fairness and distribution of regulatory outcomes. He describes justice as "those qualities of a decision process that provide arguments for the acceptability of its decisions'" (1983: 25). He identifies three competing justice models that are distinguished by their concern for 1) accuracy and efficiency; 2) appropriate outcome or service; and 3) fairness. He argues that the development of regulatory agencies can be described as a competition over these respective concerns.

The Distribution of Regulatory Benefits/Burdens (Distributive Justice)

Distributive justice questions applied to the regulatory arena consider who benefits from regulation and who is unduly burdened. There is an implicit assumption that regulation, as a component of modern welfare states, works to distribute resources in ways that enhance social development. In his study of the Cost of Living Council's efforts to implement the wage-price freeze enacted by Congress in 1971, Kagan found that, "Issues of distributive justice are particularly salient in a program that directly regulated prices and wages for an entire nation" (1978: 59). Scholars and practitioners disagree, strongly, however, on who benefits and who is harmed by regulation and whether the distribution of regulatory outcomes approximates justice or even what it means. Similarly, those most affected by regulation understand it differently. Employers and employees, for example, are likely to have different conceptualizations of what constitutes distributive justice in the regulatory context.[40]

Many scholars will argue that regulation represents an undue and unfair financial burden to the regulated.[41] Scholars who support deregulation, for example, are likely to find that regulation hampers the ability of business firms to compete, to innovate, and, in general, to be vibrant players in contemporary markets. This is true not only in the case of economic regulation, but also in terms of social regulations that require "costly" new procedures to control pollution and monitor safety.[42]

Costs are not only financial. In some studies scholars relate the problem of justice to questions of efficiency. Bardach and Kagan (1982), for example, define regulation as unreasonable (read, not just) when it involves economic inefficiency. "An instance of regulatory unreasonableness can also be experienced as an instance of government imposed injustice. For each 'victim' of regulatory unreasonableness . . . the experience of regulatory injustice is exasperating, infuriating, or, even worse, demoralizing" (1982: 28). From a completely different perspective and agenda, Lipsky's (1980) analysis of street-level bureaucracy frames justice questions in terms of bureaucratic efficiencies.

But scholars are just as likely to consider distributive questions in terms of the reproduction of social hierarchies and the injustices that accompany them. Diver (1980), for example, questions the redistributive potential of regulation. More often than not, he argues, the regulation of prices and entry (a distributive question) protects "sunk costs" from the vicissitudes of shifting demand or technological change (1980: 209). Business stratification is reproduced through regulation when the costs of compliance disproportionately burden small, marginal, or peripheral firms.

Equity is an important theme in the work of environmental sociologists who consider the disproportionate burden that lower income and minority communities shoulder in what appear to be rational, universalistic regulatory programs. Following the logic of Schnaiberg's (1975) study of the 1974 energy price increases, Lutzenhiser and Hackett (1993) demonstrate that efforts to reduce energy consumption by increasing energy prices would disproportionately affect lower income households that were more likely to face structural impediments to reducing consumption, regardless of cost (e.g., energy inefficient if not substandard housing, greater commuting distances, and the like). Bullard (1990) examines the siting of "noxic facilities" (municipal landfills, hazardous waste facilities, chemical plants, and the like) from a distributive justice perspective. He notes that "blacks, lower-income groups and working-class persons are subjected to a disproportionately large amount of pollution and other environmental stressors."[43] In an all too familiar critique of divorce mediation, Douglas Amy (1987) critiques the promises of environmental mediation for failing to recognize the imbalances of resources and expertise that parties bring to the negotiating table.

The Fairness of Regulatory Procedures

Questions of procedural justice, defined by Tyler in terms of the participants' assessments of the fairness of legal procedures, have not been directly studied by regulatory scholars. Scholars have considered who participates in regulatory decision making and who is left out and how structures of participation influence regulatory outcomes.

Scholars demonstrate that legal systems privilege certain values over others (e.g., individual rights over more collective, distributional concerns). Yeager's (1991: 6) analysis of air and water pollution regulation described above demonstrates that "the application of cost- or risk-benefit logics in rule making . . . favor the more easily accounted private sectors' costs of compliance over the less 'measurable' public interest at stake (e.g. in clean environments)." Smith and Jepason (1993) describe how the decisions about the management and allocation of marine resources diminish the importance of commercial net fishers' local knowledge about marine ecology. Fishing families must adapt their behavior to unfamiliar, and sometimes unwelcome, technoscientific knowledge. Lynch (1993), in her study of Latino environmental discourse and its relationship to mainstream environmentalism, argues persuasively for a vision of environmental justice that "requires that environmental changes be assessed from multiple perspectives and that alternative discourses be heard" (1993: 118).

The Distribution of Regulatory Sanctions

Consistent with the criminological perspective that has influenced sociolegal study of regulatory enforcement, researchers have considered questions of retributive justice, the fair sanctioning of violators. In the case of securities regulation, for example, Shapiro (1984) found that the "organizations subject to SEC investigation are not corporate giants that have been around for a long time; they are very young and very small" (1984: 41). Ewick (1985) found that in the case of organizational offenders, the most severe sanctions were reserved for firms that were financially or organizationally moribund. She refers to this as redundant regulation. Overall, observations of bias (systematic differences in the amount and type of enforcement) are linked to the characteristics of offenses, the technical abilities and interests of regulatory agencies (Shapiro, 1984), to the situational politics of regulatory action (Lynxwiller et al. 1983; Scholz 1984), as well as to attributes of the regulated entities themselves, for example, their size, economic clout, or technical prowess (Yeager 1987).

Emerging Questions

Our changing understanding of the relationship between law and power encourages us to ask new kinds of questions about justice. Rather than looking at questions of impact and process, we can begin to ask questions about the justice of law's framework and categories of action. To questions of who participates in regulatory decision making and who benefits from regulatory rules we might add questions about the distinction between the state and the economy, the normative standards, the underlying ethics, and the beliefs and expectations about government that define regulatory programs. We can ask questions about how people experience regulation and the hierarchies that define those experiences.[44] To pursue questions of justice is to pursue the very structures of knowledge that define regulatory law.

B. JUSTICE SOLUTIONS

The perspectives of power that inform regulatory scholarship offer different kinds of justice questions and different "solutions" to perceived injustice. When power limits law, the solution to injustice is to find ways to neutralize power through law. Traditionally, of course, this includes efforts to develop universalistic criteria or to impose a formalistic equality to regulatory proceedings. Recognizing the difficulties of separating procedure from substantive issues, reformers seek to "increase access" to the regulatory process, to institutionalize countervailing powers, and to use "rights claims" to pursue justice. Justice has become a proceduralism question, although in a different guise. Give more people a voice and honor the principals of fairness that the law promises.

A perspective that recognizes that law shapes power, as well as being shaped by it, suggests a different kind of solution to (in)justice, one that pushes us to think about changing the foundation and character of the regulation game, to think about new standards for regulation that rearrange the dynamics of power. The point here is that simply adding voices to an already well-ordered chorus is not likely to do much. To pursue justice we need to rethink the structure of choral music to create a new ordering and innovative solutions.

What might this new justice look like? As I think about the new possibilities, I look to ways that feminists have challenged traditional legal categories and standards in criminal law and family law, and I wonder about their applicability here.[45] What might business regulation look like if it was written from the point of view of the reasonable woman? What would environmental law look like if it explicitly connected communities and identities to ecological concerns? What would regulatory law be if it were truly preventive rather than reactive?

5. CONCLUSION

This brief review of regulatory scholarship demonstrates several distinct orientations to the relationship between law and power. I suggest that traditional regulatory scholarship assumes that law reacts to outside forces that mobilize it in particular directions. For some scholars, power is understood as the resources, broadly defined, that interested parties bring to the regulation game. For others, law's power is subordinate to the forces of production that ultimately determine or direct its effect.

I suggest a third orientation to understanding the relationship between law and power that recognizes law and legal practice as a direct participant in the making and remaking of power. Power is not only a force to bring to the regulatory arena, power is continually contested, affirmed, and sometimes transformed through regulatory practice. Law's power is its capacity to define the categories of meaningful action. Regulatory law articulates and authenticates certain experiences, values, and beliefs at the expense of others. The regulation game is a game of, not over, power. Regulatory practice is not only the imposition of knowledge/power, it is a contest over how knowledge is interpreted and used. Regulatory law is an important force in the construction of identities, as implicit in it are norms about citizenship, consumerism, employer-employee relations, and the like.

Regulatory theorizing that embraces an understanding of law's power to shape the structures of action requires a much expanded empirical focus for study. The experiences of regulated entities must take greater priority in regulatory studies. To see law's power we need to know much more about how law disciplines everyday practice. To pursue questions of regulatory justice, we need to first expose law's power in constructing our subjective experiences and the objective factors that condition them. Once those analyses are done, they must be joined to the ongoing important work on regulatory agencies, policy making, and theories of the state. Then we may have a more complete picture of power and justice in regulatory process.

NOTES

1. Consider, e.g., Kagan's (1990: 35) assessment that "Modern legal systems are shaped by a basic political struggle. One side wants government to encourage economic efficiency and growth through economic incentives and free markets. The other demands more government regulation of (or compensation for) the economic losses, inequalities, environmental hazards, and social disruptions that flow from what Schumpter (1942) called the 'creative destruction of capitalism.' "

2. The Administrative Procedure Act requires that agencies publish notice of proposed rule making in the Federal Register, provide for a public comment period, and conduct hearings before a rule can be enacted.

3. Although there is some debate about what federal regulation of the stock markets intends, I believe that it developed to insure that markets would be stable and relatively safe places to raise capital. Investor protection, more rationalized procedures for handling investments, and efforts to create at least the image of a level playing field were part of a package to encourage continued participation in the market.

4. In describing the development of public policy over markets, James Willard Hurst (1982) notes that law was used to "foster values not measured by market transactions. Especially in statute law and in administrative rules and regulations, this emphasis of policy took the form of developing canons of social income and cost accounting. But the prominence of this type of legal intervention did not negate another kind of concern for social context—regard for the general vitality of the private market itself as an institution of social order" (1982: 7).

5. The Interstate Commerce Commission (1887), the Federal Reserve Board (1913), the Federal Trade Commission (1914), the Food and Drug Administration (1931), the Federal Power Commission (1920), the Federal Communications Commission (1934), the Securities and Exchange Commission (1934), the Civil Aeronautics Board (1938), the Federal Aviation Administration (1948), and the Nuclear Regulatory Commission (1975) represent this style of market-oriented regulation.

6. According to Manning (1989: 50) this strategy stands in marked contrast to the focus of economic regulation which seeks to increase the benefits of the market model.

7. As described by Rees (1988), the central question, officially incorporated into the regulatory program, is "not *which* enforcement strategy regulators should use—cooperative or punitive—but *when*" (1988: 176).

8. Ayres and Braithwaite (1992) argue persuasively that claims for an era of deregulation are vastly overstated. They suggest that "we have not, and are not, experiencing an era of deregulation so much as an era of regulatory flux—an era when dramatic regulatory, deregulatory, and re-regulatory shifts are occurring simultaneously" (1992: 7). Lowered regulatory activity in one area (OSHA enforcement) is often being countered by increased activity in another (EPA enforcement referrals to the Department of Justice).

9. These programs approximate to some degree Braithwaite's proposal for enforced self-regulation. Braithwaite (1982: 406) proposes a system where "government would compel each company to write a set of rules tailored to the unique set of contingencies facing that firm. A regulatory agency would either approve their rules or send them back for revision if they were not sufficiently stringent." The advantage would be a more efficient, yet flexible, regulatory system and the affirmative commitment to regulation by the regulated.

10. This is not to say that the politics of law is more real here than in other areas of law. It simply appears that scholars in this field have made political struggle a more explicit part of their analyses.

11. Consider, e.g., Executive Order 12044 (1978) that required regulatory analysis to discuss economic consequences of alternatives and Executive Order 12291 (1981) that required that the benefits of new rules exceed their costs or that they were the least costly alternative.

12. The classic studies of regulation are the political and economic histories that describe the emergence and expansion of regulatory authority. Seligman's (1982) study of the Securities and Exchange Commission, Kolko's (1965) analysis of the railroads, e.g.,

illustrate this line of inquiry. (See also McGraw [1975] for a history of regulation in America, and the collection in Wilson [1980] for contemporary histories.) Together, these studies demonstrate how business and political interests interact with the legislative process to create a particular form of state intervention that meets the needs of those particular interests.

13. I combine capture of regulatory agenda after an agency has been formed with models of what has been described as "predatory regulation" (Zerbe 1980), regulation established originally at the behest of interested parties.

14. Kolko's analysis showed how business could take advantage of the inherent tensions between federal and state regulatory regimes.

15. In a contemporary discussion, Aman (1992) suggests that the limits of regulatory law are located in the institutionalization of regulatory authority. They "deal less and less directly with the burning issues of the day. As they became less visible, they became their own centers of power rather than the agents of elected representatives. The more remote they grew, the less flexible and responsive they became. Soon, these agencies were trapped by their reliance on precedent, their penchant for incremental change, and their need to adhere to a certain type of logic. . . . As these agencies matured they became more easily neutralized if not captured by the interests they were supposed to regulate" (1992: 23).

16. Citizen groups have become powerful in regulatory affairs not only for their direct influence on rule making or implementation but also through their efforts to change the venue of regulation away from the agencies and into the federal courts. In the area of environmental regulation, e.g., citizen groups filing private lawsuits against polluters have generated a significant amount of private enforcement of regulatory law (see Boyer and Meidinger 1985). As Yeager (1991) reports, between 1978 and 1983, citizens filed only 41 notices to sue and lawsuits under the water law. "But in 1983, with the evidence of the collapse in EPA enforcement and high rates of noncompliance in industry, citizens filed 108 notices and suits, and 87 more in the first four months of 1984 alone" (1985: 320). This trend continued throughout the 1980s and created a private enforcement effort that rivaled if not surpassed federal regulation over that sphere.

17. Their "tripartism" model offers a partial solution to scholars who view the increased participation by advocacy groups, particularly the use of judicial forum for handling regulatory disputes, as creating a kind of malaise or paralysis in rule making (Shapiro 1988; Melnick 1983).

18. For a good discussion of the need to systematically integrate republican and moral theories into regulatory negotiation, see Forester 1992.

19. These studies owe a classic debt to Davis (1971), who identified the importance of understanding administrative discretion. Here the focus is on decisions to respond to potential and known violations of regulatory rules.

20. For a complementary perspective, see Mendeloff (1988), who argues that unreasonably strict standard setting generates unintended consequences of less compliance.

21. They describe forbearance as "(1) overlooking violations that pose no serious risk under the circumstances; (2) not enforcing regulatory requirements that would be especially costly or disruptive in relation to the additional degree of protection they would provide; (3) granting reasonable time to come into compliance and accepting measures that would provide substantial if not literal compliance; and (4) making allowance for good faith efforts on the part of the regulated enterprise" (Bardach and Kagan 1982: 134).

22. Overinclusive rules are rules that are too general, too stringent, and too costly to enforce.

23. For different kinds of analyses that reach similar conclusions, consider also Braithwaite's (1985) assessment that persuasion is more effective than punishment in meeting

regulatory objectives and John Scholz's (1984) economic model of enforcement that suggests that cooperation is the most economically rational response.

24. The general sociopolitical climate may be a factor as well. Barnett (1990) identified two distinct orientations to environmental regulation. In the Burford era, roughly 1981–83, deregulation was the rallying cry at the EPA and across the executive agencies. The Ruckelhaus/Thomas era was more in keeping with the proregulation mandate that had established the EPA. Barnett found that under the Burford administration, there was a greater number of superfund settlements but at a cost of limiting enforcement and future fund expenditures. During the Ruckelhaus era the EPA was more likely to issue unilateral orders that induce compliance through the fund option threat.

    The power of public opinion to shape regulatory policy has been the focus of other work that describes factors that affect the regulatory agenda. (See also Schnaiberg's [1980] discussion of how shifting public opinion influences public policy choice.)

25. In a sample of Securities and Exchange Commission cases between 1937 and 1977, only 14 percent of the offenses that carried possible criminal penalties were referred to the Justice Department for criminal prosecution (Shapiro 1984, 1985).

26. Sudnow's (1965) discussion of "normal cases" provides the classic example.

27. Emerson (1992) defines organizational horizon as the organizational background that explains the current case and the expected future implications of handling a case in a particular way.

28. At the core of these analyses is the assumption that the state will operate in the long term interests of capital whether or not members of the capitalist class participate or benefit directly from state policy making (see the discussion in Poulantzas 1973).

29. As Spitzer (1987: 48) notes, "if capitalism requires uncertainty for its development *as a system*, but individual actors and organizations need to reduce uncertainty to operate and profit, then security [i.e., regulation] clearly stands in a complex and contradictory relationship to capitalist vitality and growth."

30. Calavita (1992: 9) reminds us that structural contradictions penetrate "institutions and bureaucracies of the state in different ways, posing different dilemmas, and eliciting different responses depending on the location of those institutions in the state apparatus." As a result, it is unwise to assume a monolithic, "rational" state response.

31. When Reagan created the Task Force on Regulatory Relief, then–Vice President Bush singled out forty-one programs where deregulation might produce substantial savings. Thirty-six of the programs were in the area of "social regulation," ten were under the jurisdiction of the EPA (Harris and Milkis 1989: 7). The irony in contemporary deregulatory policy is the requirement for increased government centralization necessary for its implementation. As Harris and Milkis (1989: 5) note, "By choosing to use conservative political appointees to harness liberal bureaucrats at the regulatory agencies and by relying on executive orders and the Office of Management and Budget (OMB) to impose draconian cost-cutting policies at those agencies, deregulation actually continued the twentieth century enterprise of constructing a centralized administrative state in America."

32. This perspective predicts that while the power of capital will often limit regulators efforts to enforce the law, the need for legitimacy will allow regulators some authority to punish powerful corporate offenders who violate the law (see the discussion in Barnett 1992).

33. In his study of workplace safety regulation, Noble (1986: 7) argues that the "state is neither directly governed by business, nor required by its location within the larger system or its form to serve only business interests." Rather, capitalist economic structures discourage public officials from interfering with employers for fear of undermining

business confidence and future political victories (1986: 11). Employees, for their part, act in ways that are compatible with capital.

34. Giddens (1979) argues that structure enables agency and power. He suggests that involvement in a relationship gives even a subordinate a certain degree of control over the outcome.

35. Friedland and Alford (1991: 246–47) argue that power itself is a culturally and institutionally contingent concept. They suggest, e.g., that the tendency for Americans to "decentralize" government, to "separate" powers and to foster regulation that prevents market concentration is a "culturally contingent concept of power embedded in a notion of liberty derived from the original settlers' experience of a highly intrusive, regulative English state" (1991: 247).

36. Edelman's later work points to the competing institutional logics and alternative levels at which law operates. (In her work this is represented by the intersection of legal and organizational logics.) Friedland and Alford (1991) suggest that society is best understood as a potentially contradictory institutional system. "Some of the most important struggles between groups, organizations and classes are over the appropriate relationships between institutions and by which institutional logic different activities should be regulated and to which categories of person they apply" (1991: 256).

37. In earlier work Mashaw (1985) "apologized for the inability of courts to engage in a sound review of substantive regulatory issues. Substantive rights—to a healthful environment, to a reasonably safe work place, to low-cost housing or hospital care—are imbedded in statutes of awesome complexity, sometimes, but not always, drafted to reflect the subtle politics of making haste slowly in a pluralist and federal political system" (1985: 5).

38. Here is where we find similarity to the new institutionalism: Bourdieu's concept of doxa: "immediate agreement elicited by that which appears self-evident, transparently, and normal." Terdiman (1987: 812) closely corresponds to the thinking of the new institutionalism. He differs from the new institutionalist by his insistence on linking structure to meaning. Consider, e.g., his "principles of division" which are the structured ways people differentiate themselves from each other.

39. Although I am not yet prepared to make this claim with confidence, I believe that the sociolegal scholars who are most likely to raise the question of regulatory bias are those who are also associated with the study of white-collar crime.

40. An interesting study would consider the meaning of justice from the perspectives of the full range of actors who are affected by regulatory rules.

41. Of course this position, as the others that follow, is fiercely debated.

42. Under Reagan, the Vice President's Task Force on Regulatory Relief and the Council on Competitiveness reflected this perspective directly.

43. Bullard cites a 1983 GAO report that found "race was by far the most prominent factor in the location of commercial hazardous waste landfills."

44. This means knowing as much about the experiences of dominating as being dominated. I cannot stress enough how important it is for sociolegal scholars to understand business elites (not just elite lawyers!).

45. Ecofeminists (Merchant 1989; Warren 1987; and the collection in Gaard 1993) are asking new questions about gender and the environment that could inform future discussions about regulatory justice.

BIBLIOGRAPHY

Abel, Richard L. 1982. The Contradictions of Informal Justice. In *The Politics of Informal Justice*, ed. Richard L. Abel. New York: Academic Press.

Alford, Robert R., and Roger Friedland. 1985. *Powers of Theory: Capitalism, State and Democracy*. New York: Cambridge Univ. Press.

Aman, Alfred C., Jr. 1992. *Administrative Law in a Global Era*. Ithaca, NY: Cornell Univ. Press.

Amy, Douglas. 1987. *The Politics of Environmental Mediation*. New York: Columbia Univ. Press.

Ayres, Ian, and John Braithwaite. 1991. Tripartism, Empowerment and Game-Theoretic Notions of Regulatory Capture. 16 *Law and Social Inquiry* 435.

———. 1992. *Responsive Regulation: Transcending the Deregulation Debate*. New York: Oxford Univ. Press.

Bachrach, Peter, and Morton S. Baratz. 1970. *Power and Poverty: Theory and Practice*. New York: Oxford Univ. Press.

Bardach, Eugene, and Robert Kagan. 1982. *Going by the Book: The Problem of Regulatory Unreasonableness*. Philadelphia: Temple Univ. Press.

Barnett, Harold C. 1981. Corporate Capitalism, Corporate Crime. 3 *Crime and Delinquency*, 171–86.

———. 1990. Political Environments and Implementation Failures: The Case of Superfund Enforcement. 12 *Law and Policy*, 225.

———. 1992. Hazardous Waste, Distributional Conflict, and a Trilogy of Failures. 3 *The Journal of Human Justice*, 93.

Bernstein, Marver H. 1955. *Regulating Business by Independent Commission*. Princeton, NJ: Princeton Univ. Press.

Bourdieu, Pierre. 1987. The Force of Law: Toward a Sociology of the Juridical Field. 38 *Hastings Law Journal*, 805.

Bourdieu, Pierre, and Loic J. D. Wacquant. 1992. *An Invitation to Reflexive Sociology*. Chicago: Univ. of Chicago Press.

Boyer, Barry, and Errol Meidinger. 1985. Privatizing Regulatory Enforcement: A Preliminary Assessment of Citizen Suits under Federal Environmental Laws. 34 *Buffalo Law Rev.*, 833.

Braithwaite, John. 1982. Enforced Self-Regulation: A New Strategy for Corporate Crime Control. 80 *Univ. of Michigan Law Rev.*, 1466.

———. 1985. *To Punish or Persuade: Enforcement of Coal Mining Safety*. Albany: SUNY Press.

Braithwaite, John, and Brent Fisse. 1987. Self-Regulation and the Control of Corporate Crime. In *Private Policing*, ed. C. Shearing and P. Stenning, 221–47. Beverly Hills: Sage.

Braithwaite, John, John Walker, and Peter Gabrosky. 1987. An Enforcement Taxonomy of Regulatory Agencies. 9 *Law and Policy*, 323.

Bryner, Gary C. 1987. *Bureaucratic Discretion: Law and Policy in Federal Regulatory Agencies*. New York: Pergamon.

Bullard, Robert D. 1990. *Dumping in Dixie: Race, Class, and Environmental Quality.* Boulder, CO: Westview.

Burk, James. 1988. *Values in the Marketplace: The American Stock Market under Federal Securities Laws.* New York: Walter de Gruyter.

Burstein, Paul. 1991. Legal Mobilization as a Social Movement Tactic: The Struggle for Equal Employment Opportunity. 96 *American Journal of Sociology*, 1201-25.

Calavita, Kitty. 1983. The Demise of the Occupational Safety and Health Administration. 30 *Social Problems*, 437–48.

———. 1990. Employer Sanctions Violations: Toward a Dialectic Model of White-Collar Crime. 24 *Law and Society Rev.*, 1041.

———. 1992. *Inside the State: The Bracero Program, Immigration, and the I.N.S.* New York: Routledge.

Chambliss, William. 1986. On Law Making. In *The Social Basis of Law*, ed. S. Brickey and E. Comack, 27–51. Toronto: Garamond.

Clegg, Stewart. 1989. *Frameworks of Power.* Newbury Park, CA: Sage.

Clinard, Marshall, and Peter C. Yeager. 1980. *Corporate Crime.* New York: Free Press.

Clune, William H. 1983. A Political Model of Implementation and the Implication of the Model for Public Policy, Research, and the Changing Role of Lawyers. 69 *Iowa Law Rev.*, 47.

Davis, K. C. 1971. *Discretionary Justice.* Urbana: Univ. of Illinois Press.

DiMaggio, Paul J., and Walter W. Powell. 1991. Introduction. In *The New Institutionalism in Organizational Analysis*, ed. W. Powell and P. DiMaggio, 1–38. Chicago: Univ. of Chicago Press.

Diver, C. S. 1980. A Theory of Regulatory Enforcement. 28 *Public Policy*, 257–99.

———. 1989. Regulatory Precision. In *Making Regulatory Policy*, ed. K. Hawkins and J. M. Thomas. Pittsburgh: Univ. of Pittsburgh Press.

Edelman, Lauren B. 1991. Legal Environments and Organizational Governance: The Expansion of Due Process in the American Workplace. 95 *American Journal of Sociology*, 1401–40.

———. 1992. Legal Ambiguity and Symbolic Structures: Organizational Mediation of Civil Rights Law. 97 *American Journal of Sociology*, 1531–76.

Edelman, Murray. 1964. *The Symbolic Uses of Politics.* Chicago: Univ. of Chicago Press.

Emerson, Robert M. 1991. Case Processing and Interorganizational Knowledge: Detecting the "Real Reasons" for Referrals. 38 *Social Problems*, 198.

———. 1992. Disputes in Public Bureaucracies. In *Studies in Law, Politics, and Society*, vol 12, ed. S. Silbey and A. Sarat. Greenwich, CT: JAI Press.

Ewick, Patricia. 1985. Redundant Regulation: Sanctioning Broker-Dealers. 7 *Law and Policy*, 423.

Felstiner, William L. F., and Austin Sarat. 1992. Enactments of Power, Negotiating Reality and Responsibility in Lawyer-Client Interactions. 77 *Cornell Law Rev.*, 1447.

Forester, John. 1992. Envisioning the Politics of Public-Sector Dispute. In *Studies in Law, Politics, and Society*, vol 12, ed. S. Silbey and A. Sarat, 247–76. Greenwich CT: JAI Press.

Foucault, Michel. 1977. *Discipline and Punish: The Birth of the Prison.* New York: Pantheon.

Friedland, Roger, and Robert R. Alford. 1991. Bringing Society Back In: Symbols, Practices, and Institutional Contradictions. In *The New Institutionalism in Organizational Analysis*, ed. W. Powell and P. DiMaggio, 232–63. Chicago: Univ. of Chicago Press.

Friedman, Lawrence M. 1985. *A History of American Law*. New York: Simon and Schuster.

Frietag, Peter J. 1983. The Myth of Corporate Capture: Regulatory Commissions in the United States. 30 *Social Problems*, 480–91.

Gaard, Greta, ed. 1993. *Ecofeminism: Women, Animals, Nature*. Philadelphia: Temple Univ. Press.

Gabrosky, Peter. 1990. Professional Advisors and White Collar Illegality: Towards Explaining and Exercising Professional Failure. 13 *Univ. of New South Wales Law Journal*, 1.

Gaventa, John. 1980. *Power and Powerlessness: Quiescence and Rebellion in an Appalachian Valley*. Chicago: Univ. of Illinois Press.

Giddens, Anthony. 1979. *Central Problems in Social Theory*. Berkeley: Univ. of California Press.

Gilboy, Janet A. 1991. Deciding Who Gets In: Decisionmaking by Immigration Inspectors. 25 *Law and Society Rev.*, 571.

———. 1992. Penetrability of Administrative Systems: Political "Casework" and Immigration Inspections. 26 *Law and Society Rev.*, 273.

Gunningham, Neil. 1987. Negotiated Non-Compliance. 9 *Law and Policy*, 69.

———. 1992. Private Ordering, Self-Regulation and Futures Markets: A Comparative Study of Informal Social Control. 13 *Law and Policy*, 297.

Harrington, Christine. 1988. Regulatory Reform: Creating Gaps and Making Markets. 10 *Law and Policy*, 293.

Harris, Richard A., and Sidney M. Milkis. 1989. *The Politics of Regulatory Change*. New York: Oxford Univ. Press.

Hawkins, Keith. 1984. *Environment and Enforcement: Regulation and the Social Definition of Pollution*. New York: Oxford Univ. Press.

———. 1989. Rule Making and Discretion: Implications for Designing Regulatory Policy. In *Making Regulatory Policy*, ed. K. Hawkins and J. M. Thomas, 263–80. Pittsburgh: Univ. of Pittsburgh Press.

High, Jack. 1991. Introduction: A Tale of Two Disciplines. In *Regulation: Economic Theory and History*, ed. Jack High, pp. 263–80. Ann Arbor: Univ. of Michigan Press.

Huppes, G. 1992. *New Market-Oriented Instruments for European Environmental Policies*. Boston: Graham and Trotman.

Hurst, J. Willard. 1982. *Law and Markets in United States History: Different Modes of Bargaining among Interests*. Madison: Univ. of Wisconsin Press.

Hutter, Bridget M., and P. K. Manning. 1990. The Contexts of Regulation: The Impact upon Health and Safety Inspectorates in Britain. 12 *Law and Policy*, 103.

Jessup, Bob. 1982. *The Capitalist State*. New York: New York Univ. Press.

Kagan, Robert A. 1978. *Regulatory Justice*. New York: Russell Sage.

———. 1989. Understanding Regulatory Enforcement. 11 *Law and Policy*, 89.

———. 1990. How Much Does Law Matter? Labor Law, Competition, and Waterfront Labor Relations in Rotterdam and U.S. Ports. 24 *Law and Society Rev.*, 35.

Kagan, Robert A., and John T. Scholz. 1984. The "Criminology of the Corporation" and Regulatory Enforcement Strategies. In *Enforcing Regulation*, ed. Keith Hawkins and John Thomas. New York: Kluwer-Nijhoff.

Kanter, Rosabeth. 1977. *Men and Women of the Corporation*. New York: Basic Books.

Kelman, Steven. 1981. *Regulating America, Regulating Sweden: A Comparative Study of Occupational Safety and Health Policy*. Cambridge, MA: MIT Press.

Kolko, Gabriel. 1963. *The Triumph of Conservatism: Reinterpretation of American History, 1900–1916*. New York: Free Press.

———. 1965. *Railroads and Regulation*. Princeton, NJ: Princeton Univ. Press.

Lipsky, Michael. 1980. *Street Level Bureaucracy: The Dilemmas of the Individual in Police Service*. New York: Russell Sage.

Lowi, Theodore J. 1979. *The End of Liberalism*, 2d ed. New York: Norton.

———. 1985. The State in Politics: The Relation between Policy and Administration. In *Regulatory Policy and the Social Sciences*, ed. R. Noll, pp. 67–104. Berkeley: Univ. of California Press.

———. 1987. Two Roads to Serfdom: Liberalism, Conservatism and Administrative Power. 36 *American Univ. Law Rev.*, 295.

Lukes, Steven. 1974. *Power: A Radical View*. London: Macmillan.

Lutzenhiser, Loren, and Bruce Hackett. 1993. Social Stratification and Environmental Degradation: Understanding Household CO2 Production. 40 *Social Problems*, 50–73.

Lynch, Barbara Deutsch. 1993. The Garden and the Sea: U.S. Latino Environmental Discourses and Mainstream Environmentalism. 40 *Social Problems*, 108–24.

Lynxwiller, John, Neal Shover, and Donald A. Clelland. 1983. The Organization and Impact of Inspector Discretion in a Regulatory Bureaucracy. 30 *Social Problems*, 425–36.

Macaulay, Stewart. 1963. Non-Contractual Relations in Business: A Preliminary Study. 28 *American Sociological Rev.*, 55–67.

———. 1986. Private Government. In *Law and the Social Sciences*, ed. L. Lipson and S. Wheeler, 445–518. New York: Russell Sage.

Mann, Kenneth. 1985. *Defending White-Collar Crime: A Portrait of Attorneys at Work*. New Haven, CT: Yale Univ. Press.

Manning, Peter K. 1987. Ironies of Compliance. In *Private Policing*, ed. C. Shearing and P. Stenning, pp. 293–316. Beverly Hills, CA: Sage.

———. 1989. The Limits of Knowledge: The Role of Information in Regulation. In *Making Regulatory Policy*, ed. K. Hawkins and J. M. Thomas, 55–85. Pittsburgh: Univ. of Pittsburgh Press.

Mashaw, Jerry L. 1983. *Bureaucratic Justice*. New Haven, CT: Yale Univ. Press.

———. 1985. *Due Process in the Administrative State*. New Haven, CT: Yale Univ. Press.

Mashaw, Jerry L., and David Harfst. 1990. *The Struggle for Auto Safety*. Cambridge, MA: Harvard Univ. Press.

McCann, Michael. 1988. The Making of the Modern Regulatory State. 21 *Polity*, 373.

———. 1992. Resistance, Reconstruction, and Romance in Legal Scholarship. 26 *Law and Society Rev.*, 733.

McGraw, Thomas K. 1975. Regulation in America: A Review Article. 49 *Business History Review*, 159–81.

Meidinger, Errol. 1987. Regulatory Culture: A Theoretical Outline. 9 *Law and Policy*, 355.

———. 1989. The Development of Emissions Trading in U.S. Air Pollution Regulation. In *Making Regulatory Policy*, ed. K. Hawkins and J. M. Thomas, 153–98. Pittsburgh: Univ. of Pittsburgh Press.

Melnick, R. Shep. 1983. *Regulation and the Courts: The Case of the Clean Air Act.* Washington, DC: Brookings Institute.

Mendeloff, J. 1988. *The Dilemma of Toxic Substance Regulation.* Cambridge, MA: MIT Press.

Merchant, Carolyn. 1989. *Ecological Revolution: Nature, Gender and Science in New England.* Chapel Hill: Univ. of North Carolina Press.

Meyer, John W., and Brian Rowan. 1977. Institutionalized Organizations: Formal Structure as Myth and Ceremony. 83 *American Journal of Sociology*, 340–63.

Mitchell, Timothy. 1991. The Limits of the State: Beyond Statist Approaches and Their Critics. 85 *American Political Science Review*, 77–96.

Mitnick, Barry M. 1980. *The Political Economy of Regulation: Creating, Designing, and Removing Regulatory Forms.* New York: Columbia Univ. Press.

Nader, Laura, and David Serber. 1980. Power as Process in Regulation. In *The Sociology of Law*, ed. William M. Evan, 331–42. New York: Free Press.

Needham, Douglas. 1983. *The Economics and Politics of Regulation: A Behavioral Approach.* Boston: Little, Brown.

Noble, Charles. 1986. *Liberalism at Work.* Philadelphia: Temple Univ. Press.

Noll, Roger G., ed. 1985. *Regulatory Policy and the Social Sciences.* Berkeley: Univ. of California Press.

O'Conner, James. 1973. *The Fiscal Crisis of the State.* New York: St. Martin's Press.

Poulantzas, Nicos. 1973. *Political Power and Social Classes.* London: New Left Books.

Powell, Walter W., and Paul J. DiMaggio. 1991. *The New Institutionalism in Organizational Analysis.* Chicago: Univ. of Chicago Press.

Pressman, Jeffrey L., and Aaron Wildavsky. 1984. *Implementation.* Berkeley: Univ. of California Press.

Rabin, Robert L. 1989. EPA Regulation of Chlorofluorocarbons: A View of the Policy Formation Process. In *Making Regulatory Policy*, ed. K. Hawkins and J. M. Thomas, 133–52. Pittsburgh: Univ. of Pittsburgh Press.

Rees, Joseph. 1988. *Reforming the Workplace*: *A Study of Self-Regulation in Occupational Safety.* Philadelphia: Univ. of Pennsylvania Press.

Reichman, Nancy. 1991. Regulating Risky Business: Securities Regulation and the Mobilization of Bias. 13 *Law and Policy*, 263.

———. 1992. Moving Backstage: Uncovering the Role of Compliance Practices in Shaping Regulatory Policy. In *Essays on White Collar Crime*, ed. K. Schlegel and D. Weisburd. Boston: Northeastern Univ. Press.

———. 1993. Insider Trading. In *Crime and Justice*, ed. M. Tonry and A. Reiss. Chicago: Univ. of Chicago Press.

Reiss, Albert J. 1984. Selecting Strategies of Social Control over Organizational Life. In *Enforcing Regulation*, ed. K. Hawkins and J. M. Thomas, 23–35. New York: Kluwer-Nijhoff.

Sarat, Austin, and Susan Silbey. 1988. The Pull of the Policy Audience. 10 *Law and Policy*, 97.

Schattschneider, E. E. 1960. *The Semi-Sovereign People: A Realistic View of Democracy in America*. New York: Holt, Rinehart, and Winston.

Schnaiberg, Allan. 1980. *The Environment: From Surplus to Scarcity*. New York: Oxford Univ. Press.

Scholz, John T. 1984. Cooperation, Deterrence and the Ecology of Regulatory Enforcement. 18 *Law and Society Rev.*, 179.

Schumpter, J. A. 1942 *Capitalism, Socialism and Democracy*. New York: Harper and Row.

Seligman, Joel. 1982. *The Transformation of Wall Street: A History of the Securities and Exchange Commission and Modern Corporate Finance*. Boston: Houghton Mifflin.

Shapiro, Martin. 1988. *Who Guards the Guardians? Judicial Control of Administration*. Athens: Univ. of Georgia Press.

Shapiro, Susan P. 1984. *Wayward Capitalists: Targets of the SEC*. New Haven, CT: Yale Univ. Press.

———. 1985. The Road Not Taken: The Elusive Path to Criminal Prosecution for White-Collar Offenses. 19 *Law and Society Rev.*, 179.

———. 1987a. The Social Control of Impersonal Trust. 93 *American Journal of Sociology*, 623–58.

———. 1987b. Policing Trust. In *Private Policing*, ed. C. Shearing and P. Stenning, 194–220. Beverly Hills, CA: Sage.

Shover, Neal, John Lynxwiller, Stephen Groce, and Donald Clelland. 1984. Regional Variation in Regulatory Law Enforcement: The Surface Mining Control and Reclamation Act of 1977. In *Enforcing Regulation*, ed. K. Hawkins and J. M. Thomas, 121–46. New York: Kluwer-Nijhoff.

Silbey, Susan S. 1984. The Consequences of Responsive Regulation. In *Enforcing Regulation*, ed. K. Hawkins and J. M. Thomas, 145–70. New York: Kluwer-Nijhoff.

———. 1992. Making a Place for Cultural Analysis of Law. 17 *Law and Social Inquiry*, 39.

Smith, Rogers. 1987. Political Jurisprudence, the "New Institutionalism" and the Future of Public Law. 82 *American Political Science Rev.*, 89–108.

Smith, Suzanna, and Michael Jepason. 1995. Big Fish, Little Fish: Politics and Power in the Regulation of Florida's Marine Resources. 40 *Social Problems*, 39–49.

Spitzer, Steven. 1987. Security and Control in Capitalist Societies: The Fetishism of Security and the Secret Thereof. In *Transcarceration: Essays in the Sociology of Social Control*, ed. J. Lowman, R. J. Menzier, and T. S. Palys, 43–58. Brookfield, VT: Gower.

Stenning, Philip, Clifford Shearing, Susan Addario, and Mary Condon. 1990. Controlling Interests: Two Conceptions of Order in Regulating a Financial Market. In *Securing Compliance: Seven Case Studies*, ed. M. L. Friedland, 88–118. Toronto: Univ. of Toronto Press.

Stone, Christopher D. 1975. *Where the Law Ends: The Social Control of Corporate Behavior*. New York: Harper and Row.

Stryker, Robin. 1990. Science, Class and the Welfare State. 96 *American Journal of Sociology*, 684–726.

Sudnow, David. 1965. Normal Crimes: Sociological Features of the Penal Code in a Public Defenders Office. 12 *Social Problems*, 255–76.

Susskind, Lawrence, and Jeffrey Cruikshank. 1987. *Breaking the Impasse: Consensual Approaches to Resolving Public Disputes*. New York: Basic Books.

Terdiman, Richard. 1987. Translators Introduction to the Force of Law. 38 *Hastings Law Journal*, 805.

Trubek, David, Yves Dezalay, Ruth Buchanan, and John R. Davis. 1993. Global Restructuring and the Law: Studies of the Internationalization of Legal Fields and the Creation of Transnational Arenas. Global Studies Research Program Working Paper Series, Univ. of Wisconsin.

Vaughan, Diane. 1983. *Controlling Unlawful Organizational Behavior*. Chicago: Univ. of Chicago Press.

Vogel, David. 1986. *National Styles of Regulation: Environmental Policy in Great Britain and the United States*. Ithaca, NY: Cornell Univ. Press.

Warren, K. 1987. Feminism and Ecology: Making Connections. 9 *Environmental Ethics*, 3–20.

Wilson, James Q. 1980. *The Politics of Regulation*. New York: Basic Books.

———. 1985. Neglected Areas of Research on Regulation. In *Regulatory Policy and the Social Sciences*, ed. R. Noll, 357–62. Berkeley: Univ. of California Press.

Yeager, Peter C. 1987. Structural Bias in Regulatory Law Enforcement: The Case of the U.S. Environmental Protection Agency. 34 *Social Problems*, 330–34.

———. 1991. *The Limits of Law: The Public Regulation of Private Pollution*. New York: Cambridge Univ. Press.

Yngvesson, Barbara. 1993. *Virtuous Citizens, Disruptive Subjects*. New York: Routledge.

Zerbe, Richard O., Jr. 1980. The Costs and Benefits of Early Regulation of the Railroads. 11 *Bell Journal of Economics*, 343–50.

IDEOLOGY, POWER,
AND JUSTICE

S U S A N   S .   S I L B E Y

I. INTRODUCTION

In the last fifteen years, ideology has been the central concept in an expanding collection of research on law. Unfortunately, much of this work reproduces the notorious confusion surrounding the term "ideology" in general, perhaps "the most elusive concept in the whole of social science" (McLellan 1986: 1). One can find several dozen definitions and uses of "ideology," including coherent and articulated worldviews (Verba, Nie, and Petrocik 1979; Converse 1964), false ideas (Marx and Engels [1846], 1970; Scott 1990), and claims of universality for what is actually partial and particular. To use the term "ideology" is, according to Eagleton, "just a convenient way of categorizing under a single heading a whole lot of different things we do with signs" (1991: 193).

But it seems to me that studies of ideology and law are both more and less than semiotic analyses of representation. Studies of legal ideology are analyses of law's complicity with power. With one historically important but conceptually marginal use,[1] the term "ideology" generally points to the ability of ideas to affect social circumstances. Thus sociologists have sometimes described the function of ideology as the capacity to advance the political and economic interests of groups or classes (Mannheim 1936; Marx and Engels [1846] 1970), or alternatively, the capacity to produce cohesion

(Poulantzas 1978: 88) and resolve social strain (Johnson 1968; Parsons 1951, 1967; White 1961). This general notion treats ideology as materially effective representation. From this perspective, the study of legal ideology is the study of how law's representations enact power.

Studies of legal ideology are not, however, only examinations of power at work in and through law. Studies of law and ideology also suggest that the power associated with signs and symbols is being exercised unjustly. Thus, adopting and deploying the term "ideology" is a form of social criticism. In more colorful language, Raymond Williams asserts that ideology "is mainly a term of abuse" ([1976] 1983: 157). To view legal institutions through the lens of ideology implies that the power of law is, despite its visibility and centrality in modern states, incompletely apprehended. To describe legal processes as ideological suggests that in this masquerade law *pretends* to enact justice.

Although justice is the ground of critique, it is rare to find explicit definitions in sociolegal scholarship. Nonetheless, Ewick suggests elsewhere in this volume that justice is implicitly understood as a set of "standards against which power can be held accountable." Distributive justice demands that like cases be treated alike, while substantive justice, or "justness" according to Ewick, demands that the outcomes and consequences of legal processes be reasonable and proportionate. Thus, to invoke the concept of ideology in studies of law is to focus on the ways in which the power attached to and enacted by legal institutions and representations impedes rather than promotes distributive and substantive justice.

In this paper, I argue that use of the term "ideology" in the analysis and interpretation of legal phenomenon is part of a critical project in sociolegal scholarship. Furthermore, introduction of the concept of ideology is part of a more comprehensive theoretical development toward a "constitutive" theory of law (e.g., Hunt 1993; Harrington and Yngvesson 1990; Henry 1995; McCann 1994; Merry 1990; Sarat and Felstiner 1995; Ewick and Silbey 1996). The argument develops as follows.

Sociolegal scholarship begins with a broad but simple claim that legal institutions—like any other social institutions—cannot be understood without seeing the entire set of interacting relations of which they are constituted and the environment in which they function. From this simple premise, sociolegal scholarship is a critical project because it challenges legal professionals who claim autonomy and authority to define the subject and operations of law. By insisting on seeing legal actions and institutions as just the same as, and to be studied just the same as, other forms of social action, sociolegal scholarship questions this claim to authoritative difference and autonomy. But critical research does more than engage in a struggle for a share of professional-intellectual markets (Dezalay, Sarat, and Silbey 1989). Critical scholarship in law specifically challenges not only dominant authorities in the legal profession but also confronts the dominant definitions and understandings of law.

For a long time, the sociology of law was occupied in observing, describing, and documenting the way legal institutions actually worked—what they did and how they did it. It seemed sufficient as a critical project to reveal that legal institutions did not function as they claimed. With time, however, this project became institutionalized so that it no longer represented a challenge to power because it became well accepted that what was called law-on-the-books and law-in-action were not the same. The difference became an accepted social fact—simply the way things were. Some of the critical edge of sociolegal scholarship was lost as scholars took as their task to show the legal system how it failed its ideals of law—principles—and how the legal system—rule of law—could be made to work the way it was supposed to. Often law and society[2] scholars provided technical assistance to do so (Brigham and Harrington 1989).

But contemporary critical sociolegal scholars do more. They examine and interrogate, question and impute, the very ideals and principles that law claims for itself. Critical scholars argue that the ideals and principles that legal institutions announce, even though they fail to support them, are part of how legal institutions create their own power and authority. The ideals of law, such as open and accessible processes, rule-governed decision making, or similar cases being decided similarly—despite their inaccuracy as a description of how law works—are nonetheless part of shared understandings of what law is. Although the ideals are not accurate empirical descriptions, they serve as aspirations that help shape and mobilize suppport for legal institutions. The term "ideology" has been adopted to specifically name this representational and constitutive power attached to legal language, concepts, and practices.

Legal ideologies—public understandings of what law is—shape individual consciousness so that the ideas and understandings seem like one's own. At the same time, social interactions invent as well as reproduce cultural signs, metaphors, and accounts. This is part of "a reciprocal process in which the meanings given by individuals to their world, and law and legal institutions as part of that world, become repeated, patterned and stabilized, and those institutionalized structures become part of the meaning systems employed by individuals" (Ewick and Silbey 1992: 741; Giddens 1987). The endless cycle of production, representation, reception, and re/production describes how people go along with law and do the work of legal institutions without paying attention to the fact that their own actions are what create the legal system, are what make it what it is. Although human action creates the law, it also simultaneously makes it seem "out there," a separate and distinct phenomenon from human action (Ewick and Silbey, in press). This is what sociolegal scholars call the constitutive theory of law: an understanding of law as something that helps construct social relations and is itself constructed by social relations. From this perspective, the task of sociolegal scholarship is to make visible the processes and mechanisms by which individual local action accumulates and condenses into repeated patterns, expectations, and institutions that in their turn have the capacity to shape local action. Thus, the ideological and constitutive perspective in sociolegal scholarship describes a recursive self-reproducing but nonetheless not completely determined process.

By offering a critique of the complicity of law and the collaboration of scholarship in the constitution of social relations, the proponents of the ideological perspective make a justice claim. They attempt to redress a present imbalance in the distribution of power by resisting the common theoretical and representational paradigms that sustain modern systems of domination. In effect, the ideological perspective claims that cultural texts and interpretive practices should no longer be treated as if they "enjoy a separate nature as an unphysical 'structure' or 'frame of meaning' " outside of power, independent of social relations and the probabilities of human justice (Mitchell 1990: 561). Those "unphysical frameworks or structures," embodied in concepts of mind, idea, or interpretation, are themselves effects produced by modern systems of power in which claims to knowledge are acts of power (Foucault 1980; Mitchell 1990). In other words, the series of distinctions which have organized Western thought and legal scholarship for nearly two thousand years, distinctions between mind/body, coercion/consent, law/state, knowledge/power, law-on-the-books/law-in-action, are themselves instruments of power and complicitous in the presently just or unjust social arrangements. In this way, studies of legal ideology analyze and critique the relationships among representation, power, and justice in legal practices.

In this paper I review some, by no means the entire body, of the research on law and ideology. I suggest that we might advance theoretically by noting how the components of this triad—ideology, power, and justice—are differentially deployed in the research literature. Specifically, I argue that the term "ideology" is often infused with different notions of power, and with differential commitments to making explicit the embedded justice claims and critiques.

In the next section, I review briefly how the concept of ideology was introduced as a means of mitigating the theoretical dichotomies (e.g., mind/body, idea/action) that had preoccupied philosophy and social analysis for centuries, and which were reproduced in sociolegal scholarship by the distinction between law-on-the-books and law-in-action.

The third section analyzes the alternative conceptions of power and justice embedded within studies of ideology and law. Some uses focus on local cultures and contests over alternative meanings to emphasize the uncertain reception of legal ideologies. By privileging competitive struggles, these analyses ignore institutionalized structures of power and thus undermine the possibility of a justice critique. In effect, by noticing the ways in which actors make justice claims, authors may excuse themselves from political critique. A second use of ideology reverses the emphasis from uncertain reception to ideological production. These studies often deploy a more instrumental conception of power, suggesting that ideology is a tool, and as such a tool belonging primarily to the powerful. The political critique is often more explicit, however, deriving from a view of justice as distributive equality, and ideology as a mask created to obscure inequality and the work of power.

Rather than taxonomic categories, I consider these two conceptions important but incomplete efforts in a process of theoretical development.

I will offer a third perspective that integrates these two positions with a constitutive notion of power and a more variable notion of justice. In this third perspective, ideology and hegemony are the opposite ends of a continuum where power and justice vary. At one end of the continuum, ideology is used to refer to struggles to establish dominant meanings and to make justice claims on the basis of alternative ideologies. Power may be locally contested and at the same time institutionally structured. At the other end of this conceptual continuum, the term hegemony is used to refer to situations where meanings are so embedded that representational and institutionalized power is invisible. Although moments of resistance may be documented, in general subjects do not question dominant structures and cannot make justice claims against the aspects of structure and power that are invisible. Thus, the scholar's use of the term "hegemony" is an enactment of a surrogate claim, a political critique that attempts to expose the silenced justice claims of the subjects (who are objects) of law and power. In this attention to hegemony, justice seems to lie in the possibilities of reflexive participation and communication through which object status is transformed into liberated subjectivity (Habermas 1970, 1992). The possibilities of political critique are strongest, I suggest, in this third cumulative or integrative perspective. Nonetheless, this conceptualization of ideology and hegemony leaves several unanswered questions, questions I raise briefly in the fourth section of the paper.

Having juggled these three abstractions—ideology, power, and justice—for long enough and having completed my conceptual excavation, I conclude with a concrete example illustrating how a constitutive perspective on ideology and hegemony can provide the grounds for political critique and the possibilities of resistance.

2. INTRODUCING IDEOLOGY TO SOCIOLEGAL SCHOLARSHIP

From its earliest uses, a pejorative aura attached to the term "ideology."[3] It was generally believed that "sensible people rely on *experience,* or have a *philosophy,* silly people rely on *ideology*" (Williams 1983: 157). For the longest time, the political Right and Left understood ideology as abstract and false thought. The ability to strategically manipulate appearances—with abstract and false thought—was treated as a sign of political power. In their use of the concept of ideology, political philosophers and social scientists have mixed descriptive and normative assessment.

Ideology is not simply a description of political accomplishment—successfully creating impressions useful for one's interests—but rather that which must be overcome to achieve justice. From this traditional perspective, it is the duty of philosophy and science to overcome the injustices produced by false ideas. For example, Plato justifies inequality in a city ruled by a philosophic elite, those who have the capacity for true knowledge, because he was convinced that confusion and other substantively bad results followed when cities were governed by false beliefs or mere images. His own experience of the Sophists' activities in Athens convinced Plato that any political system, good or bad, was the direct product of the beliefs held by its members, and if "mere opinion" could wreak havoc on a community, "true belief might work just as powerfully in the opposite direction" (Wolin 1960: 38). This fueled Plato's conviction that philosophy—the pursuit of real knowledge—was not only a good thing in itself, but of practical political importance and urgency. This latter approach, with its direct heirs in the Enlightenment and contemporary social science, connects the pursuit of real knowledge with the possibilities of justice and names ideology, an expression of political power, as the enemy of both truth and justice.

Since Plato first attempted to distinguish what was real and true from what was illusory and false by differentiating a concrete and incomplete world of senses from an immutable and true world of ideas, Western philosophy has been plagued by models opposing thought and action, truth and illusion. Descartes's preoccupation with the relationship between body and mind, and Locke's analysis of sensation and reflection, extended and elaborated this persistent dualism until Kant and then Hegel attempted imaginative reconciliations. In the Enlightenment, mind and the world outside of the mind—the idea and its enactment—still represented entirely separate entities and processes. However, in the age of emerging empiricism, Plato was turned on his head, and ideas—as distinct from things—became associated with the untrue rather than the real and ultimate truth. Because ideas are intangible, ideology—as either the study of ideas or as systems of ideas—was again tainted with this patina of subjectivity and untruth.

Over time, the effort to construct a science of society produced a vision of social life that was predominantly behavioral and positivist, reinforcing the pejorative associations among ideology, subjectivity, and untruth. Although many sociologists claimed otherwise, most prominently Max Weber, mainstream academic social scientists eschewed interest in anything that could not be objectively measured and empirically validated. This was interpreted to mean that anything not capable of quantitative, not only objective, measurement was sociologically irrelevant. Eventually, only that which could be measured was considered real. As a consequence, social science spent most of its energies studying behavior (that which could be "objectively" observed), relegating ideas and representations to the realm of the subjectively unreal. This laid the foundation for seeing human beings as objects rather than subjects—actors but not minds—and left little room for joining action and meaning, behavior and interpretation, other than in opposition.

This intellectual inheritance took an ironic turn in law and society research where the effort to document relationships among image, reality, power, and justice was pursued for a long time before the concept of ideology was adopted to organize empirical analyses of law. The dualisms that consumed philosophy and sociological theory were reproduced in the terminology and topics relevant to law. For example, for the longest time, the dominant conception of law as a system of rules was absorbed by competing interpretations of that rule system as the locus of reason or force. Seeking to identify the real (material) workings of the legal system, rather than the ideal (illusion) of a rule of law, sociolegal scholars reversed the terminology of the classical Platonic distinctions, resurrected the Enlightenment debates, and created their own particular duality between law-on-the-books and law-in-action. Research became preoccupied with dichotomies between law and state, equality and hierarchy, ideals and practices, and its own version of agency and structure in the debates about consent and coercion (Hunt 1993).

Tracking what came to be called law-in-action as distinct from law-on-the-books, several generations of empirical researchers identified persistent contradictions within liberal law: structured patterns of inequality, coercion, and, by implication, injustice that belied aspirations to equality and due process (Fuller 1964). There seemed to be an inescapable "gap" between the written rules or aspirations and practices of law (Feeley 1976; Abel 1980: Nelkin 1981; Sarat 1985; Silbey 1985). Thus, police practices were not merely described but described in terms of their consistency with the ideal of the rule of law and with democratic aspirations; case processing in courts was not merely detailed but measured by the demands of constitutional due process; regulatory enforcement was not only modeled but also assessed for its conformity to legislative mandates and policy interests. Repeated studies demonstrated that "the gap between the ideals of law and its performance is a central and pervasive feature of legal existence and of the consciousness of those who deal with, operate, and observe the legal system" (Trubek 1977: 544).

During this same period from the late 1960s to 1970s, criminologists in Britain were arguing that much of what was observed as a violation of law was in fact the product of law. Rather than controlling crime, law was itself crimogenic. Critical criminologists denounced the "correctionist" stance of traditional criminology by revealing the law's complicity in crime production and announcing their own commitment to diversity, crime-free social arrangements, and social equality (Taylor, Walton, and Young 1973, 1975). For example, in a classic study of mugging and street crime, Hall et al. (1978) demonstrated how law and popular culture were mobilized to create a politically useful meaning about mugging that synthesized diffuse fears about race, crime, and youth with a more general panic about structural changes in British economy and society. A spiral of signification was created in which a specific issue (mugging) became identified with what was named as a subversive minority, and then this single issue became linked with other issues that represented an escalating threat with prophecies of more trouble to follow if action was not taken. The series of representations produced one overwhelming consequence: "it legitimated the recourse to law, to constraint and statutory power, as the main, indeed the only, effective means left" of defending the British state. "It toned up and groomed the society for the extensive exercise of the repressive side of state power" (Hall et al. 1978: 278). The analysis offered a step-by-step description of how law was ideologically mobilized by showing how a popular cultural consensus was actively created that empowered the state, legitimated repressive law enforcement, and successfully claimed to have cabined broader social unrest.

In American law schools, critical legal scholars began to unpack the contradictions and specific class and group interests embedded in much legal doctrine. Offering a progressive critique, critical legal scholars systematically deconstructed the doctrinal edifices of one after another icon of American law, including contracts, torts, and corporations, as well as antidiscrimination and labor law. They decoded the representations and relationships institutionalized by legal doctrine.[4] Some analyses simply revealed logical incoherence, while others demonstrated the presence of alternative values and interests suppressed by dominant ideologies (e.g., Kennedy 1976; Kairys [1982], 1990; Frug 1984; Frug 1985). Some argued that legal education was itself a training exercise for future careers at the top of a socially dominant hierarchy (Kennedy [1982], 1990; Kelman 1987).

Faced with what looked like the false ideals or appearances of law (doctrinal texts and law-on-the-books), some researchers refused to discount the "gap" as either an atypical aberrant practice, a legally remediable lapse, or "as evidence of the total falsity of ideals . . . merely a mask behind which the rich and powerful hide their continued domination and exploitation of the poor and powerless" (Trubek 1977: 544). Some researchers called for intensive study of how the law worked, but without using ideals as a template against which to measure, assess, or interpret practices. Some began to deploy the notion of ideology as a way of paying attention to practices while refusing to ignore the role of the ideals as a part of the practice of law. Thus attention to "legal ideology" became a way of understanding and analyzing the persistent gap between the ideals and practices of law. Attention to "legal ideology" became a way of overcoming what I described above as an overly behaviorized and positivistic view of law. By adopting the concept of ideology, sociolegal scholars could build on Weber's work on legitimation, on the symbolic functions of law (e.g., Gusfield 1963; Edelman 1964, 1971), and could join traditional Marxist socioeconomic concerns to a rehabilitated interest in human subjectivity (e.g., Althusser 1969). An ideological conception of law could underwrite analyses that explored law's symbolic and material constitution and consequences.

In 1984, Roger Cotterrell published *The Sociology of Law,* a basic text built around an incisive and powerful account of law as ideology. Synthesizing the emerging literature that viewed law as an ideological phenomenon with the extensive empirical literature documenting law-in-action, Cotterrell established the centrality of an ideological perspective in sociolegal studies. He explicitly used the concept as a means of resolving the tensions between doctrinal (law-on-the-books) with cultural (law-in-action) conceptions of law. In this effort, he self-consciously moved beyond narrowly behaviorist visions, but stopped short of other analysts who threatened to include all of social life within the terrain of law. He wanted to make a place for both the traditional doctrinal materials which occupy legal professionals and are looked to by ordinary citizens, and the important empirical work on the daily life and practices of legal institutions and actors produced by sociolegal scholars. Building on both the work in critical criminology and cultural studies that documented the social processes of representation and domination in Britain and the critical legal studies that analyzed class interests in American legal doctrine, he offered the notion of legal ideology as a means of seeing how both cultural practice and doctrine combine to shape the way law works in social life.

Very soon thereafter, Alan Hunt published a long article in the *Law and Society Review* delineating "advances and problems in the recent applications of the concept of ideology to the analysis of law." He laid out what was to become known as a constitutive theory of law in which "legal ideology provides a constituent of what Althusser called the 'lived relation' of human actors" (1985, 1993: 121). Hunt identified three levels at which legal ideology functioned: the content of concrete legal norms; the content of general principles; and the content of the form of law. Importantly, he distinguished between the processes of law that produced ideological effects—that is, that mirrored or transformed phenomenal experience into reified abstractions—and consequences of legal processes that produced particular ideological content—norms, categories, or representations that might thus mystify or distort.

Together, Hunt and Cotterrell provided theoretical ground for an abundance of empirical work in which the concept of ideology has been deployed to emphasize ways in which ideals and practices of law work together to empower or to subordinate different persons, groups, positions, and understandings. These studies of legal ideology are not limited to the direct action of law such as an arrest or the disposition of a trial or regulatory process; nor do ideological analyses emphasize exclusively the written text and doctrinal principles. Rather, the analyses of law using the concept of ideology attempt to demonstrate how power is enacted in the conjoining of action and representation through cultural practices and consciousness. When law is understood as an ideological phenomenon, it accentuates the capacity of law to forge authoritative and powerful accounts of social relationships.

3. POWER AND JUSTICE IN STUDIES OF IDEOLOGY

Having adopted the concept of ideology to analyze legal phenomenon, however, researchers deployed the term in diverse ways, infusing the concept of ideology with competing notions of power and justice, producing less and more effective political critiques. Although I speak of these uses as distinct, it is more likely that one can find several versions operating in combination in any particular piece of research. I offer these distinctions, nonetheless, as analytic devices to help identify potential uses and critical capacities of the ideological perspective. Moreover, they can be understood as pieces of a developing perspective, a perspective I outlined in the introduction and return to below.

A. IDEOLOGY: CULTURE WITHOUT POWER

In some pieces of sociolegal research, ideology is equated with culture and becomes synonymous with the most pervasive and general processes of social construction. Seeking to avoid the quagmire of attributions and analyses of false consciousness, some writers focus on the mutually constitutive processes of making meaning among sentient actors and, as a consequence, perhaps inadvertently, strip ideology of its role in the processes of constituting and distributing power. In this first, "powerless" conception, Merry, for example, describes ideology as a

> set of symbols and meanings by which individuals make sense of their world and their experience, suggest[ing] that it is neither false nor true, but one of a range of ways of making the world coherent. Cultures provide multiple and competing sets of symbolic forms and meanings from which individuals choose. These symbolic systems are subject to redefinition through experience and changes in the social system itself. (Merry 1985: 61)

Fine and Sandstrom similarly assert that ideology "helps actors to cope with their lived reality and to facilitate social concourse" (1993: 25). Specifically, Fine and Sandstrom, like Merry, mesh meaning and interaction to "focus on how individuals and groups *do* ideology"; they describe "how people use and act on ideas to realize their interests and purposes in everyday situations" (1993: 25; cf. Thayer 1981).[5] Here, ideology is understood as simultaneously symbolic, affective, and behavioral sets of interconnections among social actors, not simply as beliefs but as situated action. Ideologies are (1) "based on a set of dramatic metaphors and images to which people respond on the basis of their shared experience and expectations"; (2) "not purely cognitive, but depend crucially on emotional responses"; (3) "presented at such times and in such ways as to enhance the public impression (and to justify the claims and resources) of presenters and/or adherents"; and (4) "linked to groups and the relationships between groups, which in turn depend on a set of resources in order to enact ideologies effectively" (Fine and Sandstrom 1993: 35).

These works go a good way toward understanding ideology as situated social action. There is an important emphasis on the relationship between ideology and lived experience as well as the ways in which actors in small group interactions make contextualized interpretations and judgments about their lives in a social and physical surround. "This model demonstrates how ideology and situated action are tied together recursively in a larger dynamic system of social action" (Steinberg 1993: 314). There is strong emphasis on plurality and contestation in the construction of social meanings (Merry 1990; Yngvesson 1993; Sarat and Felstiner 1995) with less attention to institutionalized structures of power and inequality (but see Seron and Munger 1996).

Consider, for example, Merry's study of working-class legal ideology. She describes how the concept of rights and legal language becomes, to use Geertz's (1973) phraseology, a "model of" society and a "model for" action. By conceiving of themselves as rights holders, disputants pursue grievances with neighbors and family members by filing suits in a local court. In one case where two children were fighting and throwing rocks, the parents filed charges and countercharges against each other alleging a variety of minor criminal actions such as threat, assault, and battery. Rather than adopting possible alternative interpretations of the incident, for example that this was just children fighting, or that it was part of ongoing opposition to racial and ethnic integration, each parent attempted to vindicate his or her child's action as a matter of an individual right infringed by the other. According to Merry, "this incident shows how social relationships can be defined in terms of legal rights," which provide a "model of neighbor ties . . . which can be brought into play when it is useful" (1985: 65). Cultural symbols such as legal rights, according to this analysis, also provide a "model for" action defining the remedies available. "Because the court was an option for both parties, their dispute was more likely to be phrased in terms of legal rights" (Merry 1985: 65). In this analysis the legal symbolism and interpretations Merry attributes to the parties seem to emerge as the mutually efficient and available one. The institutional and strategic viability of the alternative interpretations is unexplored.

In this conception, ideology is everywhere and culture is a collection of ideologies. Power is also everywhere but institutionalized nowhere. The political critique of injustice attached to the concept ideology is considerably weakened, even where traces may be found.[6] Although hierarchical relations and structured inequalities are critical variables in the constitutive perspective I described above, differences in participation and capacity are subordinated in this effort to strip ideology of its associations with false consciousness, with instrumental conceptions of power, and with naive materialism. In the effort to acknowledge the struggles through which power is enacted, and thus to recognize the agency of even the relatively powerless, this cultural perspective seems to valorize a choosing subject enmeshed in a web of symbolic and material interactions. Unfortunately, the emphasis on the choosing subject selecting from a tool kit of available symbols, metaphors, and strategies elides the actions of collectivities seeking "to privilege their visions of the world as reality," and the efforts of "others in turn [to] find the means to resist such attempts" (Steinberg 1993: 317). The analysis of working-class legal ideology seems to assume the existence of the symbolic terms—the cultural surround—from which the subjects choose and with which they negotiate. The deployment is tracked while the invention is not interrogated. In order to offer any productive purchase in the repertoire of social analytic concepts, I suggest, ideological analyses must take on the burden of specifically acknowledging and interrogating cultural production as well as reception. Yes, ideologies are "contextually produced chains of meaning" (Steinberg 1993: 317), but those contexts are structured, and constrained, even as they extend to the very personal, intimate, and seemingly idiosyncratic sinews of social interaction. The constraints—blocked paths, rejected interpretations—need to be made explicit and more visible.

B. IDEOLOGY: THE POWER OF ACTORS

In a second set of uses, power and ideology are relatively concrete and observable. Here, the role of power is an explicitly acknowledged and essential element in the constitutive and interpretive work that is described by the term "ideology." Here, ideology is articulated and power is disproportionately exercised by discrete persons and collectivities. Ideology depends directly on and develops from the agency of social actors and groups. Although the power located in collectivities, as well as private persons, may not be appropriately and proportionately represented in public institutions, power is relatively formal and visible. There are two common analyses of this more instrumental and actor-centered notion of power: a pluralist and an elite version.

In the pluralist versions of actor-centered power, the "choosing" subject of the cultural perspective is explicitly endowed with independent agency and will. That actor is identified as the central agent of social and political life, which is merely "an association of self-determining individuals who concert their will and collect their power in the state for mutually self-interested ends" (Wolff 1969: 5). This is a model of power as fundamentally and essentially private. The public or political realm is, effectively, a consequence of the intersection and accumulation of private individual agents. The classical pluralist model includes protections against injustice in the form of major imbalances of power. Private power, if unbalanced, can be checked by the existence of competing actors and groups and by a vigorous patrolling of the boundary between the public and private realms. If the responsibility for checking private power devolves to the state, however, there is a structural necessity to check the power of that public umpire. The American solutions to this "technical" problem of pluralist democracy are quite familiar: a Bill of Rights, checks and balances, and the creation of competing or countervailing powers. In this pluralist conception of power, ideologies can be checked, false ideas unmasked, truth and real knowledge achieved by the open, public competition among and between ideas (e.g., Dahl 1961; Polsby 1963). The social world is a virtual marketplace of relatively *subjective* ideologies, opinions, and attitudes competing for control of the public realm: the state and the public culture of beliefs and allegiances. Following several decades of disrepute, this model of power has resurfaced as the most popular conception of the possibilities of justice in a global economy.[7]

In a second version of actor centered ideology, power can be concentrated in elites—groups or classes—rather than in individuals. In *The German Ideology*, Marx and Engels provide the canonical statement of this elite version of the actor-centered conception of power (e.g., Mills 1956; Hunter 1953). Here, Marx and Engels use "ideology" to mean a set of ideas that are largely determined by the economic arrangements of a society. In class societies such as capitalism, ideologies are determined and distorted by class interest. Ideology is the idealized version of material conditions. In what may be a highly schematic and thus vulgarized condensation, ideology refers in this formulation to sets of ideas that reflect the interests of the ruling class, ideas that are impressed on the consciousness of the proletariat, rendering that consciousness false or mistaken about the actual conditions of life. Thus, ideology derives from the capacity of a dominant group, the capitalists, to impose their will and their worldview on others. I think this is one of the most commonly deployed accounts of ideology and can be connected to behaviorist theories of power which define power as the ability of one person to achieve intended and foreseen effects on others (Wrong 1979).[8] In this actor-centered version, like the pluralist version above, power is also unlikely to be entirely or independently public, official or formal. Nonetheless, powerful actors and groups manage to obtain what they want, including ideological conformity and subordination as well as manipulation of public authority.

Douglas Hay's classic essay "Property, Authority and the Criminal Law" (1975) illustrates well this elite conception of ideology, while laying the ground for questions taken up in the third perspective described below. Its central place in sociolegal literature merits an extended summary. Hay observes that eighteenth-century British law was replete with statutes mandating capital punishment, and in particular capital sanctions "to protect every conceivable kind of property from theft or malicious damage" (1975: 106). Not only had Parliament produced an unprecedented number of capital statutes, but it had also sanctioned an increasing number of convictions under these statutes. At the same time, Hay observed, there was a noticeably declining proportion of death sentences. Hay sets out to understand this blatant and apparent disjunction between legal prescriptions and the practices of criminal law. How was this contradiction managed and what were its consequences for British society? Deploying the conception of ideology as a means of resolving social strain or contradiction (see introductory essay), Hay suggests that the contradiction was functional, protecting the power and resources of the landed gentry exactly as it was intended to do. This is an early and very clear example of research that went beyond the observation of a gap between law-on-the-books and law-in-action to explain both the pattern and the consequences of that gap.

The major work of Hay's essay is a demonstration of how the combination of more stringent capital sanctions, coupled with a noticeable measure of legal formalism, discretionary administration, and publicly visible mercy in the form of pardons, sustained the interests of the landed gentry by establishing not merely the sanctity of property but the authority of law. The criminal law created, Hay argues, an explicit set of obligations and materially realizable bonds of obedience and deference that legitimated the status quo by "constantly recreating the structure of authority which arose from property, and in turn protected its interests" (1975: 108). Here the law served, according to Hay's analysis, to create the meaning of wealth and definitions of property by naming the actions and relationships that challenged and resisted these definitions as a crime: theft.

The law may have fabricated these relations of property but, Hay continues, "class interest and the structure of law itself shaped it into a much more effective instrument of power" (1975: 108). Because ultimate power—physical strength and numbers—lay with the populace, the landed elite required a means of subjugating their strength. By strategically deploying mercy, while invoking metaphors of equality, the law served the interests of the landed gentry. The law provided a political, apparently consensual, solution by which the "motives of the many induce [them] to submit to the few" (William Paley quoted in Hay 1975: 108).[9]

Although Hay describes the law as an instrument of power, in his analysis authority is not a reservoir of social resources (e.g., chips or trumps) held by someone or some group. Instead, he treats authority as a set of relationships enacted in performances of command and deference (Wrong 1979). As performances, authority relations are scripted, enacted through cultural representations. In Hay's analysis, law provided the scripts for the enactment of command and deference. The law was the means by which the power of the authors of the law could be institutionalized so that the authors of the script and the beneficiaries of the play became less visible. In this way, Hay describes the historical invention of the script spoken by Merry's subjects.

It is important to recognize, however, that while Hay's analysis shows how the criminal law was specifically manipulated to serve the interests of the landed classes, ideology does not belong exclusively to the powerful. There may be in any setting, institution, or political system, dominant sets of understandings, representations, and interpretations, in other words a ruling ideology that will be associated with dominant groups, classes, or persons. However, subordinate populations may also have ideologies and may draw upon them in a variety of ways, including but not exclusively struggles aimed at redistributing the balance of power. Any struggle is ideological to the extent in which it "involves an effort to control the cultural terms in which the world is ordered and, within it, power legitimized" (Comaroff and Comaroff 1991: 24). Moreover, ideologies need not be so coherent and consistent that they can be exclusively attached to the interests of any one group.[10]

McCann's (1994) study of pay equity reform provides a contemporary example of the complexities of ideological struggle. McCann argues against critics who claim that women's efforts to achieve pay equity through litigation merely reinforced rather than opposed the logic of market forces and the hierarchy of modern capitalist society. He suggests parallels with the eighteenth-century debates about property rights that Hay (1975) as well as E. P. Thompson (1975) reported. McCann suggests that even though the parties to the political struggles mobilize mainstream legal norms (e.g., claims of property rights by the propertyless in eighteenth century, claims of equal rights by those receiving less pay for the same work in late twentieth-century America), the law's adverse rulings did not silence their sense of injustice. They are undaunted if they lose particular battles; they do not believe that the law represents the only right and just outcome. They are willing and able to employ alternative, sometimes contradictory arguments, depending on the arena and the opponent. The struggle is an ideological engagement because the players retain a sense of opposition, a self-consciousness of their own role in shaping the terrain on which political struggle is joined, and an awareness that legality itself is fashioned as it responds to and enacts power.

But what about justice? The first model emphasized choosing a subject drawing from a repertoire of cultural symbols. To rebut imputations of passivity and unconscious or unknowing acquiesence to power among the powerless, researchers documented local contests and struggle. It was sufficient, for the critical project, to show that one could not predict the uses of particular signs, symbols, and ideologies. By shifting the emphasis from uncertain reception to ideological production, this second model, pluralist or elite actor-centered theories, cannot rest content with participation as a political position and measure of justice. Justice seems to be understood as distributive equality, and thus equal capacity or effectiveness in shaping the ideological terrain, rather than mere participation, is necessary to serve critical goals. By revealing inequality in symbolic and material outcomes, this more instrumental position demonstrates the failure of law to achieve justice. Ideology is deployed to describe how law obscures that inequality and its own complicity in the creation and maintenance of inequality.

C. IDEOLOGY AND HEGEMONY: CONTEST AND DOMINATION

I propose a third conception which places ideology ("struggles to control cultural terms in which the world is ordered and, within it, power legitimated") as one end of a continuum along which power and justice vary. At the other end, power is explicitly present but more diffuse than in the actor-centered conceptions. We can sort through a lot of the confusion and make much progress in understanding the relationships among ideology, power, and justice if, following Comaroff and Comaroff, we adopt the term "hegemony" to refer to this end of the continuum where power is dispersed through social structures and relations. Rather than viewing ideology as expressed in the representations of individual subjects or as the consequence of group power, in this third notion, power and hegemony derive "as if naturally, from the very construction of economy and society" (Comaroff and Comaroff 1991: 23). Here, hegemony is used to refer to those circumstances where representations and social constructions are so embedded as to be almost invisible, so taken for granted that they "go without saying, because, being axiomatic, they come without saying" (Comaroff and Comaroff 1991: 23; Bourdieu 1977: 167). But where there are articulated sets of meanings, values, and beliefs, where there is active contest over meanings, values, and beliefs, I use the term "ideology." Thus along the power dimension of the continuum, ideology and hegemony differ by the degree to which there is active contest and struggle among groups promoting alternative ideologies.

> Whereas [hegemony] consists of constructs and conventions that have come to be shared and naturalized throughout a political community, [ideology] is the expression and ultimately the possession of a particular social group, although it may be widely peddled beyond. The first, [hegemony], is non-negotiable and therefore beyond direct argument; the second [ideology] is more susceptible to being perceived as a matter of inimical opinion and interest and therefore is open to contestation. Hegemony homogenizes, ideology articulates. Hegemony, at its most effective, is mute; by contrast, says de Certeau (1984: 46), "all the while, ideology babbles on." . . .
>
> Hegemony . . . exists in reciprocal interdependence with ideology: it is that part of a dominant world view that has been naturalized and, having hidden itself in orthodoxy, no more appears as ideology at all. Inversely, the ideologies of the subordinate may give expression to discordant but hitherto voiceless experience of contradictions that a prevailing hegemony can no longer conceal. (Comaroff and Comaroff 1991: 24–25)[11]

In this third recursive and cumulative notion, ideology/hegemony integrates across the prior notions to suggest that power is neither entirely a matter of conscious intention and decision, nor a consequence of one person's or group's consolidated and complete domination of others, nor so pervasively present or absent as to be equated with culture generally. Rather, power circulates, and operates through institutions as well as cultural symbols. In addition to being the ability of some to achieve intended and foreseen effects on others (the elite view), power is also a consequence of collective forces and social arrangements. The bias of social systems, that is, the degree to which particular interests and persons are benefited (are powerful), or disadvantaged (powerless), is a consequence not only of individually chosen acts (the cultural and pluralist conceptions), but also of socially structured and culturally shaped patterns of behavior of groups and practices of institutions. Here, "domination," refers to structured patterns of asymmetry in the distribution of social resources which can be *drawn upon and reconstituted in ongoing social interaction* (see Sewell 1992). Techniques of power even in the most intimate exchanges, at the extremities of social exchange, are systematically invested, utilized, colonized, transformed, and extended by ever more general, and institutionalized or recursively reproduced, mechanisms (Foucault 1978,

1980). Ideas, meanings, interpretive frameworks, metaphors, and images are part of those apparatuses of power, and function as ideologies when contested and as hegemony when taken-for-granted.

In this continuum of ideology/hegemony, it is not the activity of the capitalist class, impressing its views on the proletariat, but the power of the commodity form, the essential structural element of capitalism, that shapes social life, transactions, and meanings. In this sense, what I am calling hegemony does not arise mechanically from class domination; instead hegemony resides invisibly in the forms of production, distribution of resources, linguistic codes, and forms of interpretation in capitalist society. In this analysis, people are produced by the things, or *by the forms of producing and distributing* things, so much so that the very construction of self, identity, mind, and meaning is masked, unnoticed, and unquestioned.

Balbus (1977) has emphasized this hegemonic character of liberal law in his analysis of the homologous cognitive processes operating in the forms of liberal law and capitalism. He claims that the generalized categories of liberal law constitute one of its primary mechanisms of domination by being, in effect, beyond question. The specific form of liberal law (open textured terms or signifiers stated as principles and ideals), Balbus argues, reproduces the essential characteristics of capitalism in what he calls the commodity form of law. In both capitalism and liberal law, generalized mediums of signification and exchange (e.g., money, individuals, rights) are used to obscure, and thus distort, the variation *within* those categories. In fact not only legal concepts but linguistic signifiers generally obscure the particularities of their use.[12] However, the openness or generality of the concepts—their metaphoric availability—also enhances investment in the categories. Different readers or audiences can see in the same term diverse meanings. Linguistic and legal signifiers thus serve as interchangeable and collective vehicles for diverse interests and purposes, sometimes competing and resistant interests. Nonetheless, these opposing forces are contained within very limited categories and formulations that can be differentially shaped and mobilized by local agents.[13] For example, by describing an aspect of experience in the language of rights, we deny the complexity, ambiguity, and contradictions of social experience that are represented by that single term. Invoking the concept of rights, a person crystallizes experience in a set of abstractions making connections with others and claims for deference and priority that may be neither empirically available nor likely. Nonetheless, the label "right" authorizes and legitimates the imagining of association and community that is denied in practice.[14]

In another classic analysis of the "hegemonic function of law," Genovese described how American slave law shaped popular consciousness, and became, by its pretensions to be an autonomous neutral institution, a vehicle for sustaining slave-owning class hegemony. Southern slave law was able to do this, Genovese argues, by disciplining both "criminal" slaves and harsh slave-owners, and thus appearing evenhanded to a degree sufficient to compel social conformity. Because slave owners turned to the courts to enforce discipline among the slaves, the law ended up disciplining slaveholders as well as slaves. By turning to law as a source of discipline, the slaveholders enabled the slaves to become, as well as themselves, creators of law. Thus, Genovese found courts acknowledging the humanity and volition of the slaves, which was necessary if the slaves were to be punishable under law as legally competent and thus reasonable human actors; at the same time, slaveholders, and courts, insisted on the status of slaves as chattel.

This contradiction within the law of slavery, while providing little protection for the slaves, nonetheless created opportunities for moral invention and resistance. The slaves were certainly not deceived and saw that they had few rights at law and that those could easily be violated by the whites. But even one right imperfectly defended was enough to tell them that the pretensions of the master class could be resisted. Before long, law or no law, they were adding a great many "customary rights" of their own and learning how to get them respected. Here, as Genovese shows, the law acted not as a simple and direct agent of the ruling class—the slave owners—but as a mediator between the ruling class as a whole and individual members. That it could do so, Genovese argued, derived from the law's hegemony, its appearance, and sometimes practice, as relatively autonomous from that class—something embedded, long-standing, historic, and independently viable.[15]

Finally, Bumiller's (1988) analysis of how victims of discrimination refused to use civil rights law to interpret their situations and to respond to their discrimination provides a contemporary example of the hegemonic power of law.[16] The study is also important because it suggests how we might identify aspects of resistance within what seems to be hegemonic law. This research gave evidence of the taken-for-granted, possibly hegemonic aspects of law because it looked not at cases at law, or grievances filed, but at what had not come to law. By looking at the nonuse of law, Bumiller documented the "legal" silence of her respondents, and thus the hegemony of state law and institutions. The people Bumiller interviewed resisted in private what was generally perceived as the encompassing—taken-for-granted—structure of cultural terms and constraints.[17]

These analyses of the hegemonic functions of law push the justice critique beyond a condemnation of inequality to an examination of the possibilities for resistance and transformation. Although all ongoing social organizations incorporate contest and struggle over the constitution of their world, most aspects of social structure[18] are taken for granted and not subject to conscious consideration and engagement. Social actors accept a good part of their social worlds as necessary, and often as natural, as perhaps they must to function at all in those worlds. Often invisible, and certainly uncontested, these taken-for-granted structures are thus unlikely to be the subject of justice claims and critiques, although they may be a source of disadvantage and injustice. Because hegemony colonizes consciousness, a central concern of critical scholarship "is to give voice to the subject: to collect, interpret, and present materials about human experiences that preserve the voice of the subjects" (Bell 1991: 245) and, in effect, to produce the surrogate justice claims that have been silenced by hegemony (Bell 1991).[19]

Moreover, because justice must be more than equal participation in an ongoing "unjust" system, the justice critique cannot be limited to denunciation of unequal participation in ideological production. Rather, the critique moves elsewhere to expose the construction of the taken-for-granted world. Thus, the task of the critical scholar analyzing hegemony is not only to give voice to the silenced but also to demonstrate how hegemony is constituted as an ongoing concern. Through social analysis, then, the critical scholar makes a space for an analysis of justice by making manifest the taken-for-granted conditions of social organization and, by implication, the possibilities of alternative social worlds. In this way, analysis hopes to disrupt hegemony's colonizing power.[20]

4. CONCLUSIONS AND QUESTIONS: A RESEARCH AGENDA

In the previous sections, I suggested that the concept of ideology was adopted to mediate persistent dichotomies plaguing empirical sociolegal research, especially distinctions between the ideal and the real, the law and the practice of law. However, ideology has taken on variable meanings in research that embody alternative conceptions of power and justice. Using the concept of ideology to describe variable cultural reception effaces the exercise of power in creating and deploying symbols, language, and interpretations. The local struggles to create convincing accounts and to control situations is described without analysis of the political or macrosocial dimensions, thus eroding the critical capacity for making justice claims and arguments. Using ideology with an agent-centered notion of power to document ideological production inverts the problem: ideology becomes a specific instrument used by individuals or groups to achieve political power. Too often, these perspectives either overestimate the power of the less powerful or ignore them altogether, making it seem as if only the powerful have ideologies. Moreover, when ideology is only the contested ground of political conflict, it seems to ignore the power that is enacted without contest. An important correction to the first cultural perspective, the second actor-centered conception tends to err in the direction of naive instrumentalism. I offered a third conception that builds on the strengths of the previous two formulations by distinguishing contested ideology from hegemony which is embedded in social structures and no longer contested.

In sum, then, when the ideological perspective is applied to law, it emphasizes the ways in which law participates in the struggles to create visions of the world that are accepted as true and real. The ideological perspective describes efforts to shape social relations by forging consequential metaphors and signs for communication and interaction. This is a critical perspective in which the law can never be seen as neutral: neither as neutral between the parties, which is an overly simplified popular vision, nor neutral in respect to the general organization of social relations. The law is a principal agent in the construction of the world because—in its concrete legal norms, in its general principles and values, and in its form and processes—it is a means of apprehending the world. Thus the persistent gap between law-on-the-books and law-in-action does not threaten either the legitimacy of law or its purported power as a means of social control and governance. The ideological perspective suggests that there is an independent, sometimes hegemonic, power exercised by the forms and ideals of law. When law functions hegemonically, its categories and symbols so suffuse consciousness that opposition and resistance are unlikely because most of the time they are unthinkable, outside the cognitively available categories. In other words, as Wittgenstein wrote, "what we cannot speak we must pass over in silence" (Wittgenstein [1921] 1961: 151).

Adopting the concept of ideology for sociolegal research, however, raises as many questions as it dissolves contradictions. Can we assume that all ideologies are equally effective? How well do different ideologies perform their functions? How do we differentiate among ideologies? If this conception of ideology identifies the connection between power and representation, it defines ideology without necessarily or linguistically distinguishing subordinate legal ideologies from dominant legal ideologies, dominant from hegemonic legal ideologies, without specifying the relationships between the distribution of power and the work of ideology. In addition, is there a relationship between forms of power (Wrong 1979) and forms and styles of ideology? Certainly Foucault (1973) suggests that forms of power vary with different epistemologies and different systems of representation. We need to understand what distinguishes dominant from subordinate ideologies, but we also need to understand how shifts occur between subordinate and dominant ideologies. In other words, how does the ideological become hegemonic? If there is movement, what accounts for it? These are empirically researchable questions, questions that extend beyond the boundaries of sociolegal research but that may have greater probability of successful analysis within sociolegal research than in other social spheres.

Consider, for example, two different versions of hegemony. In one account, a dominant hegemonic ideology persuades "subordinate groups to believe actively in the values that explain and justify their own subordination" (Scott 1990: 72). As a consequence, they readily comply with laws, rules, and regulations that more powerful groups enact to sustain and enhance their interests. A different version suggests that hegemony achieves law abidingness and conformity through "non-violent forms of control exercised through the whole range of dominant cultural institutions and social practices, from schooling, museums, and political parties to religious practice, architectural forms, and the mass media" (Mitchell 1990: 553). In the first account, subordinates provide consent; in the second, compliance and resignation are sufficient. There is a growing body of literature developing to suggest that the first, consenting version of hegemony is untenable as a model of the ways in which legal ideology enacts power. Empirical sociolegal research (much of it reviewed elsewhere in this volume) describes complex interactions between the law and compliance to law. It has never been complete. Not only does law make provision for its own violation, but cynicism about the neutrality and majesty of law has persisted alongside grandiose claims for its transcendent legitimacy (Ewick and Silbey, in press).

The "resigned compliance" version of hegemony, more commonly deployed in sociolegal scholarship, recognizes that conflict and resistance are consistent with the existence of a dominant hegemony. All that is required is that the order of things seem inevitable. "A degree of distaste for, or even hatred of, the domination experienced" is not incompatible with hegemony in this sense in which neither agreement, consensus, nor harmony is necessary. "The claim is not that one's fated condition is loved, only that it is here to stay whether one likes it or not" (Scott 1990: 75). Contemporary social theorists sometimes describe what I am referring to as hegemony when they speak of the sedimentation and institutionalization of structures of everyday life.[21] Giddens, for example, talks about "the naturalization of the present" in which existing socioeconomic arrangements, especially those that existed for several generations and centuries, come to be taken for granted (1979: 195). And Bourdieu describes how "every established order tends to produce (to very different degrees and with very different means) the naturalization of its own arbitrariness" (1977: 164). Thus, when law is understood as a hegemonic phenomenon (in contrast to contested ideology), it refers to this ability to inscribe arbitrary and varied cultural forms with the aura of the natural and inevitable.

Ideologies, even when contested, can be said to distort and mystify experience, to falsely portray unity, and to conceal class relations. But it is not "the truth"—an immutable natural reality knowable through positivist science—that is concealed. Rather, law in its ideological and hegemonic capacities masks the possibilities of alternative understandings and accounts of social relations. By suppressing alternative interpretations, ideologies also deny that they are themselves creations. In short, neither ideology nor hegemony proclaim themselves as such. For example, the ideologies of meritocracy, competitive individualism, desert, and fairness simultaneously construct and deny systems of structured inequality. Therapeutic professionalism, founded on the rhetoric of diagnosis and intervention, denies its role in creating pathologies of mind and body it then seeks to treat.

Of course, denying the existence of an ideology does not make it go away; if anything, it makes the ideology stronger because it may then operate at the hegemonic level, more deeply where it cannot be challenged overtly. Ideologies that have the ability to deny themselves, or to naturalize themselves as I have been suggesting, become hegemonic through their ability to deflect criticism and attention. The power of an ideology may well be its capacity for invisibility, similar to what Bourdieu refers to as habitus. From this point of view, law may have more than one ideology implicit in it. Some legal rules (for example, rules against murder or in favor of private property in the U.S. system) may seem "obvious" or otherwise so hegemonic that they cannot be questioned except by marginal types like academics. But other legal rules may be more questionable (like antidiscrimination laws and new rape statutes) and more ideologic. The question, of course, is whether these are properties of all ideologies or only of some particular hegemonic systems. Perhaps this is another subject for further research.

Hegemonic ideologies, even in the version that assumes only resigned compliance rather than agreement and consensus, may not merely naturalize the social world but may encourage subordinates to believe that they are just, that is, the justice that is possible. What is perceived as what ought to be—"necessity becomes virtue" (Scott 1990: 76). Imagining an alternative system becomes not only difficult, not only undesirable, but undesired.[22] Even though serfs, peasants, and other widely subordinated groups are regularly imagining alternative worlds, I suggest that hegemony may persist. The resistant imaginings Scott describes (1990: 80) merely up-end—in imagination—the system of subordination; they do not question the inevitability of stratification and inequality, merely the subordinate location (misplacement) in a world of purportedly inevitable and apparently natural inequality. Thus, in this example, the notions of inequality and stratification are hegemonic.

If law can be hegemonic, to what degree do challenges to law reject law or specific laws? Moreover, to what degree can challenges to hegemony operate completely outside the dominant discourse?[23] Can political struggles be pursued without a common ground of cultural interpretation? It may be important to begin to specify and distinguish counterhegemonic from ideological struggles in order to identify systemic confrontations from disputes within an accepted boundary (e.g., Fantasia 1988; Hunt 1993: 227–48; McCann 1994). This is especially important, if we recognize that hegemony is complex, self-contradictory, and polyvocal (Bakhtin 1981; Billig et al. 1988). To what degree does the polyvocality of an ideology contribute to its hegemonic potential? Or, conversely, to what degree does univocality contribute to the instability of hegemony?[24] Messick's (1988, 1992) analysis of Islamic law suggested that the abundance of intratextual space—the ability to forge multiple readings and yet remain within the sacred spaces—helped sustain religious/legal domination. Genovese's study of American slave law also suggested that the contradictions generated by trying to use law to enforce the physical domination of slaves sustained the legitimacy of slavery while it simultaneously provided opportunities for resistance to slavery. Does polyvocality contribute to or subvert conflict? Does it make resistance more or less likely? Does polyvocality erode the possibilities of justice critiques? Is the claim of procedural justice an example of how liberal law subverts the possibilities of substantive justice critiques?

Finally, what role does scholarship play in the ongoing struggles to forge compelling accounts of social life? In the ideological constitutive perspective

I have been outlining, scholarship cannot be exempt from a role in the constitution of the world. Because we know that our actions and interpretations produce and reproduce the world, critical scholars try to develop ways of describing what happens in social relations that unsettle dominant conventional understandings and empower alternative visions and actions. Being critical "means refusing to accept as given the dominant ways that social relations are represented" (Peller 1992). Through teaching and research, sociolegal scholars disrupt the taken-for-granted comfortable understandings of law and social relations—the way the world works—to construct accurate but unconventional alternative descriptions that may frustrate the processes of reproduction on which institutional power rests.[25] The stories we tell become part of a new taken-for-granted world.

In the institutions and profession of law that valorize history, precedent, hierarchy, and authority, empirical research has by definition this disruptive critical capacity. Because studies of law and ideology analyze not only power (the way things are), but embody justice critiques as well (the way things might be), adopting an ideological perspective on law has the capacity to enhance this critical potential. It must be said, however, that critical scholars often fall short of the mark. Ironically, justice is rarely the explicit topic of sociolegal research and more often only an implied critique. The reticence to be explicit about justice may derive from a residue of scientism that infects all social science, and with it an unarticulated belief in the possibilities and virtues of value-free scholarship. As C. Wright Mills advised, however, social scientists have a responsibility to help think through what might be as well as what is. Thus we might view those who adopt the ideological perspective as self-consciously partisan in the construction of social reality.

5. EPILOGUE: AN ILLUSTRATIVE STORY

Several years ago, I participated in a faculty seminar at Wellesley College that was part of an effort to enrich liberal education by encouraging interdisciplinary exchange. The group consisted of four social scientists, two historians, and a half dozen literary critics. The seminar was entitled "Rereading the Canon"; the readings consisted of two canonical texts, Virgil's *Aeneid* and Goethe's *Faust,* accompanied by selected theoretical essays by Bloom, Benjamin, Brecht, and others. Each session, three times a week for a month, began with one of the seminar leaders (both members of language and literature departments) introducing a passage from the text for the day. These preliminary remarks usually offered historical context, some cross-references, and other background for the passage. Very quickly, however, conversation was joined around particular interpretations of passages and themes in the work.

I began the seminar with great enthusiasm because I harbored ambitions to expand my sociological repertoire of interpretive techniques and skills. For some time, I had been impressed by erudite performances by literary scholars and by theoretical arguments about the connections between literature and social science. But I was soon disappointed. No, that is not right; I was frustrated, and more to the point, I soon became angry.

I was floundering in the seminar. Although I would faithfully prepare for each session and would listen carefully to the discussion, I could not figure out what was expected or accepted as a response to the text. I was unable to discover the grounds of interpretation. I did not know what counted as compelling evidence for particular readings. If the interpretation seemed to rest on the placement of the material in the text, I asked if order was one of the guidelines. If repetition and reiteration seemed to support a particular interpretation, I asked again if that were another important variable. Interestingly, although historical and background information was regularly presented by the seminar leaders in their introductions of the texts, it was almost never used when interpretations of the texts were debated. Each time I formulated what seemed like a "rule" or a methodological instruction, I was dismissed; I seemed to be going about this the wrong way. According to the responses, there seemed to be no specifiable rules or methods per se. I was beginning to feel as I did in college when I sat through literature classes, captivated by the texts but bewildered by the teacher and the discussion. I never knew where the class was going, or why, except to notice the pattern of particular persons' styles and interests. The relationship between the text and the analysis eluded me completely. I was becoming increasingly agitated. I also began to sense that I was treated as comic relief.

But these were not my youthful college days, and I was no longer easily intimidated by agile wordplays and facile performances. Then, I removed myself from the source of the frustration; now I responded. I talked to others in the seminar and discovered that they too—the other social scientists, that is—were also frustrated. Several of them also remarked on the familiarity between this class and their college experiences, and how this kind of frustration had made them choose to study social science and history rather than literature. The literary discussion, they said, was opaque and mysterious when they were students and remained so now as faculty.

I should probably note that although there turned out to be differences among the literary scholars, I first experienced them as homogeneous because they collectively joined in conversations that, despite their differences of method and perspective, they individually understood without naming or explaining to the others. Some turned out to be quite traditional in their approaches and methods, and others were postmodern deconstructionists. These differences were, nonetheless, obscured by the ability to read, interpret, and argue about interpretations without translation among themselves.

I had always imagined, and imagined again in this seminar, that there must be a text somewhere that would explain how to do it, how to read and interpret literature. I looked for a guide that would offer a set of rules that, while obviously not embodying the full extent and richness of literary interpretation, nonetheless would offer a novice an introduction to the techniques and methods. I sought access to what seemed to lie, and I was sure did lie, behind the visible and audible. I sought access to what in current scholarship seemed like powerful magic.

It sounds preposterous, and to a large degree offensive, to suggest that a tenured faculty member at a relatively wealthy and elite institution is colonized. Nonetheless, for that moment, I was not unlike "Christianized" peoples around the globe, who are often convinced that the white colonizing missionaries have a separate, secret bible and set of rituals (be it cricket, the telegraph, or tea parties) that account for the colonizer's power (cf. Comaroff and Comaroff 1991: 32). Some anthropologists describe the "whimsical 'unreason' of such movements as the cargo cults . . . [arising] from precisely this conviction" (Comaroff and Comaroff 1991: 32). My own desire to enter the liturgic secrets of literary interpretation were not, I believe, far removed from these native movements. Like some indigenous peoples who were observed during colonization to walk around wearing watches and eyeglasses that did not work, I too sought what seemed like symbols of the powerful. In this case power was the ability to read beyond the surfaces of texts and situations, and the visible sign was not the apparel of the colonizer but the ability to deploy literary language, tropes, and terms of art. The cargo cults, the wearing of nonfunctional watches, and the desire to enter the world of literary interpretation may each represent "early efforts to capture and redeploy the colonialist's ability to produce value." Often, however, such adoptions and appropriations are, according to anthropologists, "seen as enough of a threat to elicit a punitive response" (Comaroff and Comaroff 1991: 32).[26]

For sure, I was made uncomfortable by the dismissals and humorous tolerance of my colleagues. And I was made anxious and distressed by the game, because it felt like "their" game, from which I was excluded. Although, each time I asked, the seminar leaders denied that there were rules or specifiable criteria, clearly there were unacceptable as well as acceptable, better as well as worse interpretations. This is an example of what I earlier referred to as hegemony. If there were distinctions and rules but I could not know them, and there was no reason to suppose I lacked the capacity to know them, no wonder I felt an almost purposeful exclusion or segregation. This was distressing.

An interdisciplinary faculty seminar invokes the most basic, generally unspoken, norms of collegiality, in this case an equally shared commitment to liberal education and, to this end, a commitment to intellectual growth in all disciplines. But as the seminar unfolded, we did not seem to have equal capacity and role, and the commitment to sharing and exchange seemed elusive. The battles among disciplines are notorious, but what appeared to be domination by my literary colleagues seemed out of proportion. For several years, it appeared as if humanist scholars were waging a paper campaign against science, and especially social science. Perhaps what I experienced was just resistance against the increasing domination by science both inside and outside of the academy, as C. P. Snow had warned two generations earlier. For some social scientists, it looked as if the humanists were winning, subordinating the claims of social inquiry to the aesthetics of rhetorical performance. Nonetheless, there always seemed to be something inconsequential about it all, just another academic fashion that would in time wane in the face of what had for several hundred years seemed like the inevitable march of science.

For a moment, however, enclosed in the small hermetic world of the seminar, this seemed like real power. This was no longer just play. The metaphor of a battle with sides drawn between friends and enemies with all the usual tactics was beginning to seem all too real. Here the intellectual claims and seductive arguments of literary critics' abstract discussions about the relativity of knowledge and the indeterminacy of texts had been transported from the realm of theory to phenomenal, ontological experience. I wanted to play on the team; I had been seduced and motivated to join the seminar because I was committed to interdisciplinary exchange and because I sought access to some of the cultural capital that seemed to attach to literary scholarship. But they wouldn't let me in.

Anthropologists of colonialism have observed what I experienced in that seminar, that "with time and increasing experience, the colonized show greater discrimination, greater subtlety in interpreting [the colonialist's] embrace and its implications" (Comaroff and Comaroff 1991: 32). No longer satisfied with wearing the markers of the colonialist or speaking their language, and yet experiencing continued exclusion and subordination, dominated populations develop more diverse responses. Some will appropriate more and more of the images, ideologies, practices, and aesthetics of imperial power; others, however, will continue to be excluded, and some of those may begin to adopt practices of contestation and resistance. There is no simple formula or pattern.

In our seminar, some of the more self-identified feminists began the attack. The leaders had organized the seminar to stimulate conversations they hoped would demonstrate the excellence of canonical texts, excellence as evidenced by the textual richness, openness, and availability for multiple and complex interpretations and lines of analysis. For example, the seminar leaders offered what they claimed were feminist readings of the texts, as well as other readings from the margins. As efforts to validate plural perspectives, these readings nonetheless sustained the notion of a center and periphery: first, by the implication that these were marginal readings, and second, by the treatment of the canon as the apex or center of literary accomplishment. At the same time, the seminar leaders resisted, quite vehemently at times, any notion that the canon itself was exclusionary or represented some unjustified privilege; it was simply the best that had been thought and written. Soon, the attacks became more vigorous and were joined by other members of the seminar who could not accept the notion of "the best" as a natural or neutral category, nor a definition and specification of the margins that legitimated a privileged center.

Members of the seminar began to bring in readings for the group, readings which did not simply offer less conventional interpretations of the principal texts but analyses of canon formation written from a variety of perspectives. The seminar read histories and began collectively to create a genealogy of the canon which challenged the claim that these books were, by supposedly objective measures, superior to all other works of literature. We tried to show how the arguments for excellence, and the measures used, were themselves products of locally determined values, and that despite the ambitions of the promoters, there were no universal criteria by which to establish what constituted the very best and thus justified the exclusive attention to some works of literature. Here is an example of the movement from what I defined above as hegemony to what we called ideology. We tried to point out the incoherence of the arguments: how alternative conclusions followed from the same premises; how the premises themselves turned out to be contradictory; and how the conclusions were arbitrary or based on dubious assumptions or hidden rhetorical tricks (cf. Gordon 1988: 17).

We went further, and I think it was in our next move that we actually began to convert some of our literary colleagues. Approximately half the seminar were social scientists, after all, and we did not believe that either by trashing the canon defenders' arguments or by revealing their inconsistencies and contradictions that we would have done enough; nor did we believe that literary history or interpretation was random, whimsical, or chaotic. Indeed, it was clear that there was a pattern and a structure; it was merely implicit rather than explicit, and I had felt it consistently. My frustration had arisen from the regularity in my experience coupled with the persistent public denial[27] of the existence and political consequences of that structure. We took it on ourselves to try to demonstrate for our colleagues the organization of their own work, the consistencies of the substantive and methodological arguments, even as they insisted that there were none. Furthermore, we tried to show them that their insistence on the lack of method or substantive pattern, what sociologists call structure, was itself patterned and consequential and marked a particular cognitive and, we insisted, moral and political ground. Here is an example of a justice critique produced as an analysis of the taken-for-granted grounds of interaction. We moved from analyses of this seminar to the materials and pedagogy of other classes, and we ended up presenting alternatives from our own work and finally collectively reconstructing this course for future use with Wellesley College students.

I have used this seminar experience as a concrete example of the movement from hegemony to ideology, from the taken-for-granted and uncontested grounds of authority and power, here literary scholarship, to ideology, "an articulated set of meanings, values and beliefs of a kind that can be abstracted as [a] 'worldview' " of any social group (Williams 1977: 109). In that seminar, some of us experienced the discomfort and contradictions inherent in situations of subordination and denial. By making our observations public, we explicitly defied the foundations of hegemonic power because hegemony relies, for its effectiveness, on its invisibility and inscription within social relations. We used the conventional tactics of trashing and deconstruction.

We exposed the contradictions, as well as the latent patterns embedded in the structure of the seminar and the seminar curriculum, and we created histories and genealogies which attempted to denaturalize the canon and demonstrate its historical and institutional creation. Finally, we attached the particular practices to a specific group and its interests.

Our success, however, did not depend entirely on these tactics, nor on some special insight or talent, nor did it mirror some grand transformation in American academia. This was, after all, local politics and we were in the end colleagues within the same institution. There were alternative sources of authority available for members that derived from their status within the college, prestige in alternative fields, as well as personal resources. These resources are important because they suggest additional avenues of penetration and resistance that can develop with variations in social and historical circumstances.

Obviously not all who attended and participated in this seminar experienced it the same way as I have described here. At other times and for other purposes I too have offered alternative accounts. Nonetheless, I believe that the major elements of the story are accurate, even if my embedded interpretations are contestable and points of emphasis constructed for particular didactic purposes. For example, we could construct alternative accounts that might emphasize the relative impotence of the seminar leadership as compared to that located among some of the participants. Others might want to describe the events not in terms of a clash of worldviews, of the transformation of hegemony into contested ideology, but as the confrontation of alternative teaching styles. Because there was no dominant perspective within the seminar, and because the leaders and literary critics were open to a variety of discourses and arguments, some may claim that my discomfort derived simply from a refusal on their part to be didactic and to prefer a nondirective, mimetic teaching style. However, there is much at stake in defining the difference as style, ideology, or hegemony. The difference is the acknowledgment of power and criticisms of injustice. Talking about the difference as style implies unconstrained, free choice, without consequence or hierarchy. Talking about ideology and hegemony puts power and justice at the very center of the analysis.

NOTES

I am particularly grateful to colleagues and friends who patiently read and reread several versions of this paper as it evolved over the years from its first incarnation to this more extended argument; their criticisms and insights prevented untold errors while providing needed direction: Patricia Ewick, Austin Sarat, Kim Scheppele, Carroll Seron, the anonymous reviewers of this volume, and the participants in the 1992 Law and Society Summer Institute.

1. Destutt de Tracy (1754–1836) first used the term "ideology" at the end of the eighteenth century to refer to what he hoped would be the scientific study of ideas, thoughts, and

cultural phenomenon. Just as geology would study the geo/earth, or eventually sociology would study the social, ideology was to be the scientific study of ideas—exploring the relation of ideas to sensory reality. Ideology, as the science of ideas, was supposed to provide a nonreligious, natural, and scientific foundation (ideas) for political organization, especially in postrevolutionary France (Kinloch 1981: 5). This use, although the first recorded use of the term, is not, however, one of the uses we usually associate with the term nor among the meanings I wish to understand. Rather, the more common usages and meanings of the term refer to ideas, signs, cultural phenomena themselves, and most often the term is used to mark a boundary between appearance and reality. The adoption of this term as a concept for social analysis derives from these more conventional uses. Rather than naming the analytic enterprise, i.e., the study of ideas, the term is used as tool of that enterprise, something deployed in the analysis of ideas.

2. I shall use the terms sociolegal and law and society interchangeably to denote the community of researchers who take as their task the description and analysis of the social organization and practices of law and legal institutions.

3. For example, Napoleon Bonaparte attacked the principles of the Enlightenment as just so much "ideology," and conservative critics attacked any social policy derived from social theory in whole or in part as "just" ideology. Marx and Engels ([1846] 1970) popularized this critical meaning in their view of ideology as an idealized expression of dominant material relationships.

4. If we think about cultural critique as focusing on three related aspects of culture—production, representations/texts, and reception/reading—critical legal studies devoted most of its early efforts toward unraveling the complex constructions and embedded meanings—the representations and significations—within legal texts (see R. Johnson 1986–87).

5. Swidler's action-oriented formulation of culture provides a foundation for Merry's and Fine and Sandstrom's conceptions of ideology. Swidler conceived of culture as that which "influences action not by providing the ultimate values toward which action is oriented, but by shaping a repertoire or 'tool kit' of habits, skills and styles from which people construct 'strategies of action'" (1986: 273).

6. In her conclusion, Merry (1985: 68) suggests that working-class participation and the "active role . . . [it] plays in creating its version of legal ideology" may support state power. The working-class court users she describes may not be aware, she claims, of their collaboration and the legal system's complicity in sustaining state power. The critique, where present, reproduces just that which it sought to avoid: working-class false consciousness and a mechanical instrumental conception of power.

7. See Wilhelm Ropke (1954: 207) for a mid-century position. Most publications of the World Bank and the International Monetary Fund during the 1980s provide more contemporary examples. Of course, Adam Smith, *The Wealth of Nations* (1776), is the classical statement of this position. Smith, however, had assumed that the free pursuit of individual desire and free exchange of ideas would take place within a framework of shared expectations and morality which he had described in *The Theory of Moral Sentiments,* first published in 1759. See Lowi 1992 for a critique of the dominance of this economic model in contemporary political science.

8. For a critique of this actor-centered notion of power, see Lukes 1974; Connell 1976, 1987; Clegg 1989.

9. To the unpropertied Englishmen of the time, Hay writes, the law offered a majestic spectacle, twice a year in the Assizes and four times a year in Quarter sessions, in which entire communities would witness "the most visible and elaborate manifestation of state power to be seen in the countryside, apart from the presence of a regiment" (1975:

109). In its symbolism, management of emotions, and psychic demands, the law's rituals performed much like religion. The court spectacle became a carnivalesque occasion for the community to coalesce in defense of violated norms and the sanctity and deity of property. The interests and agency of the owners of property were removed and distanced by the court performance. This distancing, perhaps charade, was emboldened by the "punctilious attention to forms, the dispassionate and legalistic exchanges between counsel and the judge" (Hay 1975: 112) that showed to all how those administering and using the laws were themselves subjugated by it and willingly submitted to its rules. The majesty of the law that demanded equality nowhere else available in eighteenth-century England was enacted by a decorous concern for protecting the property of ordinary as well as noble Englishmen. Finally, the regular and consistent pardoning of convicted felons, Hay argues, sustained the image of an independent and just legal system. "Discretion allowed a prosecutor to terrorize the petty thief and then command his gratitude, or at least the approval of his neighbors as a man of compassion. It allowed the class that passed one of the bloodiest penal codes in Europe to congratulate itself on its humanity" (Hay 1975: 120).

10. For many years, it was a favorite occupation of survey researchers to deny American voters any ideological consciousness because the researchers were unable to establish a logical consistency among the beliefs and political positions of the surveyed population. They lacked "ideological constraint," it was said (Converse 1964; Verba, Nie, Petrocik 1979).

11. Hegemony is always dominant; ideologies may be either ruling or subordinate.

12. Wittgenstein's great achievement was to demonstrate the soundness of this argument. In his philosophy of psychology, Wittgenstein claimed in an oft quoted phrase that "an inner process stands in need of outward criteria." Here Wittgenstein did not mean some simplistic version of behaviorism but the demand for careful attention to context and to use as examples of those outward criteria. He believed that we could understand language, or any human emotion or thought process, not by developing a general theory but rather by developing alert and observant sensitivity to the ways in which people act and the organization of those actions.

13. Karl Llewellyn made a similar claim when he wrote in a book review in the *Harvard Law Review* (1926: 145), "Mortgage is a legal concept; that concept, in all its phases is important. Mortgage is also a security device. That fact, in all its phases, is even more important. The legal concept is empty, without its application." In "What Is Wrong with So-called Legal Education" (1935: 669), he continued in this vein, "Legal rules mean, of themselves, next to nothing. They are verbal formulae, partly conveying a wished-for direction and ideal."

14. The identification of the commodity form as part of the hegemonic character of liberal law derives from Marx's critique of rights. In that analysis, Marx described the alienated self as a product of the liberal state's denial to each person his or her species membership, and the institutionalization of an isolating loneliness that is then justified as human nature. The liberal state, Marx argued, abolished distinctions based on birth, social rank, education, and occupation when it declared, as it did in the American Declaration of Independence or the French Rights of Man, that all men are created equal. (Of course neither the American Declaration nor the French Rights of Man meant to imply that all persons were equal, certainly not men and women, and certainly not slaves, and in places certainly not persons without property. Thus these declarations of human equality rested upon unexamined notions of who exactly were the humans being referred to.) The liberal state thus assured to each citizen the equal right to participate in the collective sovereignty and denied the relevance of birth, social rank, education, and occupation to that participation. (From 1780 until 1870 only freed white men could be naturalized as American citizens. After 1870 freed slaves and white women were included. Persons who were neither white nor

freed black could be naturalized [Lau 1994].) However, far from denying the importance of these distinctions, Marx argued, the liberal state institutionalized these distinctions by relegating inequalities of birth, social rank, education, and occupation to the protected realm of civil society untouchable by legal action. In other words, he argued, liberal law creates a fundamental schism between man (in civil society) and citizen (in the state) which is then treated as a natural condition. In this way, Marx continued, the liberal state derives its raison d'être—the protection of political equality and the fundamental rights of man [*sic*]—as a means of confining the natural material inequality that exists in civil society. As a consequence, Marx wrote, the citizen lives in perpetual alienation with a self divided between state and society. The citizen lives in a state organized by a set of "privatized" relationships which state law claims—through the conception of rights—are beyond the law or the state to affect. Rights, in this conception, become the means by which participation is organized; but rights cannot provide fundamental or real emancipation because rights are the creations of the liberal state and the means of alienating the individual from her species consciousness—life in civil society.

Following this line, Peter Gabel extends Balbus's analysis by specifying the processes by which "the legal order substitutes an harmonious abstract world for the concrete alienation that characterizes [people's] lived experiences" (1981: 263). He defines alienation as a "paradoxical form of reciprocity between two beings who desire authentic contact with one another and yet at the same time deny this very desire in the way they act toward each other" (Gabel 1984: 1567). He argues that individuals desire intersubjective recognition—what he calls authentic connection—but deny this desire as they confront others across a "forbidding distance." As a consequence, the individual "withdraws her own self and adopts a false self," with which she confronts and interacts in the world. Thus we live in a world in which we perpetually feel "at once unconnected to everyone else and yet anxiously committed to the pretense of connection that is manifested in the reciprocity of roles" (1984: 1573). Rights provide a basis for denying this dilemma, Gabel argues. They become part of the stories we tell ourselves about how we are collectively constituted, yet remain individuals.

15. Genovese's argument parallels, to a large degree, Hay's analysis of eighteenth-century English criminal law, and thus demonstrates the continuity and development among these diverse uses of ideology and hegemony in sociolegal research. For heuristic purposes, however, I have differentially placed these pieces of research in this scheme to illustrate different emphases. Hay illustrates well concern with ideological production and class interests, especially the suggestions of instrumental deployment of "mercy," while Genovese is more explicitly concerned with questions of hegemony. As such, Genovese provides less attention to protecting particular group interests and more to the inadvertent consequences of a formalist conception of law.

16. Bumiller interviewed people who chose not to seek legal remedies when they believed those remedies were available and due them. She reported that her respondents (who claimed to have been discriminated against on the basis of age, sex, or race) refused to turn to law in order to avoid the need to speak through lawyers and the tendency of legal processes to individualize grievances. Her analysis of the respondents' stories suggested that they experienced—as Marx had theorized—that legal action and rights are alienating. The individualization of grievances and the lawyer's mediation deny people control of their own lives and isolate them from their community and cultures at a time when they may be most in need of connection and support. Their discrimination was based on their group identities and membership, but the law required that they act individually.

17. See, e.g., White 1991; Ewick and Silbey 1992, in press; Tucker 1993; Merry 1995; and Gilliom 1996 for additional studies of resistance. See Handler 1992 for a critique. What remains theoretically open, however, and discussed briefly in the next section, is the

degree to which an ideology can be hegemonic and resisted. Need struggle be manifest for it to be ideological?

18. I use "structure" to mean interpretive schema and resources through which social interactions and organizations are constituted. Structures that operate to define and pattern social life are both determinant of and at the same time highly contingent on social practice. Understood as processes rather than immutable conditions, social structures account for both reproduction of social relations and for social change. See Sewell 1992; Ewick and Silbey 1995.

19. This is a large part of the task of much critical race theory in legal scholarship. See Bell 1987, 1992; Crenshaw 1988; Delgado 1995; Delgado and Stefanic 1992; Harris 1990; Matsuda 1987, 1988.

20. See Ewick and Silbey 1995 for an analysis of how hegemony is reconstituted through narrative and how it can also be subverted.

21. This literature derives directly from Gramsci's writing on hegemony.

22. Scott (1990: 80) rejects the notion of hegemony and, in particular, questions this more empirically viable version of hegemony. He suggests that serfs, peasants, and other widely subordinated groups are regularly imagining alternative worlds; thus the naturalization hypothesis fails, he claims. These imaginings are some of the "hidden transcripts" of resistance he documents in his work. I question Scott's evidence for rejecting this version of hegemony because the resistant imaginings he describes do not challenge the inevitability of stratification and inequality. In the end Scott rejects the notion of hegemony as an explanation for compliance with power, and for why the many succumb to the few. He argues that there is not quiescence in the social world, merely the picture of it. He can make this argument only if we define hegemony as absolutely complete. But, I suggest, no sociological concept can be defined without the possibility of variation. Mitchell suggests, however, that Scott's terminology specifically misreads Gramsci. Where Scott talks about consensus—agreement and harmony—Gramsci talked about *consenso*, "which refers primarily to the 'consent' given by exploited groups to the exploitation. The consent reduced the need for the use of violence against them, but may or may not produce consensus in the sense of harmony" (Mitchell 1990: 554).

23. Some recent work on representation and law goes directly to this point. Aware of how efforts to report on social life contribute to its reproduction, some writers seek to unpack the processes by which we create social exchange and meaning by simultaneously trying to describe and destabilize the processes of representation they describe. They do not wish, e.g., to participate in an unthinking reproduction of gendered or racist representations—representations that are not merely labels, e.g., he/she, but deeply coded within syntax and social relations. This accounts, I believe, for what might seem like overly mannered and difficult writing styles.

24. See Cushman 1995 for analysis of popular cultural resistance within a singular hegemonic culture.

25. I want to make clear that I am not talking about intentionally false representations but efforts to highlight and recognize what is present but too often hidden by hegemonic ideologies.

26. I include the references to colonization to illustrate the theoretical connections and utility of the concepts of ideology and hegemony, much of which originally developed from studies of colonialism but which have been applied more generally in cultural studies.

27. Privately, one of the humanists started talking to me about my continued demands for help in the seminar. He offered me several texts that "did what I wanted"; he also acknowledged that literary people resist that kind of didactic instruction.

BIBLIOGRAPHY

Abel, Richard. 1980. Redirecting Social Studies of Law. 14 *Law and Society Rev.,* 805.

Althusser, Louis. 1969. *For Marx.* Harmondsworth: Penguin.

———. 1971. Ideology and Ideological State Apparatuses. In *Lenin and Philosophy.* London: New Left Books.

Bachrach, P., and M. S. Baratz. 1962. Two Faces of Power. 56 *American Political Science Rev.,* 947–52.

———. 1970. *Power and Poverty: Theory and Practice.* New York: Oxford Univ. Press.

Bakhtin, M. M. 1981. *The Dialogic Imagination: Four Essays,* ed. Michael Holquist, trans. Caryl Emerson and Michael Holquist. Austin: Univ. of Texas Press.

Balbus, Issac. 1977. Commodity Form and Legal Form: An Essay on the Relative Autonomy of Law. 12 *Law and Society Rev.,* 571.

Bell, Derrick A. 1987. *And We Are Not Saved: The Elusive Quest for Racial Justice.* New York: Basic Books.

———. 1992. *Faces at the Bottom of the Well: The Permanence of Racism.* New York: Basic Books.

Bell, Susan. 1991. Commentary on "Perspectives on Embodiment: The Uses of Narrativity in Ethnographic Writing" by Katherine Young. 1 *Journal of Narrative and Life History,* 245.

Billig, Michael, Susan Condor, Derek Edwards, Mike Gane, David Middleton, and Alan Radley. 1988. *Ideological Dilemmas: A Social Psychology of Everyday Thinking.* London: Sage.

Brigham, John, and Christine Harrington. 1989. Racism and Its Consequences: An Inquiry into Contemporary Sociological Research. 17 *International Journal of the Sociology of Law,* 41.

Bourdieu, Pierre. 1977. *Outline of a Theory of Practice.* Cambridge: Cambridge Univ. Press.

Bumiller, Kristin. 1988. *The Civil Rights Society.* Baltimore: Johns Hopkins Univ. Press.

Clegg, Stewart R. 1989. *Frameworks of Power.* London: Sage.

Comaroff, Jean, and John Comaroff, 1991. *Of Revelation and Revolution.* Vol. 1. Chicago: Univ. of Chicago Press.

Connell, R.W. 1976. *Ruling Class, Ruling Culture: Studies of Conflict, Power and Hegemony in Australian Life.* Cambridge: Cambridge Univ. Press.

———. 1987. *Gender and Power.* Stanford, CA: Stanford Univ. Press.

Converse, Philip E. 1964. The Nature of Belief Systems in Mass Publics. In *Ideology and Its Discontents,* ed. David Apter. New York: Free Press.

Cotterrell, Roger. [1984] 1995. *The Sociology of Law.* Charlottesville: Michie Press.

Crenshaw, Kimberle Williams. 1988. Race Reform and Reentrenchment: Transformation and Legitimation in the Antidiscrimination Law. 101 *Harvard Law Rev.,* 1331.

Crenson, Matthew. 1971. *The Un-politics of Air Pollution: A Study of Non-decisionmaking in the Cities.* Baltimore: Johns Hopkins Univ. Press.

Cushman, Thomas. 1995. *Notes from Underground.* New York: SUNY Press.

Dahl, Robert. 1961. *Who Governs: Democracy and Power in an American City*. New Haven, CT: Yale Univ. Press.

de Certeau, Michel. 1984. *The Practice of Everyday Life*. Berkeley: Univ. of California Press.

Delgado, Richard, ed. 1995. *Critical Race Theory: The Cutting Edge*. Philadelphia: Temple Univ. Press.

Delgado, Richard, and Jean Stefanic. 1992. Images of the Outsider in American Law and Culture: Can Free Expression Remedy Systemic Social Ills? 77 *Cornell Law Rev.*, 1258.

Dezalay, Yves, Austin Sarat, and Susan Silbey. 1989. D'une demarche contestaire a un savoir meritocratique. In 78 *Actes de la recherches en sciences sociales* (June), 79–93.

Eagleton, Terry. 1991. *Ideology: An Introduction*. London and New York: Verso.

Edelman, Murray. 1964. *The Symbolic Uses of Politics*. Urbana: Univ. of Illinois Press.

———. 1971. *Politics as Symbolic Action*. Chicago: Markham.

Ewick, Patricia, and Susan Silbey. 1992. Conformity, Contestation and Resistance: An Account of Legal Consciousness. 26 *New England Law Rev.*, 731.

———. 1995. Subversive Stories and Hegemonic Tales: Toward a Sociology of Narrative. 29 *Law and Society Rev.*, 197.

———. In press. *The Common Place of Law: Stories of Popular Legal Consciousness*. Chicago: Univ. of Chicago Press.

Fantasia, Rick. 1988. *Cultures of Solidarity*. Berkeley: Univ. of California Press.

Feeley, Malcolm. 1976. The Concept of the Laws in Social Science. 10 *Law and Society Rev.*, 497.

Fine, Gary Alan, and Kent Sandstrom. 1993. Ideology in Action: A Pragmatic Approach to a Contested Concept. 11 *Sociological Theory*, 21–28.

Foucault, Michel. 1973. *The Order of Things*. New York: Random House.

———. 1978. *The History of Sexuality*. Vol. 1. New York: Pantheon.

———. 1980. *Power/Knowledge*. New York: Random House.

Frug, Gerald. 1984. The Ideology of Bureaucracy in American Law. 94 *Harvard Law Rev.*, 1277.

Frug, Mary Joe. 1985. Rereading Contracts: A Feminist Analysis of a Contracts Casebook. 34 *American Univ. Law Rev.*, 1065.

Fuller, Lon. 1964. *The Morality of Law*. New Haven, CT: Yale Univ. Press.

Gabel, Peter. 1981. Reification in Legal Reasoning. 3 *Research in Law and Sociology*, 25.

———. 1984. The Phenomenology of Rights-consciousness and the Pact of the Withdrawn Selves. 62 *Texas Law Rev.*, 1563.

Geertz, Clifford. 1973. *The Interpretation of Cultures: Selected Essays*. New York: Basic Books.

Genovese, Eugene. 1976. *Roll, Jordan, Roll*. New York: Random House.

Giddens, Anthony. 1979. *Central Problems in Social Theory: Action Structure and Contradiction in Social Analysis*. Berkeley: Univ. of California Press.

———. 1987. *Sociology: A Brief But Critical Introduction*. San Diego: Harcourt, Brace, Jovanovich.

Gilliom, John. 1996. Everyday Surveillance, Everyday Resistance: Computer Monitoring in the Lives of the Appalachian Poor. 16 *Studies in Law, Politics and Society*, 275.

Gordon, Robert. 1984. Critical Legal Histories. 36 *Stanford Law Rev.*, 57.

———. 1988. Law and Ideology. 3, no. 1 *Tikkun*, 14–18, 83–86.

Gramsci, Antonio. 1971. *Selections from the Prison Notebooks.* London: Lawrence and Wishart.

———. 1988. *A Gramsci Reader.* ed. David Forgacs. London: Lawrence and Wishart.

Gusfield, Joseph. [1963] 1986. *Symbolic Crusade.* Urbana: Univ. of Illinois Press.

Habermas, Jürgen. 1970. Toward a Theory of Communicative Competence. 13 *Inquiry*, 360–75.

———. 1992. *The Structural Transformation of the Public Sphere.* Cambridge, MA: MIT Press.

Hall, Stuart, Chas Critcher, Tony Jefferson, John Clarke, and Brian Roberts. 1978. *Policing the Crisis: Mugging, the State, and Law and Order.* New York: Holmes and Meier.

Handler, Joel. 1992. Postmodernism, Protest and the New Social Movements. 26 *Law and Society Rev.*, 697.

Harrington, Christine, and Barbara Yngvesson. 1990. Interpretive Sociolegal Research. 15 *Law and Social Inquiry*, 135.

Harris, Angela P. 1990. Race and Essentialism in Feminist Legal Theory. 42 *Stanford Law Rev.*, 581.

Hay, Douglas. 1975. Property, Authority and the Criminal Law. In *Albion's Fatal Tree: Crime and Society in Eighteenth Century England*, by D. Hay et al. Harmondsworth: Penguin.

Henry, Stuart. 1995. *Constitutive Criminology: Beyond Postmodernism.* Thousand Oaks, CA: Sage.

Hunt, Alan. 1985. The Ideology of Law: Advances and Problems in Recent Applications of the Concept of Ideology to the Analysis of Law. 19 *Law and Society Rev.*, 101.

———. 1993. *Explorations in Law and Society: Toward a Constitutive Theory of Society.* New York and London: Routledge.

Hunter, Floyd. 1953. *Community Power Structure.* Chapel Hill: Univ. of North Carolina Press.

Johnson, Harry M. 1968. Ideology and the Social System. 7 *International Encyclopedia of the Social Sciences*, 76–85.

Johnson, Richard. 1986–87. What Is Cultural Studies Anyway? 16 *Social Text*, 38–80.

Kairys, David. [1982] 1990. *The Politics of Law.* New York: Pantheon.

Kelman, Mark. 1987. *A Guide to Critical Legal Studies.* Cambridge, MA: Harvard Univ. Press.

Kennedy, Duncan. 1976. Form and Substance in Private Law Adjudication. 89 *Harvard Law Rev.*, 1685.

———. [1982] 1990. Legal Education and the Reproduction of Hierarchy. In *The Politics of Law*, ed. D. Kairys, 38–58. New York: Pantheon.

Kinloch, Graham C. 1981. *Ideology and Contemporary Sociological Theory.* Englewood Cliffs, NJ: Prentice-Hall.

Lau, Estelle. 1994. What Is White? Unpublished manuscript on file with author.

Llewellyn, Karl. 1926. Review of Morton Campbell. *Cases on Mortgages of Real Property.* 40 *Harvard Law Rev.*, 143.

————. 1935. What Is Wrong with So-called Legal Education. 35 *Columbia Law Rev.,* 651.

Lowi, Theodore. 1992. The State in Political Science: How We Become What We Study. 86 *American Political Science Rev.,* 1.

Lukes, Steven. 1974. *Power: A Radical View.* London: Macmillan.

Mannheim, Karl. 1936. *Ideology and Utopia.* New York: Harcourt.

Marx, Karl. [1852] 1968. The Eighteenth Brumaire of Louis Bonaparte. In *Selected Works in One Volume,* by Karl Marx and Friedrich Engels (1968). London: Lawrence and Wishart.

————. [1843] 1975. On the Jewish Question. In *Early Writings,* by Karl Marx (1975). Trans. Rodney Livingstone and Gregor Benton. New York: Random House.

Marx, Karl, and Friedrich Engels. [1846] 1970. *The German Ideology.* London: Lawrence and Wishart.

Matsuda, Mari. 1987. Looking to the Bottom. 22 *Harvard Civil Rights and Civil Liberties Law Rev.,* 323.

————. 1988. Affirmative Action and Legal Knowledge. 11 *Harvard Women's Law Journal,* 1.

McCann, Michael W. 1994. *Rights at Work: Pay Equity Reform and the Politics of Legal Mobilization.* Chicago: Univ. of Chicago Press.

McCann, Michael W., and Tracey March. 1995. Law and Everyday Forms of Resistance: A Socio-Political Assessment. 15 *Studies in Law, Politics and Society,* 207.

McLellan, David. 1986. *Ideology.* Minneapolis: Univ. of Minnesota Press.

Merry, Sally E. 1985. Concepts of Law and Justice among Working-Class Americans: Ideology as Culture. 9 *Legal Studies Forum,* 59–70.

————. 1990. *Getting Justice and Getting Even: Legal Consciousness among Working-Class Americans.* Chicago: Univ. of Chicago Press.

————. 1995. Resistance and the Cultural Power of Law. 29 *Law and Society Rev.,* 11.

Messick, Brinkley. 1988. Kissing Hands and Knees: Hegemony and Hierarchy in Shari'a Discourse. 22 *Law and Society Rev.,* 637.

————. 1992. *The Calligraphic State: Textual Domination and History in a Muslim Society.* Berkeley: Univ. of California Press.

Mills, C. Wright. 1956. *The Power Elite.* New York: Oxford Univ. Press.

Mitchell, Timothy. 1990. Everyday Metaphors of Power. 19 *Theory and Society,* 545–77.

Nelkin, David. 1981. The "Gap Problem" in the Sociology of Law. 1 *Windsor Access to Justice Yearbook,* 35.

Parsons, Talcott. 1951. *The Social System.* New York: Free Press.

————. 1967. *Sociological Theory and Modern Societies.* New York: Free Press.

Peller, Gary. 1992. Correspondence to Duncan Kennedy, May 23, 1992.

Polsby, Nelson. 1963. *Community Power and Political Theory.* New Haven, CT: Yale Univ. Press.

Poulantzas, Nicos. 1978. *State, Power, Socialism.* London: New Left Books.

Ropke, Wilhelm. 1954. Economic Order and International Law. 207 *Recueil Des Cours.* Leiden: Sijtthoff.

Sarat, Austin. 1985. Legal Effectiveness and Social Studies of Law: On the Unfortunate Persistence of a Research Tradition. 9 *Legal Studies Forum,* 223.

Sarat, Austin, and William Felstiner. 1995. *Divorce Lawyers and Their Clients.* New York: Oxford Univ. Press.

Scott, James. 1990. *Domination and the Arts of Resistance.* New Haven, CT: Yale Univ. Press.

Seron, Carroll, and Frank Munger. 1996. Race, Gender . . . and, of Course, Class. 22 *Annual Rev. of Sociology.* 11.

Sewell, William H. 1992. A Theory of Structure: Duality, Agency and Transformation. 98 *American Journal of Sociology,* 1–29.

Silbey, Susan S. 1985. Ideals and Practices in the Study of Law. 9 *Legal Studies Forum,* 7.

———. 1991. Loyalty and Betrayal: The Discovery and Reproduction of Legal Ideology. 16 *Law and Social Inquiry,* 809.

Smith, Adam. [1759] 1976. *The Theory of the Moral Sentiments.* Indianapolis: Liberty Classics.

———. [1776] 1925. *An Inquiry into the Nature and Cause of the Wealth of Nations,* ed. E. Cannan. London: Methuen.

Steinberg, Marc. 1993. Rethinking Ideology: A Dialogue with Fine and Sandstrom from a Dialogic Perspective. 11 *Sociological Theory,* 314.

Swidler, Ann. 1986. Culture in Action: Symbols and Strategies. 51 *American Sociological Rev.,* 273–86.

Taylor, Ian, Paul Walton, and Jock Young. 1973. *The New Criminology.* London: Routledge and Kegan Paul.

———. 1975. *Critical Criminology.* London: Routledge and Kegan Paul.

Thayer, H. S. 1981. *Meaning and Action.* Indianapolis: Hackett.

Thompson, E. P. 1975. *Whigs and Hunters: The Origin of the Black Act.* London: Allen Lane.

Trubek, David. 1977. Complexity and Contradition in the Legal Order: Balbus and the Challenge of Critical Social Thought about Law. 11 *Law and Society Rev.,* 529.

Tucker, James. 1993. Everyday Forms of Employee Resistance. 8 *Sociological Forum,* 25–45.

Verba, Sidney, Norman H. Nie, and John R. Petrocik. 1979. *The Changing American Voter.* Cambridge, MA: Harvard Univ. Press.

Weber, Max. 1966. *Law in Economy and Society,* ed. Max Rheinstein. Cambridge, MA: Harvard Univ. Press.

White, Lucie. 1991. Subordination, Rhetorical Survival Skills and Sunday Shoes: Notes on the Hearing of Mrs. G. In *At the Boundaries of Law: Feminism and Legal Theory,* ed. M. A. Fineman and N. S. Thomadsen. New York: Routledge.

White, Winston. 1961. *Beyond Conformity.* New York: Free Press.

Williams, Raymond. [1976] 1983. *Keywords.* New York: Oxford Univ. Press.

———. 1977. *Marxism and Literature.* New York: Oxford Univ. Press.

Wittgenstein, Ludwig. [1921] 1961. *Tractatus Logico-Phlisophicus,* trans. D. F. Pears and B. F. McGinness. New York: Routledge and Kegan Paul.

Wolff, Robert Paul. 1969. Beyond Tolerance. In *A Critique of Pure Tolerance.* Boston: Beacon.

Wolin, Sheldon. 1960. *Politics and Vision.* Boston: Little, Brown.

Wrong, Dennis. 1979. *Power: Its Forms, Bases and Uses.* New York: Harper and Row.

Yngvesson, Barbara. 1993. *Virtuous Citizens, Disruptive Subjects, Order and Complaint in a New England Court.* New York: Routledge.

JUSTICE AND POWER IN CIVIL DISPUTE PROCESSING

❖

TOM R. TYLER

I. JUSTICE AND POWER IN CIVIL DISPUTE PROCESSING

The goal of the papers in this volume is to examine the relationship of justice and power within different areas of law and society research. Other chapters in this volume have emphasized the importance of the concept of power (see Fineman), suggesting that justice is defined largely and, perhaps exclusively, by the objective distribution of power. I will argue for a different perspective: that justice is, to at least an important extent, distinct from power. I will do so through an examination of the recent literature on civil dispute resolution.

A. THE STUDY OF POWER

Social scientists studying power have typically defined power in objective terms, focusing on the ability of people to influence the distribution of resources among the members of society. Gamson (1968) defines power as the ability to determine the behavior of others, hence "altering what would have occurred without you" (Gamson 1968), a definition shared with many others (Cartwright and Zander 1953; Easton 1958; Parsons 1958). This definition flows from Weber's definition of power as "the ability to impose one's will on others" (Bendix 1960). Similarly, Pfeffer defines power as having "the ability to achieve desired outcomes" in interactions with others (Pfeffer 1981). These definitions anchor power in reality. Power is about the ability to shape the world, not about feelings within the person. Hence, the study of power is objective in character.

Of course, power can also be treated as a subjective issue by focusing on people's judgments about their power over others. Studies of subjective power suggest that people typically exaggerate their ability to control outcomes when dealing with both the physical and the social world (Langer 1975). Studies of dispute resolution support this suggestion, finding that people have exaggerated beliefs about their ability to influence the behavior of third parties (Thibaut and Walker 1975).

2. RESEARCH ON LEGAL NEEDS

Research on the legal needs of the disadvantaged is an important research tradition within the law and society movement. Concerns about power dominate the early work on civil litigation, which includes studies of legal aid, legal services, and litigation (see Carlin, Howard, and Messinger 1966, 1967; Engel 1984). Research in these areas focused on equality or inequality in access to legal services, and on the level of outcomes which people receive from the legal system. It explored how the legal system shapes who gets what from others.

The legal needs literature was reviewed by Galanter (1974) in his classic paper, "Why the 'Haves' Come Out Ahead in Litigation." That article examines instances when the legal system acts as an agent for redistributing resources to the haves, who have had multiple experiences with the legal system (repeat players), from the have nots, who are novices (one-shot players). The legal needs literature is concerned with the potential of law to promote social change, that is, with whether individuals and groups actually gain power by appealing to the legal system. The focus of Galanter's examination is the objective distribution of resources across individuals—who gets what from others with the aid of the legal system.

An objective focus on who gets what from litigation develops out of a concern with promoting social change. One aspect of this concern is with demonstrating that legal procedures disadvantage some groups in society (Caplovitz 1963, 1974). As Caplovitz says about laws on consumer credit,

> The imbalances in the consumer credit system that have existed these many
> years are so blatant . . . that one might well ask why society has taken so long
> to recognize these injustices and to try to correct them. . . . A significant ex-
> planation for the slowness to reform the system might stem from the nature
> of the people who are most likely to suffer from these inequities. Default-
> debtors are overwhelmingly persons of marginal if not poverty-level income,
> persons of low occupational status, and persons disproportionately recruited

from minority groups—blacks and Spanish-speaking citizens. The persons who fit these descriptions do not have powerful voices in our society. On the contrary, they tend to be exploited and have little power to correct the injustices practiced upon them. (1974: 300)

In the past many disadvantaged groups have used the courts as an avenue through which to expand their "legal rights," believing that those rights—once established—would increase their access to resources within society. Interestingly, Caplovitz (1974) credits reforms in consumer credit law to such legal pressures, which he associates with the civil rights movement and the government's war on poverty.

An especially important symbolic example of legal efforts to help the disadvantaged is the *Brown v. Board of Education* decision, which culminated a long-term struggle by Blacks to achieve legal recognition of their right to equal education (Kluger 1975). This is not to say that everyone accepts the premise that legal rights can be converted into power. Some scholars in the law and society movement have questioned whether the disadvantaged are actually able to effectively gain resources through the pursuit of legal entitlements. Scheingold's book, *The Politics of Rights* (1974), for example, suggests that legal change does not actually offer disadvantaged groups an effective avenue to gaining greater power in American society.

What both proponents and critics of the "politics of rights" share is a concern with the degree to which legal rights are objectively linked to the attainment of social resources (i.e., with the objective distribution of resources). They differ about their answer to this question. In other words, the focus of the legal needs tradition is on the distribution of rights and, through that distribution, the distribution of resources. From this perspective power is the ability to use "rights" granted by the legal system to secure desired resources for oneself or one's group from other members of society.

More recently, similar concerns about the distributive consequences of court involvement in social conflicts have been raised about "alternative" dispute resolution procedures, such as community mediation (see Abel 1982). Focusing on one such program, the neighborhood justice center, Harrington (1985) argues that the "reforms associated with informalism . . . are . . . closer to an order maintenance style of exercising state authority than to matters of social justice" (1985: 2). Harrington suggests that a "focus on dispute techniques has separated the politics of problem solving from the politics of taking rights seriously" (1985: 173). As a consequence, the courts have less to do with social problems and social change. They are less involved in helping the "have nots" become "haves."

The literature on the distributive consequences of legal change fits well with an instrumental model of legal claiming, which argues that people's use of the legal system is determined by their judgments about the likelihood that their actions will be successful (Felstiner, Abel, and Sarat 1981).

It is also important to recognize that the members of some communities may not regard it as desirable to create conflict by raising legal claims, irrespective of whether those claims are likely to prevail. Greenhouse (1986), for example, studied the members of a Southern Baptist community and found that conflict had negative value within that community. In that religious community, members equated "harmony" and "social justice" and were disinclined to seek legal recourse for their problems. Cultural values, not instrumental calculations, governed people's actions.

3. THE OBJECTIVE CONSEQUENCES OF LEGAL PROCEDURES

Another possible perspective on civil disputes focuses on having the power to create desired outcomes in litigation (as does the legal needs approach), but views those objective issues from a procedural perspective. The concern in these studies is on the objective consequences of making legal decisions in different ways. For example, Handler (this volume) discusses the consequences of using varying procedures for making welfare decisions, identifying differences in the participatory opportunities provided to those involved; and Reichman (this volume) examines the quality and type of decisions made under varying forms of regulation. In each case, the objective consequences of varying procedural issues are explored. Power is reflected through use of a procedure that yields favorable consequences. For example, when regulatory decisions are being made, being consulted during the planning process can represent power if such consultation allows the nature of the plans created to be shaped in desirable ways.

The possibility of an objective approach to procedural issues is suggested by Thibaut and Walker (1975) in their original research on procedural justice. In that work the objective quality of the verdicts reached by the adversarial and the inquisitorial procedures was compared. Thibaut and Walker argue that the adversary system reaches objectively superior verdicts. For example, they demonstrate that the adversary system encourages disadvantaged parties to work harder in their own defense; giving an advantage to the party with the weaker case (Thibaut and Walker 1975).

Similar efforts to understand the objective quality of the results reached by different types of legal procedures can be found in studies of decision making by juries of varying size and decision rule (Davis 1980; Hastie, Penrod, and Pennington 1983). These studies suggest that the quality of jury decision making is higher when (1) juries are larger (twelve vs. six) and (2) when they use unanimous decision rules.

A. A Shift toward the Study of Justice

Justice can be studied as an objective issue through a focus on what "ought to be" according to some ethical standard of deservedness. Such standards can be drawn from a variety of disciplines, including philosophy, religion, and/or ethics. Each provides standards for indicating what is morally "right" or "appropriate," that is, for defining justice. Such definitions can include statements about the just distribution of rights and/or resources across people or groups (distributive justice), or statements about how such a just distribution can be obtained. Rawls's theory of justice, for example, includes both statements about principles guiding the fair distribution of social resources and a statement about an ethically appropriate procedure for making distributive decisions (by people who are "behind the veil"; Rawls 1971: 136).

Justice can also be studied as a subjective issue by focusing on whether people experience their interactions with others as fair. The subjective study of justice has focused on three issues: whether people feel that the distribution of resources across individuals or groups is fair, and, in particular, whether they feel that they have received a fair number of resources (distributive justice); whether they feel that decisions allocating resources across groups or individuals are being made in fair ways (procedural justice); and whether they feel that there are appropriate sanctions for rule breaking (retributive justice). In each case, people's subjective evaluations of the objective world are the key concern.

4. SUBJECTIVE EVALUATIONS OF EXPERIENCES WITH LAW

When studying civil litigation, the focus in a number of recent studies has been on the subjective nature of the litigation experience. Instead of evaluating litigation experiences against objective criteria specifying desirable features of procedures or outcomes, experiences are evaluated in terms of the subjective experiences of the litigants.

A shift from objective to subjective issues does not necessarily imply a need to shift the focus to issues of justice instead of issues of power. However, such a shift suggests that what should be important in defining what is studied are the factors that shape the reactions of those who deal with the legal system. A subjective focus implies that those aspects of experience that influence the thinking and behavior of people are the crucial concerns, not those issues that are central to an objective analysis of society and/or the legal system.

A. How Do People Evaluate Their Experiences with the Civil Justice System?

Several possible bases for the subjective experiences of litigants have been identified. One is the ability of litigants to gain favorable outcomes from their experience, that is, their power in the situation. In other words, litigants may care about issues of power, evaluating the legal system in terms of their ability to obtain desired outcomes when they deal with police officers, mediators, and/or judges.

Traditional subjective outcome-based explanations of reactions to experience have emphasized issues of cost, delay, and poor outcomes, suggesting that these features of the litigation experience lead litigants to feel that they have had an unfavorable experience with the legal system. The most extreme outcome models suggest that people focus primarily, or even exclusively, on the favorability of their outcomes when dealing with the legal system.

This instrumental view of people has dominated recent law and social science, in the form of the public choice, law and economics, and deterrence literatures. It suggests that people's reactions to their dealings with legal authorities are strongly affected by whether or not desired resources are obtained. In other words, it assumes that people care about having the power to shape their outcomes.

It is also possible that people care about their judgments concerning the fairness of their experience. Three aspects of fairness have been distinguished: distributive, procedural, and retributive. Distributive fairness involves judgments about the justice or injustice of the outcomes of the litigation. People may evaluate the fairness of their outcomes, for example, by judging if they received what they deserved, or "more" or "less" than they deserved. The principles of distributive justice by which people evaluate the fairness of outcomes have been directly studied by psychologists such as Deutsch (1985). Three principles have been found to be of particular importance in understanding allocation decisions: equity, equality, and need. Procedural fairness involves evaluations of the justice or injustice of the process through which those outcomes are reached. In other words, people may care about issues of how decisions are made. For example, people evaluate procedures in terms of their opportunities to state their positions, their influence over the outcomes reached, the neutrality of the third party, and many other factors. These factors are distinct, though not necessarily independent, from the favorability or fairness of the outcome of the process. Typically people believe that a fair procedure will produce a fair outcome (Lind and Tyler 1988).

Principles of just compensation for injury ("retributive justice") are also central to conflict resolution decisions, in which people are seeking recompense for a past injury. Judgments about fairness in punishment and compensation have been studied in analyses of retributive justice (Darley 1990; Vidmar and Miller 1980). Such analyses examine both the form of restitution which is appropriate for various types of injury and its amount.

B. Research on Subjective Assessments of Justice

Recent studies of civil dispute processing have approached the topic of civil dispute resolution subjectively. These studies use interviews with disputants to examine the degree to which people care about power, as evidenced by an interest in obtaining favorable outcomes from litigation ("achieving desired outcomes" [Pfeffer 1981] or "determining the behavior of others" [Gamson 1968]) and the extent to which they care about whether the outcome and/or the procedure are fair.

Lind et al. 1989, 1990 are illustrative of recent work in the area of civil litigation. They describe the results of a study of tort claim resolution via a variety of legal procedures, including trials, arbitration, settlement conferences, and bilateral bargaining. In the study, disputants are interviewed following the resolution of their cases. The concern is with their postdisposition satisfaction and feelings about the justice or injustice of their litigation experience.

The study reaches two key conclusions. First, objective indices of outcome are not good predictors of subjective reactions to the litigation experience. Whether assessed in terms of length of time to case resolution (delay), costs to the litigant, and/or amount won or lost, objective indicators do not explain much about people's postlitigation feelings. Hence, a subjective focus is quite different than an objective focus. The objective quality of the outcomes which flow from the resolution of a civil dispute have little to do with the resulting feelings of those involved. Although the Lind et al. study examines civil disputes, its findings parallel those of recent research on criminal disputes. In a study of defendants on trial for felonies, Casper, Tyler, and Fisher (1988) found that the objective quality of a defendant's sentence was a very poor predictor of the defendant's subjective reaction to the litigation experience.

The second key conclusion is that satisfaction is shaped by justice-based judgments. In the Lind et al. study, satisfaction was shaped by both distributive and procedural justice judgments. Distributive justice was assessed by establishing outcomes received relative to prior expectations. Procedural justice was assessed by examining whether the procedures experienced contained procedural elements associated with justice, including opportunities to address the decision maker, honest decision making, and treatment with dignity and respect. Their finding is consistent both with the findings of the original Thibaut and Walker (1975) research on litigation and with the results of other recent studies of civil litigation (Adler, Hensler, and Nelson 1985; MacCoun et al. 1988).

Other studies of subjective reactions to experiences with the courts have extended the findings of the Lind et al. study. First, other research has demonstrated that feelings of distributive and procedural justice shape the voluntary acceptance of decisions (MacCoun et al. 1988; Pruitt et al. 1990). Since the courts rely heavily on the voluntary acceptance of their decisions (Tyler 1989b), these findings suggest that subjective satisfaction is not simply an academic issue. Studies have also shown that people generalize from their judgments about their experiences with particular legal authorities to their views about legal authorities in general (Tyler 1990; Tyler, Casper, and Fisher 1989) and to their everyday behavior in relationship to legal rules (Tyler 1990). This generalization process has been found to be mediated primarily by judgments about procedural justice.

C. Summary

A shift from the legal needs to the justice perspective changes the focus of civil litigation studies. The first shift is from an objective to a subjective focus. Instead of being concerned with the objective consequences of litigation, studies examine the subjective feelings of those who have been involved in the litigation process. This change in approach leads to a second change. Procedural issues receive greater emphasis in the subjective approach. This is not a necessary change. As has been noted, procedural issues can be studied from an objective framework, while outcomes can be examined subjectively. However, past objectively framed studies have emphasized outcomes, while a subjective frame leads to a procedural focus. This is an empirical effect occurring because people react subjectively to procedural issues.

5. THE HISTORY OF A SUBJECTIVE APPROACH TO CIVIL LITIGATION

Accepting the subjective focus of recent justice research does not mean accepting the invasion of a foreign research paradigm into the field of law and social science. On the contrary, the concerns of the justice literature develop directly from the traditional concern of law and society researchers with the potentially destructive effects of dispute resolution procedures, such as the adversary trial process, on the ongoing social relationship among the parties to a dispute.

The recognition that the forum in which disputes are resolved shapes the impact of dispute resolution on ongoing social relationships is widespread among social scientists who study law. It is especially central to the discussions of dispute resolution within different cultures (see, e.g., Gluckman 1967; Nader 1969; for a review, see Lempert and Sanders 1986). A classic study demonstrating the importance of concerns about social relationships is Macaulay's study of suits over breaches in contracts (Macaulay 1963). Macaulay found that many businesses avoid litigation when they have differences of opinion with other businesses because of the negative effects of the litigation process on ongoing social relationships (see Lempert and Sanders 1986).

Concern about the destructive effects of litigation is also central to the classic work of Thibaut and Walker (*Procedural Justice,* 1975). Their research is motivated by a concern about the potentially destructive effects of the adversary system on relationships among the parties to a dispute. They wanted to establish how disputes could be resolved in ways that enhanced the post-dispute quality of the exchange relationships among disputants. As Thibaut and Walker note:

> One prediction that can be advanced with sure confidence is that human life on this planet faces a steady increase in the potential for interpersonal and intergroup

conflict. The rising expectations of a continuously more numerous population in competition for control over rapidly diminishing resources create the conditions for an increasingly dangerous existence. It seems clear that the quality of future human life is likely to be importantly determined by the effectiveness with which disputes can be managed, moderated, or resolved. Procedures or methods that may be put to this task of conflict resolution therefore claim our attention. (1975: 1)

6. WHAT IS GAINED THROUGH A SUBJECTIVE FOCUS?

Instead of examining whether a procedure is or is not consistent with objective standards of justice, or does or does not produce objectively fair outcomes, a subjective approach considers whether people experience a procedure and its outcome as just. This has several advantages. The first is theoretical. Psychological theories make clear predictions about the basis of satisfaction in social interactions. Thibaut and Walker (1975), for example, draw on psychological models of control (Dweck and Goetz 1978; Glass and Singer 1972; Langer, Janis, and Wolfer 1975; Seligman 1975) to make their original procedural justice predictions. Other procedural justice researchers have drawn on psychological theories about self-esteem and social status (Abrams and Hogg 1990; Hogg and Abrams 1988; Turner 1987) to make predictions linking procedural justice judgments to issues of neutrality, trustworthiness, and treatment with respect and dignity (see Tyler and Lind 1992).

In addition to having a clear theoretical base, studies of people's subjective reactions to their experiences with legal authorities can also draw on the body of methodological techniques developed through a long tradition of attitude research. This literature includes a substantial body of psychological research on the study of social attitudes (Oskamp 1977) and the experience of survey researchers (Babbie 1973; Backstrom and Hursh-Cesar 1963; Oppenheim 1966). These methodologies provide thoroughly developed approaches for selecting respondents, constructing questionnaires, and determining the reliability and validity of responses. Hence, procedural justice research rests on a well developed conceptual and methodological base.

Beyond methodological ease, attitude research benefits from a clear-cut and simple face validity. When concerned with people's subjective reactions, it seem very reasonable to use people's self-reports as evidence. For example, it seems very reasonable to believe that a person's statement that they are or are not happy is relevant to answering the question whether or not they are happy. Consider the case of a judge urged to reform the settlement conference process for resolving civil disputes (see Tyler 1989a). That judge responded by pointing out that he had conducted exit interviews with litigants in his courtroom and found high levels of satisfaction with the procedures he used. Since litigants were satisfied, he suggested, why was reform needed? Although its validity is seemingly self-evident, the value of self-report will be critically examined later in this discussion.

The apparent validity of self-report is further enhanced by the many studies showing that subjective feelings have important behavioral implications. As already noted, people's feelings have been found to predict their willingness to accept judicial decisions, as well as their general rule-following behavior. What people feel influences what they do.

7. LIMITATIONS OF A SUBJECTIVE FOCUS

An important limitation to the subjective focus is the loss of an ability to critically evaluate the quality of people's judgments. Are people's judgments to be taken at face value? If not, how can they be evaluated? Unlike objective evaluations, those exploring subjective evaluations have typically lacked a normative framework against which to evaluate people's judgments.

Why might subjective evaluations be problematic? Many factors may constrain them. First, people may be unaware of their alternatives. Having never experienced the alternatives, people may not recognize that they could be much happier than they are. As Galanter notes, many people are one-shot players in the legal system. Hence, they have little basis for knowing what they should expect.

Second, people may have low expectations. If people expect to get nothing from the legal system, they may be surprised to receive a little. Paradoxically, the system may benefit from providing people with little, since people will develop low standards about what to expect. Studies of relative deprivation suggest that people can be very satisfied with objectively low outcome levels, if those outcomes correspond with their expectations (Taylor and Moghaddam 1987). It is only when expectations change, and are therefore no longer met by obtained outcomes, that people become dissatisfied.

Silbey (this volume) articulates a clear case for the limits of a subjective analysis. She suggests that a long history of critiques of dominant cultures argue that unequal power, when it exists, allows certain groups to create hegemony in a society's ideology. Through control over the mechanisms of socialization—schools, the mass media, and so on—a dominant group can define the consciousness of an entire society, including subordinate groups that have different "objective" interests. In a culture where hegemony prevails, a certain construction of reality seems obvious to all members of society. In such a situation, people's subjective evaluations of their experience may depart substantially from their "objective" interests.

If people's beliefs reflect "false consciousness" of the type that would be reflected in a hegemonic society, then there should be a value consensus among the members of a society, even a pluralistic one. There is considerable evidence that a broad value consensus on core beliefs and values exists within American society (see, e.g., Hochschild 1981; Kluegel and Smith 1986).

Hence, evidence on subjective beliefs is consistent with the idea of ideological hegemony. On the other hand, internalization of legitimation is "incomplete" (Cook and Hegtvedt 1986), in that minorities and those in low-income groups are not as accepting of core beliefs and values as are more socially central members of American society. Hence, the glass is either half empty or half full. There is substantial consensus of beliefs, but belief differences reflecting differences in objective circumstances also occur.

Also central to the suggestion of hegemony is the argument that the subjective value consensus that exists within a society reinforces the objective interests of one group in society at the expense of others. Efforts to address this question require a model of an objectively appropriate or fair outcome distribution. Hence, efforts to address this question refocus attention on the issue of the objective appropriateness of varying distributions of resources. This is a core question examined by the legal needs literature.

Studies of American's beliefs about fair distributions of resources across American society suggest that judgments about justice in allocating resources across the members of American society (macrojustice) require more equality in distribution than is currently found in American society (Brickman et al. 1981). Hence, when issues of justice are presented at the societal level, support is found for the need to redistribute social resources.

A. The Study of Culture

Recognition of the important role of ideology in shaping individual reactions to experiences highlights another consequence of the psychological focus of procedural justice research. The sociopolitical context within which dispute processing occurs is generally ignored in procedural justice studies, which focus on the individual litigant and his or her feelings.

Although it has not been a focus of studies on civil litigation, psychologists do recognize the importance of the larger society in shaping the basis of subjective reactions to particular experiences (Tyler and McGraw 1986); although psychologists do not typically focus on social structural or cultural factors in their analyses. For examples of such analyses by sociologists, see Cook and Hegtvedt (1983, 1986), and by anthropologists, see Merry (1990) and Yngvesson (1988).

Some procedural justice researchers have been concerned with examining the impact of culture on both the meaning and the importance of procedural justice (Leung and Lind 1986). This research has examined why people in different cultures prefer different methods for resolving civil disputes. Findings in this area suggest that people do not differ in the desirability which they attach to cultural values such as interpersonal harmony. Rather, they differ in their beliefs about the influence of different procedures on those values. For example, Chinese respondents believe that adversary procedures hurt interpersonal harmony, while American respondents do not believe that adversary procedures hurt interpersonal harmony (Leung and Lind 1986).

8. PROCEDURAL VS. SUBSTANTIVE JUSTICE

The procedural justice approach is also distinctive for its focus on processes rather than on outcomes. The value of this procedural focus is suggested by the large body of consistent findings which have emerged from procedural justice studies. In other words, procedural justice judgments are key mediators of subjective evaluations of legitimacy. Studies almost uniformly find important subjective effects of procedural variations: People care about procedural justice! Furthermore, those subjective reactions involve important attitudes and predict important behaviors. Procedural justice has been linked to attitudes about the legitimacy of authorities and, through those attitudes, to the willingness to accept third-party decisions and to follow legal rules (Tyler 1990c; Tyler and Lind 1992).

Much of the power of the procedural justice research tradition comes from its challenge to the outcome perspective on litigation. The challenge posed by procedural justice findings is primarily empirically based. The results of procedural justice studies suggest that people do not react in outcome terms, as would be predicted by an instrumental model. In other words, the focus on how decisions are made flows from the results of interviews with those involved in the legal system. Those interviews reveal that people care about how their cases are resolved, not about whether they win or lose.

A. WHAT LEADS A PROCEDURE TO BE EVALUATED AS FAIR?

It is possible to understand more about the implications of people's concern with procedural justice by exploring the criteria which people use to assess whether they have received procedural justice from a legal procedure, that is, by considering the psychological dynamics underlying procedural justice.

In addition to establishing the important role of procedural justice in shaping people's reactions to their experiences with authorities, Thibaut and Walker (1975) proposed a control model of people's procedural preferences and judgments about the fairness of legal procedures. Their model suggests that the distribution of control among disputants and the third-party decision maker is the key procedural characteristic shaping people's views about both the fairness and the desirability of the procedures. Thibaut and Walker distinguish between two types of control: process control and decision control. Process control refers to the extent and nature of participant's control over the presentation of evidence. Decision control refers to the extent and nature of people's control over the actual decisions made.

Underlying the control model is the assumption that people are exchange-oriented in their dealings with third parties. Their concern is with the problem or dispute which brings them to third parties and with the way that problem or dispute is resolved. The exchange assumptions of the control model are illustrated by the assumption that people's concern in dealing with the third-party focuses only on winning the dispute at issue. It is control over aspects of the procedure related to the resolution of the dispute that is central to the control model (Thibaut and Walker 1975, 1978). In particular, the Thibaut and Walker model predicts that people (1) are not very concerned about interpersonal issues such as politeness, which are not linked to decision-making outcomes (see Tyler and Bies 1990), and (2) are not very concerned about the nature of their relationship with the authorities or institutions acting as decision makers (Tyler 1990b). Both of these concerns receive little attention in the control model because they are unrelated to the resolution of the specific dispute at issue.

Much of the research subsequent to Thibaut and Walker (1975) has followed the control model framework outlined by Thibaut and Walker, focusing on the distribution of control within various types of legal procedure (see Lind and Tyler 1988 for a review). The findings of research on control support the Thibaut and Walker suggestion that the distribution of control within a procedure influences assessments of its procedural fairness (Lind and Tyler 1988). In that respect, Thibaut and Walker's control theory has been widely confirmed.

In their original analysis of control in procedures, Thibaut and Walker placed their primary emphasis on decision control, viewing process control as an indirect means of exerting decision control. In contrast, subsequent research has suggested that process control is often more important to people than is decision control (Lind, Lissak, and Conlon 1983; Tyler 1987; Tyler, Rasinski, and Spodick 1985).

The mere fact that people care about process control does not show that they are not concerned about decision control. It may simply be that people think they can influence decisions if they have an opportunity to control the presentation of evidence. Since people tend to exaggerate their control over outcomes (Langer 1975), this could even be true when they have little objective control over the decision. To understand the influence of voice, it is important to distinguish between two functions of process control: the instrumental and the expressive (Katz 1960). To demonstrate that concerns about process control have an element that is independent of issues of decision control, it is necessary to show that people who have process control feel more fairly treated, even if that process control is not linked to decision control.

Research findings suggest that process control is valued for reasons other than its potential instrumentality in achieving favorable outcomes. First, several studies (e.g., LaTour 1978; Lind et al. 1980) have shown a poor correspondence between ratings of the perceived favorableness of procedures to the disputant (i.e., the disputant's judgment about the likelihood that using a particular procedure will help him or her to win the case) and procedural fairness ratings of the same procedures.

Second, virtually all of the studies of procedural fairness in dispute resolution have shown a process control enhancement of procedural fairness judgments, even when ratings are made after litigants have already lost their case. In the face of a negative outcome, it should be obvious to a disputant that process control has been ineffective in securing favorable outcomes. The Lind et al. 1980 study, for example, found little reevaluation of procedures after disputants knew the verdict of an adjudication.

Several recent studies show even more clearly that the process control effect involves something other than the ability of process control to influence case outcomes. Lind, Lissak, and Conlon (1983) tested the relative effects of process and decision control on reactions to conflict resolution procedures. Decision control was operationalized in this study as the opportunity to reject a third-party decision. This type of decision control is a more direct form of control over outcomes than is process control, and if the instrumental view of the process control effect were correct, decision control should have greater effects on judgments of procedural fairness than does process control. Indeed, one might expect that process control would be of little importance when disputants have decision control.

Lind, Lissak, and Conlon used the same experimental paradigm employed by the Walker et al. (1974), LaTour (1978), and Lind et al. (1980) studies, but they independently manipulated the process control and decision control contained within varying hearing procedures. The process control manipulation involved the use of adversary or nonadversary procedures similar to those used in the Walker et al. 1974 study. In the high disputant decision control condition, the judge's decision could be rejected by either disputant (in favor of the option of attempting to negotiate a settlement). In the low disputant decision control condition, the judge's decision was final and binding on both parties. In addition, the study included a manipulation of the outcome of the hearing—participants were told either that they had been awarded two-thirds of the outcome in controversy or that they had been awarded only one-third of the outcome in controversy.

The results of the Lind, Lissak, and Conlon study show that the decision control manipulation had little effect on procedural fairness judgments. Whether decision control was available or not, process control enhanced disputants' perceptions of the fairness of the procedure. These findings are contrary to those that one would expect if outcome instrumentality were the major force underlying the process control effect.

Tyler, Rasinski, and Spodick (1985) used both survey and laboratory data to test whether process control independently influences procedural justice judgments. Two sets of survey data, one involving defendant reactions to trial experiences and one involving student reactions to college courses, were analyzed to determine whether judgments about process control influenced procedural fairness judgments over and above the effect of judgments about decision control. In both surveys an independent effect was found for process control. In their third study, Tyler et al. manipulated the level of process control, the level of decision control, and the allocation setting described in scenarios. Again process control was found to have independent effects on ratings of procedural fairness. In another round of survey studies, Tyler (1987) replicated these findings.

The Tyler et al. (1985) studies mentioned earlier produced the results predicted by a value-expressive explanation of the process control effect—people cared about process control even when it did not influence decision control. But additional evidence is needed to assure us that it is expression per se, and not some other non-outcome function of process control, that is the key to the effect. Several studies have shown results that point even more strongly to expression as a key factor in procedural justice.

Among these is a field study of procedural fairness judgments of court-annexed arbitration procedures, conducted by Adler, Hensler, and Nelson (1983). Adler, Hensler, and Nelson asked open-ended questions about what disputants saw as fair or unfair in their arbitration hearings. They found that a majority of the disputants who viewed the hearings as unfair complained that they had too little opportunity to tell their story. The importance of the opportunity to tell one's story has also emerged from ethnographic studies of legal proceedings (Conley and O'Barr 1990).

A study by Musante, Gilbert, and Thibaut (1983) provides additional evidence favorable to the proposition that procedural justice judgments are enhanced by an opportunity to express views and opinions, whether or not that expression is instrumental in obtaining favorable outcomes. Musante, Gilbert, and Thibaut examined the effects of various types of participation in the design of procedures on judgments of their fairness. Participants were assembled into six-person groups. Some groups were asked to discuss and decide on the rules to be used in a later adjudication that would affect the participants' outcomes. Other groups were told to discuss their preference for the various rules, but these groups were led to believe that their preferences would have no effect on the rules actually used—participants in these groups were told that the rules to be used had already been selected. In half of these discussion-only groups the rules actually used matched the preferences expressed in the group discussion, in the other groups in the discussion-only condition, the rules actully used did not match the group's preferences. Finally, some groups were not allowed to either discuss or decide the rules to be used.

The Musante, Gilbert, and Thibaut study found that participation in the form of group discussion and decision making led to the greatest enhancement of the judged procedural and distributive fairness of the subsequent adjudication, but that group discussion alone led to some enhancement of both types of fairness relative to the condition that involved neither discussion nor decision making. These findings suggest that participation in the design of a procedure can enhance the perceived fairness of that procedure. Further, the results of the study show that procedural variation in one social decision-making procedure can affect reactions to a subsequent, related procedure. These study findings are also of considerable theoretical importance to the issue under discussion in this section: it is remarkable that the study showed some enhancement of fairness in the conditions that encouraged discussion but that explicitly ruled out any influence of this discussion on the decision.

It appears that discussion and the expression of preference, even without any action in response to the preference, is one source of favorable procedural and distributive fairness judgments.

Lind, Kanfer, and Earley (1990) provide an even more striking example of the value-expressive influence of voice. They allowed participants in work groups to voice their opinions about work goals, either before or after the goals had been assigned. Their results indicate that participating in such a discussion increases judgments of the fairness of the procedures, relative to a no discussion control group.

These findings support the hypothesis advanced by Tyler, Rasinski, and Spodick (1985) that some process control effects may be due to value expression rather than any instrumentality in achieving outcomes. In both Musante, Gilbert, and Thibaut 1983 and in Lind, Kanfer, and Earley 1990, an enhancement of fairness was observed in conditions that are purely expressive, conditions in which there was no suggestion whatsoever of control or influence over a decision-making process. Further research has suggested that this process control effect does not occur under all conditions. It is important that the decision maker be seen as giving due consideration to the views expressed, even if he or she is not influenced by those views (Tyler 1987).

Tyler (1987) used cross-sectional survey data to test four possible limitations on the process control enhancement of procedural justice judgments. Tyler tested whether the process control effect disappears (1) when the decision maker is seen as biased; (2) when the decision maker is seen as not acting in good faith; (3) when the decision maker is seen as not giving the disputant's views due consideration; and (4) when the outcomes involved were important. Each limitation was tested by selecting individuals who did not believe they had any control over the decision and who believed that the limitation in question was operative in their case. Within each subset of individuals, the procedural fairness judgments of those who had experienced varying levels of process control were compared. Tyler's results showed that only the third limitation, the lack of due consideration, diminished the process control effect. Process control enhanced procedural justice even when the decision maker was seen as biased, when he or she was seen as acting in bad faith, and when the outcomes were important, but not when the decision maker was seen as not giving consideration to the respondent's views and arguments.

A recent laboratory study showed results that are congruent with those of Tyler's finding that the consideration of arguments is an important factor in procedural justice. Conlon, Lind, and Lissak (1989) studied the effect of receiving varying levels of outcomes in the context of an adjudication. They tested whether compromise outcomes induce feelings of injustice. Conlon, Lind, and Lissak hypothesized that compromise outcomes might be interpreted as showing inadequate consideration of a disputant's views, because a compromise can be suggested without really considering the difficult issues of right and wrong that underlie many disputes. These authors suggest this might lead to judgments that the procedure and outcome are less fair when a judge issues a compromise decision than when an all or nothing outcome is issued.[1]

The study was designed in such a way that a dispute arose among the participants, and a trial was held to decide whether cheating had actually occurred and who should receive the prize that was to be awarded to the winner of the competition. Some participants were told that their team had been found innocent of all counts charged and would receive the full prize, others were told that their team had been found innocent on most of the counts and would receive two-thirds of the prize, others were told that their team had been found guilty of most of the counts and would receive only one-third of the prize, and others were told that their team had been found guilty on all counts and would receive none of the prize. Participants were asked to make judgments about procedural and distributive fairness and the extent to which the judge considered the arguments favoring their side of the case. The results suggest that issues of consideration played a central role in the formation of judgments of procedural fairness.

Overall, there is considerable evidence that the process control effect involves something beyond an instrumental desire to control outcomes. It appears that the opportunity to express one's opinions and arguments, the chance to tell one's own side of the story, is a potent factor in enhancing the experience of procedural justice. In other words, as Thibaut and Walker predict, people care about control, but the nature of their concerns about control does not correspond to those suggested by the Thibaut and Walker control model.

Research on the relationship between control and procedural preference stimulated by Thibaut and Walker has not simply confirmed their initial predictions. Instead, it has suggested that the relationship between control and procedural preference is more complex than Thibaut and Walker suggested. Subsequent studies show that one reason process control is valued is that it allows litigants to indirectly influence outcomes by influencing the decisions of third parties. In addition, however, it is now clear that the opportunity to state one's case has value in itself. Recent studies suggest that this expressive value of speech may be more important than its instrumental influence on decisions. At the same time, recent studies have suggested that such process control effects do not occur under all circumstances. Litigants only value voice if they feel that the decision maker is giving consideration to what they say.

The voice findings outlined suggest that people have a noninstrumental image of control. But what do they want from authorities, and how do they evaluate their experiences with them? An alternative perspective to the control model of Thibaut and Walker, which suggests a different basis for the evaluation of experience, is provided by the relational model (Tyler and Lind 1992).

The relational model suggests that evaluations of experience are linked to the social bonds that exist between people and authorities, bonds that extend beyond the immediate issue or problem which is being dealt with. In other words, reactions to authorities are linked to issues that define the connection between the individual and the authority.

The basic assumption of the relational model is that people are predisposed to belong to social groups and that they are very attentive to signs and symbols that communicate information about their status within groups. People want to understand, establish, and maintain the social bonds that exist within their groups. Research shows that people establish such connections if given even the most tenuous basis for group identification (Brewer and Kramer 1986; Kramer and Brewer 1984; Messick and Brewer 1983; Tajfel 1981; Tajfel and Turner 1979). They do so because positive connections enhance feelings of self-esteem and self-worth. Tyler (1989b) identified three types of relational concern: information about standing in the group; evidence about the neutrality of the decision maker; and trust in the motives of the third party.

Information about standing is communicated by the interpersonal quality of treatment by the authority. Whether people are treated politely and with dignity and whether respect is shown for their rights is linked to social standing concerns (Tyler and Bies 1990). Lind et al. (1990) refer to these issues as "dignitary" concerns.

People are also concerned about the neutrality of the decision maker. When considering neutrality, people are focusing on the dispute or problem, but not on the favorability of their outcome or on their control over that outcome. Instead, they are focusing on whether the third party creates a "level playing field" by evenhanded treatment. Neutrality involves honesty and a lack of bias. Neutral decision making also uses facts, not opinions, leading to decisions of objectively high quality.

Finally, inferences about the trustworthiness or benevolence of the third-party authority involve beliefs about the intentions of the third party. Inferences are especially important because they are used to predict both the future behavior of that authority and the behavior of other, similar, authorities.

Tyler has examined the importance of relational influences in legal settings (Tyler 1988, 1989; Tyler and Lind 1992) using interviews with people with recent personal experiences involving police officers or judges. The results suggest that the basis of evaluations is complex and multidimensional. Five aspects of procedures make independent contributions to judgments about procedural fairness. These include outcome favorability, control, neutrality, trust, and standing. The strongest influence is found among the relational variables, which exert the greatest influence in both arenas. Standing and trust are most important. Outcome favorability and control influences occur, but are not the major factors used to evaluate the fairness of procedures.

The importance which people attach to issues of standing is striking. Standing issues are particularly key to judgments about the fairness of procedures. People appear to be remarkably sensitive to evidence of the respect with which they are regarded by the authorities, evidence provided by the politeness and dignity they experience. Lane (1988) notes that one of the most important aspects of procedural justice to citizens dealing with the political authorities is that the procedures used support their sense of self-respect. Similarly, Tyler and Folger examined citizen-police contacts and found that a key issue to citizens in such contacts was a "recognition of citizen rights" (1980: 292).

Further evidence of the importance attached to issues of standing is provided by the results of two recent studies of the civil justice system (Lind et al. 1990; MacCoun et al. 1988). In the Lind et al. (1990) study, ratings of procedural justice were found to be related to judgments of the dignity of a procedure ($r = .57$). In the MacCoun et al. (1988) study similar ratings were linked to judgments that the procedure was ethical ($r = .71$), led disputants to be treated with respect ($r = .56$), and led them to be treated with dignity ($r = .35$).

The Tyler data divide standing into issues of politeness and respect for rights. Both aspects of standing are important, but respect for rights slightly dominates the influence of standing on procedural justice within legal settings ($r = .54$ vs. $r = .49$). This accords with the finding of MacCoun et al. (1988) that being ethical is more important in a procedure ($r = .71$) than that the procedure treats people with dignity ($r = .35$).

Tyler (1988, 1989b; Tyler and Lind 1992) argues that standing is less closely linked to outcome-based concerns than are neutrality or trust. An examination of the relationship among outcome favorability and distributive justice judgments and evaluations of neutrality, trust, and standing supports that suggestion. Of the three, standing is the least linked to outcomes obtained.

The most important influence on procedural justice judgments is the individual's evaluation of the trustworthiness of the intentions of the authorities involved (Tyler and Bies 1990; Tyler and Lind 1992). Concern about the intentions of the authorities reflects a focus on issues of trust or benevolence. These concerns reflect a desire by group members to understand the stable underlying motivations of authorities, motivations that allow their future behavior to be predicted. If people infer that authorities have a benevolent disposition, they can trust that, in the long run, the authorities will work to serve people's self-interest. It is for this reason that trust is a key component of legitimacy (Barber 1983).

Why do people focus on questions of trust? Trust involves questions of security, that is, people's efforts to predict how the authorities will act in the future. When asked in the abstract how the authorities would treat them if they had dealings with them, people almost universally predict that if they were to deal with the authorities in the future, they would receive fair treatment (Tyler 1990c). This expectation exists despite the widespread belief that injustice often occurs when citizens deal with the police and courts. When people are asked what generally happens when people deal with authority figures, they say that many people are treated unfairly. This discrepancy between the belief that injustice occurs and the belief that one is oneself invulnerable to being unfairly treated may suggest the presence of an "illusion of personal justice."

Other research supports the suggestion that there is a gap between beliefs about justice on the personal and societal level. Crosby (1984) noted that women workers recognized the existence of discrimination but believed that they were not personally the victims of discrimination. Similar findings have emerged from studies of ethnic discrimination (Taylor et al. 1990). Crosby argues that this gap reflects a desire for "comfortable ignorance" or distancing (Crosby and Nagata 1990). By feeling removed from discrimination, people need not feel personally hurt by it.

The suggestion that people have a need to feel secure is not a new one. Pepitone coined the term "facilitative distortion" to describe this need (Pepitone 1950). He demonstrated that people exaggerate the benevolence of those authorities on whom they are dependent. Similarly, Heider (1958) suggested that people would exaggerate the degree to which authorities were responsible for threatening problems as a way of minimizing the extent to which such events had to be seen as occurring due to chance. Walster (1966) has demonstrated that this motivation shapes people's reactions to events in their personal lives, while Tyler (1982) demonstrated this motivation in peoples' reactions to authorities by showing that people exaggerate the responsibility of the president for causing national problems when those problems are important to them.

To the extent that people need to feel the security of believing that they will not receive unfair treatment, they are likely to be sensitive to confirmation of that belief by a favorable experience with an authority, or to its disconfirmation by an unfavorable experience with an authority. When people deal with particular authorities, this belief in fair treatment is being put to the test.

What is it that matters about the intentions of authorities? The results indicate that it is the ethical dimensions of trust which dominate, not trust in the competence of the authority. The average correlation of competence dimensions to procedural justice is .50. The average correlation of ethical dimensions is .70.

Finally, neutrality effects are found. Why do people care about neutrality? People have a long-term commitment to the social group and its authorities, rules, and institutions. Instead of focusing on a single outcome, people look for evidence suggesting whether, over time, they will receive a fair level of benefits from group membership. Such evidence is provided by the existence of neutral decision makers. Focusing on neutrality—the absence of unfair procedures—as a way of assessing the reasonableness of decisions seems especially appropriate when people cannot easily determine what the correct outcome of a decision is. In dealings with legal authorities people are likely to be uncertain about what a correct outcome is, since they have very few such experiences (see Tyler 1988, 1990c) and lack knowledge about the law.

As the findings outlined make clear, the relational model suggests a fundamentally different image of how people react to legal authorities than is suggested by instrumental models, such as the control model of Thibaut and Walker (1975). The relational model suggests a much more interpersonal focus (Tyler and Lind 1992). It suggests that people don't equate either objective or subjective power, in the form of control that increases the ability to create personally favorable outcomes, with subjective justice.

As would be expected, (1) procedural justice is most important and (2) relational factors have an especially important role in defining procedural justice when the variables of concern directly involve the person's relationship with authorities. For example, procedural justice is crucial to judgments about the judge, mediator, or other third party who makes decisions or about the legal system they represent (Tyler and Lind 1992).[2] Judgments of personal satisfaction, while responsive to procedural concerns, are also more sensitive to issues of outcomes. Outcome sensitivity occurs primarily through a concern about issues of distributive justice, not through a focus on outcome favorability.

B. Why Do People Focus on Procedural Justice?

What needs might a procedural justice focus serve? One is the desire for cognitive simplicity. Efforts to evaluate the favorability or fairness of outcomes rapidly become complex. Consider an effort to evaluate one's relative inputs and outcomes from the university at which one teaches. Imagine a rapidly expanding calculus including office size and location, teaching load, administrative duties, student quality, and so on, balanced against salary. It quickly becomes quite difficult to assess both absolute and relative outcome levels. In dealings with legal authorities one-shot players have the further complication that they lack knowledge about the outcomes of others. In such instances it is far simpler to examine the fairness of procedures—assuming that fair procedures produce fair outcomes.

It is also possible to regard procedural justice as a solution to problems of interpersonal trust. In many social situations, such as those discussed by the social dilemma literature (Tyler and Dawes 1993), people's best interests are served by trusting others and acting in the group's long-term interests. Yet people are reluctant to trust, knowing that others might "defect" and do them short-term harm. If people know that the group is making its decisions using fair procedures, they can trust that, over time, their interests will be protected.

The perspective outlined also explains the striking finding that people define procedural justice most strongly by reference to the "trustworthiness" of the motives of the third-party authority with whom they are dealing. Again, if people believe that the authority with whom they are dealing is trustworthy, they need not engage in the lengthy process of calculating outcome favorability or worry about the risks of suspending the operation of short-term self-interest in an effort to promote their own long-term interests and those of their group.

A procedural focus may also be enhanced by value ambiguity, that is, the inability to determine what constitutes an appropriate outcome in litigation may not only be an issue of lack of experience. One of the characteristics of a pluralistic society, like the United States, is the lack of a common moral code from which to draw standards of right and wrong. Hence, people may lack a sense of what is an appropriate claim of entitlement.

Conflicts over appropriate entitlements also reflect political differences in conceptions about the role of the courts. For example, people differ in their views about whether the courts ought to act in ways which redistribute resources. Further, those who accept this goal may differ concerning who should receive greater resources.

Within a pluralistic society a focus on procedural, as opposed to substantive, issues is natural. Since there may be no commonly held moral or political values out of which a common sense of entitlement or distributive justice can arise, authorities may seek to increase the acceptability of their decisions by emphasizing their procedural qualities. For example, they may emphasize their willingness to allow all affected groups to participate in the deliberations through which the outcome occurs.

Consider a policy such as whether abortion should be allowed. In some societies the answer to this question is straightforward; a religious or cultural value indicates the appropriate public policy. For example, in the past, heavily Catholic countries such as Poland and Italy have not allowed abortion. In other societies, for example Germany, the legislature enacted a policy, after directly discussing the substance of the issue and considering positive consequences of allowing or forbidding abortion. In American society the abortion question is treated as an issue of "rights." Hence, its substance—the implications of abortion policy for the goals of American society—is not directly considered. Instead, discussion centers around whether or not it is a legitimate personal legal "right" under the American Constitution for women to make their own abortion decisions. One consequence of this "rights consciousness" is to encourage the shift toward a procedural focus, since the process of legal decision making is overtly accessible for evaluation, while courts eschew the role of making substantive judgments. In other words, saying that the Constitution gives women a legal right to have an abortion is not an evaluation (either pro or con) of the wisdom of deciding to exercise that right. Hence, evaluations of legal authority inevitably tend to focus on procedures.

C. Dangers of a Procedural Justice Focus

The subjective focus on procedure found among those studied is also a cause for potential concern. To the extent that those in positions of authority are not interested in the welfare of litigants, the procedural focus found among litigants facilitates their ability to beguile those with whom they deal.

In management, procedural justice findings have already spawned a literature on "impression management," which examines how managers can maximize the acceptance of their decisions by presenting them as fairly made (see Greenberg 1990). For example, Bies (1987; Bies and Shapiro 1987; Bies, Shapiro, and Cummings 1988) has examined the effect of presenting mitigating circumstances as an excuse for an unpopular decision. Bies demonstrates that managers benefit if they suggest that, following "due" consideration, external circumstances prevent granting a worker's request.

The key to the effectiveness of an impression management strategy is the willingness of people to feel subjectively satisfied with objectively disadvantaging litigation outcomes. In other words, it is based on the belief that people will be satisfied at receiving "fair" process, even if that fair process leads to an "unfair" outcome. Such a willingness has been labeled "false consciousness" (Lind and Tyler 1988; Tyler and McGraw 1986).

Since most procedural justice research on people who have had actual experiences with legal authorities is based on self-reports from litigants, such studies lack any way to evaluate the relationship between the subjective and the objective.

Laboratory studies which control on objective outcomes suggest that people typically retain their belief that a procedure is fair after it has delivered an unfair outcome. For example, Thibaut and Walker (1975) found that litigants rated the adversary system to be a fairer procedure after it had falsely convicted them than they rated the inquisitorial system after it vindicated their innocence. Of course, there are limits to this effect. Lind and Lissak (1985) identified one such limit—the procedure must be enacted fairly. When a procedure was enacted in an obviously biased way, people reacted negatively to an unfavorable verdict. However, when decision makers are judged to be acting in good faith, they appear able to make errors without damaging public respect for procedures.

Conley and O'Barr's ethnographic study of litigants in courts supports the argument that people resist evidence that judges are unworthy of their power. Their findings suggest that people will go to considerable effort to avoid interpreting an unfavorable experience with a particular judge as a negative reflection on the legal system in general (Conley and O'Barr 1990).

The effect of repeated exposure to negative experiences has not been directly examined using naturally occurring experiences. However, Tyler and Lind (1990) found that even the members of disadvantaged groups based their evaluations of the legitimacy of legal authorities more heavily on procedural justice than on outcome favorability or fairness. Since the members of such groups have suffered a lifetime of second-class treatment, it is striking that they, nonetheless, continue to base their allegiance on procedural justice judgments. Similarly, Casper, Tyler, and Fisher (1988) found that the young, largely uneducated and unemployed minorities who formed their sample of people on trial for felonies evaluated their experiences in strongly procedural justice terms. As in other studies, this sample was found to base their generalizations from their experiences to their views about the legitimacy of legal authorities solely on judgments about procedural justice (Tyler, Casper, and Fisher 1989).

D. The Implications of a Procedural Justice Approach for Civil Litigation Research

What difference does it make what perspective is used to view the civil litigation process? Consider the issue of alternative dispute resolution procedures. Traditionally civil disputes have been resolved within the courts, using a combination of formal legal processes and informal mechanisms such as settlement conferences. The formal legal process is the civil trial. It can involve either a bench trial before a judge or a jury trial. However, most cases have not actually been resolved through formal trials. Instead they have been resolved through informal settlement conferences (see Abel 1982).

During the past several decades increasing attention within the American legal system has been given to the procedures used in resolving disputes within the civil court system. A wide variety of types of "alternative" dispute resolution procedures have been developed and incorporated into the traditional civil justice system (see Goldberg, Green, and Sander 1985).

Why is there dissatisfaction with the traditional legal system and why have alternative dispute resolution programs developed? Traditional outcome-based explanations have emphasized issues of delay, cost, and poor outcomes. As the Lind et al. study (1990) demonstrates, however, such explanations are inadequate. People do not evaluate their experiences with legal procedures in terms of the objective quality of their outcomes. In other words, the subjective experience of justice or injustice does not flow from the consequences of the objective distribution of power. Instead, people focus on their evaluations of the nature of the process itself, evaluations which are distinct from the outcomes they obtain.

This finding has broader implications, beyond its implications for understanding reactions to different forms of alternative dispute resolution. Mac-Coun and Tyler (1988), for example, examined the basis of public evaluations of the criminal jury. They found that people do not evaluate the criminal jury primarily in terms of judgments about the objective quality of jury decisions (i.e., the outcomes of jury deliberations). While the objective quality of jury decisions mattered, other, process-oriented issues also shaped evaluations.

Procedural justice may also have implications for people's willingness to accept the decisions of national-level legal authorities like the United States Supreme Court. Tyler and Rasinski (1991) used data from a national survey of citizens to suggest that people are more willing to accept the right of a disliked group to march in their community if that right is endorsed by the United States Supreme Court. The extent to which such an effect occurred was linked to evaluations of the fairness of the decision-making procedures used by the court. Similarly, Tyler (1992) demonstrated that people who regard the United States Supreme Court as making decisions fairly are more willing to allow the court to decide if abortion should be a right.

E. THE DYNAMICS OF LEGAL AUTHORITY IN AMERICAN SOCIETY

A number of social scientists have hypothesized that procedural issues of justice have a key role in the evaluation of political and legal authorities. For example, the theories of David Easton (1965, 1968, 1975), Talcott Parsons (1963, 1967), and others concerned with the viability of social systems all suggest that procedures are a key underpinning of political stability. Their models view conflict and disputes as irritants to the smooth functioning of social systems. They examine the mechanisms which social systems create to preserve their viability by resolving disputes which arise within the system. Their work emphasizes the importance of having institutions whose rules and procedures for allocation and dispute resolution are acceptable to all of those within the system, and which, as a result, can make rules and decisions which will be voluntarily obeyed.

In other words, the roots of concern about procedural justice lie in an interest in the viability of the legal system. Key to that viability is the capability of rendering decisions which are authoritative, that is which are accepted by both parties; which resolve the dispute; and which restore positive relationships among the parties to the dispute.

Conversely, social scientists like Barrington Moore (1978) have focused on the origins of rebellion and revolt, that is, on the circumstances which diminish viability. Moore suggests that historically people have accepted both high levels of deprivation and the lack of opportunities for advancement. Under some circumstances, however, people rebel against the established order. In contrast to theories focusing on the stability of social systems, Moore examines their potential instability.

Social scientists and legal scholars are united in suggesting that the stability of the political and legal system is enhanced if authorities can secure voluntary compliance with their directives (Tyler 1990c). One basis for such voluntary compliance is legitimacy—the belief among members of the public that the directives of authorities ought to be obeyed. To the extent that the public regards authorities as legitimate, the ability of those authorities to govern effectively—maintaining the stability of the legal and political system—is enhanced.

One example of social science research on the legitimacy of legal institutions is found in research on the legitimacy of the United States Supreme Court. To be effective in its role the United States Supreme Court must be able to make decisions that will affect the behavior of American citizens. A decision outlawing school prayer, for example, is of value if it is followed by decreases in the occurrence of school prayer. In a classic paper which draws on the theoretical framework of David Easton, Murphy and Tanenhaus (1969) examined the basis of public acceptance of the right of the United States Supreme Court to make policy decisions in areas like school prayer, school de-segregation, and so on. Their study suggests that there is widespread support for the United States Supreme Court as an institution whose function is to interpret the Constitution, support which encourages support for unpopular Supreme Court decisions. This support is based on public beliefs about the procedures used by the court when making policy decisions (i.e., on "diffuse" system support, as opposed to "specific" system support, which develops from agreement with incumbent authorities' policies).

Legitimacy, and the authoritativeness that flows from it, can be regarded as desirable, since it enhances the stability of the existing legal system. However, this is only the case when the maintainance of the existing system is valued. If the existing system is regarded as unjust, and social change is desired, then stability is an undesirable situation.

Is people's willingness to embrace procedural solutions to distributive problems reasonable and desirable? From the perspective of the ongoing political system, such solutions are very desirable. If the goal is to maintain the stability of the political/legal system, the willingness of groups to agree to a common procedure for resolving a conflict and then voluntarily to accept whatever results this procedure obtains is highly desirable. It facilitates the effective exercise of authority.

From the perspective of a literature such as that on the legal needs of the disadvantaged, the findings of the procedural justice literature are more troubling. Given the potentially beguiling effects of a procedural focus, people may be better off trying to focus directly on outcomes and ignoring proce-dures. Interestingly, a recent study of the speeches of revolutionary leaders, which uses content analysis to identify the themes in those speeches, finds that revolutionary leaders focus primarily on questions of distributive, not procedural, injustice (Martin, Scully, and Levitt 1990). Perhaps revolutionary leaders recognize that social unrest is facilitated by such a shift in focus.

The findings of procedural justice research are of equal value to those who seek stability and those who seek change. Each group needs to understand that basis of stability; in one case to create it, in the other to undermine it. Hence, the focus of procedural justice studies on the basis of authoritativeness is not linked to a belief that stability is desirable. Those who seek to promote social change have an interest in understanding the psychological dynamics underlying stability which is equal to that of those concerned with maintaining the power and influence of existing legal authorities.

9. PROCEDURAL JUSTICE RESEARCH AND THE CRITICAL LEGAL STUDIES MOVEMENT

An important aspect of recent legal scholarship is the development of the crit-ical legal studies movement (Sarat 1993). That movement provides a critical perspective on legal institutions, regarding them as instruments of hegemony, which function to legitimate a set of rules which insure the domination of a particular set of individuals at the expense of others (Sarat 1993).

The critical legal studies movement is concerned with "how and why people put up with" an objectively unjust system of law (Sarat 1993). It examines the manner in which people deny the implications of their experience, leading it to be deprived of political force and energy. Studies of the American legal system suggest that people do, indeed, accept that system. Tyler (1990c) found strong endorsement of the personal obligation to follow legal rules, even if those rules conflicted with questions of personal morality, among a sample of 1,575 Chicagoans. For example, 82 percent indicated that they felt they should "obey the law even if it goes against what they think is right," and 82 percent also indicated that they "always try to follow the law even if [they] think it is wrong." Similarly, 79 percent indicate that "disobeying the law is seldom justified"; while 69 percent say that "it is difficult to break the law and keep one's self-respect." In other words, people regard it as a personal obligation to obey laws.[3]

From the perspective of those critical of the existing social order, the willingness of substantial numbers of Americans to uncritically accept its legitimacy is disturbing. Such uncritical acceptance of the legitimacy of authorities has been implicated, among other things, in the willingness of citizens to commit crimes of obedience—injuring innocent others in response to the orders of "legitimate" authorities (Kelman and Hamilton 1989). Unfortunately, such obedience is also an important precursor to the effective exercise of authority, so it cannot simply be dismissed (Tyler 1990c). For authorities in democratic societies to administer laws, they must have legitimacy in the eyes of the public—legitimacy which leads to voluntary acceptance of many of their directives.

Legitimacy is disturbing when it leads soldiers to kill civilians. But it is good when it facilitates the willingness of Whites in the South to accept desegregated schools, when it encourages antiabortion activists to allow people to enter abortion clinics to exercise their Constitutional right to have an abortion, and when it enables disliked groups to exercise their Constitutional right to march or hold a public rally. In each case, people's action is restrained in deference to the directives of legitimate authorities. The psychological dynamics at work in these cases are the same as those underlying "crimes of obedience" such as the massacre of civilians by soldiers (see Kelman and Hamilton 1989).

It is also important to recognize that the American legal culture is a clearly defined and established legal system. It exists without serious ideological challenges; has a long history; and, hence, is ideal for the production of cultural socialization effects. Other cultures lack such characteristics. They may, for example, have greater conflicts over the appropriate form of the legal system. Such conflicts may lead people to be more aware of the possibility of alternatives. Typically dissatisfaction with existing arrangements is only translated into a critique of the legal or political system when people have some ideological framework through which to understand that dissatisfaction (Femia 1976; Parkin 1971).

Luker (1984) examines the interpretation of the personal experience of having an abortion. Her interviews suggest that many women had illegal abortions without considering the broader political implications of abortion, since no ideology existed to support such an interpretation. Subsequently, when the abortion rights movement provided such a supportive ideology, those women interpreted their earlier experience in political terms.

Kelman and Hamilton (1989) directly examine the circumstances under which people are able to resist the orders of legitimate authorites. They find that people seldom disobey legitimate authorities without some alternative source of legitimate authority to support their actions. Historically religion has often served as an alternative source of authority to government. They argue that "it typically requires the introduction of a new ideological framework . . . to enable citizens to challenge the legitimacy of the established order" (1989: 57).

Critical legal studies scholars see the roots of the acceptance of the personal obligation to obey laws in the cultural hegemony of the legal system—people accept the legal system because they are taught that it is legitimate and fair. Lacking alternate ideologies, people are unable to translate their personal experiences of dissatisfaction into disobedience. One aspect of critical legal studies studies is a focus on the social structure and cultural beliefs ("ideology") through which hegemony occurs (see Merry 1990; Yngvesson 1988). In this respect such studies differ greatly from studies of procedural justice. Procedural justice focuses on the individual and his or her feelings, and does not generally examine social structure or cultural beliefs, except on an individual basis.

Despite its different focus, procedural justice research speaks directly to a core question raised by the critical legal studies movement—how is the legal system maintained? The findings outlined address the psychological dynamics through which people interpret their experience with legal authorities, converting those experiences into interpretations about the legal system and its authorities.

The procedural justice literature suggests an answer to the question posed by the critical legal studies movement: Why do people accept the [unjust] legal system? It suggests that people focus on procedures, not outcomes. Further, they define those procedures in terms of their status-conferring properties, not in terms of the quality or favorability of the outcomes they provide to the individual. Hence, people do not evaluate legal procedures in ways that would lead them to question the legitimacy of the current legal system.

The findings of procedural justice studies address the seeming paradox posed by critical legal studies authors: the system is unjust, yet it is accepted. The roots of an answer to that paradox lie in an understanding of the psychology of domination. That psychology is elaborated in the procedural justice studies examined here. Hence, procedural justice studies help to clarify how domination occurs.

Why do people react as they do in procedural justice studies? Why do they focus on process, not outcomes? Why do they define process in terms of trust, standing, and neutrality, not in terms of control? In particular, do these psychological processes reflect basic human psychology or the workings of cultural hegemony? These questions are not directly addressed within the procedural justice literature outlined. That literature elaborates the nature of the dynamics which occur when people deal with legal authorities, but does not explore the origin of those dynamics. An important project for the future is that proposed by the critical legal studies movement: to differentiate the effects of universal psychological processes and the effects of the manifestation of those basic processes within different cultural contexts.[4]

One possibility is that cultural forces override psychological dynamics. In such a case, proposed by hegemonic models, people's subjective feelings would reflect the definitions imposed by culture. Instead of focusing on outcomes, people are taught by their culture to focus on procedures—a dysfunctional focus in a system in which procedures legitimate structural inequality. Because of this dysfunctional focus, for example, the poor focus on the "procedural justice" of the American economic system—which gives everyone an "equal" opportunity to advance economically, instead of evaluating whether they have personally received favorable opportunities in their lives and/or whether inequality of income is actually changing in the United States (Hochschild 1981; Kluegel and Smith 1986).

An alternative view is that basic psychological dynamics resist cultural influence, remaining the same within different cultural contexts. If so, then the procedural justice findings outlined reflect the operation of basic human needs, not the distortions of an unjust cultural socialization process.

Any conflict between cultural socialization and individual psychological dynamics is especially intense when people have personal experiences with legal or political authorities. In such a situation "culture and personal experience may strongly push individuals' conceptions of justice in diverging directions" (Hall and Jose 1983: 279). For example, people may be "torn between general differentiating beliefs that they have been taught," which justify disparities in treatment and outcomes, and "specific egalitarian beliefs" suggesting that people should be treated equally "that they derive from [personal] experience" (Hochschild 1981: 255).

One example of research on personal experiences is the work of Thibaut and Walker on people's experiences with legal authorities conducting trials. Thibaut and Walker (1975) found that Americans regarded the (American) adversary legal procedure as fairer than the (European) inquisitorial legal system. This finding could be explained as cultural—with Americans adopting the view presented to them by their culture. It could also be explained psychologically—the adversary system may be responsive to basic human psychological dynamics. To test these alternative views Lind et al. (1978)

examined fairness judgments among the French, who have an inquisitorial system. They found that French respondents also preferred the adversary system and regarded it as fairer. This effect could not be explained culturally, since France has an inquisitorial legal system. It suggests that the adversary system is responsive to basic psychological dynamics, in this case the desire to have freedom to directly address third-party authorities.

The procedural justice literature addresses some but not all of the issues raised by the critical legal studies movement. It examines the psychological dynamics through which people filter their experience, elaborating those dynamics by identifying those aspects of experience which people focus on and the psychological reasons for that focus. Hence, those findings provide one building block in the larger program of research suggested by the critical legal studies agenda.

What procedural justice models are well equipped to explain is the basis of individual behavior toward legal authorities and legal rules. It has been demonstrated that people's subjective reactions to their experiences with legal authorities influence both their willingness to voluntarily accept their legal decisions and their general willingness to voluntarily follow legal rules (Lind and Tyler 1988). Since effectiveness as an authority is linked to the ability to secure compliance (to "authoritativeness"), and since voluntary acceptance is recognized to be key to an especially valuable, and perhaps indispensible, type of compliance for an authority to be able to secure (Tyler 1990c; Tyler and Lind 1992), subjective evaluations of legal authorities are an important input into their viability.

At the same time, it may also be true that the transition from the objective distributive focus of the legal needs literature to the subjective procedural focus of procedural justice studies which is outlined in this discussion may represent a reenactment among scholars of the dynamic found among respondents. Lacking a value-based consensus for evaluating the objective distribution or redistribution of resources within a pluralistic society, scholars—like members of the public—may find the study of the subjective procedural consensus underlying authoritativeness appealing. Within the context of an existing social order there is obvious face validity—at least to established authorities—to the study of the basis of authoritativeness. Certainly the problems which result from noncompliance with law—ranging from fathers' widespread nonpayment of child support orders to the recent Los Angeles riots—are widely (if not universally) regarded as undesirable. Since authoritativeness is found to rest on a procedural base, a focus on this set of concerns leads to a shift in empirical interest from distributive to procedural issues.

NOTES

I would like to thank Peter Degoey, Bryant Garth, Felice Levine, Austin Sarat, and Maria del Carmen Torralba for their comments on a draft of this paper.

1. Field studies support the suggestion that decisions which seem not to consider the merits of the case are regarded as unfair. MacCoun et al. (1988) found that disputants associated the belief that a mediator has "split the difference" with unfairness ($r = -.26$) and were less likely to accept such awards ($r = -.28$).

2. It is also possible to specify who will care most strongly about issues of procedural justice (see Brockner, Tyler, and Schneider 1992; Tyler and Lind 1990).

3. Of course, it is important to recognize that the United States is a democratic country. It should not be assumed that repressive states can expect to receive similar levels of public support. Further, such countries may not expect to govern through legitimacy and may, as a consequence, need to utilize coercion.

4. A recent effort to study the dynamics of cultural socialization is found in the work of Cohn and White (1990). This work contrasts the learning and cognitive-developmental perspectives on cultural socialization. It does so within the context of the internalization of legal rules.

BIBLIOGRAPHY

Abel, Richard. 1982. *The Politics of Informal Justice*. Vols. 1 and 2. New York: Academic Press.

Abrams, Dominick, and Michael Hogg. 1990. *Social Identity Theory: Constructive and Critical Advances*. New York: Springer-Verlag.

Adler, Jane, Deborah Hensler, and Charles Nelson. 1983. *Simple Justice: How Litigants Fare in the Pittsburgh Arbitration Program*. Santa Monica, CA: Rand Corporation.

Babbie, Earl R. 1973. *Survey Research Methods*. Belmont, CA: Wadsworth.

Backstrom, Charles H., and Gerald Hursh-Cesar. 1963. *Survey Research*. 2d ed. New York: Wiley.

Barber, Bernard. 1983. *The Logic and Limits of Trust*. New Brunswick, NJ: Rutgers Univ. Press.

Bendix, Reinhard. 1960. *Max Weber*. Berkeley: Univ. of California Press.

Bies, Robert J. 1987. The Predicament of Injustice: The Management of Moral Outrage. In *Research in Organizational Behavior*, vol. 9, ed. L. L. Cummings and B. M. Staw, 289–319. Greenwich, CT: JAI Press.

Bies, Robert J., and Debra L. Shapiro. 1987. Intentional Fairness Judgments: The Influence of Causal Accounts. 1 *Social Justice Research*, 199–218.

Bies, Robert J., Debra L. Shapiro, and Larry L. Cummings. 1988. Causal Accounts and Managing Organizational Conflict: Is It Enough to Say It's Not My Fault? 15 *Communication Research*, 381–99.

Brewer, Marilynn, and Roderick Kramer. 1986. Choice Behavior in Social Dilemmas: Effects of Social Identity, Group Size, and Decision Framing. 50 *Journal of Personality and Social Psychology*, 543–49.

Brickman, P., R. Folger, E. Goode, and Y. Schul. 1981. Microjustice and Macrojustice. In *The Justice Motive in Social Behavior*, ed. M. J. Lerner and S. C. Lerner. New York: Plenum.

Brockner, Joel, Tom R. Tyler, and Rochelle Schneider. 1992. The Higher They Are, the Harder They Fall: The Effects of Prior Commitment and Procedural Injustice on Subsequent Commitment to Social Institutions. 37 *Administrative Science Quarterly*, 241–61.

Caplovitz, David. 1963. *The Poor Pay More*. New York: Free Press.

———. 1974. *Consumers in Trouble: A Study of Debtors in Default*. New York: Free Press.

Carlin, J. E., J. Howard, and S. Messinger. 1966. Civil Justice and the Poor: Issues for Sociological Research. 1 *Law and Society Rev.*, 9.

———. 1967. *Civil Justice and the Poor*. New York: Russell Sage.

Cartwright, Dorian, and Alvin Zander. 1953. *Group Dynamics*. New York: Harper.

Casper, Jonathan D., Tom R. Tyler, and Bonnie Fisher. 1988. Procedural Justice in Felony Cases. 22 *Law and Society Rev.*, 483–507.

Cohn, Ellen S., and Susan White. 1990. *Legal Socialization: A Study of Norms and Rules*. New York: Springer-Verlag.

Cook, Karen S., and Karen A. Hegtvedt. 1983. Distributive Justice, Equity, and Equality. 9 *Annual Rev. of Sociology*, 217–41.

———. 1986. Justice and Power: An Exchange Analysis. In *Justice in Social Relations*, ed. H. W. Bierhoff, R. L. Cohen, and J. Greenberg. New York: Plenum.

Conley, John M., and William O'Barr. 1990. *Rules versus Relationships*. Chicago: Univ. of Chicago Press.

Conlon, Donald E., E. Allan Lind, and Robyn Lissak. 1989. Nonlinear and Nonmonotonic Effects of Outcome on Procedural and Distributive Fairness Judgments. 19 *Journal of Applied Social Psychology*, 1085–99.

Crosby, Faye. 1984. The Denial of Personal Discrimination. 27 *American Behavioral Scientist*, 371–86.

Crosby, Faye, and Donna Nagata. 1990. *Denying Personal Disadvantage*. Paper presented at the annual meeting of the International Society of Political Psychology, July, Washington, DC.

Darley, John. 1990. Moral Rules: Their Content and Acquisition. 41 *Annual Rev. of Psychology*, 530–45.

Davis, James. 1980. Group Decision and Procedural Justice. In *Progress in Social Psychology*, ed. M. Fishbein, 157–229. Hillsdale, NJ: Erlbaum.

Deutsch, Morton. 1985. *Distributive Justice*. New Haven, CT: Yale Univ. Press.

Dweck, Carol S., and T. Goetz. 1978. Attributions and Learned Helplessness. In *New Directions in Attribution Research*, vol. 2, ed. J. Harvey, W. Ickes, and R. Kidd. Hillsdale, NJ: Erlbaum.

Easton, David. 1958. The Perception of Authority and Political Change. In *Authority*, ed. C. J. Friedrich. Cambridge, MA: Harvard Univ. Press.

———. 1965. *A Systems Analysis of Political Life*. Chicago: Univ. of Chicago Press.

———. 1968. Political Science. In *International Encyclopedia of the Social Sciences*, ed. D. L. Sills. New York: Macmillan.

———. 1975. A Reassessment of the Concept of Political Support. 5 *British Journal of Political Science*, 435–57.

Easton, David, and J. Dennis. 1969. *Children in the Political System: Origins of Political Legitimacy*. Chicago: Univ. of Chicago Press.

Engel, David. 1984. The Oven-Bird's Song: Insiders, Outsiders, and Personal Injuries in an American Community. 18 *Law and Society Rev.*, 549.

Felstiner, William L. F., Richard L. Abel, and Austin Sarat. 1981. The Emergence and Transformation of Disputes: Naming, Blaming, Claiming. 16 *Law and Society Rev.*, 631.

Femia, J. 1976. Hegemony and Consciousness in the Thought of Antonio Gramsci. 23 *Political Studies*, 29–48.

Festinger, Leon. 1954. A Theory of Social Comparison Processes. 7 *Human Relations*, 117–40.

Galanter, Marc. 1974. Why the "Haves" Come Out Ahead: Speculations on the Limits of Legal Change. 9 *Law and Society Rev.*, 95.

Gamson, William. 1968. *Power and Discontent.* Homewood, IL: Dorsey.

Glass, D. C., and J. E. Singer. 1972. *Urban Stress: Experiments in Noise and Social Stressors.* New York: Academic Press.

Gluckman, M. 1967. *The Judicial Process among the Barotse of Northern Rhodesia.* Manchester: Manchester Univ. Press.

Goldberg, S. B., E. D. Green, and F. E. A. Sander. 1985. *Dispute Resolution.* Boston: Little, Brown.

Greenberg, Jerald. 1990. Looking Fair vs. Being Fair: Managing Impressions of Organizational Justice. 12 *Research in Organizational Behavior*, 111–57.

Greenhouse, Carol. 1986. *Praying for Justice.* Ithaca, NY: Cornell Univ. Press.

Hall, W. S., and P. E. Jose. 1983. Cultural Effects on the Development of Equality and Inequality. In *The Child's Construction of Social Inequality*, ed. R. L. Leahy, 253–85. New York: Academic Press.

Harrington, Christine. 1985. *Shadow Justice: The Ideology and Institutionalization of Alternatives to Court.* Westport, CT: Greenwood.

Hastie, Reid, Steven Penrod, and Nancy Pennington. 1983. *Inside the Jury.* Cambridge, MA: Harvard Univ. Press.

Heider, Fritz. 1958. *The Psychology of Interpersonal Relations.* New York: Wiley.

Hochschild, Jennifer. 1981. *What's Fair.* Cambridge, MA: Harvard Univ. Press.

Hogg, Michael A., and Dominick Abrams. 1988. *Social Identifications: A Social Psychology of Intergroup Relations and Group Processes.* New York: Routledge.

Katz, D. 1960. The Functional Approach to the Study of Attitudes. 24 *Public Opinion Quarterly*, 163–204.

Kelman, Herbert C., and V. Lee Hamilton. 1989. *Crimes of Obedience.* New Haven, CT: Yale Univ. Press.

Kluegel, J. R., and E. R. Smith. 1986. *Belief about Inequality: Americans' Views of What Is and What Ought to Be.* New York: Aldine de Gruyter.

Kluger, Richard. 1975. *Simple Justice: The History of Brown v. Board of Education and Black America's Struggle for Equality.* New York: Vintage.

Kramer, Roderick, and Marilyn Brewer. 1984. Effects of Group Identity on Resource Use in a Simulated Commons Dilemma. 46 *Journal of Personality and Social Psychology*, 1044–57.

Lane, R. E. 1988. Procedural Goods in a Democracy: How One Is Treated vs. What One Gets. 2 *Social Justice Research*, 177–92.

Langer, Ellen. 1975. The Illusion of Control. 32 *Journal of Personality and Social Psychology*, 311–28.

Langer, Ellen. J., Irving Janis, and J. Wolfer. 1975. Effects of a Cognitive Coping Device and Preparatory Information on Psychological Stress in Surgery Patients. 11 *Journal of Experimental Social Psychology*, 155–65.

LaTour, Stephen. 1978. Determinants of Participant and Observer Satisfaction with Adversary and Inquisitorial Modes of Adjudication. 36 *Journal of Personality and Social Psychology*, 1531–45.

Lempert, Richard, and Joseph Sanders. 1986. *Invitation to Law and Social Science*. New York: Longman.

Leung, Kwok, and E. Allan Lind. 1986. Procedural Justice and Culture. 50 *Journal of Personality and Social Psychology*, 1134–40.

Lind, E. Allan, B. E. Erickson, N. Friedland, and M. Dickenberger. 1978. Reactions to Procedural Models for Adjudicative Conflict Resolution: A Cross-national Study. 22 *Journal of Conflict Resolution*, 318–41.

Lind, E. Allan, Ruth Kanfer, and P. Christopher Earley. 1990. Voice, Control, and Procedural Justice: Instrumental and Noninstrumental Concerns in Fairness Judgments. 59 *Journal of Personality and Social Psychology*, 952–59.

Lind, E. Allan, S. Kurtz, L. Musante, L. Walker, and J. Thibaut. 1980. Procedure and Outcome Effects on Reactions to Adjudicated Resolutions of Conflicts of Interest. 39 *Journal of Personality and Social Psychology*, 643–53.

Lind, E. Allan, and Robyn E. Lissak. 1985. Apparent Impropriety and Procedural Fairness Judgments. 39 *Journal of Experimental Social Psychology*, 643–53.

Lind, E. Allan, Robyn E. Lissak, and Donald E. Conlon. 1983. Decision Control and Process Control Effects on Procedural Fairness Judgments. 4 *Journal of Applied Social Psychology*, 338–50.

Lind, E. Allan, Robert J. MacCoun, Patricia Ebener, William L. F. Felstiner, Deborah Hensler, Judith Resnik, and Tom R. Tyler. 1989. *The Perception of Justice: Tort Litigants' Views on Trial, Court-Annexed Arbitration, and Judicial Settlement Conferences*. Santa Monica, CA: Rand Corporation.

———. 1990. In the Eye of the Beholder: Tort Litigants' Evaluations of Civil Justice System Experiences. 24 *Law and Society Rev.*, 953.

Lind, E. Allan, Robert MacCoun, and Tom R. Tyler. 1991. Alternative Dispute Resolution in Trial Courts. In *Handbook of Law and Psychology*, ed. D. K. Kagehiro and W. S. Laufer. New York: Springer-Verlag.

Lind, E. Allan, and Tom R. Tyler. 1988. *The Social Psychology of Procedural Justice*. New York: Plenum.

Luker, Kristen. 1984. *Abortion and the Politics of Motherhood*. Berkeley: Univ. of California Press.

Macaulay, Stewart. 1963. Non-Contractual Relations in Business: A Preliminary Study. 28 *American Sociological Rev.*, 55–67.

MacCoun, Robert J., E. Allan Lind, Deborah R. Hensler, David L. Bryant, and Patricia A. Ebener. 1988. *Alternative Adjudication: An Evaluation of the New Jersey Automobile Arbitration Program*. Santa Monica, CA: Rand Corporation.

MacCoun, Robert J., and Tom R. Tyler. 1988. The Basis of Citizens' Preferences for Different Forms of Criminal Jury. 12 *Law and Human Behavior*, 333.

Martin, Joanne, Maureen Scully, and B. Levitt. 1990. Injustice and the Legitimation of Revolution: Damning the Past, Excusing the Present, and Neglecting the Future. 59 *Journal of Personality and Social Psychology*, 281–90.

Merry, Sally. 1990. *Getting Justice and Getting Even: Legal Consciousness among Working-Class Americans*. Chicago: Univ. of Chicago Press.

Messick, David, and Marilyn Brewer. 1983. Solving Social Dilemmas. In *Review of Personality and Social Psychology*, vol. 4, ed. L. Wheeler and P. Shaver, 11–44. Beverly Hills, CA: Sage.

Moore, Barrington. 1978. *Injustice: The Social Bases of Obedience and Revolt*. White Plains, NY: Sharpe.

Murphy, Walter F., and Joseph Tanenhaus. 1969. Public Opinion and the United States Supreme Court: A Preliminary Mapping of Some Prerequisites for Court Legitimation of Regime Changes. In *Frontiers in Judicial Research*, ed. J. B. Grossman and J. Tanenhaus, 213–303. New York: Wiley.

Musante, L., M. A. Gilbert, and J. Thibaut. 1983. The Effects of Control on Perceived Fairness of Procedures and Outcomes. 19 *Journal of Experimental Social Psychology*, 223–38.

Nader, Laura. 1969. Styles of Court Procedure. In *Law in Culture and Society*, ed. L. Nader, 69–92. Chicago: Aldine.

Oppenheim, A. N. 1966. *Questionnaire Design and Attitude Measurement*. New York: Basic.

Oskamp, Stuart. 1977. *Attitudes and Opinions*. Englewood Cliffs, NJ: Prentice-Hall.

Parkin, Frank. 1971. *Class Inequality and Political Order*. New York: Praeger.

Parsons, Talcott. 1958. Authority, Legitimation, and Political Action. In *Authority*, ed. C. J. Friedrich. Cambridge, MA: Harvard Univ. Press.

———. 1963. On the Concept of Influence. 27 *Public Opinion Quarterly*. 63–82.

———. 1967. Some Reflections on the Place of Force in Social Process. In *Sociological Theory and Modern Society*, ed. T. Parsons. New York: Free Press.

Pepitone, A. 1950. Motivational Effects in Social Perception. 3 *Human Relations*, 57–76.

Pfeffer, Jeff. 1981. *Power in Organizations*. Marshfield, MA: Pitman.

Pruitt, Dean G., R. S. Peirce, N. B. McGillicuddy, G. L. Welton, and L. M. Castrianno. 1990. *Long-term Success in Mediation*. Unpublished manuscript, SUNY at Buffalo.

Rawls, John. 1971. *A Theory of Justice*. Cambridge, MA: Harvard Univ. Press.

Sarat, Austin. 1993. Authority, Anxiety, and Procedural Justice: Moving from Scientific Detachment to Critical Engagement. 27 *Law and Society Rev.*, 647.

Scheingold, Stuart A. 1974. *The Politics of Rights: Lawyers, Public Policy, and Political Change*. New Haven, CT: Yale Univ. Press.

Seligman, M. E. P. 1975. *Helplessness*. San Francisco: Freeman.

Tajfel, Henri. 1981. Social Stereotypes and Social Groups. In *Intergroup Behavior*, ed. J. Turner and H. Giles. Chicago: Univ. of Chicago Press.

Tajfel, Henri, and John Turner. 1979. An Integrative Theory of Intergroup Conflict. In *The Social Psychology of Intergroup Relations*, ed. W. Austin and S. Worchel. Monterey, CA: Brooks/Cole.

Taylor, D. M., and F. M. Moghaddam. 1987. *Theories of Intergroup Relations: International Social Psychological Perspectives*. New York: Praeger.

Taylor, D. M., S. C. Wright, F. M. Moghaddam, and R. N. Lalonde. 1990. The Personal/Group Discrimination Discrepancy: Perceiving My Group, But Not Myself, to Be a Target of Discrimination. 16 *Personality and Social Psychology Bulletin*, 254–62.

Thibaut, John, and Laurens Walker. 1975. *Procedural Justice*. Hillsdale, NJ: Erlbaum.

———. 1978. A Theory of Procedure. 66 *California Law Rev.*, 541.

Turner, John C. 1987. *Rediscovering the Social Group*. New York: Blackwell.

Tyler, Tom R. 1982. Personalization in Attributing Responsibility for National Problems to the President. 4 *Political Behavior*, 379–400.

———. 1987. Conditions Leading to Value Expressive Effects in Judgments of Procedural Justice. 52 *Journal of Personality and Social Psychology*, 333–44.

———. 1988. What Is Procedural Justice?: Criteria Used by Citizens to Assess the Fairness of Legal Procedures. 22 *Law and Society Rev.*, 301.

———. 1989a. The Quality of Dispute Resolution Processes and Outcomes: Measurement Problems and Possibilities. 66 *Denver University Law Rev.*, 419.

———. 1989b, The Psychology of Procedural Justice: A Test of the Group Value Model. 57 *Journal of Personality and Social Psychology*, 333–44.

———. 1990a. A Psychological Perspective on Mass Tort Claims. *54 Law and Contemporary Problems*, 199.

———. 1990b. The Social Psychology of Authority: When Do People Resist an Order to Harm Others? 24 *Law and Society Rev.*, 1089.

———. 1990c. *Why People Obey the Law*. New Haven, CT: Yale Univ. Press.

———. 1992. Legitimizing Unpopular Public Policies: Does Procedure Matter? Paper presented at the Onati workshop on procedural justice, June, Onati, Spain.

Tyler, Tom R., and Robert Bies. 1990. Interpersonal Aspects of Procedural Justice. In *Applied Social Psychology in Business Settings*, ed. W. Austin and S. Worchel. Hillsdale, NJ: Erlbaum.

Tyler, Tom R., Jonathan D. Casper, and Bonnie Fisher. 1989. Maintaining Allegiance toward Political Authorities: The Role of Prior Attitudes and the Use of Fair Procedures. 33 *American Journal of Political Science*, 629–52.

Tyler, Tom R., and Robyn Dawes. 1993. Justice in Organized Groups: Comparing the Self-Interest and Social Identity Perspectives. In *Distributive Justice*, ed. B. Mellers. Cambridge: Cambridge Univ. Press.

Tyler, Tom R., and R. Folger. 1981. Distributive and Procedural Aspects of Satisfaction with Citizen-Police Encounters. 1 *Basic and Applied Psychology*, 281–92.

Tyler, Tom R., and E. Allan Lind. 1990. Intrinsic and Community-Based Justice Models: When Does Group Membership Matter? 46 *Journal of Social Issues*, 83–94.

———. 1992. A Relational Model of Authority in Groups. In *Advances in Experimental Social Psychology*, vol. 25, ed. M. Zanna, 115–91. New York: Academic Press.

Tyler, Tom R., and Kathleen McGraw. 1986. Ideology and the Interpretation of Personal Experience: Procedural Justice and Political Quiescence. 42 *Journal of Social Issues*, 115–28.

Tyler, Tom R., and Kenneth Rasinski. 1991. Procedural Justice, Institutional Legitimacy, and the Acceptance of Unpopular Decisions Made by the United States Supreme Court. 25 *Law and Society Rev.*, 101.

Tyler, Tom R., Kenneth Rasinski, and Nancy Spodick. 1985. The Influence of Voice on Satisfaction with Leaders. 48 *Journal of Personality and Social Psychology*, 72–81.

Vidmar, Neal, and Dale T. Miller. 1980. The Social Psychology of Punishment. 14 *Law and Society Rev.*, 565.

Walker, Laurens, Stephen LaTour, E. Allan Lind, and John Thibaut. 1974. Reactions of Participants and Observers to Modes of Adjudication. 4 *Journal of Applied Social Psychology*, 295–310.

Walster, E. 1966. Assignment of Responsibility for an Accident. 3 *Journal of Personality and Social Psychology*, 73–79.

Yngvesson, Barbara. 1988. Making Law at the Doorway: The Clerk, the Court, and the Construction of Community in a New England Town. 22 *Law and Society Rev.*, 409.

Marianne Constable is associate professor of rhetoric at the University of California at Berkeley. She is the author of *The Law of the Other: The Mixed Jury and Changing Conceptions of Citizenship, Law, and Knowledge* (University of Chicago Press, 1994), which won the 1996 J. Willard Hurst Prize in legal history. She is currently working on a book on silence, speech, and judgment in United States law and politics.

Patricia Ewick is an associate professor of sociology at Clark University. For the past few years, she has been studying the social construction of legality. *The Commonplace of Law: Stories of Popular Legal Consciousness* (University of Chicago Press, forthcoming), written with Susan Silbey, examines legal consciousness to determine how people interpret the role of law in their everyday lives.

William L. F. Felstiner is professor of sociology at the University of California, Santa Barbara, and professor of law at Cardiff University, Wales. He recently coauthored, with Austin Sarat, *Divorce Lawyers and Their Clients: Power and Meaning in the Legal Process* (Oxford University Press, 1995).

Martha Albertson Fineman is Maurice T. Moore Professor of Law, Columbia University School of Law. Her books include *The Illusion of Equality: The Rhetoric and Reality of Divorce Reform* (University of Chicago Press, 1991) and *The Neutered Mother, the Sexual Family, and Other Twentieth-Century Tragedies* (Routledge, 1995).

Bryant G. Garth is director of the American Bar Foundation. His recently published book, with Yves Dezalay, is entitled *Dealing in Virtue: International Commercial Arbitration and the Construction of a Transnational Legal Order* (University of Chicago Press, 1996).

Carol J. Greenhouse is professor of anthropology at Indiana University–Bloomington. Her teaching and research focus on the ethnography of the contemporary United States, and interpretive and comparative problems in the anthropology of law. Her publications include *Praying for Justice: Faith, Order, and Community in an American Town* (Cornell University Press, 1986), *A Moment's Notice: Time Politics Across Cultures* (Cornell University Press, 1996), and an edited volume, *Democracy and Ethnography: Citizenship, Culture, and the Tensions of Liberalism* (forthcoming).

Joel F. Handler is Richard C. Maxwell Professor of Law at the University of California, Los Angeles. His publications include *The Poverty of Welfare Reform* (Yale University Press, 1995) and *Down from Bureaucracy: The Ambiguity of Privatization and Empowerment* (Princeton University Press, 1996).

Hendrik Hartog is Class of 1921 Bicentennial Professor of History of American Law and Liberty at Princeton University. He is the author of *Public Property and Private Power: The Corporation of the City of New York in American Law, 1730–1870* (University of North Carolina Press, 1983), among other works, and he is completing a legal history of marital conflict in the nineteenth century.

Robert L. Kidder is professor of sociology at Temple University.

Lewis A. Kornhauser is Alfred and Gail Engelberg Professor of Law, New York University.

Nancy Reichman is associate professor and chair of the Department of Sociology at the University of Denver. Current research includes a study of the implementation of the

Montreal Protocol and a study of gender differences in the careers and compensation of Colorado lawyers.

Susan S. Silbey is the William R. Kenan, Jr. Professor, Department of Sociology, Wellesley College. Her forthcoming book, with Patricia Ewick, is entitled *The Common Place of Law: Stories of Popular Legal Consciousness* (University of Chicago Press).

Tom R. Tyler is professor of psychology at the University of California, Berkeley. His research explores the basis of people's reactions to their experiences with legal authorities. He is the author of several books, including: *The Social Psychology of Procedural Justice* (Plenum Press, 1988; with Allan Lind); *Why People Obey the Law* (Yale University Press, 1990); *Trust in Organizations: Frontiers of Theory and Research* (Sage Publications, 1996; with Rod Kramer); and *Social Justice in a Diversity Society* (Westview Press, 1997; with Robert Boeckmann, Heather Smith, and Huen Huo).

171; portrayal in *Brown v. Board of Education,* 119, 130n. 21; portrayal in coverage of Los Angeles in 1992, 117, 130n. 21; as property, 169–70, 178, 182; special education, 152–54

Children's Home, in Florida, 84

child support payments, 99, 101–2, 158–59, 338

choice: discourse of in postmodern legality, 52; existence of in discretion, 137–38; preference and obligation theories of, 213–19 (*see also* obligation; preference)

cities, images of: Los Angeles in 1992, 115–16; nineteenth-century London, England, 130n. 15

citizenplace, as a structurally autonomous place, 203

citizenship, relationship to hegemony, 301n. 14

civil disobedience, 209, 226

civility (civic order), 9, 112–13, 122, 125, 130n. 23

civil justice, 14n. 2, 310, 312–16, 332–33; heavy caseloads, 66; review of regulatory rules and procedures, 233; subjective assessments of experiences with, 313–19; women's efforts to achieve pay equity through, 285–86

civil rights, 118–22, 130n. 24, 289, 302n. 16

movement, 130n. 23, 136

texts, 9, 118–25, 139; association of diversity with violence, 114, 118–22, 126–27

Civil Rights Act of 1964, 118–20, 121–23

Civil Rights Act of 1991, 118–19, 121

civil society, as distinct from the state, 113–14, 202–3

class, 8, 14n. 2, 129n. 6, 280, 284; diversity in, 112–13; hegemony, 288–89; and legal ideology, 282–83, 300n. 6; role in discussions of 1992 Los Angeles violence, 115–16

"classical" (premodern) penality, 39, 42–46, 48, 49

Clastres, Pierre, 30–32

Clean Air Act, 255

Clegg, Stewart, 141–43

client-centered approach to legal counseling, 56–57, 73

clients (*see also* lawyer/client relationship): dependent people as, 137–38, 156–58; of human services agencies, 144–49, 154–55, 157–58

Clinard, Marshall, 244

clinical courses and programs, in law school, 70, 72–73

Clinton, William, 90–91

Codd v. Codd 1816, 189n. 20

codes of honor, enforcement of, 225

coercive power, 223–24, 234, 339n. 3; and norms as incentives, 214, 217, 223, 230n. 24, 232n. 32

Cohen, Stanley, 38

Cohn, Ellen S., 339n. 4

colonialism, 24–25, 26, 196–97, 296, 297, 303n. 26

Comaroff, Jean, 125–26, 285, 286–87, 296, 297

Comaroff, John L., 125–26, 285, 286–87, 296, 297

commerce: as factor in civil rights cases and legislation, 118–21, 122–24, 126–27; as factor in vigil over public space, 124; relationship to law, 126–27

commerce clause (U.S. Constitution), role in civil rights legislation, 119–20, 122–23, 126–27

Commission on Impaired Attorneys, ABA, 69

Commission on Women in the Profession, ABA, 63

commodity culture, as form of control, 39, 50–51, 52

common law, 25, 109–10, 228n. 4

common law marriage, Blackstone's description of, 92

communication, in practice of law, 21, 29, 63; law school courses on, 72

communitarian (participatory) approach, to discretion in social programs, 138, 150, 157

community, 7, 9, 14n. 2, 124–28, 130n. 24, 332; alternatives to formal law, 197–98, 311–12; care programs based in, 154–55; as locus of civil rights, 118–22; multiple meanings of in American

poststructuralism, approach to power,
141–43
Pound, Roscoe, 196
poverty, 82, 90–92, 126, 150, 161n. 19 (*see
also* poor, the); linked with poverty of
values, 116, 130n. 16; reform efforts
and assumptions on the family, 82,
84–85, 99
Powell, Laurence, 118
Powell, Walter W., 250
power, 1–14, 14n. 2, 128, 166–67, 281–86
critical empiricism's approach, 201–2
definitions of, 8–10, 139, 159n. 6, 231n.
31, 309–10
in dispute processing, 309–10, 312
embedded in studies of ideology and law,
275, 280–81, 290–94
in hegemony, 286–90
in human services agencies, 144–49,
157–59
issues of in legal pluralism, 194–95,
196–98, 200–201
location of in interdisciplinary seminar,
296–97
manifestations of, 139–44
of normative systems, 211, 223–25
penal, 36–38, 42–52
in the practice of law, 65–69; in
lawyer/client relationship, 22, 56,
60–65, 73
in regulatory processes, 233–35, 250–56,
259–60; and capitalist development,
245–48; extralegal, 238–48
relationship to law, 248–50, 264n. 35,
272–76
relations of, 151–56, 161n. 13; in the
family, 80–81
in Santos's structure of social relationships,
203–5
of the state: in supervision and control of
the family, 80–83; working-class legal
ideology seem as supporting, 300n. 6
three dimensions of, 139–41, 147–48,
152, 155–56, 160n. 11
treatment in sociolegal studies of language,
19–27, 29–32
Power: A Radical View (Lukes) (1974),
139–41
powerlessness, 143; informal law alternatives

as response to, 197–98; in lawyer/client
relationship, 62
powers, separation of, 238, 253, 264n. 35
practical reason, theories of, 213–19
"predatory regulation" models, 262n. 13
(*see also* capture theory)
preference(s), theories of action based on,
12, 209, 213–19, 226, 229nn. 7, 8,
15, 230nn. 24, 25; and the analysis of
power, 223–24, 231n. 32
premodern ("classical") penality, 39, 42–46,
48, 49
prenuptial (antenuptial) agreement, in Barry
case, 168, 176, 180
Price, Susan, 56–57, 73
primitive societies, 30–32, 196–97
prison(s), 39, 47–49, 52; inmates' right to
marry, 88
prisoner's dilemma, 219–20, 230nn. 26–28
private-natural family. *See* traditional family
private normative systems, 211–13
private (domestic) sphere, contrasted with
public (market/political) sphere, 84
proactivity, 137, 149, 152
probations offices, 39
procedural justice, 1–2, 4, 10–13, 40–43,
149, 158
and the critical legal studies movement,
334–38
focus on as opposed to focus on
substantive justice, 329–32
in lawyer/client relationship, 55–56,
65–66, 74; law schools' limited ability
to affect, 69–70
in modern penality, 46–48
for the poor, 136–39
in regulatory practices, 258, 259
subjective assessments of, 64, 312–30
process, 64, 156, 157; control as factor
in judgments of procedural fairness,
320–25
property, 184, 225, 227
children as, 169–70, 178, 182
rights: of Eliza Barry's father in Barry case,
188n. 18; not applicable to children,
169–70, 182; in eighteenth-century
British law, 285, 286, 300n. 9
"Property, Authority and the Criminal Law"
(Hay), 284–85